THE BEATLES AND THE 1960s

THE BEATLES AND THE 1960s

RECEPTION, REVOLUTION, AND SOCIAL CHANGE

Kenneth L. Campbell

BLOOMSBURY ACADEMIC
LONDON • NEW YORK • OXFORD • NEW DELHI • SYDNEY

BLOOMSBURY ACADEMIC
Bloomsbury Publishing Plc
50 Bedford Square, London, WC1B 3DP, UK
1385 Broadway, New York, NY 10018, USA
29 Earlsfort Terrace, Dublin 2, Ireland

BLOOMSBURY, BLOOMSBURY ACADEMIC and the Diana logo are trademarks of
Bloomsbury Publishing Plc

First published in Great Britain 2022

Copyright © Kenneth L. Campbell, 2022

Kenneth L. Campbell has asserted his right under the Copyright, Designs and Patents Act, 1988, to be identified as Author of this work.

For legal purposes the Acknowledgments on p. xiii constitute an extension of this copyright page.

Cover design: Terry Woodley
Cover image: Statue of the Beatles at Liverpool pierhead.
John Davidson Photos / Alamy Stock Photo

All rights reserved. No part of this publication may be reproduced or transmitted in any form or by any means, electronic or mechanical, including photocopying, recording, or any information storage or retrieval system, without prior permission in writing from the publishers.

Bloomsbury Publishing Plc does not have any control over, or responsibility for, any third-party websites referred to or in this book. All internet addresses given in this book were correct at the time of going to press. The author and publisher regret any inconvenience caused if addresses have changed or sites have ceased to exist, but can accept no responsibility for any such changes.

Every effort has been made to trace copyright holders and to obtain their permissions for the use of copyright material. The publisher apologizes for any errors or omissions and would be grateful if notified of any corrections that should be incorporated in future reprints or editions of this book.

A catalogue record for this book is available from the British Library.

Library of Congress Cataloging-in-Publication Data
Names: Campbell, Kenneth L., author.
Title: The Beatles and the 1960s : reception, revolution, and social change / Kenneth L. Campbell.
Description: [1.] | New York : Bloomsbury Academic, 2021. |
Includes bibliographical references and index.
Identifiers: LCCN 2020052557 (print) | LCCN 2020052558 (ebook) |
ISBN 9781350107434 (hardback) | ISBN 9781350107441 (paperback) |
ISBN 9781350107458 (ebook) | ISBN 9781350107465 (epub)
Subjects: LCSH: Beatles. | Rock music–1961–1970–History and criticism. | Nineteen sixties.
Classification: LCC ML421.B4 C34 2021 (print) | LCC ML421.B4 (ebook) |
DDC 782.42166092/2–dc23
LC record available at https://lccn.loc.gov/2020052557
LC ebook record available at https://lccn.loc.gov/2020052558

ISBN: HB: 978-1-3501-0743-4
PB: 978-1-3501-0744-1
ePDF: 978-1-3501-0745-8
eBook: 978-1-3501-0746-5

Typeset by Newgen KnowledgeWorks Pvt. Ltd., Chennai, India

To find out more about our authors and books visit www.bloomsbury.com and sign up for our newsletters.

For Millie

CONTENTS

List of Illustrations	xi
Acknowledgments	xiii

Introduction   1

1 Postwar Britain, American Rock and Roll, and the Birth of the Beatles   7
- Growing Up in Postwar Liverpool: The Geographical and Historical Context   7
- Origin Story # 1: The Beatles Reflect on Their Own Childhoods   11
- Origin Story # 2: Rhythm and Blues, Skiffle, Rock and Roll, and the Quarrymen   15
- Origin Story # 3: John Meets Paul   18
- Origin Story # 4: How the Quarrymen Became the Beatles   20

2 Postwar Germany, the Beatles, and the Birth of the 1960s   23
- Postwar Germany   23
- Hamburg: The Geographical and Historical Context   26
- Britain Meets Germany: The Beatles Arrive in Hamburg   30
- Astrid Kirchherr and the Transformation of the Beatles   33
- The Final Piece to the Puzzle: John, Paul, George, and Ringo   37

3 1963: Profumo, the Pill, and *Please, Please Me*; The Rise of the Beatles   41
- The Profumo Affair   41
- The Pill and the Beginning of the Sexual Revolution   45
- Listening to the Beatles in 1963: *Please Please Me*   48
- Critical and Popular Reactions to the Beatles in 1963   52
- The Beginnings of Beatlemania   55

4 1964: Beatlemania in Historical Context   61
- The Battle over the Civil Rights Bill in the United States   61
- Audience Reception Theory and the Beatles   66
- Comparative Analysis of Differing Views on the Causes of Beatlemania in America   69
- The Impact of Beatlemania on Women   73
- The Cultural and Political Context of *A Hard Day's Night*   76
- Popular and Critical Reaction to the Beatles in 1964   80

Contents

5   1965: Help! The Beatles and the Political Culture of the Mid-1960s   87
The Crisis of the Pound—July–August 1965   87
The Political and Cultural Context of *Help!*   91
Popular and Critical Reaction in Britain to the Beatles' Second Film
  and the Accompanying Album   94
The United States in the Summer of 1965   97
Popular and Critical Reaction to the Beatles and *Help!* in the United States   101

6   1966: The Beatles on a Global Stage   107
"Why Did Bobby Kennedy Make Fun of My Wife?"   107
Rubber Soul   111
The Beatles in Japan and the Philippines   115
"More Popular Than Jesus": The US Tour of 1966   117
Revolver   122

**7   1967: All You Need Is Love; War, Peace, the Beatles, and the
    Summer of Love**   127
Arnold Toynbee, Britain, and the Vietnam War   127
The Making of *Sgt. Pepper's Lonely Hearts Club Band*   131
Sgt. Pepper's Lonely Hearts Club Band as a Product of Its Time   134
The Summer of Love   138
Magical Mystery Tour as a Reflection of Changes in the Beatles and
  Britain at the End of 1967   141

**8   1968: Revolution, Rock Music, and the Beatles; The White
    Album in Historical Context**   145
The Spirit of '68: Paris, London, and New York   145
The Year 1968 in Rock History: From San Francisco to London   149
Rock and the Politics of Protest   155
The Making of the White Album: The Beatles in India   160
Contemporary Reactions to the White Album   163

9   1969: Woodstock, the Beatles, and the End of the 1960s   169
"Revolutionaries Who Have to Be Home by 7:30"   169
The Beatles and Their Fans in 1969   173
The Summer of '69   177
The Beatles at Woodstock   182
Here Comes the Sun: *Abbey Road*   185

**10 Let It Be: Contemporary Responses to the Beatles' Last
    Albums and the Breakup of the Beatles**   189
"Paul Is Not Dead": The Beatles as News   189
Contemporary Responses to *Abbey Road*   194

Let It Be	197
Contemporary Responses to *Let It Be*	200
The Beatles Break Up and the Fans React	202
Conclusion: Post-1960s Politics and the Absence of the Beatles	209
The Morass of the 1970s	209
The Beatles Go Their Separate Ways	212
Successors to the Beatles?	217
The Long-Term Significance of the Beatles and Their Breakup	222
Notes	225
Select Bibliography	251
Index	257

ILLUSTRATIONS

0.1	Triangular relationship between the news, Beatles, and their audience	2
1.1	Pier Head, Liverpool, 1952	8
2.1	Early Beatles, On the Way to Hamburg, August 1960	29
3.1	Beatles at the Cavern Club, Liverpool, 1963	50
3.2	Beatles' fans, Manchester, 1963	57
3.3	Fan Mail, Beatles Fan Club, 1963	58
4.1	The Beatles, *A Hard Day's Night* promotion tour, 1964	77
4.2	Beatles at Heathrow Airport, 1964	84
5.1	Help!, 1965	91
5.2	Beatles fans, Kennedy Airport, 1965	101
6.1	George and Lurleen Wallace, 1966	109
7.1	Beatles' Press party for the Release of Sgt. Pepper's Lonely Hearts Club Band, 1967	135
9.1	John Lennon and Yoko Ono, Hilton Hotel, Amsterdam, 1969	175
9.2	Woodstock Music Festival, Bethel, NY, 1969	183
10.1	Rural McCartneys, Scotland, 1970	204

ACKNOWLEDGMENTS

First, I would like to thank Emily Drewe, Abigail Lane, and Beatriz Lopez for believing in this book and for their support throughout the writing of it. Special thanks to Tedi Pascarelli for help with the research and for reading the entire manuscript and her valuable and thoughtful comments and editorial corrections. Thanks also to Melissa Davis, who read a large portion of the manuscript and provided so much encouragement and helpful feedback. In addition, much gratitude to Kalyani and the Newgen KnowledgeWorks team for the fantastic job they have done on the copy editing and production of the book.

At Monmouth University, Ken Womack offered great support and many good recommendations; he has also given me the opportunity to write about the Beatles in several of his edited books. His own work on the Beatles has provided much insight and inspiration. I am incredibly grateful to Melissa Ziobro for serving as my oral history guru and all of her helpful guidance and advice. I would also like to thank Chris DeRosa, Maryanne Rhett, Hettie Williams, Judy Nye, and Bea Rogers, particularly for their support of my courses on the Beatles. Thanks to Owen Flanagan for his musical expertise. Sherry Xie always does an amazing job of tracking down all of the books I need through Interlibrary Loan. Beth Meszaros helped me talk through the possibilities for this project before I ever started working on it; I have also benefited from the numerous research presentations she gave over the years to my Beatles classes. I would be remiss if I did not say thank you to all of the students in those classes over the past ten years, as well as my peer learning assistants, especially Sarah Lewis who took the course as a freshman and worked as my PLA for the next three years. Chris Ellwood helped me with the student newspaper archive at Monmouth. Finally, Monmouth University generously supported this book with a Grant-in-Aid for Creativity and a Faculty Summer Fellowship in 2020 so I could finish it on time.

Oliver Lovesey gave me some great ideas and helped me formulate my thoughts on the Beatles at Woodstock; a longer treatment of that subject appears in a volume he edited for *Popular Music and Society* in 2019. Robert Brosh generously shared his recent book *Rock History: The Musician's Perspective* with me at a key stage in the process. Walter Everett kindly granted me permission to quote from his remarks at a conference in September 2019 commemorating the fiftieth anniversary of *Abbey Road*. His books have been a special source of inspiration.

I could not have written this book without the willing participation of all of the people I have interviewed or supplied me with their remembrances of the Beatles and their experience in the 1960s. These include the following: Mark Angellini, Claude Assante, Roy Auerbach, Jeff Ayers, Jane Barnes, Ivan Bell, Tom Blazuki, Ross Bloomfield, Alan Chevat, Julius D'Amelio, Artie Doskow, Rebecca Duncan, Ed Eichler, Bobby and

Acknowledgments

Nick Ercoline, Marbie Foster, Stan Green, Michael Halbreich, Robin Levine, Michael McEntarfer, Lenny Mandel, Ruth Mandel, Tom Noce, Janet Nugent, Peter Orenzoff, Len Pniewski, David Scher, Bob Schiffer, Allen Sorrentino, and James Vignapiano. In addition, it was great to interview Wade Lawrence, the director and senior curator at the museum at Bethel Woods, at the site of the original Woodstock Music and Arts Festival. I especially want to thank Larry Kane for talking with me and contributing a great perspective and unique insights based on his personal experiences with the Beatles. Eraldine Williams-Shakespeare and Debora Graas helped me with the transcriptions of the interviews that I conducted for the book.

I would also like to thank my family and friends, especially my friends, Ken (Hans) and Clare Fahnestock, for helping me to keep my sanity during a global pandemic.

My wife, Millie, to whom I have dedicated this book, used to sing, "Do You Want to Know a Secret?" to me when we were teenagers and deserves my lasting thanks for so many more wonderful memories in my life.

INTRODUCTION

This book places the Beatles' career and music into the context of the political and popular culture of the 1960s, with special attention to how listeners at the time would have heard and interpreted their songs and albums. This book also examines the complex interactions between the Beatles' lives, songs, and times. Taking for the most part a year-by-year approach, each chapter views the changing sensibility of the Beatles songs, less with a view to their internal development as artists, an approach skillfully employed by Walter Everett, Kenneth Womack, and others, and more with a view to the external influences absorbed, consciously or unconsciously, from the culture surrounding them. For the purposes of this book, I have conducted interviews with about three dozen individuals who were born between the years 1949 and 1957, almost all of whom were at least 12 or 13 when the Beatles first broke through—in 1963 in Britain and 1964 in the United States. I have also consulted numerous primary sources, including many contemporary reviews and articles, to gauge further the reception of the Beatles in the 1960s.

The Beatles are the most iconic rock/pop band in history and consequently, in all likelihood, the most written about as well. Numerous biographers and writers have scrutinized and detailed every aspect of their lives as individuals and a group, as well as the music and lyrics of every song. Thanks to the work of Bob Spitz, Mark Lewisohn, and others, we do not need a book that aims at uncovering new details of their day-to-day lives or personal histories. Nor is there any shortage of analytical works on the Beatles, including some excellent ones by Jonathan Gould, Steven Stark, Devin McKinney, Kenneth Womack, and Rob Sheffield. However, the 1960s was a complex and controversial time and the role the Beatles played in it so important that there will always be room for further thought and reflections on the topic. Furthermore, each period needs constant reevaluation based on how our understanding and perception of the period changes with the times. Today, we are living at a time in which Britain has voted to abandon the European Union (though the details of that exodus are still in the process of being worked out) and democratic, cosmopolitan norms are being challenged throughout Europe, the United States, and the world. Much of the rise of these conservative trends and acceptance of authoritarian leaders represents a backlash to the changes in the values and ideals that occurred in the 1960s, inspired by a revolutionary change in youth consciousness in which the Beatles played a very large part. This book represents an attempt to reevaluate the lives, career, and legacy of the Beatles by asking some new and re-asking some old questions about the lives, history, music, and times of the Beatles.

This book therefore focuses on the interpretation and reaction to the Beatles' work by a generation that not only shaped the political culture of the 1960s but also embodied values and ideals that inspired a revolutionary change in consciousness for decades to come. Indeed, we are still living with the consequences of that change, which repulses as many as it attracts, contributing heavily to the culture wars experienced in Western democracies at the beginning of the third decade of the twenty-first century. The Beatles are very much a part of that story, making their relevance as great today as at any point in the past, aside from the enduring appeal of the music itself. Not just another biography of the Beatles, this book takes a fresh look at the role this iconic group played in the culture wars of the 1960s, and therefore of our own time.

This book places a special emphasis on audience reception theory, including a look at some of the reviews of and reactions to their work on college campuses during the revolutionary decade of the 1960s. It argues that contemporary events had a far greater impact on the evolution of the Beatles' song writing and lives than people generally recognize. Throughout the book, I will be exploring the triangular relationship between the news, the Beatles, and their audience.

Figure 0.1 illustrates the ways in which the Beatles' work does not exist in a vacuum, nor is the relationship with their fans merely a two-way street. The Beatles received feedback from their audience, all the while absorbing the impact of current events and changes in the culture of the 1960s. The Beatles' audience had lives independent of their Beatle fandom and were thus affected as well by current events and social and cultural changes. In addition, the Beatles themselves existed as news; their albums, lives, and words proved capable of generating important headlines, just as did their audience's protests, demonstrations, civil rights marches, and perpetuation of the counterculture. Young people in the 1960s made news, as much as the news affected them. This triangular relationship made for a period of dynamic and rapid change that did much to define the nature of the period in which the Beatles thrived as a group. One notorious example that illustrates well the nature of this triangular relationship occurred in 1969 when rumors that Paul McCartney had died became a news item in its own right. This story in turn had an impact on the Beatles and certainly on Beatles fans, who in turn did much to perpetuate the rumor and reinforce its importance as a news story (see Chapter 10).

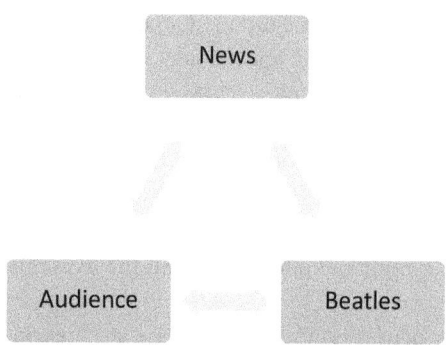

Figure 0.1 *Triangular relationship between the news, the Beatles, and their audience.*

Introduction

In addition to the plethora of biographies and other books about the Beatles, a number of publications have featured reminiscences of Beatles fans. For example, in 1982 Marc Catone solicited letters from Beatles fans and published them anonymously, giving only the initials and hometown of each writer, in a volume called *As I Write This Letter*.[1] Such sources are too valuable to pass up for any author writing about the reception of the Beatles, but I have tried not to rely too heavily on them. My interviews, most conducted in 2019, have a different perspective from people of the same generation as Catone's epistlers, looking back not at a distance of ten or fifteen years, but at a distance of fifty years. Both perspectives are valuable and needed to assess the reception of the Beatles, but we can certainly expect people to have gained some additional wisdom and perspective as they have aged, and perhaps even to see the period of their youth in a clearer relief than when they were closer to it. In addition, instead of soliciting responses, having the opportunity to interview these individuals gave me an opportunity to ask probing questions for them to consider that might have helped them remember things they might not have thought of on their own. The reader will find these perspectives scattered throughout the book and can judge how much they contribute to it.

In addition, those writing on Beatlemania tend to focus on the enthusiasm and large number of female fans of the group at the height of their popularity from 1963 to 1965. This book does include the perspectives of some of those Beatlemaniacs but also includes the perspectives of male fans, many of whom the Beatles affected just as profoundly, even if male fans did not display their feelings in the same ways that girls did. To say this is not to diminish the revolutionary ways in which young females expressed themselves in public, which they did to a degree unheard of at the time. It is merely to assert that the Beatles exerted an amazing influence on an entire generation of baby boomers that included both males and females, an influence that did not end in 1965 after the first wave of Beatlemania had peaked. In fact, in many ways their influence became deeper, stronger, and more profound in the second half of the decade. The Beatles' lyrics became more serious, their music more diverse, and their lives more complicated, just as at the same time their fans became more mature and looked for something in a rock band besides pop love songs, no matter how catchy and well-crafted those of the Beatles might have been.

The Beatles drew their inspiration from a variety of sources already present in the culture of 1960s Britain and America, and the fusion of so many different popular trends in one rock band helps to account for their becoming such a cultural touchstone for so many people. Even those individuals in their teens or early twenties in the 1960s who did not consider themselves particularly avid fans of the Beatles could not escape their influence. The Beatles' music was ubiquitous, but they affected the culture in so many other ways, from their hairstyles to the controversy that arose when John Lennon remarked in a 1966 interview that the Beatles were more popular than Jesus. Even people who did not own a Beatles record would have been aware of the rumor that Paul McCartney had died.

The Beatles transmitted their influence to their fans and the culture at large in a variety of formats in addition to the records they released, further enhancing their visibility and impact. They gave interviews to television and print reporters, as well as disk jockeys. Early in their career, they gave hundreds of live performances at clubs and assembly halls, which gave way to concerts at larger venues like arenas and stadiums when they began touring internationally in 1964. They performed on variety television shows such as *Sunday Night at the Palladium* in England and the *Ed Sullivan Show* in the United States. Especially in the early years, they frequently gave guest performances on the British Broadcasting Corporation (BBC). They even had a cartoon series based (very loosely) on their lives and exploits. Their images appeared on tons of merchandise (for which the Beatles received very little money). Perhaps most importantly, they made films that became almost as much a part of their legacy as their music, starting with *A Hard Day's Night* in 1964, and continuing with *Help!* (1965), *Magical Mystery Tour* (1967), the animated *Yellow Submarine* (1968), and at the end of their career, *Let It Be* (1970).

The fact that the Beatles' career occurred at a time of cultural revolution and social change magnified their importance. The 1960s was a decade of despair and hope, but above all hope. Racism and discrimination still flourished, but the Civil Rights movement led by Dr. Martin Luther King Jr and the legislation it inspired provided hope that African Americans would have more opportunity and greater equality in the future. The Vietnam War loomed large over the decade and sent tens of thousands of young American men to their deaths while inflicting extensive damage, destruction, and death on Vietnam and its people. However, it also provoked widespread protests and demonstrations, not only in the United States but also in Britain and around the world, leading to the hope that the younger generation would bring about not just an end to that war but to all wars. Britain faced the loss of an empire, the waning of its international stature, and the relative decline of its economy, but the Beatles provided a huge economic boost (for which Queen Elizabeth II awarded them the prestigious designation of Members of the British Empire). The Beatles also provided hope that Britain could triumph culturally on the global stage if not in other ways. The Cold War not only contained within it the threat that at any moment nuclear war might wipe out a significant portion of humanity but also implied the possibility that war would prove too costly for either the United States or the Soviet Union to contemplate ever actually using nuclear weapons. In addition, young people hoped to create a new society based on ideals that rejected the premises of both capitalism and communism but rather on simple concepts like peace and love.

The Beatles did much to romanticize these concepts and help perpetuate the idea of a counterculture that became so central to the ethos of the 1960s generation and reached its apex at the Woodstock Music and Art Festival in Bethel, New York, in August 1969. When they arrived in New York City for the first time on February 7, 1964, the Fab Four immediately infused a breath of fresh air into a country still reeling from the assassination of President John F. Kennedy the previous November and in the midst of a struggle in the American Congress over proposed Civil Rights legislation. The response the group received during their first visit to the United States was unprecedented and amazed even the Beatles themselves. American teenagers in the 1950s had thrilled to the first wave of rock and roll music, which appealed to their rebellious side, but now teenage girls were running down streets after the Beatles, trespassing, crossing police barriers, and generally acting out of control with impunity. The Beatles had inadvertently set off a revolution, even though at the time they mostly sang upbeat and catchy love songs such as "I Want to Hold Your Hand" and "She Loves You." As the decade went on their lyrics became more thoughtful and their music more ethereal, tapping into more adult concerns even as they reflected the psychedelic drug culture emerging in the second half of the decade. For example, they addressed the loneliness and alienation in modern society in "Eleanor Rigby," the bizarre imagery associated with acid trips in "Lucy in the Sky with Diamonds," and the ominous political radicalism stirring in youth around the world by 1968 in "Revolution." In the latter, they disavowed violent revolution and indicated they wanted to be part of the solution, not the problem. The solutions they offered revolved around those simple concepts of peace and love.

In one of his books, Beatles' biographer Philip Norman referred to the Beatles as "the Swinging Sixties incarnate."[2] While this moniker would carry positive overtones for some people, it would have an entirely pejorative meaning for others. Some people found the social changes and revolutionary atmosphere of the 1960s exhilarating, while others found them simply maddening. At the time, as a part of those changes, the Beatles inspired division and controversy. Yet we have now reached a point where almost everyone seems able to agree on the greatness and likeability of the Beatles, who have benefited from a kind of generic contemporary branding, which has taken them out of their historical context and sanitized them so that they can appeal to everyone from toddlers to the elderly. Even the frequently confrontational and irreverent John Lennon has benefited from the halo effect of his murder in December 1980. You rarely hear anyone speak of Lennon except in the most reverential terms anymore.

Meanwhile, fans of their music turn on the Beatles Channel on Sirius/XM radio or create their own playlists on Spotify or Apple Music and hit shuffle. Each of these listening formats has the potential to create new and interesting juxtapositions of their songs. There is nothing wrong with people having the freedom to listen to music in whatever ways they choose and the reordering of songs from their original placement on albums even has benefits and allows for comparisons that might spark interesting insights and ideas. For example, the *Love* soundtrack for the Cirque de Soleil show of the same name contains combinations of songs from different stages of the Beatles' career and reveals some pleasantly surprising musical effects and compatibilities between certain songs. However, if we are to understand the Beatles in the context of their times and comprehend what they meant to the people of that time, we have to return to the history and music of the period to reconsider their audience's response to listening to Beatles songs and albums they were hearing for the first time. To do so, as Julie Andrews sang in *The Sound of Music*, we have to "start at the very beginning"—at a time before the Beatles rose out of obscurity to help define a decade and shape a generation that would change the world.

CHAPTER 1
POSTWAR BRITAIN, AMERICAN ROCK AND ROLL, AND THE BIRTH OF THE BEATLES

Growing Up in Postwar Liverpool: The Geographical and Historical Context

On October 5, 1956, the *Empress of Britain*, the flagship of the Canadian Pacific line, prepared to set sail for Canada from the northeastern English port of Liverpool. In a wind analysis for the North Irish Sea published that same month, G. Reynolds provided an explanation of what made Liverpool, in particular, prone to uncommonly high-force winds.

> The physical explanation of these high gusts at Liverpool ... must be that almost all abnormally strong winds there occur with a wind direction of 270" or 280". Winds from this direction blow approximately 4 mi over land before reaching the anemograph [a device that measures wind] (at low water, more than 6 mi overland owing to drying sandbanks), a greater overland fetch than at any of the other stations for their most prevalent gale direction. This, together with its hill-top position, would make for a more turbulent airstream at Liverpool.[1]

One of those gale-force winds slammed the *Empress* into a concrete wall before it could get out of the dock. Despite the loss of some rivet heads and some scraped-off paint, the *Empress* managed to make it out of port, though at least ten other ships experienced delays because of the hazardous wind conditions, while others remained offshore unable to enter the Mersey River that runs through the city. This episode, which made the *New York Times*, would have been an important story for a port city like Liverpool, which largely owed its existence to the shipping industry.

No one grew up in Liverpool without an awareness of the docks and the importance of shipping to their hometown. Liverpool in the 1950s was far from its heyday as the major hub for receiving cotton and exporting manufactured textiles from the mills of northern industrial towns such as Manchester when British industry made the country the leading power in the world in the nineteenth century, but shipping was still central to the city's livelihood. Much of the city revolved around the docks, with a massive infrastructure having risen up over time to support them and the people who worked there, from churches to railways and, by the 1950s, tramlines and bus routes. George Harrison, one of the original Beatles, described the Mersey as "very prominent with

Figure 1.1 *The Pier Head, a riverside location in the city center of Liverpool, Merseyside, England, 1952. It is part of the Liverpool Maritime Mercantile City UNESCO World Heritage Site. This photo includes a trio of landmarks collectively known as The Three Graces and comprising of Royal Liver Building, Cunard Building, and Port of Liverpool Building. Courtesy of Getty Images.*

all the ferry boats, and the big steamers coming in from America or Ireland."[2] Gerry Marsden, lead singer and songwriter for the popular Liverpool group Gerry & the Pacemakers, wrote one of his best-selling hits about the "Ferry 'Cross the Mersey." The song is a romantic ode to "the place I love."

The fondness Marsden expressed for his hometown is understandable, but it did not quite convey an accurate representation of the status of the city in the late 1950s and early 1960s. When one visits Liverpool today, with its thriving pedestrian mall downtown, its polished image, its redeveloped docks, and its lovely Beatles tours to the sites associated with their lives and immortalized in their songs, it is easy to view the past and the city of the Beatles' youth unrealistically and idealistically. Liverpool, which itself had eclipsed older cities like Bristol and Chester during its rise to economic prominence during the Industrial Revolution of the late eighteenth and nineteenth centuries, had suffered a steep economic decline after the First World War, which the Great Depression of the 1930s only exacerbated. These harsh economic times preceded the Second World War, which inured Liverpudlians to further hardships and contributed to a sense of solidarity and pride of place such as people customarily cultivate when they find their city and country under attack. Liverpool suffered particularly heavily from Hitler's bombers who launched their opening salvos on the city in August 1940. Liverpool experienced sixty-eight air raids and heard over five hundred air raid warnings between the first on August 17, 1940, and January 10, 1942.[3] Tim Riley points out that "Hitler dropped 454 tons of explosives and 1,029 tons of incendiaries on the town, more than the Luftwaffe dropped on any other British city that month [August 1940], including London."[4] Harrison recalled, "Even until the day in 1963 when I left Liverpool there were still many patches full of rubble from direct hits."[5]

Liverpool, like the rest of Britain, took time to recover from the devastation wreaked by the war. Rationing was commonplace, housing shortages abounded, and through the 1950s most Liverpool households did not have an indoor toilet (including the childhood homes of three of the four Beatles), let alone a television or an automobile. A survey of 12.4 million homes in England and Wales done in 1951 revealed that "1.9 million had three rooms or less; that 4.8 million had no fixed bath; and that nearly 2.8 million did not provide exclusive use of a lavatory."[6] As for rationing, many people who grew up in the 1950s, including Keith Richards and Cynthia Lennon, frequently mention their inability to buy sweets as one of the enduring memories of their childhood. By the late 1950s rationing ended, perhaps teaching British youth something about delayed gratification.

Liverpool, like the rest of Britain, would also have had a clearly demarcated class structure based on a variety of factors that went beyond mere economic status, including regional accents, level of education, and occupation. The Beatles provide an excellent illustration of this: Paul McCartney relished his experience at school and saw it as opening up new worlds for him, so he later came off as more middle class, despite his working-class background. John Lennon, the more reluctant student, grew up in a much more comfortable middle-class environment, but always came across as someone with working-class roots. Liverpool was an ethnically diverse city, with a large Irish population dating to the potato famine of the mid-nineteenth century, as well as sizable numbers of Welsh, Scots, and Italians, with separate Polish and German communities as well. By the 1950s, these groups had largely adopted a working-class identity, with class more of a defining characteristic than ethnicity. Both Paul and John had Irish ancestors, but do not seem to have identified much with their Celtic heritage. However, by the late 1950s class did not provide the only dividing line within British society, for a combination of fashion, language, attitudes, and especially taste in music had created an increasingly large divide between teenagers and their elders.

In late July 1956, British prime minister Anthony Eden, after the Egyptian president Gamal Abdel Nasser nationalized the Suez Canal, bungled his way into a diplomatic crisis that inflicted incalculable damage to British prestige. It brought home an inescapable reality that would have affected even those who at that point had largely reconciled themselves to Britain's postwar loss of status as an imperial power. It also highlighted the dividing line that had become clear to those on both sides of it in 1950s Britain: those who could remember the Second World War and those born after about 1940 who for the most part could not. In fact, Keith Richards wrote in his memoir, "The main effect of the war on me was just the phrase, 'Before the War.'" It might be difficult for anyone who has studied the interwar period, scarred as it was by the lingering psychological and material effects of the First World War and hardships endured during the Depression, to understand why people in the 1950s would regard it at all favorably. That is, until one considers the even worse fears and deprivation experienced during the Second World War and the very real possibility that Britain might surrender or experience defeat at the hands of Hitler.

In John Osborne's 1957 play, *Look Back in Anger*, from which the "Angry Young Man" phenomenon in late-1950s English literature derived its name, the lead female character says to her father, "You're hurt because everything has changed. Jimmy is hurt because everything is the same." Her father is upset, because before—and during—the war he and his generation could cling to the vestiges of British power and prestige as providing meaning to their lives and affirming Britain's place in the world. Indian independence, which came in 1947, and the gradual diminution of the Empire thereafter, combined with Britain's humiliation in the Suez Crisis, had taken that away. It was a strong reminder that both the United States and the Soviet Union had eclipsed Britain as a world power. Cold War tensions between these two powers and the menacing threat of imminent nuclear annihilation only further antagonized the younger generation and contributed to both its anger and its apathy.

The bomb easily led to a live-for-today mentality, and the anger boiled over in a general attitude of revolt among British teenagers that belies the image of the 1950s cultivated over the ensuing decades as a period of placidity and conformity, especially in the United States. Yet it was from the United States that British teenagers took their cue. Consider the following exchange involving the teenage protagonist of Colin MacInnes's 1959 novel, *Absolute Beginners*:

> "Listen," I said to him. "No one in the world under twenty is interested in that bomb of yours one little bit."
> "Ah," said this diplomatic cat, his face coming all over crafty, "you may not be, here in Europe I mean, but what of young peoples in the Soviet Union and the USA?" "Young people in the Soviet Union and the USA," I told him, clearly and very slowly, "don't give a single lump of cat's shit for the bomb."
> "Man, it's only you adult numbers who want to destroy one another. And I must say, sincerely, speaking, speaking as what's called a minor, I'd not be sorry if you did: except that you'd probably kill a few millions of us innocent kiddos in the process."[7]

MacInnes's hero, based in London, is a jazz aficionado, who haunts the jazz clubs of the capital and loves Ella Fitzgerald, "who would soothe a volcano," and Billie Holiday, "who sends me even more than Ella does."[8] Meanwhile, teenagers in Liverpool and elsewhere were thunderstruck by a different kind of American music: rock and roll.

In Liverpool, in particular, the hardscrabble existence led by many in the grimy industrial city provides one explanation for the appeal to the youth of American skiffle and rock and roll steeped in the blues and country and western music emanating from the hot fields, dusty towns, and intolerable prisons of the American south. Teenagers might not have had television (only about 30 percent of British households did), but they did have radio, which many of them used at night to tune into Radio Luxembourg, which broadcast the latest rock and roll music from the United States.

One wonders if the storm that hit Liverpool in October 1956 or the damage to the most important ship of a major shipping line provoked much reaction among the teenage residents of the city. If it did, it more likely than not provided some measure of excitement at a time when British teenagers were finding life particularly dull. It is possible that John Lennon and Paul McCartney would have discussed the weather that day with their friends and family. Had the incident occurred a year later, they might have discussed it with each other after meeting for the first time the following summer. Although no one could have known it at the time, that meeting would have far-reaching consequences for Britain, the United States, and the world. Their partnership and the impact of the group they would form still lay ahead. When John and Paul met, although still quite young, they both already had a past, as did the two young men who would later join their group. Both the city they came from and the specific childhood experiences of Lennon, McCartney, George Harrison, and Richard Starkey, aka Ringo Starr, had shaped them as individuals and affected significantly what each would eventually bring to the group that later became known as the Beatles. Moreover, like the *Empress of Britain*, no prevailing headwinds would prevent them from getting out of Liverpool either.

Origin Story # 1: The Beatles Reflect on Their Own Childhoods

The stories people tell about their own lives always have a bit of myth to them; memories prove unreliable, even when we completely convince ourselves they are true. However, we mostly forget details—names, dates, a particular sequence of events; we place people at a scene who were not there or forget people who were. Occasionally, we might convince ourselves that something happened that did not, or that something did not happen that did, but if we remember getting hurt in a car accident, the death of a loved one, getting married or divorced, we can be sure that those events happened, barring a more severe form of amnesia. We all tell our friends, families, romantic partners, ourselves narratives of our lives that conform to some kind of pattern, that help us explain our successes and failures, and reveal something of who we are and who we want to be. Celebrities are no different than anyone else, really, in this regard, but they perhaps see themselves as having more at stake in terms of the image they want to project to the public. All of these are reasons, not to dismiss the Beatles' later reflections on their childhoods but to regard them as critically as we would with anyone else and to bear the above points in mind when reading this section, which I have based on the Beatles' own words in printed sources and interviews, especially those compiled for *The Beatles Anthology*. Furthermore, the Beatles' reflections on their own childhood are, from the vantage point of being a Beatle, more than just individual memories—they are part of a larger story— an origin story and treated as such by everyone who writes about them. We can learn a great deal about the Beatles and their later reception in the 1960s not just from learning about their childhoods but also from how they framed the narrative of their childhoods as the first origin story we will consider in connection with the band.

John Lennon had by far the most traumatic childhood of any of the four Beatles, even though Ringo suffered tremendously as a child and Paul experienced his own devastating loss with the early death of his mother. What made John's experience growing up almost unbelievably tragic owes primarily to his abandonment by both of his parents at a particularly young age. In one incident described especially well by Tim Riley, John's parents gave their 5-year-old son a choice between going to New Zealand with his father and remaining in Liverpool with his mother, with the prospect of never again seeing the parent he did not choose. John initially chose his father, before quickly reversing himself and staying with his mother, temporarily as it turned out, as she sent him to live with his aunt shortly thereafter. It is one thing to have a father leave, as Ringo's did, or a parent die, as Paul's mother did, but quite another for a young child from as early as he can remember to experience life through the prism of rejection by both parents. John himself said, "I was never really wanted," a feeling he linked to a longing for acceptance that he directly connected to his career as a Beatle. "The only reason I am a star is because of my repression," he said. This becomes a particularly key aspect of the Beatles' first origin story because, as important as each of the other Beatles were to the band's chemistry, history, and success, clearly without John Lennon there would have been no Beatles.

The question is, could the Beatles have existed if John lived what he called "a normal life"? John did not think so, saying, "Nothing would have driven me through all that if I was 'normal.'"⁹ From the outside, it would not have appeared that John had it so bad. In fact, he grew up in a comfortable middle-class environment in the home of his mother's sister, his Aunt Mimi, and her husband, his Uncle George. John would later point out that he was the only Beatle who did not grow up in government-subsidized housing, something to which he and the others all attached some significance. As surrogate parents, Mimi and George seem to have not only treated John well but also brought him up in a literate and intellectually stimulating environment and encouraged his musical career when it came to that. John counted Lewis Carroll and Oscar Wilde among the most important literary influences from his childhood. Paul claimed Lewis Carroll as an influence of his own, one of the things that he and John had in common that helped forge the bond between them. John always saw himself as a rebel though, carrying through life a load of resentment that no amount of love or approval seemed to diminish. It is a stereotype to contrast the resentful, pessimistic John with the happy-go-lucky, optimistic Paul. This broad characterization does not do justice to the complexity of each person, but it survives because of the elements of truth within it. Even so, John had many positive memories from his childhood, including attending garden parties at Strawberry Field, an orphanage run by the Salvation Army, with his close friends Ivan Vaughan, Nigel Walley, and Pete Shotton.

Paul has admitted to being sentimental about his own childhood. He acknowledged that his family gave him a comfortable enough existence growing up, but affirmed, "We were not rich by any means." Like many British families, his never owned a car, but the McCartneys did acquire a television, like many British households, around the time of Queen Elizabeth's coronation in 1953.[10] Paul had many fond memories of his parents growing up, and the loss of his mother in October 1956 clearly devastated him, his brother, and his father, despite a taboo on open displays of grief among males. Nonetheless, Paul still had his father and brother, who both offered support and encouragement to the precocious musical genius. The McCartney household crackled with music of all sorts, and his father, a former entertainer himself who knew myriad songs, encouraged Paul to learn to play the trumpet and the piano, before rock and roll steered him in the direction of the guitar. The eclecticism of Paul's musical tastes and later compositions had its roots in the musical variety he heard as a child. Unlike the other Beatles, Paul enjoyed school, drawn to English and literature in particular. (John, although an avid reader at home, was a notoriously poor student.) Music drew Paul away from taking his other interests too far, however. According to Paul, "I nearly did very well at grammar school but I started to get interested in art instead of academic subjects. Then I started to see pictures of Elvis, and that started to pull me away from the academic path."[11]

George Harrison joined the Beatles while still virtually a child, which greatly affected his development, as well as his position within the group. If George had not joined the Beatles, or found success in another band, he would have undoubtedly followed a working-class profession for he hated school. At one point, he did train briefly for a career as an electrician, just as Ringo started to apprentice as an engineer at a local factory. Still, as much as George loathed school and recalled very few good memories about it, he said that he liked playing football and had a happy home life, with relatives constantly at the house and grown-up parties he longed to join a common occurrence. Music also featured prominently in the Harrison household, ranging from Bing Crosby on the radio to English music hall numbers playing on his parents' phonograph. Ringo had very few memories of his father, saying that he probably only saw him five times in his life, but he was not prone to the mawkishness that afflicted John when it came to the subject of parental abandonment. This was partly because Ringo's mother adored and doted on him from infancy, whereas John only developed a close and loving, if complicated, relationship with his mother during adolescence. This was also partly because John lost his mother when a car driven by an off duty police officer struck and killed her. Julia died just as she and John had started to grow close, reinforcing John's sense of hurt and abandonment, not to mention anger. Furthermore, Ringo grew up in an environment that did not encourage one to dwell on such feelings. "We were the last generation to be told, 'Just get on with it,'" he reflected. Paul recalled that "none of this sitting at home crying, after his mother died," before adding, "that would be recommended now, but not then."[12] John, of course, belonged to that generation as well and this attitude manifested itself, for example, in his stoic reaction to the death of his close friend, Stuart Sutcliffe. However, by the mid-1960s, John had begun to explore and express his feelings more in his music and his life, even more so with encouragement from his second wife, Yoko Ono, when they got together a few years later.

Ringo's main source of childhood trauma came from illnesses from which he easily could have died and that caused him to miss school for long periods. Having nearly died of peritonitis from a burst appendix at the age of 6, he contracted pleurisy, which turned into tuberculosis when he was 13. He spent two years in a sanitarium, missing years of education at an important transitional time in his life. Ringo throughout his life has demonstrated a joie de vivre, which could have derived from the long months spent in hospital as a child and the realization that he had beaten the odds to survive two potentially fatal illnesses at a very young age.

When they did become old enough to spend more time outside the home, all four Beatles found Liverpool far from benign. They were constantly anxious about the "Teddy Boys," those peculiar manifestations of rebellious modernity in their mock Edwardian suits (from which their name derived, "Ted" being a nickname for Edward). The Teddy Boys aspired to toughness, often accompanied by outright violence. Paul told Barry Miles:

> I was looking out for guys on every corner who were going to beat me up. There were fights where George and I used to live in Speke. The next district, about a quarter of an hour away, is called Garston and the guys from Garston would sometimes get on a latenight bus and come to Speke. And suddenly word would go round, because it was like a frontier town in the Wild West: "The lads from Garston are coming! Fuck off, fuck off!" And you'd have to run! And they would come, forty guys from Garston would come and our bigger guys didn't run. They would go and meet them. It was very very real. It was serious fighting. George and I weren't very involved, but our moment came. There was one fight I remember in Woolton on the day I met John Lennon at the Woolton fête. We went to the pub afterwards, all getting a bit steamed up, then the word went round—God knows who it is puts that word round, there was always a runner—"The lads from …" "The teds from so and so are coming." "Jimmy Ardersly's around. He said he's goin' to get you."
>
> "What? Jimmy Ardersly? He's fuckin' said he's goin' to 'it me? Oh! My God! I didn't like all that shit. I was not that type at all. I was much more of a pacifist."[13]

Undeterred, each of the Beatles knew their way around Liverpool. Paul recalled spending a great amount of time at the docks, where he said he absorbed a fundamental practical education in theology, which led him to conclude that "God is just the word 'good' with the 'o' taken out, and Devil is the word evil with a 'D' added. Really, all that people have done throughout history is to personify the two forces of Good and Evil."[14] This consideration could help to explain Paul's cultivation of his image as the "good" Beatle, an image that has largely remained undiminished to this day. Paul has by no means been a perfect human being (no one is, of course), but if one sees himself on the side of the angels, it becomes that much easier for others to view them the same way. However, Paul's receptiveness toward his fans and his accessibility probably owed more to another childhood memory that also made a lasting impression on him. Waiting outside the stage door of the Empire Theatre in Liverpool hoping to secure autographs from a popular group called the Crew Cuts, he found them extremely approachable when they emerged. "They were very kind and very nice," he recalled, "and I thought, Well, that's possible then, stars can talk to people and I remembered that later."[15]

John went the other direction, even modeling himself after the Teddy Boys and adopting their style of dress at one point.[16] He did not imitate their penchant for violence though. "They were dockers. We were only fifteen, we were only kids—they had hatchets, belts, bicycle chains and real weapons. We never really got into that, and if somebody came in front of us we ran, me and my gang."[17] Ringo, who grew up in the city in the roughest neighborhood of any of the Beatles, experienced his share of bullying, saying, "It was really rough. In those days there were still gangs and fights and madness and robberies."[18] Like the other Beatles, Ringo eschewed violence, even though he saw plenty. "I wasn't a great fighter, but I was a good runner, a good sprinter … because if you were suddenly on your own with five guys coming towards you, you soon learnt to be. … It was quite vicious. I have seen people lose their eyes; I have seen people stabbed; I have seen people beaten up with hammers."[19] Ringo's overall assessment of his childhood was that "Liverpool was dark and dreary, but it was great fun to be a kid."[20] The precarious nature of existence in the city, however, may have provided extra incentive for young people like the Beatles to look for a way out, however wistful they might have later become about their childhoods.

Clearly, their own unique childhood experiences influenced the Beatles, as did the time and place in which they grew up. These factors all contributed to who they would become and the reception they received in the 1960s. Cynthia Lennon would later write of this time:

> The late fifties was a wonderful time to be young and setting out in the world. The grim days of the war and postwar deprivation were over; national service had been lifted and teenagers were allowed to be youthful and unafraid. It was as though the gray austerity of the forties had been replaced by a brilliant spectrum of opportunities and possibilities.[21]

For the Beatles, the opportunities and possibilities that would transform their lives came from the music they listened to with rapturous attention, the effects of which constitute a second story about the origins of the Beatles.

Origin Story # 2: Rhythm and Blues, Skiffle, Rock and Roll, and the Quarrymen

The Beatles grew up with rock and roll, which only became an identifiable genre of music around the time they reached their teenage years. They developed a strong affinity for the rock and roll music of artists such as Chuck Berry and Little Richard, whose songs they would play and perform throughout their career. A revolution of sorts took place in American popular music in the first half of the 1950s, as rhythm and blues gradually began to dominate the charts and eclipse traditional forms of popular music such as vocal pop, jazz, swing, and Tin Pan Alley standards. March 1955 saw thirteen R & B songs in *Billboard* magazine's top thirty.[22] The popularity of Fats Domino, Chuck Berry, and Little Richard indicated a change in attitudes toward music by Black artists, who entered the pop mainstream even as white performers continued to cover their songs. In addition to the growing influence of rhythm and blues, that same year a group calling itself Bill Haley and His Comets (aka, erroneously, as "the Comets") caught fire with a song called "Rock Around the Clock," which, though not the first rock and roll song, became the anthem for this new category of music. Haley introduced influences from country and western and swing music to a style of music some called "rockabilly" because of its fusion of country or hillbilly music with rock and roll. If "Rock Around the Clock" was the anthem, however, a raw musical talent emerged as a star the following year to become its first real icon.

Elvis Presley, who changed the definition of a male celebrity to one with an overt, charismatic sex appeal with his ostentatious bodily movements, hip thrusts, and seductive facial expressions,[23] had a huge influence on the Beatles and remained one of their idols after they became famous. Elvis and his less talented imitators, such as Fabian, helped prepare the way for the reception of the Beatles by cultivating a young female audience. By the time the Beatles appeared on the American scene in 1964, young girls had become accustomed to idolizing, gazing at, and displaying histrionics in the presence of male rock stars.[24] Elvis became quite popular in Britain as well as the United States, so he could have helped to prepare female fans for the Beatles there as well.

Elvis factored heavily into the Beatles' origin story in another way. There is a scene, perhaps apocryphal, in the 2009 biopic *Nowhere Boy* about the young John Lennon, in which John tells his mother Julia that he is going to be as big as Elvis, to which she replies that he is going to be bigger than Elvis. This kind of myth can easily arise around anyone who achieves a great deal of success in any field. The story of the baseball player who said at the age of 5 that he wanted to play in the major leagues and ended up making it ignores the thousands of other 5-year-old boys who said the same thing and never made it past Little League. Therefore, even if John did say something to this effect, his determination to make it big owed to a wide variety of additional factors. Most importantly, John needed a band and he needed bandmates who were just as serious about the music as he was and talented enough to help him get where he wanted to go.

Elvis did represent something important for Lennon and other aspiring rock and roll stars though. He came from a lower class background, lacked formal training, and was a man of the people who worked in a factory and as a truck driver before he recorded his first single at Sun Records in Memphis because he wanted to give it to his mother. Elvis was part of a larger trend that saw teenage doo-wop groups and other untrained or self-taught musicians rise to prominence in the 1950s, giving hopes and incentives to any aspiring musician. Origin stories like Elvis's can easily give rise to similar origin stories like those of the Beatles, who came from, what Londoners anyway considered, an uncivilized backwater. These prejudices still existed in the 1990s; when I arrived on a flight at London's Heathrow Airport in 1994, a female customs agent, upon hearing that I planned to go to Liverpool, exclaimed, "Liverpool! Why do you want to go there? They don't even speak English." Still, if Elvis could make it, so could the Beatles, which is the whole point of the scene in *Nowhere Boy*. None of the Beatles really had formal training or extensive music lessons from professional teachers, but this did not stop them from aspiring to success—nor did it need to do so, given trends in the music industry at the time.

The most important role played by Elvis in the Beatles' origin story, however, came through his music. John later recalled hearing "Heartbreak Hotel" for the first time, saying, "it was the end for me."[25] Brian Ward argues that Elvis's appeal in Britain connected to a larger fascination the British had with the music and culture of the American South. Ward shows that British attitudes underwent a change during the late 1950s because of the Civil Rights movement, which shined a light on the South's heritage of racism, segregation, and bigotry, but not before it gave rise to a new form of popular music in Britain.[26] The skiffle craze swept Britain in the mid-1950s, most clearly exemplified by the success of Lonnie Donegan's cover of "Rock Island Line," which hit #8 on the British charts in February 1956. It remained on the charts for twenty-two weeks and spawned an entire musical phenomenon among British youth.[27] Since skiffle music featured everyday household items such as jugs and washboards as instruments, skiffle bands proliferated quickly, although most bands featured regular musical instruments like guitars and drums as well but not expensive instruments like electric guitars or saxophones. Tim Riley estimates that over five thousand skiffle bands started up in England in 1955 and 1956.[28] They included successful acts like the Vipers Skiffle Group and Chase McDevitt and Nancy Whiskey, who joined Donegan in contributing hits to the British charts. Their number also featured in the Eddie Clayton Skiffle Group, the first band to which Ringo Starr belonged, and John Lennon's first group, the Quarrymen, which he formed with a group of his childhood friends.

This did not mean, however, that skiffle had displaced rock and roll as John's favorite music, only that it supplemented John's musical tastes and helped him secure his first gigs around Liverpool. John and his friend Erich Griffiths played the guitar, with Rod Davis on banjo, Pete Shotton playing the washboard, and Len Garry and Colin Hanton alternating on drums.

Another member of the group, Ivan Vaughan, played the more important role of introducing John to a friend of his named Paul McCartney. The Quarrymen played their first gig from the back of a truck in Roseberry Street for the Empire Day celebrations. They played for free, but John was happy at that point just to have the opportunity to perform in front of an audience.

Paul and George shared John's eclectic musical tastes. Although Paul had a more diverse musical background growing up than any of the other Beatles, they each listened to all kinds of music. As George Harrison said in *The Beatles Anthology*, "I don't understand people who say, 'I only like rock 'n' roll,' or 'I only like the blues' or whatever … as Beatles, we were fortunate that we were open to all kinds of music. We just listened to whatever happened to be on the radio."[29] Paul, whose musical background included a smattering of brass band and show music among other genres and listened to records by country singers like Jimmie Rogers and Slim Whitman, absolutely fell in love with rock and roll. Like John, however, Paul drew inspiration from the skiffle craze. In May 1956, both Paul and George went to see Lonnie Donegan perform at the Empire Theatre in Liverpool; Paul purchased his first guitar shortly thereafter.[30]

Nonetheless, skiffle soon took a back seat for John and Paul, who continued to listen to and marvel at the plethora of rock and roll hits coming across the airwaves of Radio Luxembourg. John credited Buddy Holly with being the one artist who inspired him to pursue rock and roll. He particularly admired the fact that Holly wrote his own songs, something highly extraordinary among performing artists at the time. It certainly set Holly apart from Elvis, despite John's admiration for the latter. Holly arrived on the scene in 1957, the same year that John met Paul McCartney. That meeting is now a legendary event that has generated its own special origin story, appropriate given how important their friendship and musical collaboration would be to the founding, success, and uniqueness of the Beatles.

Origin Story # 3: John Meets Paul

Ivan Vaughan introduced John Lennon to Paul McCartney at the now-famous Woolton fête, a fair held at St. Peter's Parish Church on the outskirts of Liverpool, on July 6, 1957. Both Ivan and Len Garry, another member of the Quarrymen, knew Paul from the Liverpool Institute, where they all attended school. Paul had just turned 15 on June 18; John was 16 but about to turn 17 in October. Paul's mother had died less than a year before he met John.

Paul already knew who John was, his reputation preceding him as something of a tough guy who you did not dare speak to without an invitation. The age difference between them also would have naturally contributed to Paul's reluctance to approach an older boy, even if he had wanted to do so. Having received an invitation from Ivan, or Ivy as his friends called him, Paul put on his trademark white sports coat, despite the oppressive summer heat that day, and prepared to attend the fête, thinking that even if things did not go well with John he might meet an attractive girl there. He had attended fairs there before and knew pretty well what to expect. He could not have known how the day would end, but he was determined to look his best, using Brylcreem to slick his hair back in a style popularly known as a "duck's arse."[31]

The Quarrymen performed at the fête that day, John wearing a checked shirt and black jeans. John consciously observed the audience that day, making mental notes of what drew positive responses from it. John and the group impressed Paul, though he noted that John played the guitar like a banjo, which was true, his having learned at that time only banjo chords from his mother. However, Paul especially liked that the group performed a song called "Come Go with Me" by the Del-Vikings, one of his favorites but a song he thought many others did not know yet.

Paul also admired John's ability to improvise lyrics on the spot to songs for which he had forgotten the words.

Paul, by contrast, knew all the correct chords and words for each of the songs he could perform. Paul had real musical talent and a fair amount of confidence for a 15-year-old, both of which immediately made a strong impression on John and the rest of the group. Len Garry took credit, along with Ivan, for spotting Paul's talent and facilitating his becoming a member of the Quarrymen. Garry said that Paul had learned to play the guitar from a friend named Ivan James, whom he alleged could play the guitar even better than Paul.[32] In his interview with *Playboy* magazine years later, John refused to admit that Paul had more talent than he did, crediting Paul's performance that day to his wider musical knowledge and education, as Paul had learned to play multiple instruments at a time when John could barely play the guitar.[33] John did say, however, that he thought Paul was as good as he was, especially singling out Paul's performance of "Twenty Flight Rock" by Eddie Cochran. According to Paul, "The Quarry Men [sic] were so knocked out that I actually knew *and* could sing 'Twenty Flight Rock.' That's what got me into The Beatles."[34] Paul's impromptu audition also included a song called "Be-Bop-a-Lula" by Gene Vincent and several Little Richard songs including "Long Tall Sally" and "Tutti Frutti." By Pete Shotton's account, the meeting lasted about twenty minutes, it taking John some time to warm up to Paul, owing to his reserved and mistrusting nature with new acquaintances.[35] John especially took note of the chords Paul played, no doubt realizing he had much to learn from the younger musician. Quite aside from Paul's facility with the guitar, he and John connected over a mutual enthusiasm for rock and roll they had seldom encountered before. At the time, John seems to have hesitated, however briefly, before asking Paul to join the band. He later remembered thinking, "If I take him on, what will happen?"[36] Eric Griffiths later said of Paul's audition, "He had such confidence, he gave a real *performance*. He could play and sing in a way none of us could, including John."[37] John himself told David Sheff in his *Playboy* interview that at the time he could "only play the mouth organ and two chords on a guitar."[38] Len Garry later acknowledged the fear that Paul might oust John from the band if he came in and took over. John did not intend to play a secondary role to anyone in his own band, but at the same time almost immediately seemed to recognize that the advantages of bringing Paul into the band outweighed any potential rivalry that might later crop up between the two. The rest of the group could barely keep up with John, despite how untrained as he was; John needed an infusion of talent if the group was going to amount to anything.

John and Paul adjourned to a local pub after the fête, where they continued to talk and get to know one another. Stories and memories vary slightly, but within a few days anyway, Pete Shotton had conveyed to Paul an invitation from John to join the Quarrymen. Pete recalled John asking him if he should invite Paul to join the group, with Pete giving his assent before John asked him to extend the invitation. Paul accepted immediately but made it clear he had holiday plans he was unwilling to jettison. This left John and the Quarrymen to play their first gig at the Cavern Club without Paul, where they drew the ire of management for mixing in some rock and roll numbers with their skiffle set, a violation of club policy at the time.[39] By the end of summer, however, Paul was practicing with the group and it was clear to the other members that John regarded Paul as something of an equal. Before long, they seem to have reached an unspoken agreement to put any potential jealousy or rivalry aside and to share leadership of the band. Their shared passion for the music and, later, the shared bond over the loss of their mothers both helped in this regard. They also began to write songs together, beginning the process that would transform the Quarrymen into the Beatles.

Origin Story # 4: How the Quarrymen Became the Beatles

The next step in the development of the group came with the addition of George Harrison, a friend of Paul who was even younger than Paul was. George's youth proved no disadvantage to the band given his musical abilities, though it did put him in a subordinate relationship to both John and Paul that would last until the group's demise. George was modest about his abilities at the time he joined the Beatles: "I was never a technical guitar player; there was always a better player around ....God knows how I ever made anything of myself. I used to sit there and practice as a kid, but I couldn't sit there forever. I wasn't that keen."[40] Nevertheless, George could never have overcome his youth and John's initial skepticism if he had not shown real talent from the beginning. Not only did he know even more chords than Paul did, but he also demonstrated the ability to solo on the guitar, performing Bill Justis's instrumental hit "Raunchy" as part of his initial audition to join the group. Still, it took time and a great deal of persistence on George's part for John to invite him into the group, simply because at 14 (at the time of his audition, which took place on the upper deck of a bus), John simply considered George too young to be in his band. John learned to play solos, but George became the designated soloist in the Beatles. One by one, the original Quarrymen dropped out (or were asked to leave), until only John, Paul, and George remained; they played with whomever they could temporarily co-opt to play the drums for them.

Despite the addition of Paul and George, and the degree to which they improved the group's sound, the Quarrymen did not experience anything close to immediate success—performing in public only a few times in 1958 and the first half of 1959. Much of the group's inactivity during this period owed to the death of John's mother, Julia, on July 15, 1958, which understandably left him depressed and withdrawn. John called it "the worst thing that ever happened to me."[41] However, the band had much to learn, and had they rushed they might have skipped over the steps necessary for their future success. Paul even had to teach John how to tune his guitar properly. It took John longer to learn chords from Paul because Paul played left-handed and John would need to learn to reverse them in order to play them right-handed. In its formative stages, the group practiced rather informally, often taking breaks to smoke and listen to records. They listened to whatever they could get their hands on, but Little Richard and Chuck Berry featured prominently in these sessions. They honed their craft without the best instruments or equipment. As Paul told Barry Miles, "the whole thing with the Beatles was we never really had great instruments, we never really had great headphones, we never really had great microphones or Pas [amps], we somehow learned to muddle through."[42] They also lacked technical training and so listening to the records and trying to imitate their chord changes became an essential part of their musical education. They became obsessed with chords, learning as many as they could from people outside the band, after which Paul and John tried to incorporate them into the songs they had begun to write together.

John and Paul both acknowledged the inspiration of Buddy Holly behind their efforts to write their own songs. There is no reason to doubt this, but both Paul and John obviously had creative impulses that they needed to satisfy or they never would have taken up this challenge. Paul already had jotted down a number of songs, complete with lyrics and chord changes, before he and John had even met, including a song called "When I'm Sixty-Four," which the Beatles would include on *Sgt. Pepper's Lonely Hearts Club Band* ten years later. John had previously tried his hand at songwriting as well. It helped that they could bounce ideas off each other when they began writing songs together almost immediately after they first met. They would meet at Paul's Forthlin Road house, which they had to themselves during the day, and Paul would write down in his school notebook whatever came to mind, after writing the heading, "A Lennon-McCartney Original."[43] By 1959, they had written a number of songs, including "Love Me Do," which would become the Beatles' first hit single in 1963. Other early Lennon-McCartney compositions included "P.S. I Love You," which became the B-side to "Love Me Do"; "I'll Follow the Sun," which turned up on *Beatles for Sale* in 1964; and "One after 909," which they revived for *Let It Be* (1970).

In the summer of 1959, the group began to gain visibility, beginning with a series of Saturday night engagements at the newly opened Casbah Coffee Club, owned by Mona Best, mother of Pete who would become the group's drummer for two years (1960–2). At the time, the Beatles bore little resemblance to the band that would burst upon the world in 1963, but they were inadvertently laying the foundation for their later success. Paul and John had begun to sing harmonies, which Paul had learned to do from his father growing up.

As for the name, "Beatles," again, accounts vary, but the consensus is that Stuart Sutcliffe, a friend of John's from the Liverpool Art College, and John came up with it. Sutcliffe had joined the band at John's request, despite his talent for painting and his lack of musical training. Stuart became the group's bass player and soon learned to do at least a passable job at it. The main impact of Stuart's joining the group at the time was that his relationship with John threatened to impinge on the friendship John and Paul had built. Paul and John must have genuinely liked one another to get along as well as they did, but Stuart was closer to John's age and the two of them had a great deal in common, including a greater sense of independence than the two younger members of the band possessed. Stuart appeared more sophisticated to John, but he also shared John's passion for rock and roll, including a particular infatuation with Elvis. Paul later explicitly stated, "When Stuart came in, it felt as if he was taking the position away from George and me."[44] They both liked Stuart though. According to George,

> Stuart was cool. He was great-looking and had a great vibe about him, and was a very friendly bloke. I liked Stuart a lot, he was always very gentle. John had a slight superiority complex at times, but Stuart didn't discriminate against Paul and me because we weren't from the art school.[45]

As much as they liked Stuart, they still frequently complained to John about Stuart's lack of skill, although this may have resulted more from their jealousy of the attention he received from John than from an actual lack of ability on Stuart's part (something about which Beatles specialists still disagree).

It may have irked Paul not to have a role in the naming of the band and he was reluctant to embrace the name "Beatles" at first. Nevertheless, he came to like that it had a double meaning like that of Buddy Holly's group, the Crickets, who seem to have provided the inspiration for the name, with John and Stuart substituting an "a" for the second "e" in "Beetles." After experimenting with several name changes, including, briefly, Johnny and the Moondogs and the Silver Beatles, the Quarrymen had permanently become simply the Beatles.

Meanwhile, Ringo Starr, who was a bit older than the other three, was gaining valuable experience as a drummer in one of the best and most popular groups in Liverpool, Rory Storm and the Hurricanes, which he joined in 1959. (George had once dated Iris, the sister of Rory Storm, whose real name was Alan Caldwell.) A year later, the Hurricanes were off to Hamburg, Germany, where Ringo would eventually cross paths with the Beatles, whose career arc took a decided jump in a city that bore a striking resemblance to Liverpool.

CHAPTER 2
POSTWAR GERMANY, THE BEATLES, AND THE BIRTH OF THE 1960S

Postwar Germany

When the Beatles arrived in the Federal Republic of Germany, also known as West Germany, in August 1960, they entered a country only fifteen years removed from the end of the Second World War, an experience that had left many Germans ashamed and embittered but others unbowed and unremorseful. Some former Nazis, most notably Hans Franck, the governor-general of Poland during the Nazi occupation, held themselves accountable and expressed a measure of remorse, but this was not typical of the Nazi party or its leadership as a whole.[1] Although the top party officials received the death penalty or lengthy prison sentences at the hands of the Nuremburg War Crimes Tribunal that had immediately followed the end of the war, many former Nazis simply blended in with the rest of the population in their chosen profession or occupation. Many Germans reacted quite negatively to the attempts of the victorious Allies to impose a regime on Germany and their efforts to eradicate traces of the Nazi past. Others, probably by far the greater number of Germans, simply sought to forget the past and get on with their lives. In doing so, they remained largely oblivious to the negative perceptions of Germany and the Germans then current in the United Kingdom and many other countries.

After the war, the Allied victors had divided Germany into four zones: American, British, French, and Soviet. Berlin underwent the same division. The Allies perhaps had good reasons for wanting to see Germany divided at the time, but the form that division took in the end resulted from the tensions between the Soviets and their Western allies. East Germany (formally known as the German Democratic Republic) under communist control and part of the Eastern European bloc aligned with the Soviets and West Germany, now a democracy, aligned with the West. This arrangement allowed West Germany to receive aid from the United States via the Marshall Plan, which served the dual purpose of helping to rebuild Europe after the war and encouraging aid recipients to eschew communism and align their interests with those of the United States. The continuing division of Berlin located within the Soviet or Eastern zone, with the western half officially remaining part of West Germany, complicated matters and provided one of the greatest sources of tension between the two sides during the Cold War.

In 1946, the influential economist Wilhelm Roepke had written, "The German problem ... appears to be one which, at best, can be solved only by a long process of moral, political, economic and social reconditioning in Germany."[2] Yet at first, the

Germans did not seem keen to undergo such a reconditioning. A new narrative quickly emerged following the war that cast Hitler and the Nazis in the role of villains, on whom the Germans could conveniently blame the trials and suffering of the German people, the horrific atrocities inflicted on persecuted civilian populations, especially the Jews, and the entire World War. Many Germans, however, did not even think the Nazis deserved such blame, so thoroughly had Hitler indoctrinated them to believe that the Jews were the enemies of Germany and a hindrance to its national destiny. In fact, 37 percent of Germans in the American sector surveyed in November 1946 said they believed that the Nazis had needed to annihilate the Jews and other non-German ethnic groups to defend the nation. This fraction matched exactly the percentage of Germans who had voted for the Nazis in the last free election held in Germany prior to Hitler's reign of terror and intimidation. Such attitudes persisted—the same percentage of West Germans in 1952 affirmed that their country would fare better if no Jews lived in it. Astoundingly, a quarter of those surveyed still stated that they viewed Hitler in a positive light.[3] In short, Roepke was right that the Allies could not simply rely on the types of political discourse that existed in other democracies; instead, they needed to select carefully those politicians who would lead the new postwar Germany.

Germany emerged from the Second World War a physically and psychologically devastated nation, with an exhausted populace facing seemingly insuperable obstacles toward rebuilding the country's homes, factories, and infrastructure, as well as any semblance of the civil society that had disappeared under the Nazi regime. In 1945, infant mortality in Berlin approached 40 percent, largely because of the widespread outbreak of dysentery caused by a damaged sewer system.[4] Dealing with their own crushing poverty and the challenges of daily survival, ordinary Germans had little interest or time in assessing the past or taking responsibility for the causes of their own dire circumstances. Economic improvement started slowly but became noticeable in the Federal Republic by 1950, even though it still had a long way to go toward full recovery. Industrial production by 1950 had actually exceeded its 1936 levels by about 33 percent.[5] German exports in 1951 exceeded those of 1948 by 600 percent.[6] Buoyed by the optimism of its postwar leader, Konrad Adenauer (1876-1967), West Germany made impressive strides toward the future even before it had begun reckoning with its past in a meaningful way. Adenauer himself had spoken of the need for Germans to put the past behind them as early as 1949.[7] West Germans embraced capitalism and the modern consumer society that took root throughout the West in the postwar era. By 1960, West Germany had achieved its "economic miracle" and its people enjoyed a standard of living that would have engendered total disbelief a decade and a half earlier.

Of course, none of this would have been possible without the American Marshall Plan aid. The United States provided $1,200,000,000 in financial assistance in the fiscal year 1948-9 alone.[8] The German economy also received a great boon when the Allies halted the dismantling of seven large German steel mills in 1949. Within a few short years, the Allies had gone from viewing Germany as a continued military threat to an important bulwark against Soviet expansion and a key player in the early stages of the Cold War. Only the beginning of the Cold War and the desire of Western powers, led by the United States, to prevent West Germany from falling under the control or influence of the Soviets facilitated a relatively quick rapprochement between the Federal Republic and the former Allied powers Germany had so recently sought to destroy.

Thus, the United States and its allies had compelling political reasons for propping up the economy of West Germany, but that did not prevent Adenauer and the government in Bonn from taking credit for the country's economic success.

In addition, West Germany shared in the general rise in global prosperity that accompanied the period of economic recovery following the Second World War. The economic successes of the 1950s had led Germans to embrace materialism and reconciled them to the democratic government of the Federal Republic. Much change occurred in Germany and the world between 1946 and 1960, but ill feelings toward the Germans among outsiders certainly lingered. It was only in the early 1960s that Germany began to face up to the terrible crimes committed in its name. The capture of Adolf Eichmann by the Israeli secret service in 1960 and his subsequent trial and execution brought to light many of the crimes of the Nazis, as did the case against twenty-two defendants in the Auschwitz trials that took place in Germany from 1963 to 1965. During the 1950s, however, West Germany had taken almost no steps toward holding legally accountable those who had committed crimes as part of the Nazi regime. Most Germans did not actually approve of former Nazi bureaucrats serving in official positions, but they either did not know who they were or lacked the power to prevent those in authority from employing them. In the meantime, the Germans continued to celebrate the valor and heroism of those who had served in the German army, or Wehrmacht, while conveniently scapegoating the Nazi leadership, especially those among the Nazi elite who had undergone trial and punishment at Nuremberg. This was one reason why the rehabilitation of West Germany under Adenauer did not completely appease the younger generation born, like the Beatles, during the Second World War but too young to remember it. History was moving very quickly and it took a while for the generation born during and immediately after the war to catch up to the immensity of the shadow the past cast over them.

In fact, a number of young German intellectuals began to criticize the postwar government of the Federal Republic for what they saw as its own bourgeois pretensions, its dullness, and its own lack of insight and understanding into the tragedy of the human condition that the catastrophic events of the twentieth century had laid bare. This period in German history mirrored that of other countries in the West. Young people grew up distrustful of authority, sowing the seeds of rebellion that would bloom in the 1960s. Furthermore, the prospect of nuclear annihilation resulting from the combination of the Cold War and the development of the atomic and hydrogen bombs cast a large enough shadow by itself.

Germans felt the sting of the Cold War much more than those in other countries because of the division of the country. They experienced what Ania Kruke has termed "Cold War angst." Surveys in West Germany in the 1950s ranked political unification among the most desired political goals. At the same time, however, a majority—almost 60 percent—believed this goal depended on the will of other powers and rested outside of the control of the German people themselves.⁹ The downside of American assistance for the German people was the surrendering of control over their own destiny to the political objectives of the United States during the Cold War. Adenauer had to balance carefully his image as a strong, independent, and perceptive leader with the reality of his government's dependence on the United States. The main consolation for many of Adenauer's supporters was that by allying West Germany with the United States, he had helped to prevent it from falling under the domination of the Soviet Union. Adenauer for the most part successfully managed to meet Roepke's challenge and steer West Germany away from the legacy of German nationalism and Hitler toward a new democratic era, but it took time and depended heavily on the country's material success and American support.

Finally, the war affected Germany in other ways, not the least of which was the imbalance between men and women among the German population, thanks to the heavy losses sustained by the German military during the war, especially on the Eastern Front against the Soviet Union. In 1960, there were still 126 females for every 100 males in West Germany.¹⁰ However, the main factors that defined postwar Germany included the tensions brought about by the Cold War, the sense of a foreign occupation, the frustration over the devastation and defeat in the war, the angst over the future, and the division of Germany between East and West. The people of the northern port city of Hamburg experienced all of these factors even more keenly, for reasons both geographical and historical.

Hamburg: The Geographical and Historical Context

Many writers on the Beatles since the 1960s have compared Liverpool to Hamburg, a port city in West Germany sitting just thirty miles from East Germany. The Beatles' first biographer, Hunter Davies, called the city "Germany's Liverpool," while Devin McKinney called it "Liverpool on the Elbe." Liverpool and Hamburg are both northern European port cities that happened to share the same latitude of 53 degrees N. Their inhabitants also shared a certain degree of hardness and toughness, as well as a strong emotional attachment to their hometown. The similarities even extended to their diet. Sailors from Hamburg largely subsisted on a local dish now most associated with the cuisine of the city called *labskaus*, consisting of a mashed-up porridge of corned or salted beef, potatoes, onions, and pickled beets, which Bob Spitz compares to Liverpool's native dish of scouse, a stew made with minced beef or lamb, potatoes, and cabbage.¹¹ However, Davies also noted that Hamburg is much larger than Liverpool and called it "a much wickeder city."¹²

Differences in their geographical location mattered too, especially Hamburg's close proximity to the border between West and East Germany. For example, Hamburg was the unfortunate recipient of many of the undesirable and criminal elements who fled from Communist control in the Soviet-occupied zone after the war. Hamburg also suffered economically because it had long served as a major trading port linking Western and

Eastern Europe, as well as the western half of Germany with that part of the country east of the Weser River, now divided because of the Cold War. Hamburg particularly feared becoming a pawn in the emerging battle between East and West in the Cold War's early stages. Fully half of Hamburg's business before the war had come from territory that now was behind the Iron Curtain.[13]

Hamburg also would have had a special historical resonance for young men coming from England only fifteen years after the end of the Second World War. The British had made raids on civilian industrial targets in Germany a priority of the Royal Air Force (RAF), partly in retaliation for Germany's attacks on civilian targets in the United Kingdom and partly in an effort to damage the Germans' morale. Hamburg had been a major target of Allied air raids, beginning in May 1940, only eight months into the war. In the course of the war, only Berlin sustained more damage from air raids than did Hamburg. In May 1943, Air Officer Commander in Chief Arthur Harris ordered the destruction of Hamburg in the hopes of crippling German industrial capacity. In a brief period in late July and early August, 8,500 tons of bombs fell on the city.[14] Hamburg, because of its economic importance, had historically suffered during foreign wars; Napoleon had imposed a near-ruinous blockade on the city in the early nineteenth century and foreign invaders in the past had frequently sacked and burned the city. Twentieth-century Hamburg was much larger though; the home of 2 million people during the Second World War, during which 55,000 residents of the city died, 50,000 more sustained injuries, and 300,000 homes were destroyed, leaving about 750,000 people homeless.[15] Hamburg lost more homes than all of Britain did during the war!

However, perhaps even worse than the physical damage suffered by Hamburg was the heavy burden placed on the city by the legacy of Hitler and the Nazi regime, which was always lurking in the background threatening to raise its ugly head. That it did in April 1961. Within ten days of the opening of the trial of Adolf Eichmann in Jerusalem, neo-Nazis attached twenty-seven cardboard swastikas to a synagogue in the Hamburg suburb of Eimsbuettel. In this context, John Lennon's frequent cutting anti-Nazi remarks from the stage in Hamburg do not seem particularly anachronistic.

Given the above circumstances, Hamburg recovered from the war surprisingly quickly and survived the division of Germany remarkably well in the decade or so following the end of the war. Max Brauer, the mayor of Hamburg from 1946 to 1960, had fled the Nazi regime in 1933 but returned to Germany after the war under American auspices. He played a key role in both the physical and political rehabilitation of the city after the war. At the end of the war, those tasked with rebuilding the city estimated that it would take ten to fifteen years.[16] Unlike many European cities, however, Hamburg under Brauer's leadership rebuilt itself and quickly removed the rubble and debris caused by the bombings, at least from those parts of the city frequented by the majority of people. It took longer to clean up the outskirts of the city and to address the housing shortage that led to serious overcrowding in some districts. However, by the end of 1953, Hamburg had emerged from the ashes of the war a rebuilt city, at least five years earlier than projected. No other German city matched its achievement. The city also managed gradually to build up its shipping to 27,500,000 tons in 1956, puzzling economists at the time as to how a city that lost so much of its immediate hinterland and access to half of its business could continue to thrive economically.

However, in 1957, Hamburg's annual tonnage shipped declined for the first time since the end of the war, an ominous sign given the disadvantages working against the city at the time. To make matters worse, Hamburg's trade with Eastern Europe dropped 22 percent that year, a figure only likely to grow larger given the political objectives of the Soviet bloc.[17] The increase in shipping Hamburg witnessed occurring in nearby East German harbors added further cause for concern to Hamburg's industrialists and merchants. These unfortunate developments had the effect of reinforcing Hamburg's ties to the West and led its merchants to look north to Scandinavia and west to Britain and the United States to recoup its losses.[18] However, they also reinforced Hamburg's anxiety about the future, which combined with the desire many people had to escape from the memories of the Nazi era to produce an urban culture given over to reckless abandon. Hamburg, like the rest of Germany, seemed to have lost control over its own destiny, despite its rapid recovery from the war and its rising levels of prosperity. The presence of a large criminal element in Hamburg meant that a black market flourished alongside traditional commerce. City authorities, instead of engaging in a futile effort to prevent such activity altogether, sought simply to regulate it, with the result that petty criminals and pimps flourished at the expense of large organized gangs or criminal organizations.

In some ways, Hamburg's seamy reputation dated to the medieval period when the city enjoyed the privileges of membership in the Hanseatic League, a loose confederation of trading ports along the Baltic capable of defending their independence from the rulers of the Holy Roman Empire. McKinney called Hamburg "a pit of misdirected tension a step away from nihilism: a culture—or anyway a subculture—that is drunken and stumbling in the dark, trembling with a hostile energy forced backward."[19] Already in 1950, a reporter for the *Saturday Evening Post* recorded that "Hamburg had the gayest, most abandoned night life of Northern Europe—and thousands of hungry and homeless on its back streets."[20] Sex, drink, and drugs featured prominently to an almost absurd degree with every taboo shattered and live sex shows available featuring every combination possible, involving men and women, men and men, women and women, black and white, in couples, threesomes, or more. All of this occurred in a culture that had made homosexuality a crime on the level of bestiality at the time of German unification in 1871. Because of its licentious reputation, Hamburg attracted people from all over looking for a place to escape, to forget, to sample forbidden pleasures, or to take advantage of opportunities to profit from such an environment. For example, Alan Williams, the Beatles representative who arranged for their contract to perform in Hamburg, noted that the city had become a central location for gunrunning associated with the Algerian war for independence from France.[21]

Furthermore, the Reeperbahn, where the Beatles lived and performed, was the seediest area in all of Hamburg, perhaps in all of Germany. It was not the kind of place normally frequented by young women like Astrid Kirchherr, who first saw the Beatles there on the invitation of her boyfriend, Klaus Voorman. The Reeperbahn had it all, from live sex shows to female mud wrestling. Gay bars flourished, perhaps in a reaction to the liberation gay people felt after the Nazis had imposed even stricter laws against homosexuality than had existed under previous regimes. Knowing that the Nazis advocated the elimination of homosexuals from society altogether, homosexuals must have truly experienced a sense of freedom and release given the relatively liberal atmosphere that followed. Transvestites openly consorted with men in these Hamburg bars, but sex of all kinds was readily available throughout the Reeperbahn and the larger St. Pauli district that surrounded it.

The culture of the Hamburg encountered by the Beatles, then, was an exaggerated mixture of postwar restlessness, guilt, defensiveness, pure escapism, and abandon, poised in the middle of the uneasy tensions between East and West that made a live-for-today attitude even more attractive. As bars competed with one another for patrons, they began to look for acts that would attract customers and give them a chance to drink and mingle while they were looking or waiting for sex or if they just wanted to get drunk or high before staggering home. Loud music blasted from the clubs along the street, adding to the level of excitement and energy that flowed through the district. Hamburg had become the European city that never slept—sleep being one precious commodity

Figure 2.1 *Early Beatles. Arnhem War Memorial, eastern Netherlands, August 16, 1960. Sitting in front of the inscription "Their Name Liveth For Evermore" are (left to right) Beatles manager Allan Williams, his wife Beryl, Williams' business partner and black Calypso singer Lord Woodbine, Stuart Sutcliffe, Paul McCartney, George Harrison, and Pete Best. John Lennon, missing, perhaps took the photograph. Courtesy of Getty Images.*

the Beatles would experience a profound shortage of upon their arrival in "Germany's Liverpool" in August 1960.

Britain Meets Germany: The Beatles Arrive in Hamburg

Alan Williams, who had arranged for the Beatles to perform in Hamburg, drove them there himself, along with his wife Beryl and a questionable character who went by the name of Lord Woodbine, whom Williams had introduced as his business partner. The Beatles became part of a Liverpool to Hamburg pipeline for rock groups, including groups such as Derry and the Seniors and Ringo Starr's group, Rory Storm and the Hurricanes. According to Cynthia Lennon, word traveled back to Hamburg from a German seaman impressed by the rock acts performing at a Liverpool club called the Jacaranda.[22] Sam Leach, an important music promoter in Liverpool during the early stage of the Beatles' career, attributed the meeting of Alan Williams and a Hamburg club owner in London's Soho district, where Williams had gone to scout musical talent, to the offer the Beatles received to perform in Hamburg.[23]

The band that traveled with Williams to Hamburg consisted of five members: John Lennon, Paul McCartney, George Harrison, Stuart Sutcliffe, and Pete Best. Their decision to go to Hamburg turned out to be of monumental importance, but at the time, it raised eyebrows and caused quite a bit of consternation among their families. John dropped out of art college, Stu put a promising career as a painter on hold, George was underage at 17, and Paul and Pete's families must have had their reservations as well. The promise of £15 a week—"more than my dad earned," Paul said[24]—alleviated any qualms he or the others had about the trip. Had they had any idea of what the lads would encounter upon their arrival, the reservations of their families would have increased exponentially. Pete Best later wrote, "We could only gape in sheer wonder when we hit the Reeperbahn, a jungle of neon and sex, where every other door seemed to lead to a place where girls were taking their clothes off or otherwise providing entertainment."[25] Stuart wrote in one letter home, "Hamburg has little quality, except for the kind you would find in an analysis of a test tube of sewer water. It's nothing but a vast amoral jungle."[26] Cynthia Lennon summed up her feelings about the city when she wrote, "Hamburg was decadent. It was sleazy. It was disgusting and it was wonderful."[27]

The Beatles' initial engagement was with a club called the Indra, which turned out to be a rather rundown strip joint owned by a gruff entrepreneur named Bruno Koschmider. The first glitch came when the group realized they had no place to stay and no money, so Koschmider agreed to put them up in the back rooms of a nearby movie theater called the Bambi. Their rooms sat near the cinema's bathrooms, which made the atmosphere of the dank place even more insalubrious. Yet these were the facilities designated for them to clean themselves, which they do not seem to have taken the trouble to do all that often. They had no shower or bathtub. The early 4:00 p.m. screenings at the theater interfered with their last opportunity to catch some shuteye before their evening's performances. Some groups might have given up on the whole enterprise at the start.

When the Beatles first arrived in Hamburg, they were unpolished, amateurish, and not particularly adroit in the art of stage presence. They drank heavily and began experimenting with drugs, particularly an upper called phenmetrazine, generally known by the brand name Preludin. They used the drug to help keep themselves awake and energetic throughout their grueling workweek. They availed themselves of the German girls who frequented the Indra, all too eager to offer themselves to these young charismatic rock musicians from England. Ringo described the Beatles at this stage of their career as "a nothing little band then. Just putting it together. In fact, they weren't really a band at all."[28] Ringo's assessment notwithstanding, they had a great deal of confidence and determination that carried them through some of the anxious moments of those early days in Germany's sin city. Facing a problematic lack of physical comforts, an exhausting schedule, and an unfamiliar environment, they quickly adjusted and came to find the place quite compelling.

They also began to rely on one another and to see themselves differently than they had when they were just one of the hundreds of rock and roll bands competing for attention in Liverpool. They may have been given an opportunity only because more polished bands would have turned it down, given the long hours and abysmal working conditions (that is what Paul thought),[29] but they astutely embraced their situation and decided to take advantage of it. The Indra did not attract big crowds, so they had the chance to experiment and try out new material, but at the same time they had to make a huge effort to keep and attract customers under the constant badgering of Koschmider to "Mach schau" (Make show). When they first started performing there, in their lilac-colored jackets, black shirts, black pants, and faux crocodile skin shoes, the place was practically empty and they actually had to perform in the street in an attempt to attract customers. They worked hard to entertain their audiences, deciding early on not to repeat a song on the same night, despite the long hours called for by their contract. This led them to perform entire albums they knew by favorite artists such as Buddy Holly, Carl Perkins, and Elvis Presley. The artists they covered ranged from Little Richard to Marlene Dietrich. They played songs by Chuck Berry, Fats Domino, Gene Vincent, and the English group the Shadows.

Ray Charles's "What'd I Say" quickly became a crowd favorite, which the Beatles learned to include in their act on a nightly basis. Although John and Paul had already started to write and perform some of their own songs, the group mainly confined itself to covers, particularly of their early rock and roll favorites.

They had committed to performing four and a half hours per night from Tuesday to Friday, and six hours on Saturday and Sunday, with breaks after every sixty- or ninety-minute set. Monday was their only day off. They had never come close to performing this much in Liverpool and the experience forged their identity as a band, sharpened their skills, expanded their repertoire, and tested their resolve. Despite the variety of music they played in Hamburg, the group also developed the distinctive Beatles sound that would soon capture the world's attention and set them on a journey that would exceed even their wildest imaginations. They infused all their music with a rockabilly feeling that perhaps revealed their limitations, as Devin McKinney suggests, but that also contributed to their own unique sound.[30] Many of their favorite cover songs that they perfected and made their own in Hamburg would appear on later Beatles' albums, such as Chuck Berry's "Roll over Beethoven," which landed on 1963's *With the Beatles*.

Their hard work paid off. As performances got stronger and more electric, people began to notice. As their act improved, the size of their audiences increased. In 2016, Paul told *Rolling Stone* magazine:

> We used to do "Dance in the Street," the Gene Vincent song. John was actually the one who said, "I'll do this—[claps hands] 'Gonna dance in the street tonight! Hey, yeah, everybody! C'mon, c'mon!'" That started to pull the students. We figured, "We got 'em sitting down. Now we'll play our stuff." And they liked it.[31]

After their initial engagement at the Indra, they moved on to Koschmider's larger and more respectable club called the Kaiserkeller, where Rory Storm and the Hurricanes also performed. It competed with a club called the Top Ten as one of the most popular clubs in Hamburg. The size and acoustics of the Kaiserkeller made them sound better and gave them a chance to perform in front of larger crowds. They also alternated sets with the Hurricanes, giving them an opportunity to listen and learn from another successful band from Liverpool, perhaps taking particular note of the group's affable drummer. They moved to better quarters, recorded a record with the English singer Tony Sheridan, and generally started to enjoy the life of successful and popular rock musicians. They later played with Sheridan at the Top Ten Club, much to the consternation of Koschmider, who decided to part ways with the group over the issue. Horst Fascher, a prominent figure on the Hamburg music scene who befriended the Beatles, recalled, "When the Beatles first came to Hamburg, they behaved quite politely. But when they got used to Hamburg, found out what they could do, and how safe their asses were, then they got a little more fresh."[32] As they gained confidence as a group, they also gained confidence as individuals. John, in particular, indulged his rebellious instincts, frequently alluding to Hitler and the Nazis and hurling anti-German slurs like "Krauts" at his audiences, as if he were asking for trouble. Fortunately, for him, Nazi sympathizers and German nationalists did not likely frequent bars where English rock and roll bands performed.

Much of the discussion about the Beatles' performance at this stage of their career has centered on the abilities of Stuart Sutcliffe on the bass guitar, or his lack thereof. You can read fifty books on the Beatles and you will likely find fifty different opinions of how well he played. Those who defend his guitar playing, like Peter Ames Carlin, note the dearth of contemporary criticism beyond that of Paul, who had (perhaps subconscious) reasons of his own for disparaging Stu. Carlin suggests that Sutcliffe was not as poor a guitar player as Paul made him out to be, that he really kept up even on the more complicated songs that the Beatles played. Most people who knew him came away impressed by how far he had come. As Stuart's sister Pauline later wrote, "He may not have been Jimi Hendrix or as a good a guitarist as he was a painter, but in early Beatles terms he cut the mustard."[33] Stuart himself said at the time, "We have improved a thousand fold since our arrival and Allan Williams, who is here at the moment, tells us that there is no band in Liverpool to touch us."[34]

Carlin suggests that Paul's real problem with Stuart was the result of a rivalry between the two guitar players over John's friendship. How could John have a musical partnership with Paul if he had become closer to Stuart? Carlin argues that Sutcliffe was a sophisticated intellectual in a way in which Paul could only aspire to be. Paul for his part said that Stuart was holding the group back and that they could not be as great as they could be in the end as long as he was in the band.[35] However, this could have also been largely because of Stuart's tendency toward aloofness on stage, cultivating a cool James Dean-like image, which did not mesh with the kind of stage presence projected by Paul, John, and George. Pete Best said Stu performed "something like a puppet."[36] This is, perhaps, ironic, since Pete himself would leave the Beatles not of his own accord, at least partly because he was so much quieter and reserved than the other Beatles. However, no one questioned Pete's drum playing at the time and drummers customarily remained in the background, unlike guitar players. Eventually, Sutcliffe left the band after an on-stage brawl with Paul provoked by McCartney's unrelenting insults, but he left without any hard feelings and, in fact, loaned Paul his bass guitar. In fact, it seems likely that Stuart simply never shared the others' extreme fervor for rock and roll and would have left eventually to pursue his art, about which he did feel passionate. Either way, Stuart was the one who most caught the eye of the woman who was to transform the Beatles and their career in a significant way—Astrid Kirchherr.

Astrid Kirchherr and the Transformation of the Beatles

The Beatles would probably have undergone a significant transformation in Hamburg even if they had never met Astrid Kirchherr; they had already ditched their lilac and brown jackets for leather ones and begun to dress more in accordance with the local culture. They changed their image and adopted more of a rebellious, edgier manner about them. They were still quite young, George not even having turned 18 yet when they first arrived, and had plenty of room to grow. Still, Astrid played an extremely important role in the lives of the Beatles and one should not underestimate her influence on them at a critical stage of their career.

Astrid was born in 1938, making her slightly older than the Beatles, but just enough to color her experiences and shape a worldview somewhat different from their own. She would have remembered the war and at least have had a fleeting sense of what it was like to live in Nazi Germany. Astrid associated with a group of young German students and artists who referred to themselves as "exis," short for existentialists, because of the influence of French philosophers and writers such as Jean-Paul Sartre, Albert Camus, and Simone de Beauvoir. England had its "mods" and "rockers" and Germany had its rockers and exis. The rockers, in both Britain and Germany, looked more to the recent past, the golden era of rock and roll and teenage rebellion, symbolized by Elvis Presley, James Dean, and Marlon Brando. The exis were modernists who rejected the traditional

German values, not to mention their abhorrence for the Nazi legacy of the world into which they were born.

The Beatles, foreshadowing the reception they would receive among varied audiences once they became stars, somehow appealed to both these groups. The Beatles had the look and attitude, not to mention the rock and roll credentials, to appeal to the rocker crowd, but Astrid and her exis friends discerned in them a responsiveness to modernist and avant-garde cultural trends. The exis' fascination with the Beatles probably had to do with the Beatles' own modernism, as displayed by the eclecticism of the music they played, their use of the stage for a kind of performance art that went beyond merely playing rock and roll, and their own youthful irreverence, especially about the past. Stuart's talent as a painter gave them—and him—even more credibility.

Astrid's boyfriend, Klaus Voorman, introduced her to the Beatles, and soon other members of their crowd followed. It is important to remember that the Beatles were not yet famous when they met Astrid. Therefore, they had no reason to suspect any ulterior motives when she initially befriended them. A photography enthusiast, she decided immediately that they would make good subjects and offered to take their pictures in and around Hamburg. "I had fallen in love with their attitude and their faces; theirs was the look I had wanted to photograph," she later wrote.[37] She also described them as "the most charming and polite men I had ever met—so different from the Germans I knew."[38]

Astrid's pictures revealed a keen eye and real photographic talent, establishing a model for how rock and roll artists would represent themselves for decades to come. In the photographs, Astrid experimented with shadows and light, to set them against a darkened background, similar to the effect on the photo used on the cover of their late 1963 album, *With the Beatles*. In Astrid's photos, the Beatles projected an air of self-confidence and maturity, probably born out of the knowledge that they had adapted themselves surprisingly easily to a foreign land and new surroundings. When the Beatles viewed the photos of themselves, they saw this as well, which could have only reinforced their swagger and self-possession. Moreover, if someone like Astrid could see them as special, perhaps the rest of the world would see it as well.

Astrid found them magnetic, while they found her refined, sophisticated, and yet mysterious at the same time. She certainly did not resemble the German groupies who typically frequented the Indra just looking for a good time. She knew about art and literature, or at least seemed to know much more than the Beatles did. Musically, her tastes ran more toward classical and jazz than to rock and roll. Astrid's personal artistic sensibilities fit with the Beatles' new image—her bedroom's color scheme included black walls, bedspread, and sheets. Gibson Kemp, Ringo's replacement on drums in Rory Storm and the Hurricanes who married Astrid in 1967, said, "she had a tremendous feel for shape and form, an unerring eye for the aesthetic, the unconventional, even the kinky, born out of a preoccupation to model herself after avant-garde Left Bank intellectuals."[39]

Becoming friends with Astrid, Klaus, and their exis friends opened the eyes of five young men from Liverpool who would have generally seen Germans depicted in a negative light back in England. Utterly enthralled by Astrid, the Beatles fastened on her as their muse. Stuart's sister, Pauline, wrote, "Astrid was much more than a girl we all fell in love with. She was a catalyst; her effect on everybody was such that it brought out the best in them, musically as well as personally."[40] Although, contrary to myth, Astrid did not invent the Beatles' hairstyle, she certainly did nothing to discourage them when they emulated a hairstyle popular with the young men in her crowd that later became known as a Beatle cut. In fact, Stuart asked Astrid to cut his hair in the same style as Klaus and their friend Jurgen Volmer, and before long the others followed suit—with the exception of Pete Best, who wanted to keep his dark, wavy hair combed back in a Tony Curtis style.

Meanwhile, Stuart and Astrid had fallen in love, although at first he found her response to him ambiguous. In one letter home, he wrote:

> I do love a girl but I will speak little of her for my mind would overflow with tenderness. She's like a rose that has run its dark leaves over the wall to look at the sun, complexion slightly pale, eyes full of fire and now full of dew. ... So saintly she might have walked the waves of a lake and the unshivered lake would have borne her tiny feet. ... Butt!!! she has a boyfriend, I'm sure she loves him and certainly he her, although no sign of affection is passed between them.[41]

Despite Stuart's initial confusion, it soon became clear that Astrid did reciprocate his feelings and their relationship began in earnest. Stu's relationship with Astrid created additional tensions within the group, as he began to prioritize his new girlfriend over the group and take umbrage with anything the others had to say about their relationship. According to John, Paul had precipitated his on-stage fight with Stuart not because he had criticized Stu's bass playing but because of a disparaging remark that Paul had made about Astrid.[42] Astrid, according to Tony Sheridan, was just as protective of Stuart.[43] In the end, Stuart decided to leave the band and remain in Hamburg to study painting and be with Astrid.

After Sutcliffe left the band, the first issue the Beatles needed to resolve was who would replace him as the group's bass player. They did not at all seemed inclined to add a new member to do it, meaning one of the three guitarists already in the Beatles would have to take over. That person turned out to be Paul, largely by default since George and John adamantly refused to consider it. However, they also needed to build on their Hamburg experience. Having succeeded in Hamburg and with little more to accomplish as a live act, they did not have record producers beating down their doors. They had recorded a record with Tony Sheridan, but those recordings, in the words of Jonathan Gould, reveal "a quartet of drastically limited instrumentalists who seem to have focused all of their efforts on doing one thing well."[44] The road to success was not a straight line, even for the Beatles. When the Beatles returned to Liverpool, they found themselves at loose ends and even began to look for other lines of work, Paul briefly taking a job in a coil-winding factory. At least as Paul tells it in *The Beatles Anthology*, he was ready to give up on the Beatles:

> One day John and George showed up in the yard that I should have been sweeping and told me we had a gig at the Cavern. I said, "No, I've got a steady job here, and

it pays £7 4 shillings a week. They are training me here. That's pretty good. I can't expect more."

And I was quite serious about this.[45]

Once John and George convinced Paul—presumably without too much pressure—to rejoin the group at the Cavern Club, the Beatles attracted the attention of a posh young record store manager looking for an opportunity to break free of his family business and chart an independent course. His name was Brian Epstein and he was about to become the Beatles' new manager. Meanwhile, Stuart had developed frequent and severe headaches, which increasingly grew worse until he died suddenly of a brain hemorrhage on April 10, 1962, devastating Astrid and deeply affecting the Beatles, especially John, who endured yet another unbearable loss. Paul later confessed to having a little guilt after Stuart died for the way he had sometimes treated him. John could have reacted with resentment and bitterness toward Paul over this and withdrawn from his friend and bandmate to avoid getting hurt again. Instead, he threw himself into the band and leaned on them for support. Both Stuart and Astrid had left their mark on the band and feature more prominently in the group's history than the Beatles and their mythmakers would later acknowledge. As Steven Stark put it, "their close involvement with [Astrid] lasted not even two years, and even then it was sporadic. By the time it ended, however, the Beatles had a different image and conception of themselves."[46]

That image would undergo further revision at the hands of Brian Epstein, who took over management of the group in early 1962. Epstein, the head of the music division at NEMS department stores, which had nine locations in the Liverpool area, had read about the group in the local music publication *Merseybeat* and he was intrigued enough to go hear them perform. He was also gay, with a penchant for handsome, young working-class men, an image that he easily could have projected onto the Beatles. The Cavern Club had recently started to feature rock and roll acts, after starting as a jazz club, and it was a dark, damp, small, crowded space that brought the audience in close proximity to the performers. Once he became their manager, he convinced them to clean up their act, changing the way they dressed and acted on stage, forbidding the group to smoke, drink, or swear, while encouraging them to adopt a more professional attitude. Eventually, they began to bow to the audience after each song. As Sam Leach put it, "Brian changed the lads' image from one of hard, aggressive rockers to smart, wellbehaved but mischievous pop stars."[47]

After they had become famous and started having hit records, while appearing regularly on radio and television, the Beatles would express some regret about the compromises they had made along the way. In the summer of 1963, Paul reflected, "Sometimes, you know, I feel as if there's nothing I'd like better than to get back to the kind of thing we were doing a year ago. Just playing the Cavern and some of the other places around Liverpool. I suppose the rest of the lads feel that way at times, too. You feel as if you'd like to turn back the clock."[48] John longed for the days when they could "naturally, express ourselves in any way that we deemed suitable" before they became "famous by compromise."[49] At the time, however, they set their sights on becoming the best rock band in the world and took advantage of every opportunity to advance themselves toward that goal. After Hamburg, they had experience, a stockpile of original songs, charisma, talent, and a great deal of faith in themselves. Although it was not obvious to their fans and may not have been obvious to themselves, it turned out all they needed to reach their dreams was a new drummer—but not just any drummer.

The Final Piece to the Puzzle: John, Paul, George, and Ringo

Pete Best had played an important role in what some argue was the most important stage of the Beatles' career, but he never fully meshed with John, Paul, and George, who often found themselves a threesome after their gigs ended. Cynthia, John's girlfriend at the time, who was in a position to know, wrote, "While the other boys mucked around, teased each other mercilessly and wisecracked their way through rehearsals, Pete said little and often seemed to be in his own little world."[50] George Harrison recalled, "Pete would never hang out with us. When we finished doing the gig, Pete would go off on his own and we three would hang together," adding that "when Ringo was around it was like a full unit, both on and off the stage."[51] Still, they seemed prepared to move forward with Pete as they began their efforts to secure a recording contract. Epstein first procured the Beatles an audition with Decca Records, which promptly turned them down after the Beatles performed material that did not seem to offer anything new beyond old-time rock and roll. In some ways, the odds were stacked against them since the music industry seemed to be moving away from traditional four-piece rock and roll groups at the time. In fact, in 1962, the head of Decca Records had famously said, "Groups are out; four-piece groups with guitars particularly are finished." However, the Beatles also had not played particularly well or adequately prepared for their Decca audition, a mistake they determined not to repeat if given another opportunity. Though disappointed, Epstein redeemed himself by getting them a recording contract in May 1962 with EMI's (Electric and Musical Industries) Parlophone label, headed by producer George Martin, who had taken charge of the label seven years earlier, mostly making comedy records, along with some classical material. EMI was the largest record company in the world and it gave Martin some leeway to experiment on his label, without the pressure to carry the company's profits. Martin heard something he liked in the group's sound, but he really decided to take a chance on them because he liked them personally and found their quirky humor at least mildly amusing. Martin recalled, "They played through a lot of things they'd been doing in their repertoire. It wasn't a question of what they could do, because they hadn't written anything that was great at the time, but they had great personalities. They had a way with them, and they charmed me a great deal."[52]

Martin, however, suggested that the band needed a new drummer to perform with them in the studio, although he had no objection with Pete Best continuing to play with them when the Beatles performed live. The Beatles' acquiescence to Martin's demand went further than he expected; they ousted Pete from the group altogether. Reluctant to deliver the bad news to Pete themselves, they exacerbated the situation by employing Brian Epstein to deliver the blow and cut themselves off from all contact with their expelled percussionist. Pete did not go willingly, writing in his autobiography, "I had no intention of leaving, not after two years as a Beatle, not having travelled this far." He told Brian he considered himself "as good, if not better, than Ringo."[53]

The decision at first backfired on the group and alienated many of their fans who adored Pete as much or more than they did the other Beatles, with only Paul rivaling him for the fans' affection. Fans queued up outside Beatles' performances with signs containing messages like "Pete Forever, Ringo Never." Pete Shotton suggested that Brian Epstein had feared as much, given Pete's good looks, especially when contrasted with the Beatles' new drummer, Ringo Starr, formerly of Rory Storm and the Hurricanes.[54] However, Sam Leach argued that Epstein never would have agreed to fire Pete Best just because Paul and George said so and that Brian saw this as an opportunity to replace a drummer who had refused to blend in with the rest of the group and conform to the image Brian was trying to create for them.[55] Leach does not exactly blame Epstein for firing Pete though, claiming that Ringo was much more of a professional than Pete was. Furthermore, Pete refused to wear the matching suits Brian had the others wear on stage and retained his pompadour haircut instead of adapting to the Beatles' style they had acquired in Hamburg.

However, John, Paul, and George certainly would not have jettisoned Pete against their will. For example, they stood up to Martin on other matters, including the decision to release their own song "Love Me Do" as their first single instead of the one Martin suggested, called "How Do You Do It," which was written by Mitch Murray and later became a hit for the Liverpool group Gerry and the Pacemakers. Had the other three gotten along better with Pete or developed closer friendships with him, they might have accepted Martin's suggestion that they replace him with a session drummer without kicking him out of the group.

Who, then, was to blame for the Pete Best fiasco and the temporary loss of goodwill among many of their fans? The fans themselves largely blamed Brian, since he had recently taken over management of the group, whereas Pete had already performed with the Beatles for two years. Martin, Epstein, and the other Beatles all contributed to the decision, but it really arose from a variety of factors that converged at a critical point in their career. John, Paul, and George could have handled it better, but this would not be the last time George Martin's instincts would prove correct. In the end, history would suggest that they made the right decision. They had not openly disparaged Pete; they just decided to move on, without looking back.

Martin said, he "was convinced I had a hit group on my hands if I could get the right song. They'd played me all their stuff and I didn't think anything was any good."[56] After "Love Me Do," the Beatles hit number one on the British charts with "Please Please Me." Within a year after that, "I Want to Hold Your Hand" became their first number one in the United States. In 1964, after the Beatles had hit it big, Astrid Kirchherr returned to Liverpool and noticed a huge difference in the city, which she had first visited in 1961. Writing in 2007, she recalled her impressions on that return visit:

One of the greatest things I noticed about Liverpool this time [1964] was all the energy and excitement that The Beatles had created. That's one of the things that I am most proud of them for. I saw a great difference in the optimism of the people, especially the young folk. All of a sudden Liverpool was on the map and success was something they could understand. On every street corner were groups of young boys strumming away at their guitars, or they were peering into Frank Hessy's shop window.[57]

The Beatles had an enormous impact on their hometown, but their impact was just as great in many other cities around the world.

On the verge of fame, the decision to hire Brian Epstein as manager and heed his advice to change their image and good fortune to land with George Martin as their producer and heed his advice to change their drummer played key roles in their success. Epstein transformed a rough, irreverent bar band into a much tamer pop group in many ways modeled on the girl groups so popular in the United States during the early 1960s.[58] Epstein encouraged the Beatles to keep their relationships hidden so female fans would think them available and at first forced John and Cynthia to conceal their marriage after they wed in 1962. As Sam Leach described the effects of Epstein's transformation of the Beatles, "It was a façade, but it was embraced by the media, the establishment and the general public. It removed resistance to their rise to fame and allowed everyone to concentrate on what they were really about: great music, the best we have ever heard."[59]

The decision to add Ringo Starr to the group as their drummer may have been as, if not more, important, however poorly the transition was handled and however unfair this might have seemed to Pete. As with Sutcliffe's bass playing, opinion on Pete Best's drum playing varies. Tim Riley strikes a good balance though, writing "Best was not a bad drummer in any sense; whether he was up to the others' level was becoming the key question."[60] Of course, one could say the same about Ringo, of whom Jonathan Gould wrote, for example, "Like Best, Starr possessed no more than a rudimentary technique on the drums."[61] However, Ringo did seem to provide the Beatles with something extra they had lacked with Pete, something only detected when listening to some of their recordings before and after Ringo joined the group. Volume I of the *Beatles Anthology* CDs provides this opportunity. Paul said, "You can hear the difference on the *Anthology* series. When Ringo joins us we get a bit more kick, a few more imaginative breaks, and the band settles."[62] Rob Sheffield notes that you can really hear the importance of Ringo to the band when comparing their version of the Shirelles' hit "Baby It's You" to the original.

The Beatles may have achieved their success and worldwide fame with Pete Best as their drummer, but we cannot ignore the fact that they did not achieve these with Pete but with Ringo. Ringo jelled with the group in a way that Pete never had, both musically and offstage. He had many similarities with the other three but just enough differences to add something unique and special to the group. He shared their sense of humor and turned out to possess his own kind of comic genius, which greatly enhanced the group's appeal and gave it an added dimension. He took care of his appearance, dressed, and cut his hair like the others, but stood out because of his rings (hence the name "Ringo"). Like the others, he hailed from Liverpool, but he was a bit older and had even more experience than they did. The story of Pete's replacement by Ringo is a tragic one, viewed from Pete's perspective, given just how much of an iconic and hugely successful group the Beatles became. Yet one could make a case that all of this happened precisely because they had found the perfect complement to the three guitarists and that Ringo Starr really was the final piece to a puzzle that has perplexed and astounded the world since 1963. That year saw the release of the Beatles' first album and their first number one record in Britain, but several other important developments occurred in 1963, marking it as the real beginning of the decade known in Britain as the "Swinging Sixties."

CHAPTER 3
1963: PROFUMO, THE PILL, AND *PLEASE, PLEASE ME*; THE RISE OF THE BEATLES

The Profumo Affair

In late 1962, a news story broke that proved irresistible to the British press, given the ways it combined espionage, sex, and a potential breach of national security, involving one of the highest-ranking members of the government and the upper echelon of British society. The backlash this particular scandal provoked threatened to topple the Conservative government headed by Harold Macmillan and elevate the Labour Party and its popular new leader, Harold Wilson, into office. The story centered on John Profumo, Macmillan's secretary of state for war, who had the previous year committed a blunder that could have come straight out of the Cold War spy novels of John le Carré or Ian Fleming. The scandal may have lacked the kind of intrigue found in stories of double agents, moles infiltrating the secret service of their Cold War enemy, or duplicitous traitors, such as the real-life spy Kim Philby, who betrayed Britain out of an ideological commitment to communism and the Soviet Union. However, the scandal had more than enough intrigue to hold the public's interest because of the serious implications that one of the most important members of the government and one in charge of national defense had placed himself in an extremely compromising position.

Profumo had engaged in a brief sexual relationship with a young woman named Christine Keeler, an affair that he later explicitly denied under oath in testimony before Parliament. British society was changing in the early 1960s, moving away from the narrow-minded attitudes toward sex and morality that had characterized the Victorian era and had lingered on into the 1950s, despite the ways in which two world wars, the Roaring Twenties, and the Great Depression all threatened to undermine them. Stephen Ward, a prominent 50-year-old London osteopath, had taken advantage of these changing sexual mores by cultivating young women in order to make them more attractive to the members of the British elite he met through his clients and with whom he wished to socialize. John Profumo was among them, a man born into a wealthy and prestigious family, who, like many members of Britain's governing class, experienced the world from a vantage point of privilege and entitlement. When he first met 18-year-old Keeler on July 8, 1961, at a weekend party hosted by Viscount Astor in Buckinghamshire, she was emerging from a swimming pool, in which she had been frolicking in the nude, at which point it seems Profumo decided he had to have her. Profumo gave her a guided tour of the Astor estate that night. He called her two days later. They began an affair shortly thereafter. Ward, who had invited Christine to stay with him at the Astor estate, in part, was fulfilling a demand unwittingly created by the Street Offences Act, which Parliament had passed in 1959, which led to a drastic decline in open prostitution, reflected in the conviction rates for the offense, which dropped from 19,536 in 1958 to 2,726 in 1960.¹ The Act had driven prostitution off the streets but created a market for high-class call girls. Ward, whose own short-lived marriage had ended in divorce in 1949, had frequently relied on prostitutes throughout the 1950s and may have had a special awareness of the potential significance of the Act. The Denning Report on the Profumo scandal called him "utterly immoral," pointing to his practice of inviting girls as young as 16 years to live in his house while he groomed them, playing the role of a more scurrilous later-day Henry Higgins. A steady stream of young girls, mostly from working-class backgrounds, flowed through Ward's house, accepting his offer to take them in and teach them the proper manners and etiquette that would allow them to interact with the upper crust of British society. Ward used the girls and had sex with many of them, even as he was preparing to pimp them out to his friends. It was for parties such as that hosted by Lord Astor that Ward had prepared girls like Christine so that he might make them available to the prominent men to whom he hoped to ingratiate himself in private social settings.

While Christine had left the home of her mother and stepfather in Berkshire and found work as a cabaret dancer in London, Ward had come from a modest family background—his father was an Anglican clergyman—and he had not attended one of the elite schools. Instead, he went to a relatively unknown public school named Canford in Dorset before traveling to the United States to study medicine at the Kirksville College of Osteopathy and Surgery in Missouri. Perhaps feeling a sense of insecurity based on his background and modest academic and medical credentials, Ward sought a place among the rich and connected. The Denning Report stated, "It pleased him to meet people in high places, and he was prone to exaggerate the nature of his acquaintanceships with them."² By contrast, Profumo had studied at the prestigious public school of Harrow, before matriculating at Oxford. The *London Times* said of him, "His infectious enthusiasm ... his lack of pomposity endear him to colleagues and opponents alike."³ His wife, whom he married in 1954, was a beautiful stage and screen actress named Valerie Hobson. Profumo rose steadily through the ranks of the Conservative Party in the 1950s, first serving as parliamentary secretary to the minister of transport, then under secretary and subsequently minister of state for foreign affairs before he gained his position as secretary of state for war in 1960.

The breakthrough in the story occurred in December 1962 when police arrested a man named John Edgecombe for firing several gunshots into Ward's London home. Inside at the time were Christine Keeler and her friend, Mandy Rees-Davies. Edgecombe had gotten involved with Christine and had exploded in an outburst of uncontrolled possessiveness. Police then made a second arrest involving an assault against Keeler by another boyfriend, a West Indian who went by the name of Lucky Gordon. In March 1963, the prosecution called Keeler as a key witness in the case against Edgecombe. Shortly thereafter, rumors started to circulate about the private life of the minister for war. Ordinarily, the implications that a leading government official had engaged in an extramarital affair or two would have merely fueled the gossip mill. The story exploded into something much bigger, however, with the revelation that Keeler had also shared a bed with a Soviet naval attaché named Evgeny Ivanov suspected of espionage—in the same period during which she was sleeping with Profumo! This constituted a serious security risk, all the more so because Profumo had top-secret knowledge pertaining to NATO (the North Atlantic Treaty Organization), in addition to British military secrets. Even if he did not pass along sensitive information in pillow talk with Christine, he had made himself a potential target for blackmail by the Soviets. Furthermore, Ivanov, as it turned out, was not only present at the same party where Profumo met Christine but had also engaged in a swimming race with Profumo in the same pool from which Christine had emerged naked that same weekend. Profumo must have been aware of the potential fallout from the affair, for he ended it after only four weeks once he found out that Christine was also sharing a bed with Ivanov.

The scandal dragged on into the summer of 1963, along with all of the political uncertainty it engendered. Wilson portrayed the affair as reflective of a larger trend of corruption and indifference associated with Macmillan's government and Conservative Party rule, while even Macmillan's supporters agreed that he had not acquitted himself particularly well in responding to the crisis. Macmillan had naively believed and backed Profumo, who denied any "impropriety" in his relationship with Christine and implausibly claimed the two had a platonic relationship. Once Profumo lied to the House of Commons about his affair with Keeler, he had sealed his fate and that of Ward as well. Profumo may have merely wanted to shield his family from humiliation and unfavorable publicity, but he should have known that it would only be a matter of time before he suffered the indignity of having to confess the truth and resign from his position in disgrace.

In fact, it took only three days following his testimony before the police received anonymous letters saying that Profumo had lied about his relationship with Christine. The press did its job of investigating and its reporting played a key role in forcing Profumo to admit the truth. Ward's reputation took an additional hit when the public became aware of his friendship with Ivanov, indicating that Ward himself may have been a spy who engineered the whole arrangement so that Christine might extract information from Profumo that she could pass along to Ivanov. Ward foolishly attempted to blackmail the government with his knowledge that Profumo had lied about the affair, but this ill-advised scheme only deepened his troubles. Then, in June, a London newspaper alleged that Ivanov had in fact sought sensitive military information from Christine that she had obtained from Profumo. The information came from a letter sent by an attorney named Michael H. B. Eddowes to Prime Minister Macmillan. It is unclear and probably highly doubtful that Profumo actually passed along any useful information to Keeler, but that is almost beside the point, given his egregious lapse of judgment.

Meanwhile, Macmillan faced calls from within his own party to resign amid displays of irreverence toward him that would have made it difficult for him to continue in office. Historians debate whether the Profumo scandal actually brought him down because Macmillan also suffered from ill health that would have soon forced him to resign anyway. Perhaps so, but the Profumo scandal could not have helped the prospects of the Conservative Party, which lost power to Harold Wilson and the Labour Party a year later.

The Profumo Affair has resonated in popular culture ever since, frequently used as a basis of comparison with any scandals that have since ensued, similar to the role Watergate has played in that capacity in the United States. As Frank Mort put it, the Profumo scandal became "the median against which other subsequent liaisons and sexual transgressions have been measured."[4] British historians have sometimes downplayed the significance of the affair; Arthur Marwick, for example, calls its historical significance "negligible."[5] However, contemporaries certainly did not perceive it this way, and, when seen against the backdrop of the social changes occurring in Britain by 1963, with the bulk of the decade still ahead, I am unconvinced by Marwick's characterization of its importance.

Mort, in fact, argues that historians have underplayed the sexual ramifications of the scandal by concentrating too exclusively on the political and foreign policy dimensions of the affair.[6] Again, that was not the case at the time; Macmillan strenuously objected to the sensationalistic treatment the press gave to sex in its coverage of the subject. The Profumo scandal brought to society's attention flaws in the Street Offences Act and revealed that the declining number of prosecutions did not in fact mean that Britain had solved the problem of prostitution; it had merely channeled it in a different direction. Furthermore, a number of recent developments, including the larger role played by television in society, the continued emergence of a unique teenage culture, and adjustments in the role of women and attitudes toward sex that contributed heavily to the Profumo scandal, hinted at the possibility of truly revolutionary social change. The year 1963, as Philp Larkin pointed out in his famous poem, "Annus Mirabilis," was also the same year when the Beatles released their first LP. In doing so, they launched the related phenomenon of Beatlemania among thousands of young girls across the UK. Larkin said 1963 was the year when "sexual intercourse began."

Indeed, the bizarre circumstances of the Profumo Affair may have played more than an indirect role in bringing the Beatles to the attention of Britain's youth. First, as its sordid details, prolonged press coverage, and eventful aftermath dragged on, the British people needed some diversion and the press, recognizing this, stood ready to provide it. Tim Riley has described the rise of the Beatles as "woven into the Profumo scandal as if mapped out by a clever screenwriter."[7] Second, the scandal seemed to point in the direction of needed changes in Britain, one badly in need of new leadership, fresh ideas, and an infusion of youthful energy. Labour Party leader Harold Wilson provided the first, and would steer his party to its first electoral victory since 1950. Fresh ideas came from a variety of sources, including a rock musician named David Sutch, who went by the stage name of "Screaming Lord Sutch" and who recorded songs with titles like "Jack the Ripper," "I'm a Hog for You Baby," and "The Monster in Black Tights." Significantly and symbolically, Sutch ran for the seat in the House of Commons vacated by John Profumo in Stratford-upon-Avon as the candidate for the National Teenagers Party. When asked about the candidate's position on the issues, his manager Tom Littlewood replied, "He sincerely believes in trying to improve the teenagers' lot and feels that if they are old enough at 18 to go to war and be shot they are old enough to vote. He intends to campaign, to push and push and push until they lower the voting age to 18. There are too

1963: Profumo, the Pill, and *Please, Please Me*

many restrictions against teenagers."[8] The youthful energy and exuberance came from the Beatles, who not only tapped into the forces unleashed by the Profumo Affair but, as Larkin suggested, arrived at the beginning of a sexual revolution.

The Pill and the Beginning of the Sexual Revolution

The Beatles had performed in strip clubs in both Liverpool and Hamburg, which must have helped them overcome any initial shyness when it came to the subject of sex. Before they went to Hamburg, the Beatles performed as a backing band for a buxom stripper from Manchester named Janice at the short-lived Upper Parliament Club in Liverpool owned by Alan Williams and Lord Woodbine. Paul McCartney wrote in an article for *Mersey Beat* in September 1962 that "we played behind Janice and naturally we looked at her ... the audience looked at her, everybody looked at her, just sort of normal." This experience undoubtedly at least helped to prepare them for what they saw in Hamburg. McCartney continued, "At the end of the act, she would turn round and ... well, we were all young lads, we'd never seen anything like it before, and all blushed ... four blushing red-faced lads."[9] While Paul may have blushed, the editor at *Mersey Beat* added a note that, since John and Stu both had experience drawing nude models in art school, it was unlikely that they did so.

"The Beatles' appearance in 1962–3 coincided with the fall of Conservatism in Sixties Britain," writes Ian MacDonald in his book on the Beatles and the 1960s, *Revolution in the Head*.[10] The event that many people saw as ushering in the sexual revolution of the 1960s was the designation of D. H. Lawrence's racy novel, *Lady Chatterley's Lover*, which many considered obscene, as one of Britain's cultural treasures. This label signaled a new understanding about sexual material available for public consumption. Both Britain and the United States had banned the novel, at least uncensored versions of it, despite Lawrence's status as one of Britain's most acclaimed novelists of the twentieth century. Lawrence had died in 1930, but in 1960, Penguin Books decided to release an unabridged version of his 1928 novel about the wife of a wealthy landowner who consummates her longing for her husband's gamekeeper. Charged with violating Britain's obscenity laws, Penguin went to court hell-bent on challenging government censorship of material that had literary or cultural significance. The judge in the case, Sir Laurence Byne, had his wife, Dorothy, read a copy of the book and annotate it for him. When the prosecutor, Mervyn Griffith-Jones, asked the jury of nine men and three women whether they would wish their servants to read Lawrence's novel, he showed just how out of touch he was with modern Britain and set the stage for Byne's landmark decision in favor of Penguin's publication.

Contemporary novels and the films based on them also revealed and contributed to new attitudes about sex, especially by those authors associated with the "Angry Young Men" literary movement of the late 1950s. Kingsley Amis's *Lucky Jim*, Alan Silitoe's *Saturday Night and Sunday Morning*, Colin Macinnes's *Absolute Beginners*, and John Braine's *Room at the Top* all fall into that category, although the movement derived its name from John Osborne's controversial play, *Look Back in Anger*. Braine's novel and the film adaptation in particular focused on issues of sex and class and the relationship between the two in a way reminiscent of the furor over Lawrence's *Lady Chatterley*.

The public did not always approve of these changes, but historians miss the point when they construe surveys indicating a strong preference for conservative moral values throughout the 1960s. A conservative strain definitely ran throughout the decade, reflected in popular attitudes in favor of the death penalty and in opposition to the liberalization of law regarding sex and divorce. More young women were getting married and the number of young men getting married before the age of 20 actually increased by 600 percent between 1945 and 1970.[11] However, these numbers ignore the fact that the population explosion that occurred after 1945 known as the "baby boom" meant that even with these increasing percentages, there were a million additional young people between the ages of 15 and 24 in the 1960s who were not married.[12] Mark Donnelly argues that the government handed permissiveness down to the people rather than the other way around by passing landmark legislation on homosexuality and divorce,[13] but the relationship between government and people is never just a one-way street.

It is one of the main premises of this book that, not only do conservatism and opposition to change coexist alongside revolutionary new social attitudes and an acceleration of social change, but that they are also likely to increase in periods when these changes are most pronounced. Furthermore, although continuity and change exist in any period of history, the historian must ask, on balance, in the end which of these holds greater historical significance. Conservative attitudes might put a break on change and reflect important attitudes at a given moment, but we must view them as themselves resulting from important challenges to the status quo, in addition to the other short- and long-term effects that those challenges might bring. The argument of this book is not that everyone embraced revolution and social change in the 1960s, but that revolution and social change defined the decade in an important way, partly because it divided society so significantly over the issue of their desirability. On the subject of sex, as Jeffrey Weeks points out, the division came over the issue of what contemporaries called the new "permissiveness."[14]

In that sense, the fact that marriage rates among young women actually increased in the 1960s or that doctors generally only prescribed the newly approved birth control pill to married women until the second half of the decade does not negate the changes in attitudes among those young men and women who remained single. Not to mention the ways in which changing ideas about sex and the role of women in society may have affected the attitudes and levels of happiness of those who did marry young. Not everyone attended strip clubs in Soho or read *Lady Chatterley's Lover*, but the numbers of people who did so increased at the same time as the numbers of women getting married in their late teens or early twenties. For example, an estimated 250,000 viewers watched over a thousand strippers on a nightly basis in London's West End by the early 1960s.[15] Similarly, not everyone watched the mischievous and glib television show, "That Was the Week That Was," but millions did tune in on Saturday nights in late 1962 and early 1963. One reporter called it a "program of extreme daring, dealing in smut, four-letter words, mockery, invective, ridicule, rudeness, crudeness, and total irreverence."[16] However conservative a significant proportion of the British public would profess themselves to be on moral matters, they stood in queues to watch movies in much greater numbers than they sat in pews in church, if they were not home watching television instead of either. In fact, church attendance continued to steadily decline, as it had since much earlier in the century.

Some of the social developments concerning sex in the 1960s, too, represented the culmination of long-term trends that occurred over the course of the twentieth century. For example, sexual freedom for women accompanied a new sense of economic independence resulting from the increasing numbers of them entering the workplace in the early 1960s. In Britain, the number of women entering the workforce had also increased steadily prior to the 1960s, increasing by 800,000 between 1937 and 1947 and by 11 percent (34 percent to 45 percent) between 1934 and 1981.[17] In addition, the age at which people had their first heterosexual experiences seems to have steadily declined over the course of the century. A survey of 18,000 British men and women conducted by the British National Survey of Sexual Attitudes and Lifestyles in the early 1990s indicated a 15 percent decline since the early 1950s.[18] Furthermore, the rise of the teenager had roots that started well before the 1960s, perhaps best symbolized in the United States by the founding of *Seventeen* magazine aimed exclusively at high school girls in 1944. *Seventeen*, with its goal of covering "everything that concerns, excites, annoys, pleases or perplexes" its female teen readers, reached a circulation of 650,000 within six months of its initial publication.[19]

Perhaps the greatest change involving attitudes toward sex was the introduction of the birth control pill, which had started with a medical test of a steroid named progestin as a possible aid to regulating women's menstrual cycles and helping them get pregnant. Dr. John Rock of Harvard Medical School conducted the test, beginning in 1954. When Rock discovered that the fifty women he tested had stopped ovulating while taking the drug, he knew that the implications of the test went beyond its use as a fertility aid, even though seven of the fifty women he tested did become pregnant after taking it.

The availability of the birth control pill represented a social and sexual breakthrough as well as a medical one. In May 1964, the Roman Catholic bishops of England and Wales reinforced Church teaching that all contraception, including the pill, violated "the unchanging nature of God's law." However, British Catholics numbered only about five million, and it is unlikely that even the vast majority followed the Church's teaching on this matter by the early 1960s. In 1963, the pill became available to married women, but it was only a matter of time before its use spread to single women, who gained legal access to it in 1967. The delay supports the notion of the sexual revolution as a progressive movement that happened over time and not all at once, but the advent of the pill's availability in 1963 still seems an important landmark along the way—even if it only encouraged more sex within marriage for the time being.

By the time the decade ended, Britain had legalized homosexuality, made divorce easier to attain, and seen millions of single women taking the pill or taking advantage of improvements in intrauterine devices (IUDs) to enjoy sex with a greatly reduced chance of pregnancy. The sexual revolution did not happen overnight and its effects would extend long beyond the end of the 1960s. It also had its antecedents in earlier developments and was part of a trajectory that covered much of the twentieth century. Yet, in retrospect, 1963 stands out as a key moment, following the aftermath of the *Lady Chatterley* trial, the introduction of the pill, and the release of the Beatles' first album, *Please Please Me*. The title of the album, taken from the name of their first number one single in Britain, had strong sexual overtones and in many ways seemed to sum up a new consumerist mentality devoted to pleasure and immediate gratification that had carried over to the changing attitudes toward sex that formed the backdrop to the beginnings of Beatlemania.

Listening to the Beatles in 1963: *Please Please Me*

On April 2, 1963, the Beatles' first scheduled performance in Sheffield occurred at the Azena Ballroom because the police expected a much larger crowd than the Stringfellow's Black Cat Club, which had originally booked them, could accommodate. About four months earlier, on November 26, 1962, Alan Smith had watched them record "Please Please Me," a song he said the Beatles hoped would break the Top Thirty, but which he predicted had a good chance to go straight into the Top Ten. Smith called it "the kind of tune you can remember after one hearing."[20] They had begun their recording sessions with George Martin in September, when they recorded the two sides of their first single, "Love Me Do" and "P.S. I Love You." The combined effect of their first single and the album named for the second single created a sensation that took Britain by storm. Music and cultural historians have suggested many reasons for the success of the Beatles and the phenomenon of Beatlemania, but it started with the music and the entirely unexpected new sound that came from a group not from London but from the provincial port city of Liverpool.

The Beatles first met George Martin in June 1962, when they arrived at EMI studios for an audition armed with a rather conservative set list of mostly covers put together by their manager, Brian Epstein. The list included standards like "Besame Mucho," which did not do the Beatles justice or allow them to display their true talents. The Beatles had a recording contract, but unbeknownst to them they still needed to gain Martin's approval before they could actually record anything. Martin saw potential in the group, but perhaps more importantly, he liked them almost immediately and decided to work with them. The pairing of the Beatles with Martin would have historic consequences, but only because the Beatles had already largely perfected their live act and Martin already had experience and proven himself adept at producing live recordings.

However, John and Paul's original compositions did not initially impress Martin and they soon clashed over which song they would release as their first single, Martin favoring a catchy pop tune written by Mitch Murray called "How Do You Do It," which later became the first number one hit by a group from Liverpool named Gerry and the Pacemakers. The Beatles wanted to release one of their original songs, "Love Me Do."

Martin reluctantly agreed to let the Beatles have their way. However, he suggested that McCartney sing lead instead of Lennon so that John could concentrate more on the harmonica portion of the song. Martin nevertheless resisted the temptation to feature McCartney exclusively as the band's lead singer or the band's front man, choosing instead to give John and Paul equal roles as leaders of the group, with George Harrison and Ringo Starr playing essential but clearly secondary roles (something that affected George much more than Ringo as time went on).

Brian Epstein described in *Mersey Beat* a grueling recording session in which the backing vocals required fifteen takes, writing that John's mouth was numb from playing the harmonica so much. He described Martin's reaction to the result as one "of great delight."[21] EMI released "Love Me Do" on October 5 with little publicity and low expectations. Bob Spitz writes:

While "Love Me Do" had a nice little pop groove to it, reinforced by John's portentous bluesy harmonica (fashioned after the one Delbert McClinton played on "Hey! Baby"), its stripped-down lyric and molasses-paced beat, which quite needlessly jolts to a standstill at the end of the break, failed to convey the bold energy the Beatles personally felt toward rock 'n roll.[22]

Spitz provides an apt description of the song, but "Love Me Do" still had a fresh and distinctive sound to it and did not resemble anything playing on the radio at that time. Even though "Love Me Do" was only a modest chart success, peaking at number 17, Tony Barrow, the Beatles' press secretary, noticed a difference in the crowds at Beatles shows. "The crowd went wild," he recalled about the first time he ever saw them perform live.[23] While the group's Liverpool fans continued to demonstrate their loyalty by attending Beatles' shows in droves, young fans from the surrounding areas began traveling into the city for a chance to watch the group perform.

When Martin first heard the Beatles play "Please Please Me," sung by John and Paul in a slow beat with a Roy Orbison-style falsetto on the chorus, he suggested the Beatles play it about twice as fast. The Beatles, to their credit, followed Martin's advice and punched up the song considerably. This innovation turned the song into a real rocker and transformed it into something markedly different from the slower paced "Love Me Do" that had preceded it. The song jolts the listener immediately with the first line, "Last night I said these words to my girl," delivered with startling intensity and proceeds at breakneck speed with no room to breathe until reaching the pleading title line, "Please please me, oh yeah, like I please you." Alan Smith described the background as a "the solid, insistent beat, defying you not to get up and dance."[24] The cover of their first album seemed to announce the Beatles arrival in the world of popular music as a fully formed group, with a photograph shot at an angle so that the lads appear positioned diagonally looking over a railing at EMI studios, smiling down with beaming faces, dressed in suits, looking neatly polished and groomed. The graphics announced the arrival of THE BEATLES, in yellow block print in the corner of the cover in the space left by the diagonal positioning of the four members of the group. Rodney Nevitt has traced the influence

Figure 3.1 *The Beatles performing at the Cavern Club, Liverpool, February 16, 1963. Courtesy of Alamy Photos.*

of pop art on this first album cover, noting that it "links with the modern architectural record of post-war England." He connects the arrival of the Beatles with Harold Wilson's call for a new modern Britain shaped by the "white heat" of technology and for a new Labour Party.[25] This cover, the last that the Beatles would not choose themselves, marks a stark contrast with the cover for their next album, released in November 1963 and titled *With the Beatles*. Their second album cover shows the four at eye level directly facing the viewer in black and white with half of their faces appearing almost as a silhouette. They wear identical black turtlenecks instead of the identical suits in which they now performed and that they wore on the cover of their first album. The back covers of both the albums informed their listeners which songs were covers and which were originals, identified on *Please Please Me* as composed by McCartney–Lennon. (Songwriting credits would be reversed on all subsequent recordings to read "Lennon-McCartney." Paul had deferred to John and Brian to keep the peace, although he clearly preferred "McCartney-Lennon"). In addition, both back covers identified who sang lead on what songs. Even Ringo took a turn singing lead on the albums, performing on the first album the Dixon–Farrell composition, "Boys," with which the US girls group the Shirelles had had a hit, and belting out "I Wanna Be Your Man" on *With the Beatles*.

The album *Please Please Me* started with their original rocker "I Saw Her Standing There," the same song the Beatles opened their first set with at the Azena Ballroom.

When Joe Cocker heard the live performance that evening, he later recalled, "Thinking how tight they sounded ... It was like they'd been working at it for years."[26] They had. The music critic Rob Sheffield calls "I Saw Her Standing There" "the best first song on a debut album, ever."[27] Walter Everett notes the distinctive use of a bass ostinato by Paul on the song, copied from Chuck Berry's "I'm Talking about You," but linking it to a number of popular rock and roll songs with which the Beatles were familiar, including standards they covered such as "Good Golly Miss Molly" and "Dizzy Miss Lizzy."[28] The album ended with another rocker, a cover version of the Isley Brothers' hit "Twist and Shout," on which John Lennon performed a searing, raw vocal, getting everything out of a shot voice caused by a sore throat and a full day of recording. George Martin knew the Beatles needed to get everything right on the first take or John's throat would not hold out. They needed two takes, but John and the lads obliged Martin with one of the great rock and roll recordings of all time. Lennon, who had needed several lozenges to inure his throat to the pain of singing the song, later said, "My voice wasn't the same for a long time after, every time I swallowed, it was like sandpaper. I was always bitterly ashamed of it, because I could sing it better than that, but now it doesn't bother me."[29]

Martin and the Beatles would not have dared record an album of all originals at this stage, even if John and Paul had had enough material that they considered worthy of putting on an album. They settled for an almost equal balance of eight originals and six cover songs. Among the other covers on the album, "Anna (Go to Him)" in particular displays the Beatles virtuosity and their ability to transform a ballad into something special. They hit just the right notes and instead of the soulful pleading of Arthur Alexander's original, John practically screams out in urgency and desperation, capturing a level of emotion that one feels as well as hears when listening to the song. John does not so much surpass Alexander's interpretation of the song, which has its own haunting beauty, as he transforms it and makes it into something that makes it seem as if he has written the song. Their original song, "P.S. I Love You," the flip side of their single "Love Me Do," is a simple enough song but it features especially strong harmonies of John and Paul and uses both major and minor chords in ways that Martin found interesting. The other original songs featured on the album were "Misery," "Ask Me Why," "Do You Want to Know a Secret," and "There's a Place," in addition to the singles "Love Me Do" and "Please Please Me." Graham Nash recalled hearing the Beatles sing "Misery" to him backstage at one of his shows at Stoke-on-Trent and thinking, "the minute I heard it, I knew it was a smash hit."[30] Listeners heard, interspersed with these originals, the Goffin-King song "Chains," a David/Williams/Bacharach composition called "Baby It's You," and the traditional pop standard "A Taste of Honey," which beat out "Besame Mucho" for a place on the album. The end result was an album that rewarded its buyers with a value they did not have a right to expect at a time when artists and groups released albums mainly to capitalize on the popularity of their singles by unloading lesser songs that did not have the potential to become hits.

In August, they recorded their next single, "She Loves You," with a song called "I'll Get You" on the B-side. They released the record on August 23 and performed both songs the next day on BBC's popular *Saturday Club* program. The host of that program, Brian Matthews, estimated its weekly audience as between 25 and 30 million, mostly young, listeners.[31] The Beatles' frequent appearances and performances on BBC radio not only enabled fans to get to know them but also gained acceptance for a group that spoke with Liverpool accents and whose speech patterns many listeners would find unfamiliar. In 2002, Bill Harry, the creator of *Mersey Beat*, reflected about how unfortunate the success of the Beatles was for other groups from Liverpool because they essentially monopolized the Liverpool sound, but that is not entirely true. Gerry and the Pacemakers, Billy J. Kramer and the Dakotas, The Searchers, and Cilla Black were all Liverpudlians who had success in the 1960s, while other groups from the provinces featured prominently among the British Invasion groups that rode the coattails of the Beatles. Herman's Hermits hailed from Manchester, the Hollies came from Salford near Manchester, and the Animals originated in Newcastle-upon-Tyne, just to name a few. The Beatles performed a total of thirty-nine times on the BBC in 1963 alone, quickly moving from guests on established shows like *Saturday Club* to shows featuring them exclusively under the title of "Pop Goes the Beatles." They had already become a British institution by the end of the year, as reflected in a special Boxing Day program featuring the group titled "From Us to You."

In one interview, Paul, responding to a question the Beatles would repeatedly face in the early years of their success about how long the band would last, replied, "Well, obviously we can't keep playing the same sort of music until we're about forty ... sort of old men playing 'From Me to You.'"[32] Paul expresses a desire to team up with John to write songs for other artists once the Beatles' career as a group ended, as if that end were already imminent. As it turned out, they were only getting started.

Critical and Popular Reactions to the Beatles in 1963

It is more difficult to assess critical reactions to early Beatles' recordings, including their first LP, than their later ones because the popular press in Britain did not yet regard popular music as an appropriate subject for serious treatment or critical analysis. Furthermore, the first two Beatles albums, *Please Please Me* and *With the Beatles*, were not even released in the United States; instead, the 1964 album, *Meet the Beatles*, featured select songs from both of these UK albums. The US reaction to the Beatles was further muted by the release of their early singles on obscure record labels, including Vee-Jay out of Chicago and Swan from Philadelphia, which had difficulty getting their records played on the radio. It would be decades later until Walter Everett and Ken Womack, among others, would explore the innovative techniques George Martin used to record the Beatles, even on their earliest records, which Martin recorded in both mono and stereo.[33] Even after the Beatles hit number one on the *New Musical Express* and *Melody Maker* charts with "Please Please Me" in February 1963, the mainstream press still failed to take note of their success.

1963: Profumo, the Pill, and *Please, Please Me*

However, the album and early singles did receive coverage in music papers and a few other random publications. Such early contemporary reviews as do exist do shed light on the Beatles' reception at this still early stage of their career. A reviewer, writing that year in *J2 Magazine*, a paper aimed at Catholic girls in France, wrote of an album released in France under the title *The Beatles Hits* that "One either likes or dislikes this cocktail of Western, or rock, and of Irish ballads; a cocktail enlivened with punch and humor ... English that comes from within itself."[34] The Beatles had indeed incorporated a wide range of musical genres into their repertoire, though most people first learned of them and primarily knew them through their early rock and roll hits like "Love Me Do," "Please Please Me," and "She Loves You." According to Mark Lewisohn, "Love Me Do" received the most positive attention from a publication called *The World's Fair*, which catered to Britain's 11,000 jukebox owners. Reviews cited by Lewisohn included such encomiums as "a most promising first disc" and "quite a catchy little tune, which strongly features the now almost inevitable harmonica." Another reviewer echoed this by saying, "Sounds very much like a big hit to me." However, *Disc Date with Don Nicholl* only gave the record an "ordinary" ranking of two stars, saying, "The Beatles sound rather like the Everly Brothers or the Brooks [Brothers] according to whose side you're on."[35] *New Musical Express* called "Please Please Me" "a really enjoyable platter, full of beat, vigour and vitality—and what's more, it's different."[36] Maureen Cleave described the Beatles in the *Evening Standard* as "a vocal-instrumental group, three guitars and drums, and they don't sound a bit like The Shadows, or anybody else for that matter."[37] The Beatles' second album, *With the Beatles*, released in November, garnered a positive review from Peter Jones writing in the *Record Mirror*, who called the album "fantastic."[38]

Elijah Wald has argued that the Beatles marked the end of an era in popular music rather than a new beginning. He called them "the summation of all the trends of the previous few years wrapped into a particularly attractive package."[39] When recording *Please Please Me*, George Martin had been influenced by traveling to Liverpool to watch the Beatles' live show at the Cavern, which he decided was how he wanted to approach the album. "I just selected all the stuff I knew they could do at the drop of a hat. I got them down to the studio and said, 'Right, we're going to record "Roll over Beethoven," we're going to record "Money," we're going to record "Chains," and so on,'" he later recalled.[40] Their engineer Norman Smith said,

> I tried to get the sound of The Beatles singing and playing as they'd perform onstage. I thought if I didn't do it, I'd lose the excitement. In other words, I laid down the backing tracks first, then laid on the words. It was important to create the live sounds as it happened, and I did get them exactly the way they performed onstage.[41]

The Beatles included a hodgepodge of earlier styles of music on both of their first LPs, reserving rock and roll classics like "Roll over Beethoven" and "Money" for their second album. On *With the Beatles*, they also intermingled alongside eight new originals Smokey Robinson's R & B hit, "You Really Got a Hold on Me," the Marvellettes' "Please Mr. Postman," another staple of their early live shows, and the ballad "Till There Was You" from the Broadway musical and extremely popular movie, *The Music Man*. Of the cover songs, Peter Jones in his review seemed to favor the Barrett Strong song "Money," which he noted was unavailable in Britain at the time. Jones called the Beatles' cover "a roar-up of the highest order. Big, brash, bright."[42] They also included eight originals on the album, including their own distinctive version of "I Wanna Be Your Man," which they had given to the Rolling Stones, who had a hit with it in their own blues-rock style. George made his songwriting debut on *With the Beatles* with "Don't Bother Me," while Paul and John wrote the other seven originals. Jones found "All My Loving" "maybe a trifle 'ordinary' by Beatles' standards … but compensated for by some pungent lead guitar from George."[43] The other original songs on the album included "It Won't Be Long," "All I've Got to Do," "Little Child," "Hold Me Tight," and "Not a Second Time." They are all perfectly good songs with catchy beats and clever if not particularly profound lyrics, but whether they represent a marked improvement over the originals on *Please Please Me* is certainly up for debate. Significantly, the Beatles did not release any of the songs on *With the Beatles* as a single.

It is a little easier to gauge popular than critical reaction to the Beatles' music in 1963. "Please Please Me" had quickly progressed up the charts in Britain, reaching number one by the end of February. It spent a week co-occupying the top spot with Frank Ifield's "The Wayward Wind," before taking sole possession of number one at the beginning of March. Maureen Cleave reported sales of "Please Please Me" running as high as 50,000 copies a week. In his autobiography, the American rock star John Fogerty, who went on to lead his own enormously successful band, Creedence Clearwater Revival, wrote that he heard "Please Please Me" every day his senior year in high school as he drove to the gas station in California where he worked after school. Fogerty was even more impressed by the B-side, "From Me to You," even though he still did not know the name of the group who performed these songs, mistakenly thinking that the disk jockeys kept saying "Shields" instead of "Beatles."[44] (Beatles fan Paula Myers told Gary Berman she thought "Please Please Me" was by the Everly Brothers.[45]) In September, the Beatles virtually owned the charts, with *Please Please Me* outselling all other LPs and "She Loves You" the top selling single in the UK. Even their record, "Twist and Shout," outsold all other records in the EP category. By the time that they released *With the Beatles* in November, they had sold 250,000 advance copies of their second album, the largest such number in British musical history, according to Peter Jones. This pushed their total record sales in excess of three million copies.

In conclusion, even if the Beatles' original contributions to their first two albums still blended the musical styles already developed by other artists, the sacrosanct manner in which their growing legions of fans regarded the group and the lengths to which they were determined to go to demonstrate their allegiance and devotion was something new and original. The mainstream press still refused to offer critical reviews of their music, but they could not help but cover the amazing new phenomenon that the press itself dubbed "Beatlemania."

1963: Profumo, the Pill, and *Please, Please Me*

The Beginnings of Beatlemania

Beatlemania seemed to catch British and American society unawares, but its development in Britain occurred gradually over the course of a couple of years, starting in Liverpool and spreading outward from there. Sam Leach dates the precise start of Beatlemania to a Beatles' gig at the Tower in Liverpool on November 9, 1961, when he witnessed a "frenzied scene that beggared belief." Leach wrote:

> The entire dance floor was crammed with ecstatic young girls crying and screaming, pushing forward to catch a glimpse of their idols. The noise was incredible, and I had to cover my ears, I was barely able to tell which songs the lads were singing. Young girls sobbed uncontrollably. The girls nearer the back were standing on tables and chairs, waving their hankies and imploring their favorite Beatles to look at them. It was madness.[46]

Something was different about the group after their experience in Hamburg and their fans clearly noticed, but from the beginning, Beatlemania was just as much about the fans as it was the Beatles. Beatlemania was about a larger shift in the culture that signaled the start of something entirely new. Leach said he had never seen anything like it. Neither had anyone else.

Graham Nash first saw the Beatles in Manchester in 1962, when Pete Best was still playing with the group, and even then, Nash wrote, "every girl in there stopped dead in their tracks. Man, it was like four Marlon Brandos had walked in. … They hadn't even played a note, and the girls would swoon and faint."[47] Maureen Cleave thought their looks had a lot to do with the popularity of the Beatles. She described them as "scruffy, but scruffy on purpose."

> They wear bell-bottom suits of a rich burgundy color with black velvet collars. Boots of course. Shoes seem to have died out altogether. Their shirts are pink and their hairstyles are French. Liverpool lads of 12 and upward now have small bouffant Beatle heads with the fringe brushed forward.[48]

Ian Inglis has argued that their success depended upon their acceptance in the music industry, which depended on them *not* departing from the model followed by other pop groups at that time. He credits Brian Epstein for recognizing this and getting them to conform, at least until 1966, to industry standards. Inglis argues that the Beatles differed from other pop groups in those early years only in the size of their success and following, but not in the path that they followed to stardom.[49] For instance, the Beatles' first appearance on the radio took place as early as March 8, 1962, during a live broadcast of an episode of "Teenager's Turn" on BBC recorded the previous day at the Playhouse Theatre in Manchester.[50] They followed this appearance up with numerous radio spots and performances that facilitated as well as recognized their growing popularity.

At the time, writing in *Tiger Beat* magazine, Ken Ferguson defined Beatlemania as simply "a form of hysterical worship instigated by four young men who call themselves The Beatles."[51] He attributed the phenomenon to the waning popularity of Elvis Presley and Cliff Richard among young people and the need for something new at which teenage music fans could direct their screams. Elvis had indeed declined in popularity after a stint in the army when he began to focus on an acting career that produced a string of corny movies with variations on the same plot. Cliff Richard's records still sold and he still had plenty of fans, but he never had much success in the United States and within Britain remained a standard, if successful, pop star. Unlike Elvis and Cliff Richard, the screams at Beatles shows would become so deafening that the group could not hear themselves play, nor could the audience who were ostensibly there to hear the music. The causes of Beatlemania in Britain and the United States varied somewhat (see Chapter 4), but in both places understanding the reasons why people liked the Beatles and understanding the phenomenon of Beatlemania are two different things.

In Britain, after the origins of Beatlemania in Liverpool in 1961 and its expansion in 1962 to other parts of Britain, 1963 produced a dynamic that began as early as January, when police presence began to appear at their shows, and continued steadily, reaching a crescendo late in the year. On February 20, 1963, the Beatles made their first appearance on the BBC radio show, "Parade of the Pops," on which they gave live performances of "Love Me Do" and "Please Please Me." On February 25, they began touring with Helen Shapiro, a popular young singer who would not turn 16 until September. By then, their record sales had skyrocketed, foreshadowing the full-scale eruption of Beatlemania in the autumn. According to Peter Brown, Epstein's personal assistant, record stores in Britain had preordered half a million copies of their new single, "She Loves You," before John and Paul had even written the lyrics![52] The song became the largest seller of any single in British history until Paul McCartney's "Mull of Kintyre" surpassed it fifteen years later.[53]

In addition, the Beatles already had an Official Fan Club in London, dating from 1962, which would reach 80,000 members by 1965.[54] Freda Kelly, Epstein's secretary and the president of the Official Beatles Fan Club, described what it was like to run the Beatles' original fan club in Liverpool.

> It [fan mail] came in sackfuls day after day. Two or more a day sometimes. I would look at all this mail, not just letters, but packages and boxes, and I would close my eyes and think, Oh my, where are we going to put it all? What have I done to deserve this? ... We would put the sacks side by side and mark each one that came in the door—Monday, Tuesday, Wednesday—and eventually we would get through it. Then it just became too much.[55]

A turning point on their road to becoming a national phenomenon occurred with their performance on the heavily watched television program *Sunday Night at the Palladium* on October 13, 1963. Reluctant to invite them to appear at first, Lew Grade, the booking agent for the show, succumbed to the pressure produced by the flood of letters he received requesting that he do so. Their first appearance on national television turned the Beatles into the overnight sensation journalists and later historians frequently described them as being. Their performance on *Sunday Night* preceded a Royal Command Performance at the Prince of Wales Theatre in London the next month, bolstering their

Figure 3.2 *Frenzied Beatles fans watching the band perform in Manchester, November 20, 1963. Courtesy of Alamy Photos.*

reputation and expanding the awareness of them among the public and the press. Their courteous demeanor and exemplary behavior inoculated them against some of the fears that could have easily developed from their cult-like following among British teenagers, another part of Brian Epstein's plan to make them respectable representatives of the music industry.

Beatlemania in the autumn of 1963 was not new, but it was different. The Beatles' road manager Neil Aspinall recalled, "They'd had a lot of madness in Liverpool, but they knew all the kids there. They didn't try to jump on you or overturn the van or rip the wing mirrors off suddenly. Suddenly this absolute craziness was going on, which was very exciting, but difficult to deal with."[56] Ringo Starr also noticed the difference:

> Home and family were the two things I didn't want to change, because it has all changed "out there" and we were no longer really sure who our friends were, unless we had them before the fame. The guys and the girls I used to hang about with I could trust. But once we'd become famous, we soon learnt that people were

Figure 3.3 *Workers at the Beatles Fan Club in London empty one of many sacks of fan mail. November 1, 1963. Photo by Chris Ware. Courtesy of Getty Images.*

with us only because of the vague notoriety of being a "Beatle." And when this happened in the family, it was quite a blow.[57]

George Harrison opined that the press was just trying to sell papers and suspected that they had built the Beatles up to such enormous heights to have the ability to tear them down later,[58] but this theory ignores the underlying reasons why the Beatles and Beatlemania sold papers in 1963 in the first place. The Beatles' reception in Britain in the fall of 1963 occurred against the backdrop of the Profumo scandal and the accompanying disillusionment with British politics and the British ruling class. The Beatles, like Ian Fleming's James Bond novels, written between 1953 and 1964, reassured the British people, albeit for different demographics and in different ways, that Britain still had something in which they could take pride. Historians of American popular culture have stressed the importance of the diversion the Beatles provided in the wake of the Kennedy assassination. In Britain, they became a distraction not only from the political crisis unfolding in 1963 but also from the Cold War and the decline of British power and prestige abroad, dating to the end of the Second World War and highlighted by the way in which the British had stumbled through the Suez Crisis in 1956.

Still, the role of the press in the creation of Beatlemania raises the question of whether or not the phenomenon was merely a product of hype that did not match the actual influence the Beatles had on youth culture. For example, David Fowler argues that the Beatles had little influence over the rebellious young people who described themselves as "mods" and who posed as the leaders and trendsetters of the younger generation. He suggests that the Rolling Stones had greater impact on youth culture than the Beatles did because Beatles fans tended to be girls under the age of 14 who would have lost interest in the Beatles by the time they were 20.[59] As the rest of this book will show, however, it does not seem to have actually been the case that young people who became fans of the group in the early years lost interest in them by the end of the decade. Furthermore, the Beatles became trendsetters in 1963 and continued to impact popular and youth culture throughout the decade, including their enormous impact on other groups in Britain and America, unless one subscribes to a particularly narrow definition of popular culture that almost seems designed to exclude them. Beatlemania in Britain benefited from the press and the attention the phenomenon received from the press, but it started with the Beatles, who would need to respond constructively to it in order for it to thrive and continue.

Either way, by the time 1963 ended, the Beatles were ready for their rendezvous with the throngs of adoring fans awaiting them in the United States, where their appearance on the popular *Ed Sullivan Show* would take the phenomenon of Beatlemania to ever-greater heights. According to one version, Ed Sullivan had first heard about the group when he witnessed mobs of fans awaiting their arrival at Heathrow Airport and inquired about the cause of the entire hubbub. News of Beatlemania soon traveled across the Atlantic with him, creating a wave of curiosity and some skepticism as to whether any mere rock and roll group could live up to all the hysteria. Reporting on the British phenomenon for readers in the United States, Frederick Lewis reported in December that "To see a Beatle is joy, to touch one paradise on earth, and for just the slimmest opportunity of this privilege, people will fight like mad things and with the dedication normally reserved for a Great Cause, like natural survival." Compared to the Beatles, he wrote, "Elvis Presley is a conservative tenor of considerable diffidence."[60] The Beatles themselves knew that they would have a difficult time living up to these outsized expectations. They also knew that their records had not sold particularly well in the United States compared to their sales in Britain. In fact, obtuse executives at Capital Records, which owned the US rights to Beatles' recordings, declined their option to release them. They would soon see the folly of their ways.

CHAPTER 4
1964: BEATLEMANIA IN HISTORICAL CONTEXT

The Battle over the Civil Rights Bill in the United States

The year 1964 marked a significant turning point in the long history of the Civil Rights Movement with the passage of both the Civil Rights Act and the Economic Opportunity Act. Simultaneously, 1964 witnessed a major shift in the history of American popular culture with the arrival of the Beatles and the accompanying phenomenon of Beatlemania. Both came fast on the heels of the assassination of President John F. Kennedy on November 22, 1963. In early February, as the Beatles arrived in New York in advance of their appearance on the popular *Ed Sullivan Show*, a race riot was taking place in Cleveland, and other incidences of racial violence and controversy were sweeping the nation. A momentary pause in racial tensions followed Kennedy's death, during which time whites and Blacks seemed to unite in their shock over the assassination. The proposal of a major Civil Rights Bill that February, therefore, seems critical to understanding the atmosphere in the United States when the Beatles first arrived there and the reception they received when they did. This is not to suggest a simplistic causal relationship between the Civil Rights Movement and Beatlemania, but rather to observe simply that Beatlemania did not occur in a political vacuum. The political atmosphere in the country was one factor that might help to explain why people in the United States reacted the way they did to the Beatles, especially since that reaction differed qualitatively from what occurred in countries like Sweden and France around the same time.[1] The Beatles were part of a changing society, and 1964 provides a great example of this.

It has become fashionable to link the Kennedy assassination with the arrival of the Beatles and the onset of Beatlemania in the United States, with the Beatles providing an antidote for the despair and depression experienced by the country after Kennedy's death. Before dealing with the causes of Beatlemania in the United States, however, it is important to note that the Kennedy assassination itself did not occur in a vacuum either. Most importantly, it took place in Dallas, a southern city with a long history of racism and racial discrimination. In fact, at least two other physical attacks on prominent Democrats had occurred in the city in the month prior to Kennedy's arrival. One involved then vice president Lyndon B. Johnson, who along with his wife, Lady Bird, endured an attack by a right-wing mob after a speech in a Dallas hotel. The other occurred when an angry demonstrator hit previous presidential candidate Adlai Stevenson with a placard. Oswald's act had shone a bright light on the dark side of the city's history of prejudice and bigotry. Lawrence Wright, who grew up in Dallas and was 16 at the time of the Kennedy assassination, writes in his memoir *In the New World: Growing Up with America from the Sixties to the Eighties* of the shame he experienced at the realization that his hometown would remain forever linked with this tragic event. In retrospect, Wright argued, Kennedy's assassination seemed almost inevitable, with Dallas the most logical place for it to occur. As Wright put it, "the world decided that Kennedy had died in enemy territory that no matter who had killed him, we had *willed* him dead."[2]

Though in retrospect it seemed people should have anticipated the assassination, the shock of the actual event was real, too, as was the depression many people throughout the country experienced, especially young people, who had been so optimistic and inspired by the youngest and most charismatic president in US history. A 2002 study by American Demographics compared the psychological response of the 9/11 terrorist attacks in the United States to that following the Kennedy assassination. It found that Americans experienced higher levels of anxiety and stress following the Kennedy assassination than they did in the months following 9/11.[3] In the aftermath of Kennedy's death, a majority of people reported finding it difficult to carry on with their daily activities; indeed, it seemed as if the country as a whole came to a virtual standstill. However, once the calendar turned to a new year, the country, if not yet fully recovered, seemed ready to get on with business, including addressing the important issue of the Civil Rights Bill being debated in the House in January. An early indication that the nation might be ready to move on this issue came on the 21st when the *Atlanta Constitution*, one of the foremost newspapers in the South, endorsed the bill. The editorial, written by the editor, Eugene Patterson, did so on the grounds that the hopes that Southern businesses would end discrimination of their own accord to prevent the need for federal legislation had not come to fruition. Patterson stated unequivocally the paper's opposition to discrimination in public accommodations.

Nevertheless, Southern senators hoped to water down the bill considerably if they could not halt its passage altogether. On February 9, the date of the Beatles' first appearance on the *Ed Sullivan Show*, several senators from Southern states voiced their staunch opposition to the bill, if for no other reason than to reassure their constituents that they would at least put up a fight. On February 20, Senator Richard B. Russell of Georgia told the press that they would do everything in their power to defeat the proposed legislation. When reporters cornered him after a strategy meeting with his colleagues, Russell remarked, "We don't mind around-the-clock sessions. We will be glad to be there 24 hours a day."[4] This opposition did not stop Vice President Hubert H. Humphrey from telling a convocation of Democrats in New Jersey the following month that the Senate would pass the Civil Rights Bill. Humphrey appealed to the reputation of the United States abroad in the midst of the Cold War, stating, "We're going to win it because we know that internationally it is imperative that we come to the world with clean hands."[5]

Meanwhile, the emergence of the Nation of Islam and the 1961 conversion of Cassius Clay (who changed his name to Muhammad Ali in 1964) foreshadowed the split over the tactics and ultimate aims of the Civil Rights Movement. Ali's voice achieved greater prominence when he was crowned heavyweight boxing champion on February 25,

1964. His meeting with the Beatles in Miami one week earlier therefore carried greater symbolic significance than books on the Beatles usually assign it. The Beatles had wanted to meet with Sonny Liston, who was favored to beat Clay in their championship fight, but Liston turned them down. The disappointed Beatles consented to meet with Clay, though John Lennon in particular did not want to settle by meeting with the challenger instead of the champion. Nonetheless, coming in the midst of the debate over the Civil Rights Bill, the Beatles' decision to meet with the outspoken Clay, already a controversial and polarizing figure, in a southern city, albeit a cosmopolitan metropolis like Miami, foreshadowed the Beatles' opposition to segregation, even if they had not intended to make a political statement at the time. Ironically, in May, Muhammad Ali suggested that integration was not an appropriate goal for African Americans, who, he argued, could only gain the respect they deserved once they had formed a separate state. Ali called the Civil Rights Bill "counterfeit money," while also voicing his opposition to the National Association for the Advancement of Colored People (NAACP).[6] This statement foreshadowed divisions in the Civil Rights Movement later in the decade and cast a pall over the hopes that the bill would move the country closer toward racial harmony.

Larry Kane was a young news director at a Miami radio station and was one of four reporters who interviewed them when they arrived there. He ended up accompanying them and covering them as a reporter on their US tour later that summer and joined them again on their 1965 and 1966 US tours. The Beatles were very much aware of the Civil Rights issue, according to Kane, who came to know the Beatles very well. Kane stated:

> They were extremely partisan when it came to disengaging in racism and felt that people should be judged by who they are and not by what they looked like. John was very much in the groove of showing his empathy and sympathy toward people of color in the United States and was not afraid to talk about it. McCartney, too. It is interesting that Epstein told them not to talk about things like that and they did any way.[7]

The Beatles' refusal to perform before segregated audiences in the South removed any doubt about their stance.

In fact, Kane asked them directly if they knew they would be performing before a segregated audience at the Gator Bowl in Jacksonville and other southern cities, at which point the Beatles took a firm stand on the issue. The South had a long history of separating crowds into sections specifically designated for Blacks and whites, whether the performing artist was Black or white. Responding to Kane's query about Jacksonville, Paul McCartney responded emphatically, "We're not going to play there," a sentiment with which his bandmates were in full agreement. John Lennon flatly stated at the time, "We never play to segregated audiences, and we aren't going to start now." The Beatles would cancel the concert at the Gator Bowl and forego the anticipated revenue if expected to play before a segregated crowd. The concert organizers had in fact never formally announced that the crowd would be segregated, but this was standard practice in the South and word must have reached them beforehand because when the Beatles showed up for their September 11 concert they found a fully integrated audience waiting to hear them play. After this, the standard copy of the Beatles' performance contract devised by Brian Epstein stipulated that the Beatles "not be required to perform in front of a segregated audience." It should be pointed out that by the time of the Jacksonville concert, the Beatles had the force of the Civil Rights Act behind them, making it technically illegal for the concert to be segregated. Nor were the Beatles the only artists who took a stand against segregated audiences, a position a number of stars like Chuck Berry had taken even in the 1950s. Furthermore, their position involved far less risk than those protesters who integrated lunch counters and other public spaces, participated in Freedom Rides, or took measures to ensure that African Americans not only had the right but also the ability to vote. However, the race issue being a long way from resolution when the Beatles took their stand in 1964, they would reiterate their condemnation of racism and white supremacy when they returned to the South before a concert in Atlanta in 1965, and it may have still been on Paul's mind when he wrote the song "Blackbird" in 1968.

Meanwhile, racial tensions had escalated in June when three civil rights workers went missing in Mississippi. They were there as part of a campaign to register African Americans to vote and encourage them to go to the polls that November. The year 1964 was an election year and people expected the contest to have huge ramifications for the country in general and the issue of civil rights in particular. Shortly after the young men disappeared, the FBI arrived, with the total backing of the Justice Department, to conduct a full-blown investigation. The missing men, two white volunteers and one African American, later turned up dead, as feared by the campaign's organizers. As this suspenseful and tragic story played out in Mississippi, in neighboring Alabama, Governor George C. Wallace was speaking out against the Supreme Court for banning prayer in schools and against the Civil Rights Bill then on the floor of the Senate. When Wallace went to Dallas, less than a year after the Kennedy assassination, to speak to the US Junior Chamber of Commerce National Convention, he received a five-minute standing ovation.[8] Dallas did not seem so eager to shed its reputation as a hotbed of racial bigotry.

Nevertheless, on July 2, President Johnson signed the Civil Rights Bill into law, only five hours after the Senate had passed it. The passage of the Civil Rights Act met with predictable resistance in the American South, although the Mississippi Economic Council, comprising the state's most prominent business leaders, pleaded with the state's residents to respect the new law and advocated that new regulations on voter registration and voting be "fairly and impartially administered for all." The governor of the state, Paul B. Johnson, did not follow suit, however. In 1962, Johnson's predecessor, Ross Barnett, had attempted to block James Meredith from becoming the first Black man to attend the University of Mississippi, a right Meredith later gained through a federal court decision. Johnson, who had served as lieutenant governor under Barnett, now advocated challenging the prohibition of discrimination in public accommodations in the courts, indicating his strong disapproval. Meanwhile, in Alabama, Wallace remained implacably opposed to the act, virtually to the point of defying federal law.

Despite these signs of opposition, what struck contemporaries was how swiftly and peacefully desegregation occurred in most parts of the South. Veteran Senators Russell of Georgia, Allan Ellender of Louisiana, and Strom Thurmond of South Carolina all spoke out in support of respecting the act once it had passed. In the spring of 1965, the writer Walker Percy argued that Mississippi might have had a better record at adapting to the new federal regulations on civil rights than Alabama. However, that might not have been saying all that much, given, as Percy acknowledged, that white students at the University of Mississippi were still throwing stones at Black students attempting to enter the campus.[9] The situation in Mississippi epitomized the problem with the Civil Rights Bill in the Deep South. However much the majority of the population complied with the new law, which did bring sweeping changes to the South, it would only take a minority of die-hard resisters to cause major problems for the federal government and raise racial tensions across the country in the process.

In November 1964, Martin Luther King Jr. traveled to Norway to accept the Nobel Peace Prize. When he returned, determined not to rest on his laurels and not to allow President Johnson to rest on his, King immediately met with Johnson to push for a federal voting rights act. Having just won reelection by a landslide over the conservative Senator Barry Goldwater, Johnson had something of a mandate but was still reluctant to move on a voting rights act so soon after the passage of a major Civil Rights Bill. Goldwater had voted against the Civil Rights Bill and ended up carrying Mississippi, as well as the entire Deep South, in the presidential election by a seven to one ratio, one indication of the depth of opposition Johnson still faced in the South. Johnson's support of Civil Rights had effectively destroyed the Democratic Party in the South, which would have occupied an even worse position had it not been for African American support for the party, a dilemma it has faced ever since. Johnson did not oppose a voting rights act, he told King, but he doubted whether he could achieve it given the strength of the opposition he had faced from Southern senators and overcome to achieve that year's legislation. King was persuasive, however, and within a year, Johnson had signed the voting rights act King wanted into law.

The year 1964 therefore carried with it important and revolutionary social changes, backed initially by the Johnson administration and the federal government, with assistance from the Supreme Court. Johnson's dream of a Great Society and a War on Poverty were just the types of broad goals many young people would have embraced when they thought that the Kennedy administration would usher in a new, shining age. After Kennedy's death, "Camelot" remained an ideal, fostered in particular by Jackie Kennedy, who told the writer Theodore White that she and the president had often enjoyed listening to the soundtrack to the play, which had enjoyed great popularity on Broadway in 1963. Jackie was afraid that people would soon forget her husband and she wanted them to remember that, as the song went, "That once there was a spot for one brief shining moment that was known as Camelot." The comparison stuck and became part of the magic and mystery associated with Kennedy's thousand-day presidency.

Johnson never had the romantic allure of a Kennedy, but he sought to create a new, better version of America, with the assistance of several new federal programs. These programs included Head Start, which focused on improving the health, nutrition, and education of children from low-income families; the Office of Economic Opportunity; and the Equal Employment Opportunity Commission, established to enforce the new laws against discrimination in the workplace. These programs, along with the Civil Rights Act itself, owed a great deal to Johnson's political acumen and his ability to manage the Senate, based partly on his long years of experience there. Admittedly, progress moved slowly; for example, in 1965 only 2.5 percent of eligible Black children attended desegregated schools in eleven Southern states (though this was double the number who had attended such schools the previous year).[10] Johnson's pragmatic and hard-nosed practice of realpolitik helped to make some of Kennedy's quixotic dreams a reality. In doing so, he helped, in his own unwitting way, to foster the dream of the younger generation's utopianism and to revive hope in the aftermath of the traumatic effects of Kennedy's death.

When the Beatles arrived in the United States in February 1964, therefore, they arrived in a country that had just endured a great national tragedy, but one that was already poised to move forward. This readiness manifested itself primarily in the proposal, debate over, and ultimately the passage of the Civil Rights Bill of 1964 and accompanying legislation that seemed to put America on the verge of vast social changes. This was a time of continuity and change, with the Beatles adding a tipping point in favor of the latter. Yet the Beatles were only one part of the equation that added up to Beatlemania; the other part consisted of the fans, whose reaction we need to assess not only against the backdrop of social issues confronting the United States at the time but also in the context of the understanding provided by the concept known as audience reception theory.

Audience Reception Theory and the Beatles

The Beatles arrived in the United States on the heels of the success of their hit single, "I Want to Hold Your Hand," which featured the pleasant tune "This Boy" as the B-side. Reception theory encourages an examination of the meaning that audiences assign to popular cultural artifacts or phenomena and stipulates that audiences are capable of providing their own interpretations independently of those that the purveyors of culture may wish to assign. As Ott and Mack put it, "Reception scholars primarily seek to understand the personal meanings that individuals make of mass media texts in relation to their lived social systems and experiences."[11] Such texts might include a novel, television broadcast, film, song, interview, music video, or any kind of performance or artifact available to the public. Scholars differ, however, on the extent to which power enters into the relationship between the audience and those responsible for mediating what they get to see or hear. For example, during the Payola scandal of the late 1950s, it became widely known that deejays accepted kickbacks from agents and record companies to play songs by their artists to the exclusion of those artists whose songs might have been just as good but did not have the financial wherewithal or connections to get airtime. Another blatant example of the role of power in influencing popular culture would be the refusal of some radio stations, especially in the South, to play what they called "race music," songs by Black artists or by white artists who sounded Black, something that made Elvis Presley so controversial in the early stages of his career. In the case of the Beatles, Capital Records' initial decision not to release the group's early singles in the United States, relegating them to lesser labels, restricted the number of people in the United States who had the chance to hear those recordings. Therefore, for many people, including Larry Kane, "I Want to Hold Your Hand" was the first Beatles song they heard, even though the group had placed songs such as "Please Please Me" and "From Me to You" on the charts the previous year. These songs never achieved much success in the United States, "Please Please Me" peaking at # 35 during its first release and "From Me to You" at # 116. "She Loves You," also released in 1963 and arguably as good a song as "I Want to Hold Your Hand," failed to make the US charts at all during its first release.

While power clearly has its place in understanding the history of popular culture and its reception in a given society, the problem with using it as an overarching explanatory force is that it denies agency to the individuals and groups that comprise an audience and thus runs counter to the entire thrust of reception theory. In the case of the Beatles, radio promotions encouraging listeners to go to Kennedy Airport to greet the Beatles upon their arrival on February 7, 1964, may have influenced the more than three thousand fans who did so (some estimates run much higher). However, those who went still made individual decisions based on something that they heard or saw in the Beatles that appealed to them. Reception theory, therefore, becomes quite useful when attempting to assess the extent to which Beatlemania and the hysteria resulting from their adulation was a creation of the fans and the extent to which the hype itself provoked the fans into their frenzied reaction to the group. Reception theory is, in fact, central to the goal of this entire book in offering a reassessment of the Beatles' reception for the rest of the 1960s, after the initial infatuation phase of Beatlemania had ended.

CBS had first announced the Beatles' arrival date, as well as the dates of their first two appearances on the *Ed Sullivan Show* (February 9 and 16) as early as December 13, so in theory Beatles fans had almost two months to anticipate these momentous events. However, no amount of hype or promotion could have provoked the scale of the response the Beatles engendered when they arrived and performed on national television, drawing an audience of around 73 million, at the time the largest television audience in history. This performance gave the audience a chance to make up their own minds and they clearly liked what they saw. The size of the crowd that greeted the Beatles upon their arrival on August 18 for their second tour of the United States, which would take them to twenty-three cities, had in fact tripled to around nine thousand people.

Furthermore, any attempt to explain Beatlemania in the United States as a product of media hype falters on the causes of Beatlemania in Britain and Ireland, where the phenomenon predated media attention to it. Reports, such as those contained in the article Frederick Lewis wrote for the *New York Times* on December 1, 1963, may have prompted readers' curiosity, though whether many of the young preteen and teenage fans of the Beatles would have read about them in the *Times* seems a dubious proposition at best. Among other manifestations of Beatlemania, Lewis reported that four hundred girls from Catholic schools in Dublin had fought police for an hour in an effort to procure Beatles' tickets.[12] This could have equally led to bemusement on the part of readers who failed to understand what all the fuss was about as a desire to understand, much less imitate, such behavior. As one homemaker named Elise Hamilton told the *Daily Princetonian*, the student newspaper for Princeton University, "I read an article in the *New York Times* in which the author said the Beatles would prove to be too amateurish for the sophisticated teenagers of our country."

In preparing Americans for the arrival of the Beatles, clearly record sales and radio would obviously play a far more important role than they did in Britain, where the group's live performances had initially attracted a large number of fans. In a 2014 study by Krause, North, and Hewitt of people's music listening experiences, the authors found that choice and control over the music they listened to was the single most important factor in determining how much they liked the music and how much attention they paid to it while listening.[13] This fits with reception theory in making agency a prime characteristic of people's musical listening experiences. While today's consumers have gained a much wider range of choices of what they choose to listen to and how they choose to listen to it, choice was hardly absent in 1964. By that time, teenagers with increased purchasing power could buy records and play what they wanted when they wanted, choose what radio stations they listened to on their personal transistor radios, and change the station to another on the dial if they did not like what one station was playing. In other words, promotion could only go so far in accounting for listeners' actual tastes or what records they bought.

Additionally, Ed Sullivan knew that the Beatles would attract viewers and thus help him with his ratings and sponsors; he certainly was no fan of rock music and had previously promoted Elvis on his program for the same reasons. In other words, Sullivan was not attempting to arbitrate popular taste; he was attempting to capitalize on it. We still need to assess the causes of Beatlemania and examine more closely the reception of the Beatles in 1964. In accordance with reception theory, we will assert that the audience itself played a role in actively choosing to watch, listen to, and become fans of the Beatles for reasons that transcended the goal of capitalists and entrepreneurs to sell records, concert tickets, and merchandise.

Before we do, however, we need to address one more explanation for the Beatles' success that seems to run counter to reception theory: that they succeeded because they followed a traditional path to show business success, following Brian Epstein's advice to dress in identical suits, bow after performances, and conform to accepted standards of stage demeanor and proper decorum. This explanation asserts that Epstein had made them acceptable to what audiences expected from a stage act, thus paving the way for their popularity with the masses.[14] In addition, an appearance with Prime Minister Harold Wilson on March 19, 1964, who presented the lads with their Variety Club Awards, further strengthened their establishment credentials and conferred upon them an additional layer of respectability. It would be foolish to deny that the Beatles' appearance had nothing to do with their reception by their audience, whether in Britain or the United States. It certainly helped that by the time they arrived in the United States

1964: Beatlemania in Historical Context

they had polished their appearance and their act and adopted a level of professionalism missing from their gigs in Hamburg or their early appearances at the Cavern Club and other spots around Liverpool. Yet, to place too much emphasis upon their appearance and stage demeanor would ignore the main reason for their popularity—their music and, in particular, the importance of their most recent release prior to their initial visit to the United States: "I Want to Hold Your Hand." More than a half century's familiarity with the song may have blunted how it sounded to people at the time and just how revolutionary it was when first released. Richie Havens, upon first hearing the song, said he thought, "Finally. Something New."[15] Bob Spitz provides one of the best descriptions of what made the song so different, calling it:

> a two-and-a-half-minute rave-up that fairly jumped off the grooves. From the unsparing two-chord intro, there was no letting up. Oh yeah, I'll tell you something. … The energy was impossible to let go of. Part easygoing pop, part joyous rocker, part roller-coaster ride, it came at the listener from every angle, with rhythmic jerks and handclaps and inadvertent detours from the standard four-chord structure. As if the overheated arrangement wasn't tantalizing enough, the Beatles' performance was extraordinary, from John and Paul's slashing harmonies to Paul's sudden full-octave leap into falsetto, capped off by stirring confessions—"I can't hide, I can't hide"—that seem to gain in fervor each time they are sung.[16]

Jane Barnes was in the sixth grade in 1964 and missed the Beatles' first appearance on the *Ed Sullivan Show*. She did not initially buy into the hype about the Beatles, describing herself as "a tomboy" who "did not do a lot of girlie girl stuff." Nevertheless, she caught the Beatles' next two appearances on Sullivan's show and the music "really struck me, it really hit me," she said.[17] As we will see in the next section, scholars, writers, and journalists have offered a variety of explanations for the causes of Beatlemania in 1964. Many factors undoubtedly contributed to the phenomenon. However, any explanation that does not place a high emphasis on the Beatles' music and the initial response it drew from its listeners will not only be incomplete but also come dangerously close to misunderstanding the popularity of the Beatles altogether.

Comparative Analysis of Differing Views on the Causes of Beatlemania in America

Although many pop music fans had heard the Beatles on the radio before February 9, 1964, for millions more the group's appearance on the *Ed Sullivan Show* that night marked the first time they ever heard the Fab Four. The Beatles themselves had little understanding of the cultural and historic forces they were about to unleash. "They had no idea what they would become," said Larry Kane. Even Peter Brown, who had already witnessed first-hand the advent of Beatlemania in Britain, described the spectacle encountered by the group when they arrived in America as "slightly incomprehensible."

Yet many fans, critics, and scholars, ranging from historians to psychologists, have still tried to comprehend and explain the causes of Beatlemania.

The Beatles did arrive in America with a great deal of publicity, especially fomented by disk jockeys like Murray the K, who played their records endlessly and encouraged listeners to form a huge welcoming party for the group at the airport. In his book on the British Invasion, Barry Miles gives Murray some of the credit for the size of the crowd that first greeted the Beatles.[18] Indeed, some casual observers and skeptical journalists quickly dismissed the Beatles as artists and Beatlemania as a fad resulting from mere hype. It did not take long for others, however, to realize that something larger and indefinable was taking place that they could not simply chalk up to mere marketing. By the end of the decade, after the Beatles had not only become a super-group but also achieved apotheosis as rock gods, scholars were taking them very seriously indeed. Writing in 1969 in the *Journal of the History of Ideas*, Evan Davies surmised, "The intensity of Beatle Mania is indicative of strong and complex motivational factors, some appearing to have a religion and love basis."[19] Writing much more recently, Robert Pielke has also attached to Beatlemania a "quasi-religious significance."[20] There was always something ineffable and mysterious about the Beatles' relationship with their fans that defied rational explanation.

Some contemporary explanations did focus on the actual effects of listening to the music. Johnny Pearson, the director of the British television program *Ready, Steady, Go*, advanced the opinion that "what stands out most is their sense of timing and the way they have of never varying the tempo they start out with. Like the best conductors, they achieve their effects through dynamic variation."[21] The Beatles did produce sounds and combination of sounds that were distinct and that sounded new, even to musicians like Richie Havens, John Fogerty, Roger McGuinn, and David Crosby, the latter two members of the Byrds. The way in which their music represented such an amalgamation of styles and musical influences, drawing from rock, rhythm and blues, country, folk, and other genres, broadened their appeal. As we have seen, their early albums included traditional pop songs like "Till There Was You" and "A Taste of Honey" and kept them from being pigeonholed musically. Without the music, it is safe to say Beatlemania would not have existed; if people did not like what they heard on the radio or the *Ed Sullivan Show*, people would have quickly lost interest. The Beatles' music was brilliant; it remains popular among people of all age groups even fifty years after the band broke up.

Beatlemania, however, was a historical phenomenon rooted in a particular time and place. Simple answers will not suffice to explain complex historical phenomena; in history, multicausal explanations are always preferable to mono-causal explanations. Their music was an obvious factor, a sine qua non of Beatlemania. However good the music though, it was not the sole cause of the phenomenon. No doubt, the group's infectious personalities and droll, often self-deprecating, sense of humor contributed to their popularity. Their long hair and cheeky attitude made them rebellious enough to appeal to young fans, while their suits and clean-shaven appearance made them seem far from sinister to parents and authorities. Perhaps for some fans, especially younger fans, the combination of their music and their appealing personalities was enough. Jane

Barnes, only 11 at the time, in a recent interview struggled to explain how other factors might have contributed to their appeal, at least for her.

> I think their music was great and it seemed approachable, they were certainly nice looking. They were cute, they were friendly, they seemed very safe [and] welcoming and so I think people related to that. I have a hard time understanding the full cultural phenomenon because they were introduced to me at a time when I was just starting to learn music and appreciate music. They were the first group I knew; it wasn't like I was listening to other groups and said "oh my god here [come] the Beatles" and went crazy.[22]

Larry Kane writes, "One of the untold stories of the early Beatles years was their outright appreciation for their fans, demonstrated by their attempts to guarantee them access when security said otherwise."[23] One Beatle fan who grew up in North Carolina later wrote, that upon seeing them on *Ed Sullivan* for the first time at the age of thirteen, "What captivated me was not so much their hair or clothes, but rather the energy and the electric atmosphere they created."[24]

A variant on the musical explanation for the Beatles' success in the United States comes from those who attribute it to the dearth of good popular music at the time. To some people, rock and roll seemed to have declined from its early success, which had emanated from rock legends such as Fats Domino, Chucky Berry, Bill Haley, Little Richard, Jerry Lee Lewis, Buddy Holly, and, of course, Elvis Presley. These early rock artists were not only talented, innovative, and creative, but they gave early rock a kind of edge that mirrored teenage angst and rebelliousness. By the early 1960s, Chuck Berry had gone to prison, Little Richard had found religion, Jerry Lee Lewis had become persona non grata for marrying his underage cousin, Elvis had lost credibility by joining the army, and Buddy Holly was dead, the victim of the ill-fated plane crash that also killed rock stars Richie Valens and the Big Bopper. Despite the music industry's attempt to fabricate or promote teen idols such as Fabian, Frankie Avalon, and Bobby Rydell, none stirred the kind of excitement generated by Elvis before them or the Beatles afterward. Their songs were popular enough (Bobby Rydell placed twenty singles on the pop charts in a five-year period), but they suffer by comparison and music historians have not generally regarded them highly. Dominic Sandbrook is among those who have favored this explanation for Beatlemania, seeing the Beatles as stepping into a vacuum created by the "fairly moribund condition" of American pop music at the time.[25]

However, others have contested this assessment of the state of popular music prior to Beatlemania and the ensuing British invasion. Andre Millard observes that the early 1960s were "golden years for Motown and for artists like Ray Charles and James Brown" and he points to songs such as Tommy Roe's "Sheila," Del Shannon's "Runaway," Bobby Vinton's "Blue Velvet," and Neil Sedaka's "Breaking Up Is Hard to Do" as classics that belie the negative reputation of the period's pop music.[26] Bob Spitz also refuses to follow a Beatlemania-by-default line of thinking. In fact, he argues, "Love Me Do" did not perform better on the American charts because of "too much competition," from the likes of Little Eva's "The Loco-Motion," The Four Seasons' "Sherry," and Chris Montez's "Last Dance," among others.[27]

Melissa Davis identifies "their Englishness" as a major factor in their appeal in America, something that made them seem sophisticated and cultured in a way that belied their Liverpudlian and lower-middle-class roots, which stood as obstacles for them to overcome rather than advantages at home. With references to the popularity in America of English literature, movie stars, films, Broadway shows, and other cultural exports, Davis writes, "Given the status of English culture and personalities, as well as their perceived attributes, it is possible that the Beatles entered a more friendly arena than they had imagined they would find."[28] The "Englishness" of the Beatles certainly provides a plausible explanation for the reception of the Beatles in America and for why fans reacted with a hysteria that differed in degree if not in kind from the reaction of teenagers to Elvis Presley, Frank Sinatra, and the other American teen idols that preceded them.

The idea that the Beatles provided some kind of psychological salve for the collective trauma experienced by Americans less than three months after the Kennedy assassination has become so commonplace that it is the first thing many people mention when asked about the impact of the Beatles' arrival in the states in 1964. When asked about the impact of the assassination on the Beatles' reception, Larry Kane said, "At the time, it was very difficult to assess that. ... There's no question in my mind that at the time and in the future, the Beatles did a great job of changing the subject."[29] Andre Millard may have underestimated the profound effects of the murder of a popular president on the American public, but he, for one, does not think the Kennedy assassination had much to do with Beatlemania. He writes, "Although the sadness of the tragic death of a president might have prepared the way for the joyous reception of the Beatles, it seems rather a stretch to assign the causes of Beatlemania to the aftermath of an assassination, especially when more than two months had elapsed before the Beatles arrived."[30] Millard and others see the phenomenon much more in the context of a growing affluent youth market with independence and money to spend, combined with a business environment in which the media and record companies found ways to capitalize on it. However, during an interview for the Living History Project carried out by the 6th Floor Museum in Dallas, when asked how long they remained depressed after the Kennedy assassination, both Jan Sittel and Betty Duke-Ruhd responded: "until the Beatles!"

Finally, because so many of the fans that participated in Beatlemania were female, some writers and commenters have offered explanations for the phenomenon that focus primarily on gender. For Steven Stark, the Beatles' experience with strong women growing up and their general respect for women allowed them to identify with their female fans to a greater degree than other bands, something that these fans could ostensibly perceive when they heard or watched the group.[31] For social historian Susan Douglas, Beatlemania was not primarily about the Beatles but about their female fans (herself included), who used the Beatles as an outlet for their pent-up energy and rebelliousness that they found difficult to release in any other way.[32] Ehrenreich, Hess, and Jacobs also argue that for young girls for whom sex was either forbidden or dangerous, the Beatles became safe objects of lust and desire on whom they could project all of their fantasies without actually having to consummate them or risk pregnancy and shame.[33]

Furthermore, the Beatles presented themselves as harmless and friendly stars who cared about their female audience, bobbing their heads instead of shaking their hips or thrusting their pelvises (*a la* Elvis), cultivating a relatively androgynous appearance, and singing a number of songs with a female-centric perspective, including some originally performed by girl groups or female singers. Larry Kane said, "Paul McCartney went out there every night and made love to the audience with his face. He knew exactly what he was doing. He also knew that the girls liked him a lot." This gendered perspective is critical to understanding Beatlemania, but its main flaw is that it does not account for the large number of young male fans who also idolized the Beatles at the time. Having said that, it is certainly possible to recognize the validity and contributions of viewing Beatlemania through the lens of gender, while also acknowledging that even this explanation does not tell the whole story of the phenomenon. In summary, the Beatles' music was arguably the most important factor in the group's appeal, but Beatlemania itself was a product of the convergence of characteristics of the Beatles and their music that made them appealing to fans and the personal and societal circumstances in which those fans discovered the Beatles. Fortunately, the Beatles gave us another lens besides their music through which to view their experience and the reaction of their fans in 1964: that of a film, which serves as both a window into and a commentary upon both that experience and the fans' reaction. The film was called *A Hard Day' Night*, but before we consider the film and its own cultural milieu, we should not leave the subject of Beatlemania without some further consideration of the impact it did have on the Beatles' female audience and the 1960s more generally.

The Impact of Beatlemania on Women

It was inevitable that the cacophonies of screaming female adolescent Beatlemaniacs would give way to a different demeanor once they grew a little bit older. They would change in other important ways as well, of course. For instance, when one pays attention to the way that these young girls dressed in 1964, their clothes look decidedly old-fashioned for the most part. Their hairstyles are still more reminiscent of the 1950s than of either the long down-to-the-waist hair of the hippie chicks or the sleek bob cut popularized by English hairstylist Vidal Sassoon or models such as Lesley Hornby, better known as Twiggy. In a few years, many of these same young women would march against the Vietnam War, adopt radically different modes of dress and change their hairstyle, and form the basis of a nascent feminist movement as advocates for women's liberation.

Although their outrageous behavior represented a violation of societal norms, it was all too easy for the critics to present Beatlemania as a fad that temporarily hypnotized hare-brained teenage girls prone to displays of feminine emotion and hysteria and thus reaffirm certain gender stereotypes that implicitly confirmed notions of male superiority. However, Susan Douglas calls Beatlemania a "critical turning point in the evolution of girl culture that wasn't foolish at all, and was particularly dangerous to the status quo."[34] It should have been clear to anyone watching these thousands of girls screaming for the Beatles, asserting their independence, and displaying disregard for authority and social conventions that they would not all find contentment assuming traditional roles as wives and mothers at home doing the cooking and the cleaning. Having found power in numbers as consumers of mass culture, it would not be long before the young female fans of the Beatles would find other ways of asserting their power and independence.

The 1960s would bring many changes to women's lives and attitudes; it would be foolish to see Beatlemania as the catalyst for all of them. More women worked outside the home, even after they got married, the pill changed the lives of both married and single women, and women began to dress and wear their hair differently, generally in ways that gave them greater freedom and deemphasized the gender differences between men and women, Mary Quant's miniskirt notwithstanding. A debate would emerge within the women's movement about clothing that reinforced the image of women as sex symbols, but at the time, Quant defended her designs, saying that they reinforced women's strength, assertiveness, and comfortability with their own sexuality. The number of women working outside the home in Britain increased from around 20 percent at the beginning of the 1950s to around 33 percent in the early 1960s to nearly 50 percent in 1972.[35] However, it would be equally foolish to assert that a phenomenon that affected the lives of so many girls and young women at a critical stage in their maturing process would have no lasting impact upon them. Beatlemania had thus unwittingly transformed those who had fallen under its spell in ways that neither the Beatles nor their fans would have understood.

Early women's liberation marches displayed some of the same joy and sense of togetherness inspired by the Beatles among gregarious women who now bonded over a cause instead of a band. In one famous incident from 1968, a crowd of around a hundred women in Atlantic City congregated to crown a sheep in protest against the sexist Miss American Pageant and then refused to speak with any male reporters about the incident. Both the Beatlemaniacs and the feminists of the later 1960s were part of a generation that had seen great strides made in the direction of Civil Rights in the 1960s, but few toward gender equality, at least as far as the law was concerned. For example, a 1965 federal law in the United States made discrimination based on race, religion, or national origin illegal, but not because of gender. Even the feminist icon Gloria Steinem, who was 30 years old at the time of Beatlemania in 1964, would adopt some of the styles and fashion choices inspired by the Beatles in the 1960s and help shatter the old-fashioned image of feminists associated with the suffragists of the nineteenth and early twentieth centuries.

These developments did not happen by design, but just because the Beatles did not set out consciously to inspire a feminist movement it does not mean that they understood nothing about their female audience. They wrote songs that appealed to women because they evinced a penchant for sentimentality ("And I Love Her," "You've Got to Hide Your Love Away," "Yesterday") or an understanding of the female perspective "She Loves You," "You're Going to Lose That Girl," "There's a Place." They covered songs by girl groups that spoke mostly of the female experience, such as "Please Mr. Postman," "Chains," and even "Boys." Deep down the vast majority of girls who fell head over heels in love with the Beatles must have realized that they were unattainable, and that this was part of the attraction they felt in the first place. The Beatles were no doubt aware of this and capitalized on it, supporting their fan clubs and even making Christmas videos for them in addition to the broad smiles and eye contact they exhibited when on stage and at a safe distance from their fans. As Steven Stark has asserted of the Beatles: "their background, the loss of their mothers, and their love for one another allowed them to transcend stereotypes and write songs that girls and women could take as liberating in ways that hadn't been true in rock's past."[36]

Nor did that attraction diminish necessarily over the course of the next few years. Once the group stopped touring in 1966, the hysteria associated with their public appearances of course disappeared, and yet the group somehow managed to remain as popular as ever, a phenomenon we will explore in later chapters. The popular perception is that their audience shifted from more predominantly female to male, yet both assumptions are either exaggerated or entirely wrong. Katie Kapurch, for example, argues that the Beatles' 1967 landmark album *Sgt. Pepper's Lonely Hearts Club Band* (see Chapter 7) had important resonances with girl culture, including the title of the album itself, since "lonely hearts" generally has female resonances. Of course, those devoted fans of the Beatles in 1964 would have had a predisposition toward noticing this and following the Beatles, even as their musical styles changed and they began to experiment with marijuana, LSD, and, in the case of John Lennon at least, even harder drugs. In addition, as Kapurch notes, these young women would also have found lessons related to their increasing amount of independence and freedom in songs such as "She's Leaving Home," about a teenage runaway and her parents' inability to understand her.[37] She also takes special notes of the song "With a Little Help from My Friends" as one that girls in particular could relate to, while female concerns are also present at the center of "Lovely Rita" (work) and "When I'm Sixty-Four" (domesticity).[38]

Of course, not all female Beatlemaniacs would become proto-feminists; as Barbara Ehrenreich readily admits, many became groupies whose main goal was to sleep with any rock star who would have them.[39] In addition, Gillian Garr notes the negative impact the Beatles had on the careers of 1960s girl groups who did not write their own songs or play their own instruments, which the Beatles had made au courante among rock bands, inspiring thousands of newly formed and predominantly male groups to do just that. Indeed, at first, Beatlemania had merely prepared the way for the British Invasion of other English male rock groups such as the Animals, Herman's Hermits, Gerry and the Pacemakers, the Dave Clark Five, the Kinks, and the Rolling Stones to achieve popularity and commercial success in the United States. However, the Beatles, who had themselves drawn from different genres beyond rock and roll even in their earliest albums, did not just prepare their fans for groups that sounded similar to them. As Rebecca Duncan put it, "the Beatles opened up our minds to popular music; it became part of our generation so we listened to a lot of different stuff."[40] Furthermore, Kapurch also notes the influence that the Beatles had not only on future female rock stars Ann and Nancy Wilson, who formed the band Heart, and Chryssie Hynde of the Pretenders, but on the immediate formation of the girl group, the Shangri-las, in 1963. Finally, Ehrenreich and her coauthors see the influence of the Beatles not only on androgynous male rock stars like David Bowie and Boy George but also on androgynous female stars such as Grace Jones and Annie Lennox, while also perceiving a thread stretching from Beatlemania to Cyndi Lauper's 1983 girl culture anthem, "Girls Just Want to Have Fun."[41] Susan Douglas wrote, "Without ever saying so explicitly, the Beatles acknowledged that there was masculinity and femininity in all of us, and that blurring the artificial boundaries between the two might be a big relief."[42]

The impact of Beatlemania could be long-lasting and reinforce solidarity among women even years later, as Jane Barnes describes from her experience:

> Ten years ago when I moved to Raleigh as a college professor, there was a bunch of us college professors—all women—who used to get together and socialize. We all were very different, [from] lots of different backgrounds, [including] English, history, and science, while I was in business. We became friends and there was a group of us who found that we were all crazy about the Beatles and so even in our late 50s there was this group of women—six of us—who found that we had all been Beatlemaniacs and crazy about the Beatles and so we started doing Beatles things again. So we went to see the movie *Across the Universe* and we have gone to see some of the mock bands. We have [get-togethers] in my house where we would watch *A Hard Day's Night* or play Beatles Trivia or something like that so even after all these years, we found something else we all have in common, and we all bonded over this.[43]

Anyone who doubts the long-range impact of Beatlemania or dismisses it as a fad propelled by emotional and immature teenagers should consider Jane Barnes and her highly educated, professional friends bonding over the experience of watching *A Hard Day's Night* a half-century after its initial release in 1964.

The Cultural and Political Context of *A Hard Day's Night*

When the Beatles agreed to do a film after their first US tour to capitalize on their popularity and recent success, they did so on the condition that they would play themselves. In doing so, their film, although obviously a fictionalized and mediated portrayal of themselves and their experience as Beatles, would come closer to depicting the reality of their lives and situation than, for example, the formulaic and entirely contrived films in which Elvis starred around the same time. Brilliantly directed by Richard Lester and based on a very funny and somewhat-true-to-life script by Liverpudlian Alun Owen, the film did much to capture each of the Beatles' individual personalities and helped viewers to get to know them a bit better and distinguish the four of them from each other much more easily. This effect more than counterbalanced the ways in which Owen may

Figure 4.1 *The Beatles during A Hard Day's Night promotion campaign, 1964. Photo reportage of Max Scheler for the magazine Stern, with photographer Astrid Kirchherr, who had befriended The Beatles during their time in Hamburg. Courtesy of Bridgeman Images.*

have oversimplified the dominant personality traits of these complex individuals; at least fans and viewers now saw them as individuals. The less-than-idealized representations of the lads had little effect on their popularity and they may have even enhanced it. As film historian Bob Neaverson has written, "*A Hard Day's Night* was one of the first pop musicals to represent pop stars in anything other than a clean-cut, conformist, one-dimensional manner."[44]

A Hard Day's Night appeared, however, in a wider cultural context than that of Beatlemania, which the film took for its main subject. London was starting to emerge as a cultural center for music, movies, and fashion, much of it aimed at a younger crowd that would soon give the city the reputation as "Swinging London." The film opened in London on July 6, 1964; in Liverpool on July 10; and in the rest of Britain on August 2. Like the Beatles themselves, it would serve as a reflection of what was popular at the time and influence what would become popular in terms of hairstyle, clothing, dancing, and general demeanor. The realistic, pseudo-documentary style of the film drew inspiration from both pop art and recent films such as the Boulting brothers *I'm All Right Jack*, though without that film's omniscient narrator. Scenes are short, and within them, we get rapid changes of shots from a variety of camera angles. This technique accelerates the speed of the film and mimics the fast pace of modern life. Stephen Glynn has observed a modernist approach through the film's self-criticism of its own material, as when George accidentally stumbles into a meeting with a marketing wizard named

Simon who quizzes the Beatle about some new clothing styles and the next teen fad, the date on which it would supposedly arrive marked on his calendar.[45]

A Hard Day's Night did not exist within a political vacuum in 1964 either. In some ways, the film reflects a sense of confidence and optimism, with the Beatles representing the potential for success and affluence that seemed to permeate the decade. The Labour Prime Minister Harold Wilson's pronouncements about the benefits of technology and the promise of the modern age built on the Conservative Harold Macmillan's appeal to the electorate that they had "never had it so good" only a few years previous. Technology is front and center in *A Hard Day's Night*, as the film gave its viewers a behind-the-scenes glimpse of the cameras and control boards that went into the making of a modern television broadcast, for example. At one point in the film, Ringo wanders through a construction site, which could serve as a metaphor for building a new Britain. However, as he escorts a well-dressed woman through the site, placing his coat over puddles so she will not have to step in the mud, he lastly places his coat over what turns out to be a hole into which the unsuspecting woman completely disappears. The scene adds another dash of slapstick humor to the film and perhaps we should take it at face value. Still, might it not also serve as a warning of unsuspected danger as Britain was attempting to step into a new age?

Indeed, filmed in black and white, *A Hard Day's Night* could serve as a reminder of the past as much as a harbinger of the future. Early in the film, the Beatles ride a train, the quintessential symbol of the Industrial Revolution of the nineteenth century that helped propel Britain to world power. In fact, it is on the train where a middle-aged man perturbed by their very presence reminds them that he "fought the war for your sort." Alongside the optimism connected with the decade, the 1960s also continued to witness high levels of anxiety about Britain's decline and older viewers might have found the Beatles' disrespect for authority, which manifests itself in this scene and a number of others throughout the film, as additional reasons for concern. In the film, John, Paul, George, and Ringo (but especially John) continually taunt their fictional manager, Norm, played by Norm Rossington, and disobey his orders virtually every chance they get. In addition, they refuse to turn down their radio for the veteran who chastises them on the train, with John imploring him to "give us a kiss." They make fun of the television producer, played brilliantly by Victor Spinetti, and cause him endless anxiety that they will not be on time for "the final run-through," which he deems so crucial to the success of his program. They constantly long to escape from the confines of their captivity, experiencing in one scene, set to "Can't Buy Me Love," a playful moment when they run and dance around a field in all their youthful exuberance. When the scene ends, and the property owner chastises them for trespassing, their response is a hardly contrite "We're sorry we hurt your field, Mister." American viewers could certainly appreciate the humor and the realities of the nascent generation gap, which would grow wider over the course of the decade. However, British viewers would have picked up more on the portrayal of the Beatles as Northerners invading London as outsiders, as well as their threat to the class divisions that still meant so much in British society.

Critics generally responded well to the film, Andrew Sarris of the *Village Voice* going so far as to call it "the *Citizen Kane* of jukebox musicals." Peter Jones, writing in the *Record Mirror*, found it "every bit as good as expected."[46] As for the music on the accompanying album, much of it written by Paul and John for the film, Jones was generally complimentary. He particularly liked the title song, "Can't Buy Me Love," and "Tell Me Why," which he said sounded "unmistakably Beatlish." He thought George "swings amiably" as lead vocal on "I'm Happy Just to Dance with You," "pushed along by Ringo's percussion." He thought that "I Should Have Known Better" was "just fine," while "If I Fell" had "a stack of compulsive charm." His only quarrel seemed to be with "And I Love Her," which he noted was "not typically Beatle in sound."[47] Yet this was exactly the kind of romantic ballad that would have broadened the appeal of the Beatles to older listeners/viewers.

The film attempted to replicate the hysteria that accompanied Beatlemania, but John Lennon called the film "a comic-strip version of what was actually going on," saying, "The pressure was far heavier than that depicted by the film." Extras posing as Beatles fans—not much of a stretch based on the enthusiasm they displayed at the mere sight of a Beatle—received the equivalent of $11.00 a day and a box lunch. In truth, the film contributed to as much as it reflected Beatlemania as it reinforced and contributed to the Beatles' expanding popularity. The film opened in New York on August 12 and in five hundred additional theatres throughout the United States the following day. Rebecca Duncan was only 11 and living in Warren, Ohio, at the time, but she remembers going to the theatre and "wanting to be one of the girls, but there were many other girls a lot louder" than she was in the theater.[48] James Vignapiano saw the film as a 14-year-old at a theatre on 9th Street in south Brooklyn. He said:

> I will never forget that opening chord to "A Hard Day's Night" hit the screen and here they [the Beatles] are running down the sidewalk, and you are sitting in the movie theater and the screen is [so] big. I just remember looking at everybody and everybody's head was tilted up towards the screen and their eyes were as wide as anything.

James said he remembered everyone he knew going out to buy a guitar the next day, an effect of the film often only attributed to the Beatles' first appearance on the *Ed Sullivan Show*.[49] Bob Schiffer, who grew up in Manhattan, was 16 when he saw the film upon its release that summer and what he mainly remembered was "screaming and screeching," but he liked the Beatles and so he remembered liking the film, especially the music.[50] People who have grown up with YouTube and the Internet may not appreciate how unique and special an experience it was for young people to have the opportunity to go to a movie theatre and see their idols on the big screen. Janet Nugent, who grew up in Baltimore, talked about the opportunity to see the Beatles in *A Hard Day's Night* as a 13-year-old Beatlemaniac: "You're longing for these people you know you are kind of in love with so when you see them on the screen that's wonderful and you love everything they do on the screen. Everything was wonderful; everything was like either laughable or tearful."

The film firmly established an image of the Beatles in people's minds and influenced how people would receive and view them at a critical moment in their career. Did the Beatles reveal too much of themselves and thus make themselves even more likeable and vulnerable to fans who believed the group belonged to them? Alternatively, did the film offer a distorted version of the Beatles and obscure the true nature of their personalities, thus transforming them into commodities? Devin McKinney thought more the former. To McKinney, by playing themselves, the Beatles gave themselves "far less buffer against the various ways the world chooses to engage with *them*." McKinney argued that the Beatles played themselves "not a mythos of themselves, on the chopping block of world response."[51] Ken Womack, on the other hand, takes almost the opposite approach, viewing the film as an exercise in mythmaking, and as creating a fictional image of the group that did not correspond to reality.[52] However, both McKinney and Womack seem to agree that the film created unrealistic expectations of the fans concerning their newfound idols. Womack seems to blame the medium and by implication the Beatles themselves to some extent; McKinney, on the other hand, blames the audience for projecting on to the Beatles what they wanted to see and then turning on them when they did not live up to that projection. Either way, *A Hard Day's Night* serves as an important factor in analyzing the contemporary responses to the group at this point in their career, when it might have seemed that the Beatles could only go downhill from there. Instead, it turned out they were just getting started.

Popular and Critical Reaction to the Beatles in 1964

A Hard Day's Night affected professional musicians as well as ordinary fans. Graham Nash wrote, "David [Crosby] and Stephen [Stills] saw *A Hard Day's Night* and knew exactly what they wanted to do." Crosby even adopted the twelve-string Rickenbacker electric guitar after George Harrison used it in the film.[53] However, not everyone was immediately enthralled. According to Nash, "Neil [Young] didn't give a shit about *A Hard Day's Night*."[54] Bob Dylan took immediate note of the Beatles' success: "I had heard the Beatles in New York when they first hit. Then, when we were driving through Colorado we had the radio on and eight of the top ten songs were Beatles songs."[55] The constant airplay of the Beatles again raises the question of whether DJs played them so often on the radio because of market demand from the fans or whether they had created the success of the Beatles by doing so. Either way, ever since their first appearance on the *Ed Sullivan Show*, the group's popularity seemed to know no bounds.

James Vignapiano recounts a telling anecdote about how he came to watch the Beatles on the *Ed Sullivan Show* in Bolly's Candy Store on 5th Avenue in Brooklyn and the effect it had on him:

> My father wanted no part of it. He liked Ed Sullivan but he wanted no part of the Beatles. So we all gravitated over to the candy store and we were standing there

five deep eating milk shakes and whatever just to hang out and he had this little TV up in the corner of the candy store and that was the first time we saw them. When they came on, it was like silence, which was unbelievable. There were no girls screaming; it was just basically a bunch of guys and the owner and his family but there was silence because everybody was just soaking this in. Who are these guys with this mop top haircut? And that was the first time I saw them and from that moment on, like a lot of other people, I was hooked. I was done.

When as a young girl Robin Levine first saw them on the *Ed Sullivan Show*, she said the first thing she noticed was that "they were all playing instruments," but then she realized that "there was harmony, and the things that they were singing about were more connected with me. It felt like I was listening to something new and they were coming from England and … the sound was so new and different." Levine's impression echoes the impression of Bob Dylan, who said, "They were doing things nobody was doing. Their chords were outrageous, just outrageous, and their harmonies made it all valid."[56] The experience of watching the Beatles on that winter night in early February had a profound effect on the life of Michael McEntarfer.

The next day in school, it was all the kids talked about, although I remember both my parents and teachers criticizing them and not understanding why we liked them so much. I was glued to the radio and made regular trips to the two record shops in town looking for new records. Watching them on *Ed Sullivan* made me and my friends want to form a band and do what they did. It directly led to me playing in a band all through high school. We played many Beatles songs—and that same band still reunites every summer and we still play.[57]

Of course, the response of the fans at their concerts provides evidence of their popularity, which remained extremely strong among fans of the group throughout the year. Marbie Foster saw the Beatles at Convention Hall in Philadelphia as a senior in high school in 1964. She described the whole experience as "so thrilling," remembering:

The minute that the Beatles came on stage everybody jumped up on their chairs and started to scream. You really could hardly hear anything that they were saying and you really couldn't see anything, all you could see is the top of their heads and everybody was constantly screaming for the whole concert, and all I could think of was "Wow! I am in the same room with the Beatles."

Michael McEntarfer saw them at Toronto's Maple Leaf Garden in 1964, the first concert he ever attended. Here is how he described the experience:

My main memory is the non-stop flash bulbs that created a strobe light effect. And the flash bulb strobe light effect continued for the entire set. My second main memory is the sound of screaming girls—such that we could not hear anything else. With each song, we would struggle to tell what song they were singing. Invariably we would catch a phrase or lick and we would say (shout) to each other "hey, I think they're doing 'All my Loving' and then we would try to determine the next song." Several times, I can recall turning around and telling the girls behind us to shut up—but of course it did no good because the entire arena was screaming. But honestly, it was both annoying and thrilling at the same time. The screaming was all part of the Beatles' mystique. So it seemed not only ok but also perfectly appropriate for the time. We were seated on Paul's side of the stage and every time Paul looked or waved our way, the screaming increased. I remember one girl tossing her sweater in Paul's direction after one of his waves. And of course, there were kids jumping down from the crowd onto the back of the stage as well as rushing the stage from the front. The police were kept busy grabbing these kids. The set lasted 45 minutes with no encore and it was certainly the most thrilling 45 minutes of my 13-year-old life.

Bill Harry, reporting in *Mersey Beat* on an appearance by the group at the Apollo Theatre in Ardwick in October 1964, observed, "The screams, yells and shrieks continued almost unabated throughout the whole of their 28-minute spot."[58] Larry Kane, who attended over sixty Beatles concerts while covering their various tours, said "Every girl, maybe every boy was convinced they were in love with one of them. So, when you see those tears, they're not just tears of joy. They had this incredible glow ... They were convinced one of them was singing to them."[59] For those not so blessed as to see the Beatles in concert that year, the radio seemed to feature an almost endless loop of Beatles music, as Bob Dylan discovered in Colorado. However, the airplay the Beatles received on the radio and the role of DJs like Murray the K and Cousin Brucie (Bruce Morrow) only accounted for part of the listening experience of fans. Fans also had access to their singles and albums like *Meet the Beatles*, released for the US market in January 1964 in advance of their arrival in the states. Nick Ercoline remembered listening to the album and "probably driving my parents crazy because I played it over and over all the time."[60]

Not everyone experienced Beatlemania the same way, obviously. Ivan Bell, no doubt like many others, did not buy any of their early records even though he heard them often enough because "they dominated the airwaves." He was among those who did not come away from watching them on the *Ed Sullivan Show* terribly impressed, although he thought that was mainly because there was so much hype that no group could have lived up to it for him.[61] Peter Orenzoff, who was living in Britain in 1964, was among those young male rock and roll fans who preferred the Rolling Stones to the Beatles. A self-described "contrarian by nature," he thought the Beatles too packaged, with their "nice little suits." "They were the good guys; the music was okay, but I had gravitated more towards groups like The Animals and the Stones that were earthier, more raw," he stated. Part of the appeal of the Stones came from the stage persona of Mick Jagger. Orenzoff noted, "Lennon and McCartney were encumbered by playing the guitar at the same time [as they were singing]. Jagger had poetic license to prance around and gyrate and

[this] added a certain element that the Beatles didn't have."⁶² A 1964 survey conducted by the *Daily Princetonian* to assess the popularity of the Beatles drew a range of responses from a broad cross-section of the population including high school and college students, as well as random members of the public. One student responded by criticizing their hair, another their singing, while a homemaker and a tile layer both described them as "ridiculous." Elise Hamilton said she was surprised to see they had become so popular and wanted to know whether they had any talent. It seemed, however, that most of the criticism came from either young males or older females.

For many younger female fans, it was a different story. The Beatles came to mean something much more personal to them. Rebecca Duncan recalled her experience as a young Beatle fan:

> I had Beatles cards and the teen magazines and anything I could get my hands on. I mean it was all in my notebooks for school and [I had] all that stuff hidden away, and I would sneak and look at it when I was supposed to be learning. To be honest, it was just a total distraction from anything in our lives for a number of years; it just thoroughly consumed me and my close girlfriends. … I just remember fantasizing about whether I would want Paul McCartney to be my boyfriend or my father. I thought he might adopt me and that it would be really fun [for him] take me over to England.

Larry Kane used to receive letters from Beatles fans saying things like "Will you tell George to meet me at the top of the city hall in Chicago at midnight so we can begin our lives together." Janet Nugent simply said, "When you fall in love with someone you don't know what that ingredient is and I was in love with the Beatles as much as a thirteen-year-old could fall in love." Critical opinion, like the popular reaction to the Beatles, was divided with the balance tipping toward a much more favorable than negative response in Britain and vice versa in the United States. Writing in December 1964 and looking back on the tremendous growth in the Beatles' popularity that year, Geoffrey Canon wrote, "The Beatles were bound to succeed as soon as they got a record released, because their sound was vastly superior to anything else being released at the time." As the year closed, however, he found the Rolling Stones "the more interesting group," mainly because of their lack of conformity and unpolished stage act.⁶³ Most articles about the Beatles in the United States focused more on Beatlemania than any serious consideration of their music, though Theodore Strongin did design to offer a critique in the *New York Times*, in which he described the group's vocals as "hoarsely incoherent, with the minimal enunciation necessary to communicate the schematic texts."⁶⁴ Gil Faggen complained in *Billboard* that radio stations were trying to "out-Beatle" one another and implied that radio stations had gone overboard with their contests, promotions, extensive news coverage, pilgrimages to England, etc.⁶⁵ It seemed as though the Beatles might become victims of their own hype, with the public and media placing entirely unreasonable expectations on them. *Newsweek* magazine ran a famous cover story on February 24 that was almost entirely dismissive of them. Many writers wondered how long the Beatles'

Figure 4.2 *The Beatles wave at fans and press as they leave Heathrow Airport for Liverpool, July 11, 1964; from left to right, John Lennon, Ringo Starr, Paul McCartney, George Harrison. Photo by Terry Disney. Courtesy of Getty Images.*

"fad" would last, a question they repeatedly had to answer in interviews with the press. For the time being though, they were riding high.

While the Beatles conquered America in 1964, their popularity hardly seemed to wane in Britain. When the Beatles returned to London in July, perhaps several thousand fans greeted them, chanting loudly and continuously, "We Love the Beatles." The Beatles in 1964 projected a kind of innocence that seemed to match the spirt of that year quite well in retrospect. The passage of the Civil Rights Bill projected optimism about the future and the United States seemed at least to be making progress toward an equal and more just society. Although much work remained, this in some ways marked a high point of the Civil Rights Movement. The Beatles were also at the height of their popularity and everything seemed to be going quite well for them and for their country.

However, the Beatles' last album of 1964, *Beatles for Sale*, foreshadowed trouble ahead. Besides the somewhat cynical title, the photo of the group on the album cover shows them looking haggard and worn, years if not decades older than they appeared only months earlier on *Ed Sullivan* or in *A Hard Day's Night*. Being a Beatle was hard work, as reflected in that film's title, just as it took a great deal of hard work and effort to get the Civil Rights Bill through the Senate the summer the film was released. The Beatles had intertwined a tour of Australia with a stop in Hong Kong in between their tours of Britain and the United States, filming *A Hard Day's Night*, and writing and recording two new albums. The year 1965 would be an extension of 1964—for the Beatles, for Britain, for the United States, and for much of the rest of the world. The Beatles' enormous success would continue, but the unrelenting pace and the demands and pressures of fame would begin to take their toll. In Britain, the bloom was about to come off the rose of Harold Wilson's dynamic new Labour government that promised to move the country into an exciting new future. In the United States, the voting rights act signaled a continuation of progress on Civil Rights, but race riots and divisions within the Civil Rights Movement and the country's further descent into the imbroglio of the Vietnam War presaged a darker future. If *A Hard Day's Night* could serve as a useful theme for 1964 as a whole, a key to understanding the year 1965 might lie in the title of the Beatles' next film: *Help!*

CHAPTER 5
1965: HELP! THE BEATLES AND THE POLITICAL CULTURE OF THE MID-1960S

The Crisis of the Pound—July–August 1965

While Beatlemania soared toward its pinnacle and as the decade the press would soon start calling the "Swinging Sixties" reached its midpoint, the British government under Labour Prime Minister Harold Wilson found itself struggling to cope with Britain's reduced economic position in the world. One of its main problems stemmed from the inflated value of the British pound, which as of March 31, 1965, was worth about three times the amount of a US dollar. When the Wilson government took over in October 1964, Treasury experts gave an unfavorable report on Britain's balance of trade and suggested devaluation as a possible measure of redressing this imbalance. Wilson also discovered upon taking over that his government had inherited a deficit of almost £400 million. Wilson thus had arrived in power only to face an immediate economic crisis. James Callaghan, Wilson's chancellor of the exchequer, rejected proposals from Lord Cromer, the governor of the Bank of England, to restrict consumer spending by devaluing the pound or to call a general election. Wilson and the rest of his cabinet all agreed that both were out of the question. Another option was to restrict imports as a way of bringing about deflation, but Wilson and his cabinet rejected this option as well. Simply blaming the predicament on the previous Conservative administrations was going to do Wilson little good at this point. To ease pressure on the pound, Callaghan opted for a combination of tax increases and cuts in public spending instead in the hopes that he could buy time for the government to find its footing.

Britain's unfavorable balance of trade resulted from a combination of circumstances, including the high demand for foreign goods among British consumers and their ability and willingness to pay for them. On one level, the British government had made an enormous success of creating and implementing the welfare state after the Second World War, providing as high a level of security and standard of living as anywhere else in Europe. Even the National Health Service had managed to create what Arthur Marwick has called a blend of "some commercialism and freedom from universalist control of the state [that] could coexist with the maintenance of the ideal of a high-level national service."[1] However, on another level, British industry and economic growth lagged behind that of other Western nations, meaning more British pounds were leaving the country than were being raised through the goods the country exported. Foreign traders would only accept payment in British sterling because it had greater value relative to other currencies. Therefore, a devalued pound would have reflected more the true value of the pound and potentially worked to Britain's economic advantage by allowing British importers to pay less for goods.

The crisis of the pound, however, was symptomatic of a larger problem: anxiety about British decline in the world. The prospect of devaluing the pound raised serious concerns about the country's long-range prospects and exacerbated fears and anxieties about national decline already present because of the 1956 Suez debacle and the winding down of the British Empire. By 1965, the British had recognized the independence of almost all of their overseas colonies. Therefore, the devaluation of the pound had acquired enormous symbolic and psychological significance to the point where British politicians, including Wilson, seemed to regard it as an economic Rubicon from which Britain could never turn back and one that would lead to untold future disasters. On the one hand, the British people seemed comfortable with their modified version of socialism and the idea of living in a welfare state, but on the other hand, they still wanted their country to carry some weight in the world and to compete on equal terms with other nations economically. They wanted the benefits of living in a country with a safety net where everyone had access to fundamental benefits like health care, without sacrificing opportunities for personal affluence and economic growth. This was a difficult balancing act for any government, but proved especially so for that led by Harold Wilson.

Part of Wilson's concern about devaluation stemmed from the one time when a previous Labour government had actually undertaken a devaluation of the pound. The postwar administration of Clement Attlee had taken that step in 1949, which dramatically altered the future prospects of the Labour Party. It did not help that Attlee called for a general election in February 1950, before any positive effects of devaluation on the economy could manifest themselves. Labour retained a narrow majority, but lost seventy-eight seats while the Conservatives picked up ninety. Just twenty months later, in October 1951, the Conservatives swept back into power, which they would not relinquish until Wilson's 1964 victory thirteen years later. Furthermore, Labour's four-seat majority was so narrow that Wilson thought it even more imperative not to take a step as drastic as devaluation that could work to the advantage of the Conservatives. Labour had been out of power for so long that Wilson seemed to emulate the first Labour Prime Minister Ramsay MacDonald, who in the 1920s refrained from departing too far from mainstream views to convince the voting public they could trust a Labour government. By contrast, Attlee had a far larger mandate to bring about sweeping social and economic changes following the Second World War.

Wilson became extremely frustrated in early 1965. As he wrote in his memoir, "the trade figures were exacting their toll, and press speculation forecasting an early election, to be followed by a Conservative government was not helping [the pound] sterling."[2] Pressure mounted on the prime minister to consider devaluation, which he knew to be a short-term palliative that would not solve Britain's fundamental problems. Wilson's biographer, Ben Pimlott, argues that Wilson feared international disapproval as much as he did domestic repercussions when it came to the issue of devaluation.[3] One bank officer said in early August, "No [foreign] government that can do something is going to stand idly by without doing it and allow Britain to go over the edge."[4] Yet Wilson also faced international pressure to devalue the pound, based on a lack of confidence that Britain could survive economically without doing so. Bankers and the financial community thus split on the issue. Even more importantly, though, Wilson had made a promise, as much to himself as to the British public, that he would avoid devaluation of the pound at virtually all costs. Wilson sought to project to the public an air of steady confidence and competence, a kind of classless technocrat who could solve Britain's problems to the benefit of all. Adopting such an extreme measure as devaluation, especially so early in his term, would have indicated a panicked reaction far from the image Wilson sought to convey. He also liked to appear on television in a sweater and smoking a pipe so people would identify with his working-class roots, even though he was perfectly comfortable in a suit and actually preferred to smoke cigars, at the time a symbol of aristocratic privilege. Devaluation also would have meant cutbacks on government spending and that the British pound would not go as far in purchasing foreign goods, thus reducing personal purchasing power, which would not have gone over well with the working classes or the British public as a whole. This was not what they had elected Wilson to do.

Concerns about the value of the pound persisted throughout the spring, but Wilson still ruled out both devaluation and the calling of a general election. Then crisis hit in July when Britain reported massive losses of gold reserves, leading to a collapse in investors' confidence that the pound could hold its value. Gold reached its highest price since it had spiraled the previous November, provoking the first crisis of Wilson's administration. British foreign currency and gold reserves dipped below $140 million, leading to a severe crisis for the pound. Wilson responded in late July by placing a six month moratorium on public expenditure, save for the construction of planned industrial buildings, housing, hospitals, and schools. He also tried to discourage people from selling off their pounds by promising that he would not devalue the currency.

On August 5, however, rumors still circulated that the government was considering devaluing the pound, raising the ire of the ministers in the Labour government. Such speculation only intensified as foreign speculators began to sell their pounds at a devalued rate, which the press thought might force the government's hand in favor of devaluation. Export companies began buying shares in gold mines and industrial properties on the premise that they would benefit if the government devalued the pound. The government also had to quash rumors that it had recalled Lord Cromer from a foreign holiday to deal with the crisis and that Cromer had threatened to resign. One rumor even had Wilson himself on the verge of resigning, which he also strongly denied. These rumors proved unfounded, but they had the potential to exacerbate the crisis if the government could not quell them. Furthermore, the government had already tried cutting spending, encouraging exports, raising taxes, adding additional taxes on imports, and had few remedies left to try short of devaluation if the crisis did not abate.

Fortunately, by August 10, the value of the pound had started to rebound, presaging an end to the immediate crisis. Wilson's firm denials that he was considering devaluation had helped to restore confidence in the pound. He declared once again that his commitment to maintaining the value of the pound was "permanent." The government received another boost when July export figures showed unexpectedly high numbers.

Denis Healey, Wilson's secretary of state for defense, used the report to remonstrate the "moaning minnies," who, he said, had underestimated Britain's economic prospects. Healey also noted that Britain's contributions to Europe's defense amounted to a billion US dollars, an amount almost equal to the trade deficit that existed at that time. The press took note of this, but an editorial in the *Birmingham Daily Post* on August 12 still questioned whether Healey should have "raised hopes on the strength of one month's figures" and presciently argued that positive economic trends would continue "by continuous effort, not by premature self-congratulation."[5] Healey might also have noted that the appearance that the United States was ready to step in to support the pound with a financial aid package if necessary had also helped to alleviate the crisis.

The immediate crisis had passed, but Healey's ebullience would in fact prove premature. First, the crisis had left the country shaken and uncertain as to when or if the next one might arise. Second, Britain had hardly resolved its long-term economic prospects, however much it benefited from the general rise in prosperity shared by the West, and indeed much of the rest of the world, in the 1960s. Third, in December 1965, Brian Abel-Smith and Peter Townsend, two professors from the London School of Economics, published a book called *The Poor and the Poorest*, exposing the levels of poverty that remained in the country and calling attention to those left behind by the rising levels of wealth in the country. Finally, in November 1967, Wilson relented and agreed to devalue the pound, decreasing its value from $2.80 to $2.40. Even this did not have the desired economic effects and did little to stem Britain's economic decline. In short, the crisis of the pound in the summer of 1965 only foreshadowed darker days to come.

However, the British people might have had trouble seeing this in the summer of 1965. The crisis of the pound had not reached the point where it significantly affected the lives of most ordinary people or the affluence now enjoyed by the younger generation. The Beatles themselves would have proved a distraction from the bleak economic news with their best-selling records and numerous television appearances. By the summer of 1965, it had gotten to the point where the Beatles themselves worried about overexposure, John Lennon saying, "We were in the papers, we were on the wireless, we were on the telly, we had a film out. It was saturation point."[6] In addition, the Beatles had further enhanced the cultural capital Britain enjoyed in America and around the world. People still loved the Beatles, but their enormous popularity was bound to produce a backlash eventually, something of which the Beatles themselves seemed increasingly cognizant of as time went on. In fact, one slight controversy not of their making erupted in May when Harold Wilson, in his own attempt to distract the public from the deepening monetary crisis, designated the Beatles Members of the British Empire (MBE) for their contributions to British commerce. Finally, while the pop music of the Beatles and other groups infused 1960s Britain with a bright, energetic, upbeat new sound, the bright colors of the highly fashionable pop art seemed to belie any dark economic clouds that loomed on the horizon. Significantly, both of these cultural trends featured heavily in the Beatles' new movie, *Help!*

The Political and Cultural Context of *Help!*

By 1965, the Beatles had unwittingly started the process of melding together the experiences of a generation coming of age in a period of rapid social change and impending political disorder. This generation would soon engage in heated divisions over the Vietnam War and experience the radicalization of youth politics that would culminate in the revolutionary year of 1968 a few years later. Already in February 1965, President Lyndon Johnson had authorized a military operation against North Vietnam called "Rolling Thunder" that would continue for three years, even though at the outset it was only supposed to last for eight weeks. In August 1965, the Beatles contributed two cultural milestones that would come to symbolize both the height of their popularity and a kind of turning point in their career, namely their concert at Shea Stadium in New York and the release of their second feature film, *Help!* The concert at Shea Stadium signified that Beatlemania had intensified if anything over the course of the eighteen months since their first appearance on the *Ed Sullivan Show*, while their songwriting for the film *Help!* and its accompanying album showed Lennon and McCartney struggling with themes that were more adult and confronting some of the darker consequences of fame and their meteoric rise to stardom. *Help!* represented a dramatic departure from the Beatles' first film, *A Hard Day's Night*, in that it took its inspiration not from the Beatles' actual lives but from other cultural reference points, most notably the series of James Bond movies based on the novels of Ian Fleming, starting with the release of *Dr. No* in 1962.

Figure 5.1 *Help!* LP by The Beatles, the original 1965 mono version—Parlophone PMC1255 (first pressing). Courtesy of Alamy Photos.

Lennon and McCartney did not tailor the songs for the film to fit the script, but instead produced an assortment of traditional Beatlesque rock and roll numbers combined with a distinct folk-rock sensibility that showed the influence of Bob Dylan, whom they had met in New York and whose records they had begun listening to obsessively. Dylan embarked on a highly successful tour of Britain in May 1965, perhaps helping to prepare the way for the reception of the transition to a more folk-rock style of music on *Help!* Songs like "You've Got to Hide Your Love Away" and "Ticket to Ride" evince some of this influence, particularly the former, but the title track had its own significance. John spoke frequently about how much he liked the song "Help!" because it came from the heart and really reflected the way he felt at the time. Yet the most distinctive and unique Beatles song of 1965 was not really a Beatles song at all, but a solo number written and performed by Paul McCartney called "Yesterday," to which George Martin had added a classical vibe with the inclusion of a string quartet on the record. *Help!* was an important film and album simply because by this point everything that the Beatles did carried added weight and significance and invited careful scrutiny by their fans and critics.

In fact, the Beatles had already transcended the realm of popular culture and had become part of the political culture of Britain, where politicians in need of support from the youth vote pandered to them and expressed their fondness for their music as if they could appropriate the group for their own purposes. Both Harold Wilson and his Conservative predecessor as prime minister, Sir Alec Douglas-Home, did this during the election campaign of 1964. Douglas-Home even suggested in one light-hearted comment that the Beatles run for Parliament as members of the Conservative Party. Meanwhile, Harold Wilson counted the Beatles among his constituents, went out of his way to have his picture taken with them, and bestowed multiple awards on them, including the prestigious MBE.[7] However, while such machinations may have carried some weight with the young, they alienated or even offended some older voters unsold on both the popularity of the Beatles and the general trend of politicians and the media pandering to the youth at that time.

The decade of the 1960s had begun with a certain amount of optimism in both Britain and America about the prospects for the future amidst the shift to a consumer society enjoying myriad home appliances and conveniences hitherto unavailable and changing styles—in music, fashion, and home décor. By 1965, many people in both countries would have had good reason to believe those promises fulfilled. Everyday life carried with it a general aura of modernity that made most people feel they did live in an exciting new age with at least more comfortable and convenient lives than previous generations had enjoyed. Television, viewed in the convenience of one's own home, to a large extent replaced radio and feature films as a window to the outside world, while the ads on television and in glossy magazines marketed the latest fashions and convenience goods from candy bars to laundry detergent. The phenomenon of Mod culture, with its bright colors and stylish fashion designs, took off in Britain between 1964 and 1967, largely because of its depiction on television and in magazines during this period. The influence of the Mods on teenage culture went beyond fashion and extended to music, politics, and society.[8] Pop art was not solely a British phenomenon, but through the success of

British artists such as Peter Blake, David Hockney, and Richard Smith, Britain could lay claim to being at the forefront of this modern cultural phenomenon.

Additionally, it became easy to criticize British culture of the 1960s for its obsession with celebrities, among whom the Beatles now counted. The rise of superstar models such as Jean Shrimpton and Twiggy, actors such as Terence Stamp and Julie Christie, or the jet-setting Princess Margaret and her celebrity-photographer husband, Antony Snowden, all spoke to a new kind of fame based on who you were or how you looked rather than on what you did. This celebrity culture was one indication that the 1960s just might be more style than substance. The fact that British culture was becoming more youth-driven also could have served as a warning sign, given the fickleness and lack of experience characteristic of teenagers, although many people saw these as virtues in the new, fast-paced society of the decade. Unlike French or German youth culture, with its adherence to existentialism, to which Astrid Kirchherr had exposed the Beatles in Hamburg, British youth mostly eschewed any sort of idealism or overriding philosophy that might have added heft or meaning to their daily existence.

Meanwhile, the crisis of the pound provided an indication that trouble might lurk ahead. Indeed, Britain's financial problems made their way into popular culture through a different kind of group: the comedy troupe known as the Cambridge Circus, starring John Cleese, Tim BrookeTaylor, and David Hatch, among others. In one skit, they quote Harold Wilson as responding to an offer from the United States to buy the Queen with the question, "Elizabeth who?" The laughs came at the expense of Wilson and his relationship with the Queen, but the fictitious proposal touches on the dire financial situation faced by Britain in early 1965 that only became worse as the year went on.

Yet another indication of the plight of Britain, though, came in the form of the Beatles' film *Help!* In Britain, as Simon Winder has argued, Ian Fleming's novels and the James Bond films helped people forget about the declining status of their nation and hold on to their belief that their country could still play an outsized role in the world through their identification with this fictional super-spy. Significantly, much of Bond's success, in the films anyway, relied upon brilliant gadgetry and high-tech wizardry that emphasized his connection with the technological aspirations of the new age; by comparison, Fleming's novels are decidedly low-tech, with Bond relying more on his own cunning.[9] The Bond films *From Russia with Love* and *Goldfinger* were the highest grossing films in Britain for the years 1963 and 1964, respectively. By choosing to parody the James Bond genre, the Beatles were throwing all of their cultural cachet behind a project specifically designed to undermine the one symbol of continued British greatness (aside from the Beatles themselves) that helped those most concerned about the fall of the British Empire to feel good about themselves. As Winder put it, "As a large part of the planet slipped from Britain's grasp one man silently maintained the country's reputation. When a secret organization with stolen atomic weapons planned to destroy Miami Beach it was not the Americans who would save the world, but a solitary Englishman, mucking about for wholly implausible reasons in the Bahamas."[10] The Beatles, upon hearing that the Bahamas might be a desirable place to house their earnings as a potential tax shelter, decided that they would like to go there and suggested the islands as a desirable film locale. What were the Beatles doing in *Help!* then but "mucking about for wholly implausible reasons in the Bahamas"? They did not deliberately choose the Bahamas because of any association with James Bond, but viewed in this context, the film takes on added cultural significance. Instead of saving the world like Bond, however, they, by their own admission, stayed stoned most of their time there, signifying a lethargic, indolent response to whatever crisis Britain happened to be in at the time. The Beatles *Help!* thus arrived at a kind of watershed moment during the 1960s, timed for the historian's convenience at almost the exact midpoint of the decade. If the Beatles had unwittingly contributed to a kind of hedonistic individualism through their early records focusing on young love and happiness and to materialism through their record sales and commercialization (as suggested by Ian MacDonald[11]), their songs on *Help!* adopted a more serious tone in response to the culture of the mid-1960s, even while at the same time the film lampooned other aspects of its pretensions. The Beatles seem nowhere nearly as engaged in their second film as they had in the first. Paul McCartney admitted on the Ron Howard documentary *Eight Days a Week* that making a second film was simply not as exciting as doing a first, while also acknowledging the Beatles' heavy use of marijuana during the making of *Help!* The songs, though, hold up in a way in which the film does not, for musically and lyrically the Beatles remained as engaged as ever. We must bear this in mind when assessing the reception of *Help!* in 1965, for people did not always make the distinction, though it was there for anyone who cared to look or listen.

Popular and Critical Reaction in Britain to the Beatles' Second Film and the Accompanying Album

In 1965, Beatlemania showed no signs of abating in Britain or the United States as crowds besieged the group wherever they went and their concerts and public appearances continued to require a heavy police presence. Given the tremendous popularity of the group and the enormous success of their first film, *A Hard Day's Night*, Walter Shenson, the producer of *Help!*, thought he had an easy hit on his hands, without having to demand too much of the Beatles. He and director Richard Lester saw an opportunity to build upon the individual screen identities established in the first film that allowed the Beatles once again to play themselves, without having to repeat the script or premise of *A Hard Day's Night*. Furthermore, in addition to the Beatles not wishing to repeat themselves, in 1964 their fellow Liverpudlians, Gerry and the Pacemakers, had quickly made and released their own film, *Ferry Cross the Mersey*, very much copying the same basic premise of *A Hard Day's Night*. Shenson, therefore, commissioned a fictional script that would take advantage of Ringo's inclination and ability to act, while requiring minimal effort on the part of the other three Beatles. Filmed on location in the Bahamas, the Austrian Alps, and closer to home on Salisbury Plain, the locations perhaps enhanced the visual effects of the film, but they inflated the budget, without adding anything to the plot and reinforced the ways in which it aspired to be similar to the Bond films.

The film definitely had problems, including the extent to which it had veered away from the relative modesty and indifference to their fame they had displayed in *A Hard Day's Night*. The notion that the Queen would house the Beatles at Buckingham Palace to ensure their protection from the villainous cult attempting to kill Ringo and secure the sacred ring that he cannot remove from his finger, while intended as a satirical comment on the extent of their fame, might have come across as them taking themselves a little too seriously. The thinness of the plot, the contrived dialogue, the unenthusiastic song performances, the way in which the Beatles generally seemed to sleepwalk through the film all contributed to its lackluster quality. *Help!*, full of what Bob Spitz has called "a patchwork of generic wisecracks that sounded flat and artificial,"[12] simply lacked the freshness and spontaneity of *A Hard Day's Night*. The film did have its moments and anyone who simply wished to see the Beatles on the screen in color or to enjoy their music could still perhaps come away satisfied. In one scene, the four Beatles enter a building with four separate doors only to enter the same apartment, which they all share, a commentary on the desire of each Beatle to retain his individuality while acknowledging the extent to which they were virtually inseparable.

Help! does not take itself seriously and does not expect its fans to do so, and in its sheer zaniness it tried to capture some of the energy and silliness of the Marx Brothers films. However, the consensus, among critics and even most Beatle fans today, is that this film was rather a disappointment after the first and that it does not hold up nearly as well, even though some fans retain a special affection for it. Fans felt like they really got to know the Beatles when they watched *A Hard Day's Night*, but it is hard to imagine that they felt the same level of connection watching their cavalier cavorting, staged shenanigans and contrived jests in *Help!* The Beatles are even less "real" in this film than in the first, which had to some degree played into unreliable stereotypes to distinguish them from one another. Larry Kane, who at the time knew the Beatles as well as anyone outside their inner circle, said he found the "quiet" George was not particularly quiet, while in his estimation the "funny" Ringo was the most serious of the four.[13] However, in *Help!* the Beatles did not just play a semi-fictionalized version of themselves; to an even greater degree, they played actors (which, aside from Ringo, they were not), playing the Beatles. In doing so, they distanced themselves even further from their fans rather than allowing them further into their world.

Awash in nostalgia and with the benefit of hindsight, it has been easy to view the film as yet another triumph on the Beatles' march from success to success through the 1960s. In their fifty-year retrospective on the film, Paul Skellett, Simon Wells, and Simon Weitzman called it "a defining moment in The Beatles' history, and by extension, the history of the world they occupied."[14] Critics at the time took a rather dimmer view of the film. In one review, Elspeth Grant, while praising Lester's ability to think up comical gags, wrote that the film is "so desperately *busy* that—as one rarely has time to get a real laugh off one's chest—one ends up frustrated and exhausted."[15] In another Peter Harcourt also found Lester's technique "wearying" while a movie review in the *Daily Mail* said it reduced the Beatles to "robots."[16] Finally, Philip French seemed to twist himself in knots trying to find a way to praise the film, writing, "its innovatory character lies precisely in its apparent lack of originality, its depth in the consistency of its two-dimensionality, its complexity in its simplicity."[17] For many people, Ringo's performance and growth as an actor provided one of the few redeeming features of the film.

A prickly Lennon shot back at the critics, "Did you know twice as many people have seen *Help!* in the couple of days it's been on as saw *Hard Day's Night* in all the time it was out? And they come up with all this rubbish about it being a flop!"[18] As Candy Leonard has noted, "Fans didn't know the Beatles were high on pot during most of the filming of *Help!*, or that it was filmed in the Bahamas so they could explore tax shelters—it was another Beatle movie and it was in color!"[19] Still, Lennon would indirectly shift some of the blame for the project to Brian Epstein, saying that the Beatles had always trusted his judgment and he had never steered them wrong. However, according to film historian Stephanie Fremaux, the Beatles played a much larger role in the production of this film than they had with *A Hard Day's Night*.[20] Moreover, Lennon's defense of the film did not stop people from wondering if the Beatles had made a significant mistake in allowing themselves to be showcased in this particular vehicle. The film's director, Richard Lester, was actually quoted as questioning whether he had "done right" by the Beatles with this film. In her review, Grant noted this and wrote, "I must say I think he did righter by them in *A Hard Day's Night*."[21] Even Lennon admitted that he was "disappointed with the way the film turned out."

Help! was in many ways more of a period piece than *A Hard Day's Night*, even though both naturally reflected key aspects of the time in which they were shot. Perhaps because the second film was in color, it highlights the fashions and material culture of the 1960s in ways not as visible in the black-and-white first film. Devin McKinney calls *Help!* "pure splash, deep color, and King's Road corduroy; at the same time it's cynical about itself, weary and mean, its bent to the morbid at odds with the shopwindow pop milieu which gives it its look and sensibility."[22] In addition, although Lester tried to downplay the influence of the Bond movies on the film, Beatles' film historian Bob Neaverson argues that the screenplay, written by Marc Behm and Charles Wood, "includes many quintessentially 'Bondesque' ingredients."[23] Behm had previously written the script for another satirical spy movie, the 1963 romantic comedy *Charade*, starring Carey Grant and Aubrey Hepburn, and was definitely familiar with the Bond genre.

Meanwhile, in his review of the soundtrack album in the *Record Mirror*, Richard Green called attention to the diversity of the music employed by the Beatles, describing it as a combination of "ballads, rock and roll, folk, country and western and a helping of straight pop." Among the songs Green singled out for praise, he particularly liked "Another Girl," which featured "some good guitar phrases and an insistent beat," making it a good, fast number for Mod dances. He also admired "Ticket to Ride," on which the group sounded "as great as ever," and "Yesterday," his favorite track, which he describes as a "slow, sombre and painful song," on which the "string quartet lend(s) a mournful quality as Paul tells how he lost his love the day before and is very, very hurt and alone." He singles out "I Need You," which featured Harrison on the vocals, for faint praise, saying, "The cha cha rhythm carries the song along, but it is not outstanding."[24] Other reviews were uniformly favorable, but Green's assessment of the songs on the album stands out for its perspicacity and it is hard not to say that his review of the album has stood the test of time.

For the most part, the record-buying public continued to show its support. If anything, the message of songs like "Help!" belied the hubris that seemed involved in putting out such a shallow film. If they had distanced themselves from their fans in the film, they revealed more of themselves to them in their music. John really was crying out for help, while "You've Got to Hide Your Love Away" also revealed an interior emotional world that seemed lacking in their earlier work. Released on August 4, the single "Help!" spent fourteen weeks on the British charts, including three weeks as number 1. On August 18, it was already the number 1 single in the *Liverpool Echo*'s top twenty, ahead of the Fortunes' "You've Got Your Troubles" and the Animals' "We've Gotta Get Out of this Place." On October 1, the single remained number 19 in Britain, at the time making the Beatles the only Liverpool group on the charts, much to the chagrin of the columnist for "Teen Beat" in the *West Lothian Courier*.[25] That same month a folk group out of Hull calling itself The Silkie had their only chart hit with a cover of "You've Got to Hide Your Love Away." A columnist reviewing the record said the song would be familiar to anyone who had seen the film *Help!*, adding parenthetically "and who hasn't?"[26] That aside provides a good encapsulation of the reception of *Help!* in Britain. Everyone went to see it—it was the second most popular film in Britain in 1965, behind only the equally nonsensical *Mary Poppins*—and most people enjoyed it even if the critics did not. Nevertheless, they still liked the group primarily for its music and the Beatles' future success would depend ultimately on that, not on their careers as budding film stars.

The United States in the Summer of 1965

In the summer of 1965, a young man named Jim Morrison had just graduated from film school at UCLA, unsure what he wanted to do with the rest of his life. Having made several short films as a student, he spent the summer after graduation living in Venice Beach and writing poetry, including poems that would provide the lyrics for some of the best-known songs of the rock band he would soon join that would call themselves the Doors. Morrison lived like someone willing to suffer for his art, sleeping on the roof of an abandoned warehouse and living on canned beans and Owsley's White Lightning, supplemented by frequent trips on LSD. The government had not yet declared LSD illegal and, although the Federal Drug Agency labeled it "dangerous," intellectuals such as Ken Kesey and Dr. Timothy Leary had become strong advocates for the mind-enhancing qualities of the drug popularly referred to as acid. Morrison and his bandmates referenced LSD in the name of their group, which they took from a novel by Aldous Huxley called *The Doors of Perception*, to which they regarded LSD as providing the entry point. Meanwhile, up the coast in San Francisco, a plethora of new rock bands had begun forming that would lead the *San Francisco Chronicle* that December to refer to the city as "the Liverpool of America." The Beatles and the rest of the British Invasion groups would soon be facing some serious competition from the West Coast of the United States. In the summer of 1965, besides the Doors, groups like Jefferson Airplane and the Grateful Dead were just getting started, while the LA group the Byrds and the San Francisco group the Beau Brummels already had hits that mimicked to a large degree what the Beatles were already doing.

The summer had opened with President Johnson confirming US policy in Vietnam, which he stated involved using limited force to put pressure on the North Vietnamese communists to negotiate a peace settlement. Johnson made the statement in order to put a halt to growing domestic criticism of his policy in Southeast Asia. In fact, that summer would mark a dramatic escalation of US military involvement in Vietnam and the corresponding intensification of antiwar protests and demonstrations. Opposition did not just come from the young or liberal intellectuals; Republican Senators and Representatives had started to make noise about halting their support for Johnson's Vietnam policy if he continued to send American soldiers into danger. The US government had already begun preparing the way for a vastly greater presence in Vietnam in April with the construction of a massive naval base at Cam Ranh Bay, consisting of an infrastructure of roads, docks, and warehouses over an area of about one hundred square miles. Cam Ranh Bay had the capacity to handle many more troops than the maximum number of 200,000 that supposedly represented the upper limit of American troop involvement in Vietnam. That same month Johnson dispatched 42,000 American troops in an invasion of the Dominican Republic to intervene in another civil war, though this action did not provoke the same level of outcry that had started to accompany US involvement in Vietnam.

As alarming as perspicacious observers might have found these developments, alongside the rising demonstrations and currents of antiwar sentiment, Americans had plenty of opportunities for mindless escapism that summer. The surprise-hit film of the summer was a United Artists movie shot in Paris called *What's New, Pussycat?* The film featured an international cast that included the British actors Peter Sellers and Peter O'Toole, the sultry veteran Austrian actress Romy Schneider, the Swiss bombshell Ursula Andress, the French star Capucine, and two young American comic actors, Paula Prentiss and Woody Allen. Burt Bacharach, who wrote many radio hits in the 1960s and 1970s for the likes of Dionne Warwick, B. J. Thomas, and the Carpenters, wrote the music for the film, including the title song, which became a hit for the Welsh superstar Tom Jones. Its scatterbrained and somewhat disjointed plot loosely revolves around the relationship between the promiscuous Michael, played by O'Toole, and his fiancée Carole, played by Schneider, who tries to make him jealous by cultivating a flirtatious relationship with Michael's anxiety-ridden friend, played, of course, by Woody Allen. The film bears some resemblance to the style, if not the content, of *Help!* The apparent need for sexy or undemanding entertainment evident in the popularity of these two films also seems reflected in the mere titles of the other films popular in the United States that summer. The list includes such mindless fare as *Up from the Beach*, *Ski Party*, *Tickle Me* (starring Elvis Presley), *Wild on the Beach*, the Dave Clark Five's Beatlesque *Catch Us If You Can*, and (I'm not making this up) *How to Stuff a Wild Bikini*. Even the obligatory westerns among that summer's blockbusters consisted of the comedy *Cat Ballou* and a film called *The Sons of Katie Elder*, the first starring the unlikely pairing of Jane Fonda and Lee Marvin, the second the equally incomprehensible combination of John Wayne and Dean Martin.

Some of the cultural changes foreshadowed by 1963 and 1964 became more visible in the summer of 1965. An increasing number of young men began wearing their hair longer, women began to dress more casually, women's hemlines started to rise up the thigh, and both young men and women began to adopt casual attitudes toward sex. Music began shifting as well, with drugs starting to influence the music and lyrics of songwriters such as Bob Dylan and the aforementioned Jim Morrison. All of these changes had their roots earlier in the decade and anticipated those changes to come in the next few years.

One of the most notable developments of the summer occurred in late July, when thousands of folk music fans gathered for the annual Newport Folk Festival, which turned out to be far more turbulent and controversial than anyone could have anticipated. The organizers reported 76,000 tickets sold, while even more listened to the music emanating from the festival in a nearby parking lot. In March 1965, Dylan had released his album *Bringing It All Back Home* that created the new blend of music that critics would identify as folk rock. The album contained the massive hit and drug-inspired "Mr. Tambourine Man," made even more popular because of the cover version by the Byrds, along with such rock-oriented songs such as "Subterranean Homesick Blues" and "Maggie's Farm," which Dylan would perform in Newport that summer. When Dylan played his new songs at Newport, accompanied by an electric guitar no less, he provoked a stir among the organizers and audience at the concert, many of whom, along with Robert Shelton covering the festival for the *New York Times*, were not impressed by Dylan's new style of music. Shelton wrote, "Bob Dylan, who seems unable to sneeze without causing controversy, introduced very unpersuasively his new fusion of folk and rock 'n' roll."[27] However, as Murray Lerner's documentary film, *Festival*, makes clear, reaction to Dylan's 1965 Newport performance was decidedly mixed; even Shelton acknowledged that the crowd demanded more, not less, from Dylan and some members in the audience said they were upset because they could not hear, not because of what Dylan was playing. Nevertheless, Dylan's performance at Newport became a dividing line in the history of popular music from which there was no turning back.

It did not take long for two simultaneous events to drive Dylan and Newport out of the headlines. On August 13, the Beatles arrived in the United States to begin their second tour of the country. On the same date as their arrival, some one hundred police officers and three hundred deputy sheriffs had cordoned off a twenty-block area of the predominantly African American Watts section of Los Angeles where riots had started two days earlier. The event that triggered the riots took place on August 11 when an officer of the California Highway Patrol named Lee Minikus pulled over an African American driver whom he observed driving in what he considered a reckless manner. Minikus and his suspect, Marquette Frye, a 21-year-old African American, stopped at the corner of 116th and Avalon, located in the Watts neighborhood. Frye's 22-year-old stepbrother, Ronald, was with him and a crowd observing the stop took umbrage with Minikus's conduct and attempted to intervene, even though Frye would later say that the stop was not worth a riot and he, improbably, became lifelong friends with Minikus.[28] A precipitant of the riots was the excessively hot weather that week, exacerbated by the heavy layer of smog that hung over the city. The root causes, however, derived from a decades-long history of racial discrimination, inequality, and racial profiling and brutality toward minorities on the part of the Los Angeles Police Department. Many African Americans, primarily from the South, had migrated to Los Angeles since the end of the First World War, believing they would encounter greater opportunities and less racial prejudice than they had in their place of origin. Their experience would not substantiate those hopes. At the time of the riots, the LAPD and the white community seemed oblivious to this reality and history. The police said they did not understand what had caused the riots. A reporter for the *New York Times* described Watts as having "a pleasantly suburban aura that belied the low income of most of its residents."[29]

The riots continued for several days, accompanied by a number of incidents of arson and widespread looting. By the fifteenth, the National Guard and other nearby police forces had fortified the efforts of the LAPD to contain the rioting, but proved unable to quell the unrest. As of August 15, twenty-one people had died, 600 were wounded, and some 1,400 were arrested, while estimates of property damage ran as high as $100 million. Sheer panic struck many white residents of Los Angeles and its suburbs. In the wake of the riots, racial hatred and fear spread throughout Los Angeles and into the San Fernando Valley, where some whites began to form vigilante groups to protect themselves from the attacks they believed imminent from African Americans. Reported episodes of racial violence took place in Burbank, Hollywood, Long Beach, Pasadena, and Venice, as well as in Pacoima in the San Fernando Valley and other mainly white areas. The shock waves emanating from the Watts riots reverberated throughout cities across the United States, many of which faced situations similar to those that had provoked the violence in Los Angeles. "Suddenly," Larry Kane later observed, "those who believed in the possibility of peaceful racial coexistence in America found their ideals shattered."[30]

On August 27, in another part of Los Angeles, the Beatles spent a historic but very awkward evening visiting Elvis Presley at his home in Beverly Hills. Trying to maintain a façade of politeness, Elvis welcomed the Fab 4 and sent them home with gun replicas as a souvenir. The Beatles did not quite know how to act around their idol and their initial attempts at humor and mild ribbing of Elvis for his recent string of mediocre singles and second-rate movies fell flat on the King and his entourage. Bob Bonis, their American tour manager who accompanied them, later recalled, "They were really nervous before they met him."[31] Los Angeles was the penultimate stop for the Beatles on their 1965 North American tour, which had included previous stops in New York (where they performed at Shea Stadium and recorded another appearance for *The Ed Sullivan Show*), Toronto, Atlanta, Houston, Chicago, Minneapolis, Portland, and San Diego. On August 31, they wound up their brief 1965 summer tour at the Cow Palace in San Francisco. If their meeting with Elvis left them feeling flat, their final concert left them feeling scared. As the crowd surged through the barricades set up to protect the stage, some

Figure 5.2 *Beatles fans greet the group at Kennedy Airport, August 13, 1965. Courtesy of Getty Images.*

people were injured, including a security guard hit in the head by a Coke bottle and a pregnant woman who had fallen amidst the stampede, causing Paul McCartney to stop the concert to plead for the police to assist her. They had arrived in New York less than a month prior, but in that short time the Beatles contributed to the major cultural shifts taking place in this transitional year, primarily through their iconic concert at Shea Stadium and the release of their second film, *Help!*

Popular and Critical Reaction to the Beatles and *Help!* in the United States

The Beatles' US tour of 1965 lasted only seventeen days, half the length of their 1964 tour, primarily because the Beatles had found the first tour too arduous. When the Beatles failed to sell out concerts in Kansas City and Portland, music industry pundits began to speculate on whether Beatlemania was dying.[32] Such speculation proved premature, if not completely unfounded. The Shea Stadium concert, which drew a crowd of over 55,000, provided the first indication that the Beatles remained a singular phenomenon in the music and entertainment industry. The promoter, Sid Bernstein, called attention to the gross from that concert, $304,000, at the time the largest in history. The Beatles themselves made $160,000 from that concert alone. Yet Bernstein noted he had only charged between $4 and $5 a ticket and could have easily sold as many tickets if he had charged three times those amounts.[33] WINS disc jockey Murray "the K" Kaufmann agreed, saying Bernstein could have gotten $10 or even $12 a ticket, but Brian Epstein had insisted on keeping the price down, in reach of most Beatles fans and increasing the likelihood of a sellout.[34] Speaking in Ron Howard's 2016 documentary about the 1965 tour, Larry Kane said, "The fact is they had to play stadiums. [Police and local authorities] would tell them 'you can't play in 5,000 seat theaters and have 50,000 teenagers going crazy outside.'"[35]

For those who had the opportunity to see the Beatles in concert that summer, it became a seminal experience. Janet Nugent won tickets to the Shea Stadium concert in a contest sponsored by WCAO in Baltimore. "A lot of my friends' parents would not have let them go at age fourteen, but my parents fully trusted me and more importantly, they knew how important it was to me and it was going to be pretty traumatic, if they didn't, so they let me go."[36] Jane Barnes was only 12 when she saw the Beatles perform at Comiskey Park in Chicago that summer, sitting in the first row behind home plate, her tickets courtesy of her uncle, who worked as head of advertising at WBBM in Chicago. She says that, reflecting back on the top three events of her life, she would put that concert on a list with her marriage and attending the Olympics, "it was that important to me."[37] This was all in spite of the fact that fans could hear little if anything of the actual music in large stadium venues such as Shea and Comiskey. Even the Beatles could not hear themselves playing, John Lennon saying of the Shea Stadium concert, "I could not hear anything. I would be watching Paul's head bobbing to see where we were in the song." Nugent affirmed this, having been a member of the crowd. Having seen the group in Baltimore the previous year, she said, "they were totally drowned out; if you thought you couldn't hear anything in Baltimore, you [absolutely] could not hear anything in New York." Yet when asked if this disappointed her, she replied, "No. You wanted to hear them, but the sheer excitement of being there and knowing that these people that you idolized were near you. ... It was nirvana." She continued, "I don't think I have ever felt that way since then and I don't think I ever will feel that way again and I am grateful for that experience; it was sheer bliss." Barnes recalled a similar experience in Chicago. She remembered, "you could barely hear them but just being there personally with them, being that close was just unbelievable [as was] the electricity in the crowd."

Of course, there had always been critics and naysayers; this had not changed in 1965. The *Daily Princetonian*'s question of the week for June 24, 1965, "Do You Approve of the Beatles receiving the Order of the British Empire medal from Queen Elizabeth?," practically invited criticism of the hype the group had received in Britain and the United States. Jean McKee, then a junior at Princeton High School, replied, "No I don't think they deserved it. I don't like the Beatles period." Her classmate, Marissa Rossi, said, "I don't think they deserve it because there must be hundreds of others who have done more for England than they have." Positive responses ranged from the 22-year-old John Marcus's "They're magnificent. They deserve anything they can get" to "I think they helped promote England in their own way and I can't agree with those who are sending their medals back," the opinion of Mike Figueroa, who worked at the time as a waiter at the Nassau Inn. Curiously, Arlene Panicaro, another junior at Princeton High, opined, "I think if you're going to give the medal to some singing group the Rolling Stones should have gotten it, they are much better singers." No one could deny the Beatles' success, however, or their position as the leading rock group of their time. In his August review of *Something New*, a Beatles' album released for the US market, Mark Slobin, writing for the *Michigan Daily*, the student newspaper at the University of Michigan, noted the talents of overseas groups such as the Zombies and Them, while acknowledging that "Over and beyond the hustle-bustle of such little groups reign the grand and glorious Beatles."[38]

The film *Help!*, released in the United States on August 25, ten days after the concert at Shea, seems to have been generally more well received by critics and fans in the United States than in Britain. Brosley Crowther in the *New York Times* gave it a kind review, calling it "a lively, funny picture in many insinuating ways," although he referenced the negative opinion of others by adding, "There's no need to work up a panic or despair over the future of the screen." Crowther summed up the attitudes of most Beatles fans, writing, "While it hasn't the wit or substance of the Beatles' first film, 'A Hard Day's Night'—it misses the winsomeness and freshness of that forthright, cheerful kind of kidding of themselves—it does have a friendly, wholesome spirit, a delight in absurdity and the youthful exuberance and musical fervor of the famous mopheaded rock 'n' roll quartet."[39] Mike McEntarfer, a huge Beatles fan who in the 1960s bought every Beatles single, EP, and LP released in the United States, usually on the day of release, said recently at the time he liked *Help!* better than *A Hard Day's Night*, primarily because *Help!* was in color, though now he prefers the Beatles' first film. He recalled hitchhiking with his bandmates to a neighboring town to see the film, and on the ride home, "I'm sure we drove the driver crazy as we recited our favorite lines from the film in our best Liverpudlian accents."[40] James Vignapiano also liked *Help!* because it was in color but was struck too by how different the music was than in their previous film. He still found the group "charming and funny," but took special note of how much they had progressed musically. Roy Auerbach remembered seeing the movie at age 15 and thinking it "silly," while noting that he still liked it because of his high level of "tolerance for silly movies." He thought *A Hard Day's Night* had more social commentary than *Help!*, which he called "just a fun laugh."[41] Jane Barnes, on the other hand, thought the film, "almost contrived … as if somebody threw it together to try to make some money off the Beatles."[42]

What American fans and critics such as Crowther seemed largely to miss at the time, as they had with *A Hard Day's Night*, whether they liked the film or not, was the ways in which the film satirized the British establishment and undermined the positive national feelings that their success had actually helped to promote. *Help!* carried the subtly subversive message that the younger generation could not trust the older generation, and therefore accorded perfectly with the general direction of American popular culture and the germinating political radicalism of American youth, whether they realized it or not. Taken out of the context of its times, it seems like another funny, silly movie, but placed within the broader context of the mid-1960s, it would have a huge influence in the United States as it did in Britain on changing styles, popular culture, and general youth attitudes that ranged from cheekiness to cynicism to outright rebellion. The enormous popularity of the Beatles and the film would ensure that millions of young people saw it, exposed to the barely disguised subliminal messages evident when giving the film a close viewing today.

Meanwhile, the soundtrack album became the best-selling LP in the country, as had *Beatles VI* only three weeks after its release two months earlier. The song "Help!" became an even bigger hit in the United States than it did in Britain, reaching number 1, staying there for nine weeks, and keeping Bob Dylan's "Like a Rolling Stone," the greatest song of all time according to *Rolling Stone* magazine, from getting to the top of the charts. "Like a Rolling Stone" combined the pop-rock sensibility of the Beatles with Dylan's folk-inspired lyrics, causing more comment on the transition from rock and roll to folk-rock. In the August 21 edition of *Billboard*, Aaron Sternfield identified Sonny and Cher's "I've Got You, Babe" and the Byrds' cover of Dylan's "All I Really Want to Do" as additional examples reaching the charts that week. Cher even reached the charts with her own cover version of "All I Really Want to Do."[43] Interestingly, when one interviewer questioned Dylan himself about the Beatles in 1965, he said,

> "The Beatles are great, but they don't play rock 'n' roll." Asked to elaborate, he said, "Rock 'n' roll is an extension of twelve-bar blues; it's white, seventeen-year-old, kid music … rock 'n' roll is a fake kind of attempt at sex, you know."[44]

Apropos of Dylan's comment, Slobin in his review of *Something New* called the Beatles' cover of Chuck Berry's "Rock and Roll Music" a "sly jest" that moves "smoothly from rock to cha-cha-cha beats." At this point, however, it did not matter if they did not play rock and roll or if they had joined the move toward folk-rock pioneered by Dylan himself. They were the BEATLES and no one else compared to them in the eyes of most pop music fans and critics.

At the beginning of the fall 1965 television season, a much more momentous annual event for viewers than it has become in the age of Netflix and satellite and cable packages that run to hundreds of channels, a new cartoon series for children joined the ABC Saturday morning lineup on September 25 at 10:30 a.m. Eastern Standard Time. The series was called simply "The Beatles" and it provided yet another way for young fans to experience the music and a representation of the personalities of their favorite group. For five-and-a-half minutes twice within the half-hour program, they were able to hear one of their favorite Beatles songs, accompanied by a storyline involving the four Beatles that loosely connected to the lyrics of the song. Some of the episodes featured situations similar to those encountered by the group in *A Hard Day's Night*, but others had the Beatles more or less living normal lives, going out to public places like parks or museums that the real Beatles would have found it extremely difficult if not impossible to do.[45] The series provided yet another indication of the myriad ways in which the Beatles had entered and influenced popular culture, despite the fact that the Beatles had little, if anything, to do with the series.

The summer of 1965 had therefore represented a central phase in the career of the Beatles, just as it marked a key transitional midpoint of the 1960s as a whole. The abbreviated tour of 1965 foreshadowed their dissatisfaction with touring, helping to ensure that 1966 would be the last year when they would go on tour. The film *Help!* portended not the continuation of the Beatles' career as potential movie stars but their growing boredom with the medium; they would never make a film like either of their first two again. In lieu of both, they would focus more exclusively on their music, while also beginning to find time for their own individual relationships and personal maturation. Robbie Robertson, who played in Bob Dylan's band on his 1965 tour in Britain, met the Beatles backstage after Dylan's concert at the Royal Albert Hall on May 27. He later said, "we were astonished at how naive they were, how very sweet, and nice, and everything. They all had on matching boots and matching clothes, and they talked about mystical things that were very corny."[46] I am not sure he would have had the same impression if he had met them six months later. Already on the *Help!* album, introspective songs such as "Help!," "You've Got to Hide Your Love Away," and "Yesterday" signified a new direction in the songwriting of Lennon and McCartney. Even "Ticket to Ride" deals with the theme of sadness and lost love from a lover who, like the singer in "Yesterday," looks at himself and reflects on what he did to cause his girl to leave. In addition, "Yesterday" had introduced classical instrumentation, blurring the boundaries between musical genres (and the recording divisions at EMI, the company with whom the Beatles had originally signed) and opened musical possibilities the Beatles would continue to explore on later albums. These songs all pointed toward the future and the maturation of the group that would show up on their next album, *Rubber Soul*.

CHAPTER 6
1966: THE BEATLES ON A GLOBAL STAGE

"Why Did Bobby Kennedy Make Fun of My Wife?"

By 1966, Governor George C. Wallace of Alabama had emerged as a prominent figure on the national stage, someone perhaps capable of putting together a coalition of political conservatives and religious fundamentalists that might lift him to the presidency itself. The Watts riots in Los Angeles the previous summer had heightened fears among many white southerners who believed those riots could spark further civil unrest in their region of the country. The only thing that angered those white southerners hostile to desegregation more than civil rights demonstrators led by figures such as Martin Luther King Jr. was the intervention of the federal government to assist the efforts of African Americans to achieve integration and equality. In 1966, white supremacists still held a grudge against Robert Kennedy because of his efforts as attorney general to assist the cause of civil rights, particularly his intervention to aid James Meredith in becoming the first African American to enroll at the University of Mississippi. On June 11, 1963, Wallace had personally stood at the door to Foster Auditorium at the University of Alabama to block two African American students, Vivian Malone and James Hood, from entering. Wallace appealed to angry white southerners by fashioning himself an outsider crusading against northeastern liberal elites like the Kennedys.

George Wallace stood on the front lines of a raging culture war that included complaints toward local CBS affiliates for what Southern conservatives perceived as the network's biased coverage of racial tensions and incidents in the South. As Walter Cronkite, the venerable anchor of CBS News well known as one of the most trusted men in America, later wrote, "They maintained that our reports were biased in favor of the blacks and that they distorted the position of the whites by suggesting that all white southerners were as violence-prone as those we pictured on television."[1] Wallace's "stand" at the University of Alabama, however, spoke for itself and forced President John F. Kennedy to send in the National Guard to secure the students' entrance, juxtaposed against Alabama state troopers who supported Wallace. The president had to go on television to defend the interjection of federal troops into Alabama, making sure that he alluded to the racial discrimination that existed in the North as well as the South, in an effort to appease—however slightly—Southern sensibilities. The effort failed. In March 1966, when the University of Mississippi invited former Attorney General Robert Kennedy to speak at its law school, Kennedy received thinly veiled death threats from a local organization calling itself the Association for the Preservation of the White Race. In fact, the president of that association, Gordon Grogan, warned that Kennedy's visit could result in "another planned assassination."[2]

Neither John nor Robert "Bobby" Kennedy had begun the 1960s as crusaders for civil rights. As attorney general for his brother, Bobby had actually attempted to dissuade civil rights activists from direct action protests that would inflame tensions in the South and potentially harm his brother's chances for reelection. For example, he secured a tax exemption from the Internal Revenue Service for a Voter Registration Project to channel the movement in a less confrontational direction. However, Bobby also had to contend with Federal Bureau of Investigation (FBI) Director J. Edgar Hoover, a staunch political conservative hostile to the Kennedys, who used devious and underhanded methods such as wiretapping and infiltration to undermine the Civil Rights movement. Bobby Kennedy found it necessary to assert his influence as attorney general over the FBI as tensions escalated in the South, much to the consternation of Hoover. When Bobby assumed the position of attorney general, the FBI had exactly three agents in Mississippi; when he left office, it had over 150 stationed there.[3]

Hoover's FBI even blackmailed Martin Luther King Jr. by threatening to expose his marital infidelities, going so far as to imply it would do so if King did not take his own life. King did not take the bait; instead, under pressure from within his own Civil Rights movement, he helped organize a protest march from Selma, Alabama, to the state capital in Montgomery in early 1965 to further the cause of securing voting rights for African Americans. Selma had a wide disparity between the number of African Americans in the city (over 50 percent) and those registered to vote (about 3 percent), a discrepancy enforced by a racist bully named Jim Clark who served as sheriff. Even so, the real target of the march was Governor Wallace, who represented a much larger obstacle to the marchers' ultimate goals of racial equality and desegregation. The 1965 Civil Rights campaign in Alabama, the highlight of which was the Selma to Montgomery march, resulted in about three thousand arrests, including that of Martin Luther King Jr.

Since Alabama's constitution prohibited Wallace from running for reelection in 1966, he attempted to have the constitution changed to allow him to serve a second term. He thought that too much was at stake in his battle with the federal government over civil rights for him to step away from politics at that time. Furthermore, Wallace hoped to position himself better for a potential presidential campaign by retaining the highest office in his state. His efforts failed, however, when a handful of senators blocked the bill after it had passed in the Alabama House of Representatives. Deprived of his opportunity to run for reelection, Wallace turned to his wife, Lurleen, who had amiably fulfilled her duties as first lady of Alabama by graciously hosting dinner parties and working on behalf of a variety of charitable causes. A columnist once described her as "just pretty enough to be attractive to men, but not so beautiful as to cause jealousy among women."[4] A faithful and supportive wife, she overcame her natural reticence and lack of interest in politics and agreed to run for governor simply because her husband asked her to do so. Like the vast majority of women of her generation, Lurleen lacked a college education, something that made her feel self-conscious on the campaign trail. When a reporter asked about his wife's qualifications, Wallace gave the trenchant response that "my wife is honest, and being honest is ninety-five percent of being a good governor."[5]

1966: The Beatles on a Global Stage

Figure 6.1 *George and Lurleen Wallace, November 8, 1966. Governor George Wallace and his wife, Lurleen, appear confident of victory after they voted at the courthouse. Mrs. Wallace is running for governor to succeed her husband, who is prevented by law from running for another term. She has promised her husband will keep running things if she is elected. Courtesy of Getty Images.*

The Wallaces in fact faced opposition from within the state, even from within their own party. In what Jeff Frederick has called the dawn of a "new social and political order," Alabama had recently undergone redistricting to allow for proportionate representation of urban areas less likely to support the governor and his efforts to perpetuate his power by acting as puppet master for his wife.[6] This led George to take Lurleen on a barnstorming campaign tour across the state to rally as much support for her as he could. For about two months, George and Lurleen traveled the state, speaking to as many as five crowds a day, seven days a week. The Wallaces' campaign rallies often featured country music performers, affirming the association of country music in the South with conservative political causes. Country music held the possibility of unifying urban and rural southerners in a rapidly changing political landscape that threatened to divide them. After a musical prelude, Lurleen, a Hank Williams fan herself, would speak briefly and somewhat vapidly; a *New York Times* reporter compared her performances to those of "a star pupil declaiming on Flag Day at the school assembly."[7] George would follow with a much longer speech to much more raucous and enthusiastic applause than the polite and restrained response afforded to Lurleen.

Meanwhile, Bobby Kennedy's commitment to civil rights and to ending the war in Vietnam had grown into causes he now regarded as moral imperatives, only intensifying his rivalry with Wallace. Then, while visiting Tuscaloosa, Alabama, in March, responding to a reporter's query about his presidential ambitions, Bobby Kennedy slyly volunteered only the comment, "my wife [Ethel] isn't running for president." Wallace seized upon the remark, asking, "Why is Bobby Kennedy making fun of my wife?" He then attacked Kennedy for wanting to send blood to the Vietcong, misrepresenting a comment Kennedy had made in 1965 defending the right of Americans to send blood to whoever needs it, including those in North Vietnam. Kennedy never mentioned the Vietcong, the name for the communist army in South Vietnam, to whom Wallace was referring. The pugilistic governor essentially used Kennedy as a foil to encourage voters in Alabama, and supporters throughout the South, to view Wallace as a defender of southern womanhood and American patriotism against the liberal elites who would impugn or threaten them.

Elsewhere that summer, as the Wallaces' campaign marched on in Alabama, the alumni of the David Starr Jordan High School in Watts attempted to commemorate the one-year anniversary of their neighborhood tragedy by staging a festival that would bring the district some much-needed positive attention. An ugly incident had occurred in May when the beatings of two reporters in the area led to the arrest of eleven African Americans. These occurrences seemed like they might portend more trouble as the anniversary of the 1965 riots drew closer. After that incident, the mayor of Los Angeles, Samuel W. Yorty, accused "left-wing agitators" of stirring up trouble and assured residents that the police would quell any new disturbances. The organizers of the festival hoped to forestall this by turning a potentially divisive and volatile situation in a constructive direction that might renew pride in the neighborhood. The planned festival, centered in the area where the riots broke out, featured a carnival, two jazz concerts, a bazaar, and an art exhibit, as well as a parade and a beauty contest. About 35,000 people attended that first festival; the second Watts Summer Festival a year later attracted an attendance upward of 130,000.

By contrast, August 1966 also saw an attempt by Wallace to push a bill through the Alabama legislature that would allow him to defy federal regulations on desegregation. The House approved the measure by a resounding vote of 76 to 9. The bill also called for appropriations of $3.8 million to offset in part the $30 million in federal funding the state stood to lose because of its passage. On August 31, the Senate passed the bill, making school desegregation illegal in the state of Alabama. The South was clearly not going to resign itself to desegregation and the end of white supremacy in the region. During Bobby Kennedy's visit to the University of Mississippi earlier that year, the Association for the Preservation of the White Race, deciding that the assassination of another Kennedy in the South would probably not reflect well on them or the region, held what they called a "wave-in" of demonstrators waving their rebel flags in solidarity at an Oxford hotel. The Democratic Party of Alabama still used "White Supremacy for the Right" as part of its motto; while some party members had begun a movement to have the phrase removed, many others had reacted with consternation, resisting any change whatsoever. Opposition to such changes came especially from small farmers and rural communities beset by the rise of industry and corporate agriculture. In November, Alabama voters elected Lurleen Wallace the 46th governor of their state; she took office in January 1967 and served in that role until her premature death in May of the following year.

Thus played out in Alabama a struggle that would symbolize a larger fight for the soul of the nation—a struggle between those committed to preserving the existing order dominated by middle-aged and older white men and those advocating a more inclusive society that provided opportunities for leadership and success for the young, for women, for African Americans and other minorities. Additional dimensions of the struggle involved the conflict between rural and urban Americans and between those residing on the East and West Coasts and those residing in the South and Midwest. At its core, the struggle pitted people who believed the country's mission involved a commitment to Christianity as a national creed and those who held a secular belief in progress, freedom, and equality for people of all creeds.

A year earlier, the Beatles had visited Atlanta as part of their US tour, where they confronted some of the same racial issues that had led them to take their stand against having segregated audiences at their concerts a year earlier. In 1966, as the Beatles' popularity soared to even greater heights, they made their presence felt on the global stage with tours that took them to Germany, Japan, the Philippines, and back to the United States. However, the world was different in 1966 than that the Beatles encountered just two years earlier when they first achieved worldwide success in ways that the Beatles did not quite understand. When the year began, the Beatles were still relatively innocent, politically speaking, but events of that year directly involving them would awaken in them a new consciousness, similar to that experienced by an entire generation around the same time. The rivalry between George Wallace and Bobby Kennedy in 1966 foreshadowed conflicts that would define the rest of the decade and, indeed, that continue to resonate in American politics in the twenty-first century. Yet, just as the world had changed, so had the Beatles, now a more grown-up version of themselves, as evidenced by the album they released just as 1965 was ending. They called it *Rubber Soul*.

Rubber Soul

Earlier in their career, the Beatles had found great success when they serenaded their female fans with love songs, but in the songs they composed for their new album in the latter half of 1965, they continued to explore deeper, more introspective themes. Their previous album, *Help!*, had already evinced a higher level of maturity in their songwriting than their previous albums (see Chapter 5). Drawing continued inspiration from the trippy lyrics of Bob Dylan, Lennon, McCartney, and now Harrison, each sought to expand their own songwriting into new realms of transcendent meaning and verbal imagery. Perhaps most notable was their changing attitude toward women, who now appeared in the lyrics of Lennon and McCartney as fully realized individuals in their own right and not simply as the objects of their lover's desire. The Beatles were growing and maturing, right along with many of their fans, and they began to process their own emotions and views of the world through more of an adult perspective. EMI released *Rubber Soul* on December 3, 1965, and printed 750,000 copies in anticipation of the Christmas rush.

The Beatles also expanded their musical repertoire on the album, infusing their songs not just with traditional elements of folk, rock, and pop but also incorporating styles and genres ranging from R & B to raga rock, psychedelia to rockabilly, while helping to create the incipient genres of folk rock, power pop, and baroque pop. The Beatles had always successfully borrowed from multiple musical styles and artists, but now it seemed like nothing was off-limits where their musical creativity was concerned. Still, the title of the album was revealing; although the Beatles would employ a diverse range of musical styles and genres on the album, *Soul* was its unifying concept. The term "Rubber Soul" implied an elasticity to the soul music the Beatles had cut their teeth on, while what they did with the genre inspired other artists to move in a more soulful direction. For example, Felix Cavaliere of the Young Rascals said the album directly inspired songs like their hits "Groovin'" and "It's a Beautiful Morning."[8]

Brian Epstein's assistant Peter Brown observed that, starting with *Rubber Soul*, "Now, instead of producing an album that was just a disconnected hodge-podge of hit songs …, the albums had a sense of collective identity, a mood and a sound linking them." Brown described that sound as "strikingly different; more melodious, haunting."[9] George Martin said, "For the first time we began to think of albums as art on their own, as complete entities."[10] Other changes characterized this album as well. For example, George Harrison debuted his experiments with an Indian instrument called the sitar. According to Martin, "The Beatles were always looking for new sounds, always looking to a new horizon and it was a continual but happy strain to try to provide new things for them. They were always wanting to try new instruments even when they didn't know much about them."[11] Walter Everett suggests that another thing that made this album sound so different from previous releases was McCartney's decision to play his Rickenbacker bass on almost every track, reserving his famous and lighter Höfner bass mainly for live performances.[12]

The Beatles managed with *Rubber Soul* to transform their music in a way that kept their previous fans happy while at the same time attracting new fans who had not taken them very seriously before. Bob Schiffer liked the Beatles before December 1965, but said, "With the release of *Rubber Soul*, I was totally hooked from then on." Schiffer said that, not only did he buy every Beatles album released from that point forward but that upon hearing *Rubber Soul* he went out and bought all their previous LPs. He remembered hearing it "all over the place" in his college dormitory and began to learn to play Beatles songs on the piano, inspired by such beautiful songs on the album as "In My Life." "I was just sort of enchanted by the whole album," he remembered.[13] Ed Eichler was 16 years old when *Rubber Soul* came out. As the son of a father who was a professional pianist, songwriter, and record producer and as someone who played in a band himself, Eichler had a much stronger musical background than most people did who listened to the Beatles at that time. He, too, took note in the change of the Beatles' direction, describing *Rubber Soul* as having "a more sophisticated sound." He said he thought at the time he was old enough "to appreciate the harmonies and the quality of their sounds as opposed to some of the very early Beatles stuff," which he regarded as "very simple, more teeny bopper stuff."[14] James Vignapiano, who was only a year younger than Eichler and, like him, had a strong musical background, concurred. He noted, "Their harmonies and the recordings [on *Rubber Soul*] were so much better" [than on their early albums], which consisted more of "raw music." Like many people I spoke with for this book, Vignapiano listened to this album with his friends and said "this was the album that really blew us away … we just loved it."[15]

Tom Noce, who turned 17 the same month as the release of *Rubber Soul*, also said he thought the album marked a real shift for the Beatles and that, for him, "the breadth of the album cemented them as not just another passing band."[16] Noce moved to southern California around the time *Rubber Soul* came out and became a Beach Boys fan, but he said the Beatles "tore up the rubric … they said here we are, this is us" and people responded. Mike McEntarfer recalled, "When *Rubber Soul* came out I recognized that their music had suddenly evolved to a new level. Music critics seemed to take it more seriously. My friend and lead guitar player in our band went to his house to listen to it after school and I still remember that afternoon."[17] Several contemporary reviews of the album verify these astonishingly similar recollections. One British reviewer wrote that the Beatles had not merely produced an "unbelievably sensational album, but were also setting trends in this world of pop."[18] Another British reviewer marveled at "the constant stream of melodic ingenuity stemming from the boys, both as performers and composers. Keeping up their pace of creativeness is quite fantastic."[19]

The American critic Greil Marcus called it "the best album they would ever make."[20] A reviewer named Eden summed up his review in *The Record Mirror* thusly: "Another Beatle album has been released, so what? SO … WOWWWWWWWWWW!"

Of course, not all Beatles fans liked the new direction, at least not immediately. Wade Lawrence, who grew up in the 1960s and now serves as museum director and senior curator of the museum at Bethel Woods, the site of the original Woodstock Music and Arts Festival in 1969, compared the reaction of Beatles fans to *Rubber Soul* to that of folk traditionalists reacting to Bob Dylan's electric performance at Newport earlier that year. Lawrence said it took him several times listening to the album before he decided that he liked it, unlike their earlier songs, which "were snappy and easy to hum and immediately you liked them or didn't like them and you usually liked them."[21] Richard Green of the *Record Mirror* dissented in labeling the album a disappointment, suggesting, "Over half the tracks, if recorded by anyone but the Beatles, would not be worthy of release." In particular, Green described "You Won't See Me," "Think for Yourself," "The Word," "What Goes On," and "If I Needed Someone" as "dull and ordinary."[22]

Green's opinion was the exception at the time, however, and since then it has not stood the test of time. *Help!* had some amazingly creative songs on it and was an important step forward in the evolution of the group, but every song on *Rubber Soul* had something innovative about it. Beatle fans in the United States received a slightly different version of *Rubber Soul* than that released in the UK. Capitol Records from the start had reserved the right to manipulate the albums to maximize profit; in this case, the North American version had only twelve songs compared to the fourteen record-buyers in the UK received. The UK version opened with "Drive My Car." In this song, an aspiring Hollywood actress convinces the singer (Paul) to take a job as her driver, even though she has yet to acquire the automobile that serves as the central motif of the song. ("But I've found a driver and that's a start.") The American version opened instead with "I've Just Seen a Face," an incredibly catchy and fast-paced song composed by Paul with echoes of country and skiffle music that does not even appear on the UK edition. In the next number on both versions, "Norwegian Wood (This Bird Has Flown)," an obviously independent woman, informs the singer (John) that she has to go to bed because she has to go to work in the morning. He "crawled off to sleep in the bath," waking to find her gone, leaving him with nothing to do, apparently, but start a fire. The song has often been interpreted to end with the singer burning the place down, but the lyrics do not actually state this; it could be interpreted as the singer simply lighting a joint to get high before he walks home. Either way, Ian MacDonald has called "Norwegian Wood" "the first Beatles song in which the lyric is more important than the music."[23]

"Nowhere Man" reflects John's sense of drift and loneliness and represents one of the most distinct songs on the album, deeper in meaning than the idiosyncratic "Norwegian Wood." The *Record Mirror* described the song as "slow, melodic, pleasant" and opined that it "would make a fine single." (The record reached # 3 on the US charts.) Another meaningful and insightful song primarily composed by John, "In My Life," reflected a mature sensibility that recalled positive memories of past friendships and relationships while the singer affirmed his commitment to the person who means the most to him. "You Won't See Me" and "I'm Looking through You" both reflect the tensions in Paul's relationship with Jane Asher, a prominent actress and just the type of independent career woman John had in mind when composing "Norwegian Wood." The songs deal with the kind of problems inherent in adult relationships. "Michelle" was perhaps a more traditional pop love song, but McCartney added some French lyrics that gave the song a distinctive cosmopolitan flavor that made it seem mature and sophisticated. Wade Lawrence described it as "a beautiful love song" and remembered one incident in which the song transfixed him and a group of Boy Scouts on a hike that had to stop and listen to the song from beginning to end when it came on a transistor radio.

Other songs on the album included "Think for Yourself," "Wait," and "Run for Your Life." One could construe the first of these, written by George Harrison, as his message to Beatlemaniacs not to idolize their musical heroes. "Wait" is an upbeat folk-rock take on a long-distance relationship that had real-life overtones and shifts to a lower key when the rock star singer assures his girlfriend that he's been "good" or at least "as good as I can be" (given the constant temptations provided by groupies during life on the road?). Although the UK and US versions of the albums began with different songs, they inexplicably both ended with the Lennon composition, "Run for Your Life," a dark lyric with a deceptively happy tone to it. Here the singer gleefully threatens violence ("I'd rather see you dead little girl than to be with another man") against his lover, perhaps the most cringeworthy song by today's standards since the Crystals' "He Hit Me" (And It Felt Like a Kiss), released in 1962 and written by the husband and wife songwriting team of Gerry Goffin and Carole King. A song the Beatles left off the album was called more optimistically "We Can Work It Out," released as a single the same day as *Rubber Soul* with "Day Tripper" on the flip side. "We Can Work It Out" was another song written primarily by Paul based on his complicated relationship with Jane Asher, but its message has been interpreted as applying to everything from the racial divisions in the United States to the Vietnam War.[24] However, as Paul and the rest of the Beatles would discover in the course of their travels in 1966, people would not always see it their way (as Paul implored the girl in the song to do) and they could not always just work everything out.

The Beatles in Japan and the Philippines

Before the Beatles set off for Asia, they made a return trip to Hamburg, which did not exactly turn out to be some pleasant trip down memory lane. The tour did not get off to a good start. George explained well the awkward circumstances attending their return to one of the most important scenes of their youth, saying, "The bad bit was that a lot of ghosts materialized out of the woodwork—people you didn't necessarily want to see again, who had been your best friend one drunken Predulin night back in 1960. It's 1966, you've been through a million changes, and suddenly one of those ghosts jumps out on you." Paul shared a similar view of the situation: "We had an old booking that had to be honoured. It was strange to see all our old friends in Hamburg. ... But we knew and they knew that we'd got famous in the meantime, and that we shouldn't really be playing that sort of gig."[25] Nonetheless, the Beatles got through it as they always did and then set off for Tokyo.

Scheduled to perform five concerts there in a three-day period, the Beatles arrived in Japan only to encounter thousands of hostile demonstrators upset that this English group would defile the almost sacred Nippon Budokan Hall by performing Western rock and roll. Tony Barrow, in his second year on tour as the Beatles' press officer, managed to find out from some Japanese students at the Tokyo Hilton what all the fuss was about and that some Japanese traditionalists had actually made death threats against the Beatles. Barrow learned that the Japanese considered the Budokan sacrosanct as the site of one of their national sports, sumo wrestling, but he seems not to have realized at the time that it also contained shrines to Japanese military heroes. Japan was in the midst of its own culture war, between nationalists who were intent on preserving Japanese traditions and resisting the influence of the West and those who sought to embrace the West and move away from Japan's nationalist past that had brought such destruction on the country during the Second World War. Japanese nationalists still bristled at the American occupation that followed that war and barely made a distinction between their disdain for the Beatles and their contempt for Western culture in general. Barrow had Japanese students translate the local newspapers for him or otherwise he might not have even known about the death threats. Although he chose at the time to keep the threats from the Beatles, they nevertheless must have wondered about the sudden presence of police guards preventing them from leaving their hotel room unaccompanied. The Beatles not only had round-the-clock guards, but the police permitted no one else on their hotel floor and staffed the elevators at all times. They escorted the Beatles to and from their concerts with military-style precision.

The Beatles performed their shows in the shadows of a strong military presence surrounding the stage at the Budokan because of the death threats made against them. Some five hundred police officers stood among the 10,000 spectators who witnessed the Beatles' first concert there. The fans who did make their way in to see the group seemed positively thrilled, Japanese teenage girls proving themselves capable of shrieking with the best of their Western counterparts. Still, the military presence put something of a damper on the concerts, which lacked the energy and frenzy that generally accompanied their earlier live shows. In addition, the Beatles' newer compositions from *Rubber Soul* and *Revolver* (see below) did not as easily adapt to live performances or allow the Beatles to replicate what they had done in the studio. Technology had still not caught up with the sound the Beatles sought to convey through their music, one factor in the group's decision to stop touring altogether by the end of the year. They dutifully and professionally performed their thirty-minute sets and recovered from their initial culture shock to perform a bit more enthusiastically by their second concert in the Budokan. Still, they were glad to leave Japan, little knowing that an even more disturbing situation awaited them in the Philippines.

A dictator named Ferdinand Marcos, who had persuaded the United States to support his regime as another stalwart against communism in the midst of the Cold War and had risen to power by promising social and economic reforms that would bring prosperity to the country and lift the Filipinos out of poverty, governed the Philippines with an iron fist. The Beatles performed in Manila on July 4, a date that commemorated both Philippine and American independence, a connection Marcos reinforced by declaring the day of the Beatles' concert Philippine–American friendship day. Devin McKinney explains:

> Obviously the Beatles have not been invited to Manila merely to play their music. At the very least, they are here as an opiate for the masses; at most, they are here to implicitly endorse Marcos's self-described "democratic revolution" by honoring the nation's most vaunted revolutionist on a day commemorating, in a perverse juxtaposition, both its independence and its grim pacts with the West.[26]

Hoping for a public relations coup by having the Beatles not only perform in the Philippines but also visit the Presidential Palace, the move backfired on Marcos, though at great cost to the Beatles as well. Trouble started when Brian Epstein declined an invitation for the group to attend a reception given by the first lady of the Philippines, Imelda Marcos, without consulting the Beatles because he knew the degree to which they cherished what little time they had to themselves on the road, given the long hours and hard work they put in. While Mrs. Marcos, her three children, and about two hundred guests anxiously awaited the arrival of the Beatles at the Presidential Palace, the Beatles never arrived. Marcos's 7-year-old Ferdinand, whom his family called "Bong Bong," allegedly remarked, "I did not think knights would be discourteous."[27]

The Beatles got wind of the reception—and their failure to show up—only later as events unfolded. Paul, ever the people pleaser who never wanted to disappoint a fan, admitted to feeling a bit guilty, but at the same time knew that the Beatles had done nothing wrong. Marcos and his wife, of course, did not see it this way and took their absence as an insult, leading to some very rough and anxious moments as the Beatles and their entourage quickly tried to exit the country. Once again, the group received death threats; however, unlike in Japan, the police in the Philippines had turned into adversaries, not protectors, making the situation a great deal more terrifying. At one point, riled up Filipinos allegedly kicked Brian Epstein after shoving him to the ground. Even after the Beatles left, they were gone but not forgotten as newspaper columnists continued to rail against them. Caloocan city, a town north of Manila, banned the sale of Beatles records and passed an ordinance prohibiting public venues such as restaurants, hotels, or cinemas from playing their music. A council member in Quezon City proposed a ban on Beatle-style haircuts. McCartney later speculated that Marcos might have known Epstein had declined the invitation and staged the reception anyway to make the Beatles look bad. Since the incident did not exactly show the Marcos regime in the best light and he later had to apologize for the shoddy treatment of the Beatles as they were leaving, this is perhaps unlikely, but it was reasonable for Paul to think this.

Desperately needing a hiatus from touring, the Beatles had planned to stop in New Delhi on their way back to Britain for a brief respite and to allow George to explore further his newfound passion for Indian culture. At first, only George and Neil Aspinall, the Beatles' road manager, planned to disembark in India, but in Japan, the rest of the group decided they could use a brief holiday as well. After the stress of their visit to the Philippines, however, the group just wanted to get home and planned to stay on the plane straight through to London. Unable to do so because the flight to London was completely booked, they ended up staying over in New Delhi nonetheless. George Harrison had indeed developed a sincere interest in Indian culture and spirituality. In August, he told a reporter, "I have become fascinated by Eastern culture and traditions, and am busy learning all I can about them."[28] He would need every bit of whatever insights he had then gleaned from an Eastern approach to help him cope with what the Beatles were about to face on their US tour that month. In both Japan and the Philippines, they had found themselves in the middle of cultural and political circumstances that thrust them into a spotlight far different from what they were used to. Even more unexpectedly, they encountered an eerily similar situation when they returned to the United States.

"More Popular Than Jesus": The US Tour of 1966

When Marc Catone solicited letters for his 1982 book of fans' recollections of the Beatles, one respondent from New York wrote, "When the Beatles talked about religion, drugs, etc., I got interested because I wanted to know where they were coming from and what they were into. ... They were an invaluable source of growth for me and helped open me up to a new world of ideas."[29] The cerebral John Lennon made one of the most provocative statements of the decade about religion when he told British journalist Maureen Cleave that the Beatles were "more popular that Jesus." John's full comments on the subject read:

> Christianity will go. It will vanish and shrink. I needn't argue about that; I'm right and I will be proved right. We're more popular than Jesus now; I don't know which will go first—rock "n" roll or Christianity. Jesus was all right but his disciples were thick and ordinary. It's them twisting it that ruins it for me.[30]

Most people whom Lennon's comments offended took umbrage with his hubris at even comparing the Beatles to Jesus Christ and his flaunting of the group's popularity. However, one can read in John's comments a much more serious tone that belied his later attempt to explain them away as a lament that Jesus was perhaps not as popular among the young as he should be. Lennon did not merely suggest the fact of the Beatles' popularity; he insisted that time would prove him right that Christianity would continue to "vanish and shrink," implying that this had little to do with what Jesus might actually have said or done but what his followers had done in his name. John aimed his critique more at Christians than at Christ, giving them even more potential cause for offense than the short phrase "more popular than Jesus" actually implies. Cleave even noted in her article that John took the topic of religion seriously and had recently done a good deal of reading on the subject.

John's recent reading had included a best-selling book called *The Passover Plot* by Hugh J. Schonfield, which had advanced the thesis that Jesus had capitalized on the high level of messianic expectations among the Jews of his time and determined to fulfill them, co-opting the support of his disciples to help him achieve his goals. However, as Devin McKinney notes, if John intended his remarks to echo Schonfield's thesis, they actually bore little resemblance to it; in fact, Schonfield's book suggested rather the opposite, that Jesus had spectacularly succeeded in his mission, as evidenced by the worldwide success of Christianity 2,000 years later. John was in his own rather inept way trying to articulate a central point he had gleaned from Schonfield's text: that Jesus' disciples were more to blame than he was for the distortions that had crept into Christianity.[31]

Whatever his intent, John's remarks to Cleave on the subject received very little attention among the British press or public when the interview first appeared, only gaining traction later in the United States and then spreading around the world. The reaction in many other countries, including South Africa, the Protestant Netherlands, Catholic Spain, and, unsurprisingly, the Vatican, would more closely mirror the negative reaction John's comments received in the United States than the relative indifference with which the British greeted them. As the Beatle fan who wrote to Catone implied, it was not just that John said what he did that bothered people; it was that those same people knew that millions of young people would be hanging on his every word and taking them as a new kind of Gospel—which is perhaps what Lennon intended all along.

Beatle fan Bob Schiffer acknowledged, "We paid more attention to John aside from the music than we did to anyone else [in the Beatles]. He was such an intriguing character. He had so much to say."[32] John made his comments for and about a British audience, but perhaps he should have realized at the time that the Beatles now occupied a world stage and that around the world others might view his comments with less nonchalance than that with which people in Britain reacted to them.

Then again, perhaps it is unreasonable to expect Lennon, however well informed, to have realized that the United States in particular was in the middle of a cultural revolution that freaked out many conservative Christians who felt under siege from a variety of movements and forces. As George Wallace's political machinations in Alabama demonstrated, white southerners had felt threatened enough by the Civil Rights Movement led by the Reverend Martin Luther King, Jr; by 1966, an incipient Black Power movement had arisen, associated to a large degree with an African American organization calling itself the Nation of Islam. King was at least a Baptist minister, but radicalized African Americans increasingly not only rejected white power but also Christianity itself. While in southern California, Watts attempted in 1966 to move beyond the violence of 1965 (see above), race riots simultaneously erupted across the nation in other major cities, including Baltimore, Brooklyn, Chicago, Cleveland, and Omaha.

Moreover, Christian conservatives had cause to fret over directions in modern philosophy and even theology, which had begun to veer in the direction of agnosticism, if not atheism, a trend that reached a popular audience when *Time* magazine published a cover story on April 6 raising the question, "Is God Dead?" The reception that Lennon's comments on Christianity received need to be understood in this context. Furthermore, they fed into general suspicions that already existed that the Beatles and rock music in general represented the work of the devil, an association that dated to the early rock and roll music of the 1950s because of its sexual provocativeness. One of the main perpetrators of this association in 1966 was a preacher named David Noebel who wrote a series of jeremiads such as *Communism, Hypnotism & the Beatles* (1965) and *Rhythm, Riot and Revolution* (1966).

Even so, Lennon's comments about Christianity almost faded away unremarked in the United States as they largely had in Britain. A spark, however, fed into the larger concerns percolating throughout the American South addressed in the opening section of this chapter. A year earlier, the Beatles had arrived in the United States just as the Watts riots in Los Angeles were starting; they arrived in August 1966 to find themselves in the midst of the kind of furor they thought they had left behind in Japan and the Philippines. Two deejays from a radio station in Birmingham, Alabama, first seized upon John's remarks and decided to make them a cause célèbre. Tommy Charles and Doug Layton were not reacting to the original article in the *Evening Standard*, which had appeared on March 4 and generated little to no response on either side of the Atlantic. They responded instead to a reprinting of John's comments in a teen magazine called *Datebook*, which appeared on July 29, just two weeks before the Beatles arrived for their 1966 US tour. A 26-year-old reporter named Al Benn serving as the bureau chief for United Press International (UPI) in Birmingham happened to hear them on the radio and wrote a news story about the topic, which immediately went national. The controversy gained legs as other radio stations in the South called for boycotts against the Beatles, angry mobs burned them in effigy, and the Ku Klux Klan threatened terrorist activity to disrupt one of their concerts in Memphis.

In an attempt to forestall any more trouble than necessary on the tour, Brian Epstein had hastily arranged for John to speak at a press conference to explain his remarks, hoping that a display of contrition would appease the Christians in the Bible Belt baying for his blood. "If I'd said, 'Television is more popular than Jesus,' I might have got away with it!" Lennon astutely observed to a national television audience. Lennon then tried to make it sound as if he had not intended to disparage Christianity, implying that he was lamenting its decline rather than celebrating it. This did not quite square with Lennon's actual comments, even though thirty years later Paul McCartney was still trying to place them in the context of declining church attendance in Britain as something that the Beatles both noticed and regretted. Paul want so far as to say, "We were actually very pro-church; it wasn't any sort of demonic anti-religion point of view that John was trying to express."[33] They may have noticed the decline in Church attendance, but it is doubtful they actually regretted this, except in perhaps some overgeneralized feeling that their fans had misplaced their religious devotion on themselves.

There is also no doubt that John issued his apology as part of an expedient intended to forestall trouble on their American tour, but watching it the viewer can see both his discomfort at having to address the situation in the first place and a bit of defiance. His televised remarks included:

When I first heard about the repercussions, I thought "It can't be true—it's just one of those things." And then when I realized it was serious, I was worried stiff because I knew how it would go on, and the things that would get said about it, and all those miserable pictures of me looking like a cynic, and it would go on and on and get out if hand and I couldn't control it. I can't answer for it when it gets that big, because it's nothing to do with me then.

John followed up on this theme in an interview with Leonard Gross, the European editor of *Look* magazine, telling Gross, "I'm slightly cynical, but I'm not a cynic. One can be wry one day and cynical the next and ironic the next."[34] He admitted as part of his apology that he was not a practicing Christian, but he clearly did not want people to regard him as a total cynic either.

Lennon's somewhat half-hearted apology largely muted the controversy, but it had already generated enough ill will among both their critics and the Beatles themselves that it soured the band further on the entire idea of touring, while causing many Americans never to think of them in quite the same way again. Here I should point out that hostility to Lennon and his comments did not just emanate from the South. For example, one Baptist minister in Cleveland, Reverend Theodore H. Babbs, threatened to "revoke the membership of any member of my church who agrees with John Lennon's remarks about Jesus or who goes to see the Beatles."[35]

Despite the bonfires of Beatle records in the South and the amount of attention John's comments generated—everyone I interviewed for this book remembered hearing about them—the controversy seems to have had little effect on the opinions of most Beatle fans on how they viewed the group. Roy Auerbach, who grew up in New York City, remembered, "Having been pretty areligious, I certainly had no personal angst over his making a statement like that. I thought it was probably a little bit injudicious, but it didn't bother me at all per se."[36] Bob Schiffer, another New Yorker, said he remembered talking about the controversy to his friends and speculating about whether John's statement about the relative popularity of the Beatles and Christianity was mathematically true. Still, he said, "it wasn't something that offended me. I just thought it was interesting and surprising that he said that."[37] Tom Blazucki, raised a Catholic in Baltimore, admitted to feeling a bit better after hearing John's explanation of his comments during his televised press conference, but said they did not affect or change the way he viewed the Beatles.[38] Janet Nugent also came from what she described as a "good Catholic family" in Baltimore. An avid Beatles fan, she admitted to struggling a bit with John's comments. Harking back to that time, she said she "probably tried to think he didn't mean it," but she found it difficult to process because "they were always sold as such good boys." She supposed she tried to rationalize it and even remembered hoping that John might have been misquoted. Aware of the record burnings in the South, she remembered finding it "very hard" when anything negative came out about the Beatles.[39] Wade Lawrence grew up in Memphis and he did recall having a number of Baptist friends, many of whom "completely turned their backs on the Beatles because they were sacrilegious and there was a lot of conservative backlash." At the same time, Lawrence recollected that "the radio stations still played them, at least the one I was listening to" and that he personally had no difficulty reconciling his faith with what John had said.[40] Indeed, even radio stations hostile toward Lennon did not always stop playing the Beatles. One radio station in Atlanta defended Lennon on the grounds of free speech even though it still condemned his remarks as foolish, while a station in Fort Knox, Kentucky, began playing Beatles records for the first time to condemn their hypocrisy, though this seems little more than a ruse to capitalize on the controversy and attract listeners.[41]

This small cross-section of responses seems to indicate two things: (1) People paid attention to and cared about what the Beatles had to say; and (2) They did not automatically subscribe to whatever the Beatles had to say, but generally did not let it affect their fandom even if they disagreed. Even the anonymous V.H., who wrote the letter to Catone quoted at the beginning of this section, added, "I never thought whatever The Beatles thought; I always perceived them critically."[42] Auerbach believed that, despite the burnings of Beatles records and merchandise in the South, the Beatles remained as popular as ever in many places across the country.

Devin McKinney, however, argues that we should not be so quick to dismiss the religious dimensions of the Beatles popularity.

> Kids, American kids especially, laded the Beatles with the aspirations, the psychic fears and physical intensities which religion had traditionally sought to absorb.

> ... It became common later in the '60s for fans—by this time better described as followers to play their Beatles records in a churchly environment assisted by candles, incense, mystical chants, even sacramental wafers of LSD; to study Beatle lyrics and Beatle iconography like Biblical scholars.[43]

McKinney speaks to a larger point about the significance of the "More Popular than Jesus" controversy—the extent to which the Beatles had become cultural touchstones because of their enormous popularity in a rapidly changing and increasingly revolutionary time. Meredith Eiker wrote a witty tongue-in-cheek column for the *Michigan Daily* at the University of Michigan actually comparing the Beatles story to that of Jesus, noting, for example, the similarities between the stage of the Cavern Club, the legendary birthplace of the Beatles, and the typical depictions of the manger scene Christians venerate as the birthplace of Jesus. Like Jesus, the Beatles had to deal with hostile crowds, with Eiker noting that many people had predicted the Beatles' imminent demise while others threatened violence against them. John, in fact, would continue to compare himself to Christ, especially in his 1969 song, "The Ballad of John and Yoko," where he predicted, "They're going to crucify me." By 1966, the Beatles did seem to have ascended to semi-divine status in the eyes of many of their fans, who waited anxiously for their next revealed text, and the clues that it might hold toward an understanding of the world or the meaning of life: two purposes that any religion ostensibly serves. In 1966, that text came in the form of the Beatles' most innovative album yet, released just a week before their 1966 US tour. They called it *Revolver*.

Revolver

Writing about *Revolver* in his 2016 memoir, Robbie Robertson of the Band recalled:

> [The Beatles] had transitioned out of their early period, when they had seemed innocent and sweet, especially in comparison to the world we had come out of. But seeing them here, even seeing the artwork on their new record—it all added up to a new, powerful musical direction.[44]

The Beatles had only heightened expectations of what their next album might hold after they had stunned the world with *Rubber Soul*, which many fans already considered the group's masterpiece. In late May 1966, the Beatles had provided some indication of their musical direction with the single, "Paperback Writer," with "Rain" as the B-side. Both songs indicated a move in the direction of psychedelic rock. The Beatles had begun to enter a phase of their career when, both mirroring and contributing to the emergent counterculture of the mid- to late 1960s, they began to turn inward and explore different levels of individual consciousness instead of focusing on the larger problems afflicting society as a whole.

Of all the tracks on *Revolver*, the song that best exemplified that trend was the last one on the album, a highly experimental and dreamlike soundscape of electronic noise called "Tomorrow Never Knows." By now, the Beatles had embarked on their experiments with LSD in addition to marijuana, leading to experiences that would have a profound effect on their music. John had read a book called *The Psychedelic Experience*, by Harvard professor, Dr. Timothy Leary and his coauthors Richard Alpert and Ralph Metzner, two professors of psychology. In this book, the authors had extolled the positive effects of LSD use, comparing them to those achieved by Eastern mystics after years of self-discipline and meditative practice. "Tomorrow Never Knows" opens with the invitation to the listener to "relax, turn off your mind, and float downstream" to music that sounds like a constant meditative chant amplified by electronic effects to create a kind of constant background hum instead of using rhythm or melody to carry the song forward. The Beatles' fascination with innovative recording techniques, including double tracking, tape loops, and reverse tracking, especially evident on songs like "Tomorrow Never Knows" and "I'm Only Sleeping," gives the album a sound unlike that heard, not just on any Beatles record but on any previous recordings by anyone. Robertson remembered, "What caught my ear immediately was the use of the recording studio as a musical instrument—incredible experimentation with sounds and effects, quite the opposite of a Bob Dylan record."[45]

If *Rubber Soul* had impressed Beatles fans and attracted new fans to the group, *Revolver* seemed to make an even stronger impression. As if the Beatles had not already displayed a unique level of musical talent and songwriting ability, James Vignapiano said, "For me personally and most of my friends, [*Revolver*] was the changing point where everybody just said 'Wow, these guys are they are not messing around. They are for real.' " He thought the album "totally different than anything they had done."[46] Vignapiano was not the only person with whom I spoke who identified *Revolver* as one of his favorite Beatles albums. For him it came down to *Revolver* or the White Album (see Chapter 8); for Roy Auerbach, the choice boiled down to *Rubber Soul* or *Revolver*. Auerbach stated that he liked the Beatles and thought they were "fantastic," but saw *Revolver* as a "real break," again something very "different" from what they had done before. Certainly not all Beatles fans applauded this shift away from the kind of music that they so dearly loved from their idols. Ruth Mandel recalled that in 1966 "the earlier music [of the Beatles] still resonated because it's just awfully good happy music." She noted, however, speaking to why the Beatles' new direction resonated with her generation, that with *Rubber Soul* and *Revolver* "the themes of their music got darker and more complicated but then so did our experience of life."[47]

Again, the Beatles had managed to please reviewers as much as they did their fans. In the *Record Mirror*, Peter Jones and Richard Green agreed that *Revolver* was "full of musical ingenuity" and, though they found it "controversial," they acknowledged that no one ever "made progress without running the risk of criticism."[48] A reviewer writing in *Melody Maker* observed, "There are still more ideas buzzing around in the Beatles' heads than in most of the pop world put together."[49] Interestingly, another music critic, who saw the album as "definitely a musical creation of exceptional excellence," complained that *Revolver* was not getting enough attention, writing that "several of the numbers included in the LP are already well on their way toward becoming contemporary standards, but the whole process is occurring with an amazing absence of fanfare and discussion."[50]

Fans would have noticed the marked difference between *Revolver* and their previous albums from the opening track, George Harrison's *Taxman*, which not only sounded different but also dealt with a subject unlike any the group had addressed before. Before the listener even hears any music, they hear coughing and a countdown into the song, which leads into George's electric guitar playing a riff, which seemed to place it in a different genre altogether, one that reflected the shift some groups were making from rock and roll to hard rock. In the song, Harrison complains about Britain's draconian tax code and a "soak the rich" philosophy that carried antiestablishment overtones, even though most Beatles fans would almost certainly have benefited from the tax policy the song condemns. Two songs selected from the album for a double A-sided single, "Eleanor Rigby" and "Yellow Submarine," could not have been more different in tone or content. Of the two songs, "Yellow Submarine," with its catchy pop vibe and psychedelic lyrics celebrating a communal spirit among fellow travelers through the 1960s, proved slightly more popular than the haunting and ominous "Eleanor Rigby" did, with its dark and shaded classical echoes and lyrics depicting the despair and loneliness of modern life. Although now regarded as a classic, at the time Peter Jones found the song "pleasant enough" but also "rather disjointed." Writing almost forty years later, Devin McKinney poetically described Eleanor Rigby as "at once an impeccably wrought chamber piece and a twisted, miserable thing. It is as safe as prosodic analysis can make it and as creepy as Marley's ghost, and its tension is between the passivity of the lyrics—stiff as a tableau, even when describing action—and the violence compressed in the music."[51] The song is significant because it marks a transition from Paul writing to or about people whom he knew to telling a story about fictional characters that still leaves room for analysis of its deeper message or hidden meaning. It comes across as an indictment of modern society, with its warnings about "all the lonely people" and its pessimistic conclusion that "no one was saved."

"Yellow Submarine" spent nine weeks on the *Billboard* charts, peaking at # 2, while "Eleanor Rigby" occupied the charts for eight weeks, rising only as high as # 11. (Ten years later, another single from the album, "Got to Get You into My Life" made it to # 7 and charted for sixteen consecutive weeks.)[52] Among the other songs on the album, the happy-go-lucky joyousness of "Good Day Sunshine" only serves to highlight the morbid fascination with death exhibited in the immediately preceding "She Said She Said," while the pleasant mellowness of "Here, There and Everywhere" follows the strange sounds of George's Indian-influenced "Love You to." Each song on the album represents its own little masterpiece with its own separate niche, but collectively the album achieved something like magic, leaving Beatles fans in wonder that the creative ingenuity of their favorite group had reached new heights none of them had anticipated.

The popularity of the album also manifested itself in the large number of cover versions of its songs that quickly appeared, some even offered for sale before the release of *Revolver* itself. In a separate review of some of these covers in the *Liverpool Echo*, the writer rather liked Marc Reid's version of "For No One," the Fourmosts' adaptation of "Here, There and Everywhere," and the Tremeloes' cover of "Good Day Sunshine." However, he said of Bill Withers' rendition of "For No One" that he "charges through this ballad with all the sensitivity of a buffalo," while Glen Dale had made Good Day Sunshine "sound like a fairground Bingo caller with a rusty microphone." The *Echo*'s reviewer's main criterion for judging cover version of songs from *Revolver* consisted of how close to the original the artist came on the grounds that the Beatles knew what they were doing and no one knew better than they did how to interpret one of their songs. For this reason, even the best of the cover versions of their songs could not compete with the Beatles' own. Therefore, even when the Beatles chose to use distortion of the music on a track like "Tomorrow Never Knows" fans and critics alike tended to give them the benefit of the doubt, even if, or perhaps precisely because, they had never heard anything like it before.

Revolver came not only as a revelation but also as a relief to Beatles fans, since the group had not released an album in eight months and, earlier in the year, rumors had circulated that the group was in the process of breaking up. Despite Brian Epstein's ardent denials of the rumors, when the British press ran a story in March on the Beatles' impending breakup, two hundred protesters demonstrated outside of his London home. Even with the release of *Revolver*, however, Beatles fans had reason for anxiety about the group's future. A reviewer in *Melody Maker* thought the most distinctive thing about the Beatles' latest album was the extent to which the individual efforts of each of the Beatles stood out. Their decision to stop touring after the final concert of their US tour at San Francisco's Candlestick Park on August 29 did not bode well for the future either. On stage, the Beatles had lost much of their verve and spontaneity, seen in their early concerts and so much on display in *A Hard Day's Night*. Moreover, the music on *Revolver* had become so electronically sophisticated that it did not lend itself to live performances, even if the Beatles had not decided to stop touring.

Then, again, by 1967, many fans, especially those entering or already in college, had more serious concerns to grapple with than the future of the Beatles, as race riots spread through the cities of the United States, antiwar protests and the draft increasingly intruded on popular consciousness, and segregationists such as George Wallace threatened to divide the nation. In this sense, even though the Beatles did not address such issues directly on *Revolver*, the maturation of the Beatles and the more experimental nature of their music resonated with fans for whom, as Ruth Mandel put it, "we couldn't live in a bubblegum music bubble."[53] However, if the Beatles were not yet ready to address directly such burning issues as the Vietnam War, others were more than ready to do it for them.

CHAPTER 7
1967: ALL YOU NEED IS LOVE; WAR, PEACE, THE BEATLES, AND THE SUMMER OF LOVE

Arnold Toynbee, Britain, and the Vietnam War

On the morning of August 4, 1964, President Lyndon Johnson told a select group of Democratic members of Congress that he had strong reasons to believe North Vietnamese Communists had fired upon US destroyers in the Tonkin Gulf off the coast of Vietnam. Johnson informed them of his plan to ask Congress for a resolution that would allow him to retaliate against the North Vietnamese. After no one present at the meeting opposed the idea, Johnson sought and obtained the Gulf of Tonkin Resolution from Congress on August 7, now widely thought of as a crucial moment in the escalation of American involvement in the Vietnam War. Though serious doubts later arose about the incident as to whether or not North Vietnamese ships were even present at the time of the alleged incident, the Resolution gave Johnson the cover to conduct a war in Vietnam without having to ask Congress for an official declaration of war. Johnson steadily escalated the war from that point forward, essentially without oversight or accountability. However, its effects soon began to show up, not only in the press and on the evening news but also in towns and cities where the wounded and body bags carrying the dead started arriving home.

By 1967, pockets of antiwar resistance, protests, and demonstrations had spread throughout the United States and the world, including Britain. Protesters demonstrated not just against the war per se but against the capitalist system and political establishment that continued to make such wars possible. As the British radical journalist John Hoyland wrote in 1967, "what we're fighting is suffering, oppression, humiliation—the immense toll of unhappiness caused by capitalism."[1] The protesters primarily consisted of young people, sometimes under the sway of Marxist ideology, sometimes under the influence of the emerging counterculture, and sometimes out of a general and sincere desire to right the wrongs of the world and the belief that peace was better than war, love better than hate. "Make love, not war" became one of the primary slogans of the youth culture in the 1960s. However, the antiwar movement also drew support from members of the clergy of all denominations, teachers, professors, and intellectuals, among others. About 250,000 protesters showed up to rallies in New York and San Francisco in the Mobilization to End the War in Vietnam in the spring of 1967. Around the same time, the antiwar movement gained a valuable and respected ally in the distinguished British historian Arnold Toynbee, one of the most famous public intellectuals of the twentieth century.

Arnold Toynbee (1889–1975) had completed in 1961 his twelve-volume, 7,000-page magnum opus *A Study of History*, which despite its ridiculous length was widely embraced by the reading public in Britain and the United States. In March 1947, Toynbee made the cover of *Time* magazine, a tribute to a man who fed the public's hunger for a general understanding of history even as academic historians, who were perhaps jealous of his publishing success and popularity, pursued narrower interests. As a generalist, Toynbee faced much criticism from his contemporary professional historians that steadily tended toward specialization. The renowned British historian Hugh Trevor-Roper, for example, called *A Study of History* "huge, presumptuous, and utterly humorless." Toynbee anticipated such criticisms but remained undaunted by them. He told Ved Mehta in 1962, "As soon as I put pen to paper I knew that whatever reputation I had would go up in smoke." He even faced ridicule within his own household. His first wife, Rosalind, whom he divorced in 1946, called the project Toynbee's "nonsense book."

Toynbee's main thesis, if such an enormous work could possess one, was that one could only understand history when considered at a universal, as opposed to a national, level and that all civilizations follow general historical principles. They succeed, for example, to the extent to which they develop appropriate responses to the challenges they face. Societies that do not face any or many challenges do not tend to develop much at all, providing one explanation for the vast disparity that exists among humans in different cultures around the globe. With regard to Vietnam, Toynbee believed that the United States was on the wrong side of history and its war effort in Vietnam ran contrary to a general trend toward nationalism and self-determination in Asia in the 1960s.

Meanwhile, in Britain, Wilson's government tried to walk a fine line between retaining friendly political and economic ties with the United States without supporting its military presence in Vietnam. Wilson even reached an agreement with Soviet Premier Alexei Kosygin, who visited Britain in February 1967, to issue a joint communique calling for "a speedy end to the Vietnam War." Polls taken in the summer of 1966 indicated only one-third of the British people supported the war and half of them favored immediate American withdrawal from Vietnam.[2] Wilson hoped the Anglo-Soviet call for peace would put pressure on President Ho Chi Minh of North Vietnam to sue for peace, which might lead the British public to view Wilson as opposing the war without the Americans viewing him as hostile to their interests. Risking opening himself up to charges of being soft on communism, the Laborite Wilson also committed to closer relations with Moscow, including the establishment of a hotline between 10 Downing Street and the Kremlin and a commitment to work with Kosygin toward achieving détente in Europe.

As the year dragged on, however, any slim hopes that the North Vietnamese were ready to begin peace negotiations began to dissipate. The recalcitrance of the North Vietnamese raised the prospect of an endless war of attrition that would continue until one side gave up, a grim prospect for the Vietcong, but an even grimmer reality for the United States, given the growing antiwar sentiment in the country. In March, Toynbee told Alden Whitman of the *New York Times* the United States could not win the war in Vietnam "unless the American Army is prepared to stay there forever."[3] Toynbee also argued that, despite their shared communist ideologies, the Vietnamese had a much greater fear of Chinese than American interference in their affairs because of their geographical proximity to China. Speaking at a Stanford University think tank in June, Toynbee sharpened his criticism of the American establishment and the Vietnam War, while reaffirming his support for the antiwar movement. He said, "It is not disloyal to dissent. The thing that disconcerts me about the American concept of loyalty—this is very rude of me—it has a very German tinge to it. My sympathies would be with the man whose conscience would not let him drop the napalm bomb."[4]

Toynbee was certainly not the only one to believe American policy in Vietnam misguided and based on false assumptions. U Thant, the Burmese secretary-general of the United Nations, gave a speech in July in which he said that peace in Vietnam would only be possible once the United States acknowledged that the North Vietnamese were fighting a war for national independence, not a war of communist aggression. U Thant described the Vietnam War as "totally unnecessary." Meanwhile, opposition to the war was growing in Britain and around the world. In October, British peace organizations such as the Campaign for Nuclear Disarmament and the British Council for peace in Vietnam marshaled their combined resources to stage a series of antiwar demonstrations in key cities, including London, Manchester, Edinburgh, and Glasgow, to support a major rally planned by American war protesters in Washington, DC.

Across Europe, as well as in Japan and Australia, similar protests arose in conjunction with the demonstration in Washington. Protesters in London, Washington, Paris, Stockholm, Copenhagen, and Genoa connected in a six-way telephone hookup to affirm their solidarity.

Much of the opposition to the war both domestically and internationally focused on the US bombing campaign in North Vietnam, which had inflicted widespread damage without bringing any degree of military success to the Americans or persuading President Ho Chi Minh and the North Vietnamese to enter into negotiations for peace. Johnson believed otherwise and remained convinced that bombing would eventually pressure the North Vietnamese and bring them to the negotiating table. At the same time, however, Johnson worried that the economic impact of the war on the United States, although slight compared with the Second World War or even the Korean War,[5] would hurt both his aspirations for creating the Great Society through his social programs and his chances for reelection in 1968. He faced opposition, not only from student demonstrators but also from within the Democratic Party for the ways in which the war detracted from domestic priorities and had adversely affected relations with US allies, including Britain.

Johnson also feared the effects of mounting American casualties and had to wonder how long the American people would endure the sacrifice of their young men. In one week in early March, American casualties numbered 232 dead and 1,381 wounded, the worst week of the war to that date;[6] by October, the total number of casualties since 1961 had reached 100,000. Privately tormented by such numbers, Johnson clung to the hope, which he expressed frequently in the press in 1967, that Ho would simply give up and withdraw from South Vietnam as long as US troops could prevent him from making significant progress there. As much as Johnson hated the war, he found the idea of giving up and rendering the sacrifices Americans had already made moot even more abhorrent. Had he listened to Toynbee and U Thant, Johnson might have understood how delusional this thinking was, rooted in his failure to acknowledge that Ho Chi Minh's main goal was reunification of his country. Like Mao Zedong, the leader of the Communist Revolution in China who held power until his death in 1976, Ho was a nationalist first, a communist second.

Toynbee, therefore, had good reason to be pessimistic about the prospect for peace in Vietnam, even as he tried to warn Americans that the United States could not win the war. Wilson's efforts to facilitate peace in Vietnam, although they may have temporarily appeased his domestic critics, had little effect, in either Washington or Hanoi. Kosygin's support for peace in Vietnam had more to do with his desire to restrain China's influence in the region, with equally futile results, though he would not have worried as much if he had understood the extent of Ho's fierce commitment to Vietnamese nationalism. Ho Chi Minh had no reason to stop the conflict, recognizing that his troops in South Vietnam could avoid defeat indefinitely by retreating or escaping across the border into Cambodia and reentering the South at a more propitious time. Johnson and the American military hierarchy at the Pentagon could not acknowledge the possibility that the most powerful nation on earth could not defeat a tiny Asian country. As for the American bombing campaign in North Vietnam, Toynbee remembered the effects of the Blitz and the Nazi bombs that rained on Britain during the Second World War. As he stated in his interview to the *New York Times* back in March, "Certainly bombing the North is not going to help. Being bombed only makes the Vietnamese more dogged and more determined. Look at my country, Britain." Toynbee was right. The war would continue.

The Beatles were not oblivious to the Vietnam War. Paul McCartney credited his awareness of the immorality and folly of the war to an impromptu meeting he had in April 1966 with the celebrated British philosopher and antiwar activist Bertrand Russell, who even at the age of 92 remained as politically engaged and outspoken as Toynbee. Paul's nervousness at the meeting betrayed itself when he almost knocked over a lamp while talking to the nonagenarian sage who had helped found the Campaign for Nuclear Disarmament in Britain prior to speaking out against American involvement in Vietnam. Paul later described how the meeting came about to Barry Miles: "Somehow I got his number and called him up. I figured him as a good speaker, I'd seen him on television, I'd read various bits and pieces and was very impressed by his dignity and the clarity of his thinking, so when I got a chance I went down and met him." He described the meeting as "Nothing earth-shattering. He just clued me in to the fact that Vietnam was a very bad war, it was an imperialistic war and American vested interests were really what it was all about. It was a bad war and we should all be against it. That was all I needed."[7] Paul later relayed this to his bandmates, who were receptive to what Paul was saying. If things happened as Paul described, he had actually adopted an antiwar stance before John did and influenced the future peacenik in that direction.

Nonetheless, even if the Beatles had made up their minds about the war in 1966, they still did not choose direct engagement, instead focusing on their own artistic vision and their next album. As usual, however, the Beatles proved perfectly in tune

1967: All You Need Is Love

with the times and their audience. By the summer of 1967, young people in Britain and the United States seemed to need something to take their minds off the war. Lacking the perspicacity of Toynbee, they still cherished hopes that love would conquer all and that peace would triumph over war. Like the Beatles, they increasingly looked to drugs and music as the means toward greater self-awareness and spiritual insight. When the Beatles released their next album, after a year's wait, young people responded to it in ways the Beatles could not have anticipated, any more than they anticipated the extreme reactions that Beatlemania had engendered. Recorded in the five months preceding its release, the Beatles called their new album *Sgt. Pepper's Lonely Hearts Club Band*.

The Making of *Sgt. Pepper's Lonely Hearts Club Band*

On June 1, 1967, the Beatles released their new album, *Sgt. Pepper's Lonely Hearts Club Band*, in both mono and stereo mixes, the former receiving much more lavish attention from the Beatles' producer, George Martin, even though most people would buy the stereo version of the album.[8] Frequently hailed as the first concept album, the Beatles did not start from that premise. John Lennon personally denied that the songs he contributed to it had anything to do with the Beatles performing a concert under the fictitious name of "Sgt. Pepper's Lonely Hearts Club Band." Lennon alleged, "All my contributions to the album have absolutely nothing to do with this idea of Sgt. Pepper and his band, but it works, because we said it worked, and that's how the album appeared."[9] One of Lennon's contributions to the album, "Lucy in the Sky with Diamonds" helped to establish the album though as belonging to the relatively new genre of psychedelic rock. The song is a tribute to lyrical improvisation that brazenly expects the listener to imagine a world with "marmalade skies," "newspaper taxis," "plasticine porters," and "a girl with kaleidoscope eyes" as part of a glorious dreamscape only a drug-addled mind could truly appreciate. It is, indeed, difficult to imagine even a fictional Victorian military band meant to serve as the Beatles' alter egos serving up such trivial and meaningless fantasy unless under the influence of drugs themselves or if they were actually part of an imaginary world such as Lewis Carroll's wonderland, which was always one of Lennon's major literary sources of influence. In fact, the album had started as a project intended to pay tribute to an idealized version of the sites and reconstructed memories of the Beatles' childhood in Liverpool. However, under pressure to come up with a single to fill the void of new Beatles' records until the album came out, the Beatles released the two songs they had based on this loose theme, Paul's "Penny Lane" and John's "Strawberry Fields Forever." The Beatles now needed a new concept for their album, if a concept album this was to be. McCartney provided the group with a starting point for the album, which turned out to be the title track, "Sgt. Pepper's Lonely Hearts Club Band." In the song, they introduce themselves as a band taught to play by Sgt. Pepper twenty years ago, along with an invitation to listeners to "enjoy the show," before introducing the singer of the next number (which turns out to be Ringo) as "Billy Shears." Having already decided to stop touring permanently, the Beatles offered their fans an album that at least created the illusion of a live performance. Neil Aspinall contributed the idea to include a reprise of the title song at the end of the album, to which the Beatles added a slight change in the lyric to include lines like "We hope you have enjoyed the show" to mimic the conclusion of an actual concert. According to George Martin, Paul said at one point, "Why don't we make the whole album as though the Pepper band really existed, as though Sergeant Pepper was doing the record."[10] This gave Martin the idea to arrange the songs on the album in between as one would a concert set-list, with the closing song "A Day in the Life" serving as a kind of encore.[11]

As for the rest of the songs on the album, John and Paul drew inspiration from a variety of sources, including television and the newspapers, but the album would also reflect their continued preoccupation with interpersonal relationships, especially in songs like "Getting Better" and "When I'm Sixty-Four." In addition, songs like "She's Leaving Home" and "Good Morning, Good Morning" include further commentary on the loneliness of the individual in modern society previously explored in songs like "Nowhere Man" and "Eleanor Rigby."

John Lennon said of *Sgt. Pepper* that, aside from the title track and its reprise, "Every other song could have been on any other album." This is perhaps true, at least on one level. "Getting Better," for example, would have fit perfectly on *Revolver*, while there is no good reason why "With a Little Help from My Friends" could not have worked on, say, *Abbey Road*. The 1968 White Album was so eclectic that it could have conceivably accommodated any of the songs from *Sgt. Pepper* if the Beatles had withheld them. On another level, however, one could argue that the exact combination and order of the songs on *Sgt. Pepper* made the album what it was: a perfect reflection of a moment in time between the relative innocence of the early 1960s and the bitterness and rancor with which the baby boom generation would close the decade. The final song on *Sgt. Pepper*, "A Day in the Life," embodied as much as any other song from the period the kind of detached sensibility that evoked the chaos and unpredictability of the times. The Beatles spoke to a generation constantly torn between engagement with politics and social issues and withdrawal from myriad other problems that plagued contemporary society including the Vietnam War.

The irony of the album ostensibly replicating a live performance was the amount of time the group spent in the studio, using recording techniques never intended for live duplication. The Beatles worked on the album for five months, during which they experimented with elaborate and innovative techniques in the studio with the assistance of George Martin and studio engineer Geoff Emerick. In 1966, the Beach Boys, whose rivalry with the Beatles until 1966 had mostly been one-sided on their part, had responded to the challenge of *Rubber Soul* with their own critically acclaimed masterpiece, *Pet Sounds*. On *Pet Sounds*, the Beach Boys' creative genius Brian Wilson had introduced a wide array of sounds in a beautiful and harmonious collage that produced the most pleasing effect to the ear in songs like "God Only Knows" and "Caroline No." For example, the clip clopping of horses' hooves that open the former provides accent and background to the amazing harmonies and soaring instrumentation that transform a simple pop ballad into a true work of art. Recording pieces of songs bit by bit, some at different studios to get exactly the desired acoustic effects, and blending them in the studio with the magic of an alchemist and the skill of a Michelangelo, Wilson had revolutionized the process of making an album that eclipsed anything even the Beatles had ever done.

McCartney and the Beatles had picked up the challenge and responded with the almost equally innovative *Revolver*. However, it surely did not help Paul's rather fragile ego that a poll in *New Musical Express* had ranked the Beach Boys as the best group of 1966, leading to further speculation in the press about "the decline and fall of the Beatles."[12] McCartney now wanted to construct an album unlike any previously recorded, even *Pet Sounds*. In fact, from this point forward, Paul became the unofficial leader of the group and the main creative inspiration behind their albums, singles, and movies for the rest of their career as a band. In collaboration with George Martin, he provided much of the leadership for the sound of *Sgt. Pepper*, though John made major contributions, including providing the main inspiration for the masterful "A Day in the Life," though still collaborating with Paul on the finished product. In addition, John's offerings included "Being for the Benefit of Mr. Kite" and "Lucy in the Sky with Diamonds," perhaps the defining song on the album. Paul wrote half the songs on the album, including the title track, as well as "Fixing a Hole," "When I'm Sixty-Four," and "Lovely Rita."

Paul employed four accomplished French horn players on the title track to give the song the actual sound of a Victorian brass band. One of them, John Burden, described the way they worked thusly: "I wrote out phrases for them based on what Paul was humming to us and George Martin."[13] Sounds of people cheering and applauding on the track helped to replicate the feeling of a live performance. Walter Everett credits a Lowrey Heritage Deluxe DSO organ for creating the combined sounds of harpsichord, vibraphone, music box, and guitar stops that produce the keyboard arpeggiations at the beginning of "Lucy in the Sky with Diamonds."[14] In addition to the Indian instrumentation prominent on "Within You Without You," George Harrison's one contribution to the album, on "Getting Better" the Beatles employed an Indian percussion instrument called a tabla, which they had first used on "Love You To" from *Revolver*.[15] Paul and John wrote one song for Ringo to sing, as had become customary for each of their albums. They gave him the second track, "With a Little Help from My Friends," which features a cowbell and Ringo on both the drums and tambourine, while contributing to the positive and psychedelic vibe on the album and providing an additional sense of togetherness and connectivity between the Beatles and their fans.

In addition to the music on the album, the cover in which it was packaged became one of the most distinctive icons of the popular culture of the 1960s. The cover and an interior, replete with colorful photographs and printed lyrics, the first pop album to include copies of the lyrics with it, made *Sgt. Pepper* almost as much a visual as an aural experience. The cover featured a collage of various people, ranging from historical figures to movie stars, and famous authors to idiosyncratic choices such as the avowed proponent of modern witchcraft, Aleister Crowley. Thus in addition to Sir Robert Peel, a nineteenth-century English prime minister, and Karl Marx, we find Mae West and Marlon Brando. Along with Aldous Huxley and Dylan Thomas, one can spot the psychologist Carl Jung and child star Shirley Temple (twice). Interestingly, Bob Dylan is the only contemporary musician featured on the cover, although the cover does include a doll wearing a shirt bearing the message, "Welcome the Rolling Stones." Stuart Sutcliffe is there, along with the Beatles themselves, standing front and center in full faux Victorian military regalia, yet decked out in bright colors of yellow, pink, baby blue, and orange instead of the drab colors usually associated with military uniforms. Standing alongside them, we see wax figures of the early Beatles in suits, now consigned to history, replaced by a more psychedelic version of themselves. In the foreground, flowers spell out the word "Beatles" in front of a drum identifying the group as "Sgt. Pepper's Lonely Hearts Club Band."

Sgt. Pepper enjoyed glowing and enthusiastic reviews from the start. A reviewer from *Hit Parader* saw the album as "expanding the outer limits of popular music" and proving that the Beatles' "dominance as the world's Number One group remains undiminished."[16] *Time* magazine said the album contained "the most original, expressive and musically interesting sounds being heard in pop music." The article continued, saying of the Beatles, "They learned to bend and stretch the pop-song mold, enriched their harmonic palette with modal colors, mixed in cross-rhythms, and pinched the classical devices of composers from Bach to Stockhausen."[17] However, as usual, reviewers still found things to criticize. Not everyone liked the artificial effects studio experimentation had on the music. Even the reviewer for the *Hit Parader* disparaged some tracks, including "Lucy in the Sky with Diamonds" and "Being for the Benefit of Mr. Kite" as resembling a "computerized assemblage of words and sounds." This reviewer put "She's Leaving Home" in the same category, a song that became one of the most divisive among the critics. The composer Ned Rorem considered it "equal to any song that Schubert ever wrote."[18] However, the *Hit Parader* review considered it the most disappointing song on the album, labeling it "no more than a tear-jerking cliché." Richard Goldstein wrote a particularly harsh review in the *New York Times*, calling the album "busy, hip, and cluttered," while singling out "A Day in the Life" for praise in "an otherwise undistinguished collection of work." Goldstein called "She's Leaving Home" "a melodramatic domestic saga."[19] Writing in his autobiography years later, however, Goldstein acknowledged that at the time he had missed the larger significance of *Sgt. Pepper*:

> *Sgt. Pepper's Lonely Hearts Club Band* ... would redefine not just the Beatles but my generation. It's hard to imagine the impact of this record unless you understood the central role rock played for us. Its messages were rubrics for life, but without clear instructions; it was up to each person to put it all together, to assemble meaning and take action.[20]

Sgt. Pepper's Lonely Hearts Club Band as a Product of Its Time

When Mark Catone was collecting letters for his 1982 book on fans' memories of the Beatles in the 1960s, an individual identified only as L.W. from Arlington, Massachusetts, wrote, saying, "*Sgt. Pepper* conjured up so many images, that I remember feeling as

1967: All You Need Is Love

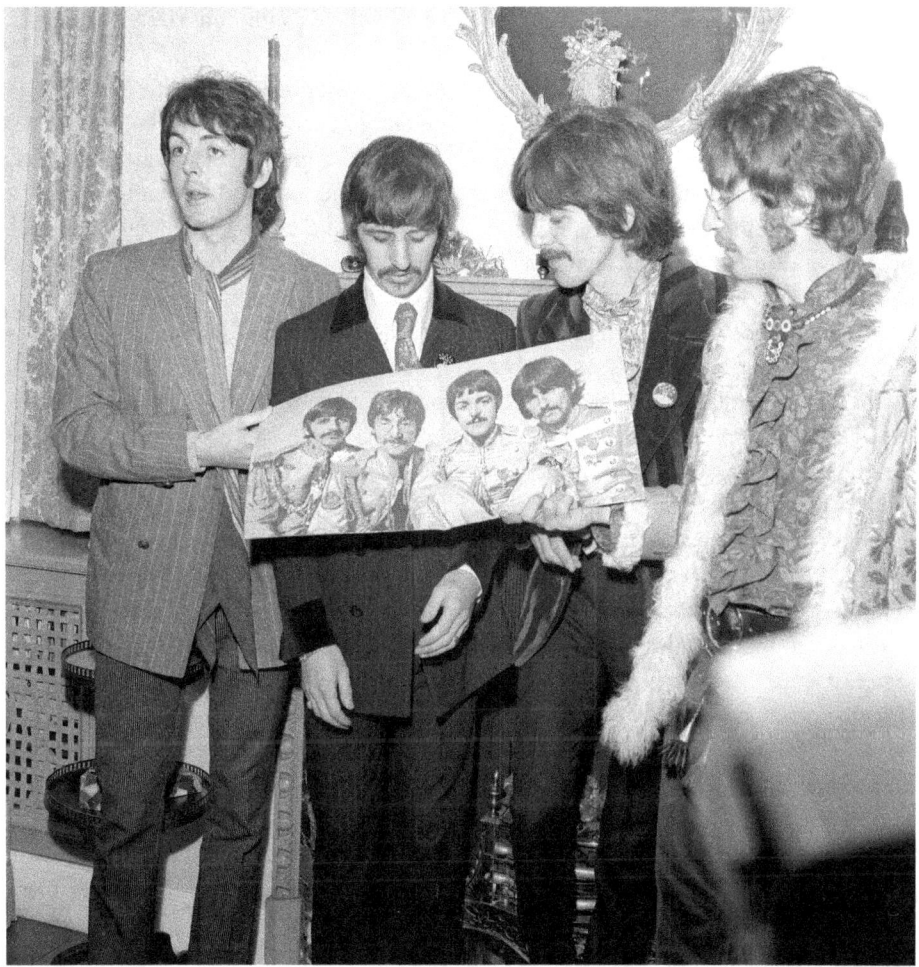

Figure 7.1 *The Beatles Release Sgt. Pepper, May 19, 1967. Paul McCartney, Ringo Starr, George Harrison, and John Lennon of the Beatles attend a press party at the home of manager Brian Epstein supporting the release of Sgt. Pepper's Lonely Hearts Club Band. Courtesy of Getty Images.*

if I had walked into a new dimension of colors, feelings, and ideas after I had heard it."[21] Later writers, most notably Elijah Wald, would criticize the Beatles for destroying rock and roll by transforming rock into an art form divorced from live performances and remote from anything that their fans could hope to replicate in their garages or at high school dances.[22] Ian MacDonald described the profoundly disorienting effect of listening to Beatles' records by the time of *Sgt. Pepper*: "The Beatles' works grew increasingly multi-focal, the conventionally dominant lead vocal vying for the listeners' ear with disconcerting harmonies, instrumental counter-melodies, backwards tapes, and distracting sound effects."[23] Dominic Sandbrook adds in agreement with MacDonald: "For many contemporary listeners, *Sgt. Pepper's Lonely Hearts Club Band* was an extraordinary, often confusing experience, with its continuous stream of sounds, its studio banter, steam organs, sitars and even farmyard barking, and its combination of cartoonish psychedelia, circus vaudeville, driving rock music and gentle ballads."[24]

Yet what the Beatles had done was not so much to change the expectations of their fans as to meet them, producing an album that, like all great works of art, seemed to express itself in language that its audience readily understood and responded to as if it revealed a vision of what they had known all along. *Sgt. Pepper* is an album for which what people imagined they heard was as important as what they did hear; this makes it difficult for the historian to analyze its effects by merely scrutinizing the album itself without recourse to the memories of fans such as L.W., quoted above. There was an important difference in this regard between *Sgt. Pepper* and earlier Beatles' albums. Every other Beatles' album contained singles the fans could have heard on the radio. In addition, albums like *Rubber Soul* and *Revolver* existed in alternative versions for the British and American market, while some Beatles' albums released in the United States, like *Beatles' 65* or *Yesterday and Today*, consisted of hybrids of singles and tracks of various albums. Conversely, fans only had access to the songs on *Sgt. Pepper* by listening to *Sgt. Pepper*, which contained no songs the Beatles released as singles and was the first album recorded after the Beatles had gained control over the contents of their American releases and therefore was identical on both sides of the Atlantic. The unique nature of *Sgt. Pepper* in this regard gave the album almost the status of revealed scripture, leading fans to search for subtle yet discernible truths in both the sounds *and* the lyrics, while viewing the album's cover as a new source of iconography that would yield messages aimed at the counterculture as well.

For younger fans who were not quite ready to adapt to the Beatles' psychedelic phase or to enhance their appreciation for "Lucy in the Sky with Diamonds" or "Within You Without You" by dropping acid, new pop groups emerged on the scene to provide them with catchy love songs resembling those that characterized the Beatles just a few years before. For example, the American band the Monkees, a contrived pop group of four males—the English lead singer Davy Jones, and the Americans Mike Nesmith, Peter Tork, and Mickey Dolenz—had their popularity reinforced by starring in their own weekly half-hour television show. They had a string of pop hits, including "I'm a Believer," "The Last Train to Clarksville," and "Daydream Believer." If you were between the ages of 11 and 13 in 1967, chances are you would have been much more enthralled with the Monkees' television series and their first two albums than with *Sgt. Pepper*. However, for teenagers, the Beatles' latest album seemed to open up a completely new world and to shape the identity of a generation. Furthermore, even for younger fans, Beatles' music was so ubiquitous that summer they could not help but be aware of it. Hearing "All You Need Is Love" for the first time that summer at a campground in Pennsylvania, this author, then 12 years old, thought the world had just become a better place because of the existence of that song. Indeed, that seemed to be the purpose of that song, as demonstrated by its broadcast via satellite around the world in an effort to show the efficacious potential of this revolutionary new technology. Peter Orenzoff, who spent part of his teenage years in England, was a devoted fan of the Rolling Stones and, until

1967, had little use for the Beatles. However, when he watched that satellite broadcast, his thinking began to shift, especially when he saw Mick Jagger and Marianne Faithfull, who had done a wonderful cover of the Stones' "As Tears Go By," on the broadcast with the Beatles. Orenzoff did not abandon his allegiance to the Rolling Stones or become an avid Beatles fan, but he did say that from that point he did begin to gain a greater appreciation for their music.[25]

In fact, even the Rolling Stones patterned their next album, *Their Satanic Majesties Request*, after *Sgt. Pepper*, which became a kind of endorsement of the Beatles, in the same way in which the Beatles had granted the Beach Boys greater credibility by paying tribute to *Pet Sounds* by emulating their work. For some Rolling Stones' fans, however, who were wrapped up in their imagined rivalry with the Beatles (the two bands were actually quite friendly and noncompetitive), the Stones' attempt to follow the Beatles' lead proved something of an irritant. This was especially true because *Their Satanic Majesties Request* represented such a departure from the combination of blues and hard rock that had come to characterize most of the Stones' musical output. Celebrated rock critic Jon Landau even wrote in *Rolling Stone* that the album had "put the status of the Rolling Stones in jeopardy." Landau described the album as "a kind of meandering undercurrent of production effects and electronic gimmicks, meandering instrumental breaks which do not follow the songs they are a part of, and an attempt at either creating, or possibly satirizing, *Sgt. Pepper* type unity."[26] Orenzoff perfectly encapsulated the reaction of a Rolling Stones fan to *Their Satanic Majesties Request*:

> The Beatles were always considered, at least then, the leaders, which annoyed me. The Stones were considered the followers at least until "(I Can't Get No) Satisfaction" came out, and even past that. When the Beatles came out with *Sg. Pepper*, the Stones responded with their *Satanic Majesty's Request*. The Beatles did "Eleanor Rigby," while the Stones did "Ruby Tuesday." So, in the mid to late 60s even though "Satisfaction" changed the whole dynamics and became an anthem to people my age, the Beatles were always considered one step ahead of the Stones, which as an avid Stones fan really annoyed me.[27]

Alan Chevat did not consider himself a Beatles fan until 1967. Before that, he was a blues fan, who was more likely to listen to the great American country blues guitarist Huddie Ledbetter, better known as Leadbelly, than he was to the Beatles or AM pop radio in general. Now a retired attorney, Chevat recently recalled, "When *Sgt. Pepper* came out, there was something about it, an excitement about it; that's when overnight I became a Beatles fan." Stan Green, who like Chevat, attended Stony Brook University in New York in the late 1960s, said of the Beatles," they were spokespersons for us; they represented us." He remembered that he started appreciating both their message and their musicianship "from *Sgt. Pepper* onwards."[28] Bob Schiffer had a job taking care of the boats on a lake in the Catskills in the summer of 1967 and remembered hooking up a long extension cord running from the boathouse to the lake so he could listen to records; the album he remembers listening to the most that summer was *Sgt. Pepper*.

The Beatles and the 1960s

Like all great works of art, *Sgt. Pepper* both influenced its time and was a product of it. The antiwar movement, the hippie counterculture, the desire of young people to assert their individuality, and their nonconformity with middle-class values all antedated *Sgt. Pepper* and helped to prepare the way for the fervor with which it was received. The fact that the Beach Boys' *Pet Sounds* had preceded *Sgt. Pepper* speaks to the Beatles' latest effort as a product of its time rather than a unique creation ex nihilo, just as the Rolling Stones' 1967 album, *Their Satanic Majesties' Request*, came largely in response to *Sgt. Pepper*. Nonetheless, artists do not imitate or respond to other artists unless they think a particular work of art worth responding to or unless they see their response as contributing something further toward answering a need in the culture of the times. Furthermore, the striking originality of the Beatles' conception for the album, the vigor with which Paul McCartney in particular pursued his musical and artistic vision for it, and the ways in which the Beatles expressed their own individuality in their new hairstyles, clothing, and laid-back demeanor perfectly resonated with a culture attuned to value each of these qualities.

Moreover, the songs and the music on the album resonated with the times in an almost alchemical way. The title song invited Beatles fans to join the group in an escapist fantasy that many young people found appealing. "With a Little Help from My Friends" suggested a feeling of love and togetherness that spoke to a communal ideal flourishing at the time. "Getting Better" was perhaps more aspirational than realistic given the turbulence of the times, but this was a hopeful time in which youth were ready for an optimistic message, just as "Fixing a Hole" suggested a reordering of priorities and the belief that even something as empty as a hole in the culture or one's soul could be mended. "She's Leaving Home" spoke to the quiet desperation of a young girl whose parents gave her "everything money could buy" but who had to escape a quiet, empty life "after living alone for so many years." It paired perfectly with the happier song released by the Mamas and the Papas in 1967 called "Twelve-Thirty (Young Girls Are Coming to the Canyon)," which referenced all the young girls flocking to Los Angeles' famous Laurel Canyon neighborhood, which became a center for pop music and the counterculture in the late 1960s. While "Lucy in the Sky with Diamonds" and "A Day in the Life" were more cryptic, they perhaps resonated the most with listeners, who were content to let the music waft over them and to allow themselves to feel whatever the music evoked in them.

When Ringo Starr talked about the album for the *Beatles' Anthology*, he did not just talk about the album; he talked about the times. "It was Flower Power coming into its fullest. It was love and peace. It was a fabulous period, for me and the world," he stated.[29] It was the Summer of Love.

The Summer of Love

The summer of 1967 saw San Francisco become the center of American popular culture and the counterculture, particularly the neighborhood known as Haight-Ashbury where hippies migrated from around the country in search of a psychedelic version of the Promised Land Americans had hoped to find in California since the 1848 Gold Rush. Briefly, for three days in the middle of June, just as schools let out for the summer, the center shifted about 120 miles south for the Monterrey Pop Festival, joining *Sgt. Pepper* as another crossroads in the history of pop music. The Beatles' smash album played for the crowd at Monterrey during breaks between the festival's live performances. When talking about the summer of 1967, music fan Roy Auerbach spoke of a "West Coast invasion" that succeeded the earlier British invasion. He identified Jefferson Airplane along with the Doors, Moby Grape, the Grateful Dead, and Jimi Hendrix as among the bands and artists he thought had started to take rock music in different directions by the time *Sgt. Pepper* came out.[30] Jefferson Airplane, a San Francisco group that had originally called itself the Great Society, had one of the most popular albums of that summer, aside from *Sgt. Pepper*. Their *Surrealistic Pillow*, released two months earlier in April, reached # 3 on the *Billboard* charts and featured two smash hits, "Somebody to Love," which peaked at # 5 on the charts, and "White Rabbit," which reached the # 8 position. The latter has become an iconic anthem to the use of psychedelic drugs in the 1960s. John Phillips of the Mamas and the Papas, the author of one 1960s anthem, the Mamas and the Papas' "California Dreamin,'" wrote another called "San Francisco (Be Sure to Wear Flowers in Your Hair)" recorded by Scott McKenzie. Released in May, it became a kind of theme song for the hippie movement and the Summer of Love.

In July, *Time* magazine described the hippies as a "wholly new subculture, a bizarre permutation of the middle-class American ethos from which it evolved." The article continued, "Hippies preach altruism and mysticism, honesty, joy and nonviolence. They find an almost childish fascination in beads, blossoms and bells, blinding strobe lights and ear-shattering music, exotic clothing and erotic slogans. Their professed aim is nothing less than the subversion of Western society by 'flower power' and force of example."[31] The tourist hippies and pie-in-the-sky newcomers to the Haight district drew the ire and resentment of some of the more radical groups who saw themselves as having a serious agenda of radical social change. These groups included the Diggers, who took the name of a radical, proto-communistic sect that had emerged out of the English Revolution of the mid-seventeenth century. Others took umbrage with the hippie movement for other reasons. In his 2015 memoir, journalist and music critic Richard Goldstein remembered, "I could tell from their disregard for money that they were securely middle class, while I came from a background where dropping out meant only one thing: poverty."[32]

Not all young people were turning on and tuning out though, as student activists continued to oppose the war and advocate for political and social change. By fall, it seemed as though young people, having collectively indulged themselves with a summer vacation, were ready to reengage with the seriousness the times demanded. At a teach-in at the University of Michigan in October 1967, Eric Chester, representing a group calling itself the Voice Political Party, responded to a French speaker who praised the connection between intellectuals and labor in his native country. Chester said that Americans lacked an "ideological heritage, an understanding of how their society runs," making revolution more challenging for radicals in the United States.[33] They were learning, however. Ruth Mandel, who grew up in Pittsburgh, attended several demonstrations in Washington in the 1960s, including the march in October 1967 during which protesters famously (and unsuccessfully) attempted to levitate the Pentagon. For her, as for many others, the period was one of startling intensity and even fear. Looking back on those demonstrations, she recalled, "People understood that you might get your head bashed in. It was very polarizing and scary and I have a special resonance with that because I am Jewish and although my family came here before the Holocaust, they came at the turn of the twentieth century so they left because of pogroms." Even though she is Jewish, she said her parents never told her about the Holocaust, which she did not know about until she was 15. Having recently learned the extent to which a government might persecute its own people, this drove her in the direction of social activism, at great personal risk. She said she even learned to shoot a gun so she could protect herself in the event of anything like the Holocaust happening in this country.[34]

Another session at the teach-in in Ann Arbor was devoted to "The Impact of the War on American Society." Reporting on this session for the school newspaper, Michael Dover noted that a rare point of agreement among those attending was the deleterious effect the war had on race relations in the United States. During the summer, as the temperature heated up, so had racial tensions, erupting into clashes between Black rebels and police, leaving twenty-six dead in Newark and forty-three in Detroit.[35] Nick Ercoline, who would later gain a measure of fame when a picture of him holding his future (and current) wife, Bobbi, appeared on the cover of the soundtrack album of the 1969 Woodstock festival, spoke of the 1960s as a "major time of change." Here is how he described the changes he and his generation experienced at that time:

We were going from the "Leave it to Beaver" family where dad wore a suit and necktie and on Sunday, mom wore her little pillbox hat and her dress and everybody got dressed up and we all went to church and then all got together on Sunday for meals and things like that. By the time we hit the [mid] 60s, we had seen a lot of changes, [including] civil rights marches and race riots. The pill was changing the way that we looked at sex. There was a women's movement and so many women were moving into the workplace. And, of course, we had the Vietnam War going on. We had a lot of war protests, which helped drive the music of the day in my opinion.[36]

In the midst of this period of radical social change and political discontent strode the Beatles, beloved of almost everyone under 30, radical enough to appeal to the hard-core leftists but popular enough to charm the politically uncommitted despite their drug use and shift toward the counterculture. Nonetheless, Paul McCartney stirred up a furor in the press with the admission that he and the other Beatles had already tried LSD while speaking effusively about the experience. In addition, on June 20, Capitol Records released in the United States a compilation album called *Yesterday and Today*, featuring a selection of songs from *Help!*, *Rubber Soul*, and *Revolver*, as well as the singles "We Can Work It Out" and "Day Tripper." The hideous cover design the Beatles selected showed them in white butcher coats ornamented with beheaded baby dolls and slabs of raw meat. Although some albums with this controversial cover made it to market, many American distributors refused to release the album, causing Capitol to hastily arrange for a more innocent cover, showing the Beatles in casual poses around a trunk, with the exception of Ringo, who stands rather formally behind it while fixing a dreamy stare at the camera. Had the "butcher cover" received wider distribution, it might have done more to knock the Beatles off their pedestal and offset the positive vibes emanating from *Sgt. Pepper* in the Summer of Love. Few fans were actually aware of the butcher cover in this pre-Internet age, but as it was, the Beatles took a hit in some circles, as if the album cover represented the dark side of the brighter and more colorful psychedelic appearance the group cultivated on *Sgt. Pepper*.

Having released *Sgt. Pepper* to such acclaim, the Beatles took a well-earned respite from recording and, now that they had stopped touring, could enjoy their first summer off since they were teenagers with relatively few distractions. However, for them the Summer of Love came to a premature and tearful end when they suffered the loss of their beloved and loyal manager, Brian Epstein, to a drug overdose on August 27. Brian's death left the Beatles adrift and needing leadership. They were loath to hire another manager but lacked the necessary experience and financial acuity to handle their own business affairs successfully. They talked about going to India to regroup, something they had planned to do anyway after meeting the Indian guru and proponent of transcendental meditation, the Maharishi Mahesh Yogi. However, after they decided—against George's wishes—to postpone their Indian trip, the Beatles opted to throw themselves back into work, which had always provided a level of comfort for them. Paul continued to provide leadership for the group and proposed a film for their next project, but one completely unlike *A Hard Day's Night* or *Help!* Paul wanted to base the film loosely on the practice of some companies in the British tourist industry of offering outings to surprise destinations, in other words mystery tours. John Lennon described the Beatles' new film venture as "a lot of laughs, some off-beat characters, a few very glamorous girls, a bit of dancing and quite a bit of magic."[37] The Beatles would call the film *Magical Mystery Tour*.

Magical Mystery Tour as a Reflection of Changes in the Beatles and Britain at the End of 1967

Not everyone had followed along with the Beatles throughout the transformation of their music as it evolved from *Help!* through *Sgt. Pepper*. The Beatles had changed too much, however, in those intervening two years for anyone to expect them ever to return to what they had once been. Gone were the seemingly carefree lads of *A Hard Day's Night* whose main concern was showing up at scheduled appearances on time. Nor were the Beatles any longer the stoned madcaps traversing the world James Bond style in *Help!* Of their decision to make another film in 1967, George Harrison said, "For years we looked around for a screenplay that was suitable, but in the time that had elapsed since *A Hard Day's Night* and *Help!*—although it was probably only two years—it was as if we'd gone through five hundred years mentally." Harrison continued, "We didn't see any way of making a similar film of four jolly lads romping around singing catchy little tunes. It had to be something that had more meaning."[38] Furthermore, *Magical Mystery Tour* initiated the Beatles' post-Epstein career, meaning it offered them an opportunity to redefine themselves as masters of their own destiny. Anyone expecting anything like a reprise of their earlier films should have known better, just based on the transformation of the group's music since then, even if they had not paid attention to the statements made about the film in the press prior to its airing. The result was a chaotic, plotless series of seemingly random scenes on and off the bus carrying the Beatles and an odd assortment of character actors and members of their personal entourage through the British countryside. The Beatles interspersed within these improvised scenes a set of new songs that, with one or two exceptions, many Beatles fans did not find up to the group's usual high standards.

The Beatles were somewhat staggered by the initial reactions to the film by critics and television viewers, many of whom deluged BBC switchboards to complain about the outlandish fare the network had offered them for viewing on a national holiday. Tom Noble of the *Los Angeles Free Press* summarized the general assessment of the film by reviewers as "a rambling unhomogenized mélange of disconnected dolly shots, spotty color, and general weirdness that fails miserably."[39] What largely went unnoticed at the time was just how significant the Beatles' decision was to show the film on television in the first place, making it freely accessible to their fans who did not have to go to the movie theatre to see it. The BBC timed the release on Boxing Day, a holiday celebrated in Britain the day after Christmas, to ensure a maximum audience. No doubt, many of those inundating the BBC switchboard with calls of complaint about the film came from people who were not Beatles fans and had tuned in either to see what all the fuss was about or simply because they wanted to watch something on the television and had limited options. People are accustomed to watching a film with a narrative, however thin. They probably expected the same of this film, even if they had never seen a previous Beatles film. Yet those previous films had left even Beatles fans completely unprepared for what they would encounter with this one.

Paul, who had the idea for the whole mystery tour concept for the film, was defensive in an interview he gave to the *Daily Mirror* on December 28 just two days after the film had aired. "It wasn't supposed to be about anything," he asserted. "It wasn't supposed to have a theme or a plot. We did it as a series of disconnected, unconnected events. They were not meant to have any depth." Still, McCartney acknowledged, "I got the general impression there was something wrong with it."[40]

People in the United States were aware of the negative press the film had received and some were equally stunned. Ross Bloomfield, an avid Beatles fan at the time, summoned up his recollections of the reception of *Magical Mystery Tour*:

> There was a huge flap over *Magical Mystery Tour*. I wasn't used to that. You know, I expected excellence. Of course, "The Fool on the Hill" is a great song. There were definitely good songs on it, but I think maybe the Beatles had almost gotten too overconfident at that point that they could do anything and it would be good just

because it was them and they didn't really have much of a script or a plan. They were just going to ad-lib through it. It didn't work out so well.[41]

Still, not everyone was so critical of the film, which received a better reception in the United States than it had in Britain. Noble, disagreeing with the critics whom he summarized, actually called it "the best of the Beatle films." He described it as "superb, brilliant, great, heavy, boss, light entertainment, good clean fun, a Message Picture, an entertaining nightmare, and it has good rock and roll music." He thought it far better than *Help!*, which he described as "boring." In Noble's view, *Magical Mystery Tour* contained a "surrealism more frightening—and at the same time grotesquely amusing—than anything Salvador Dali ever dreamt up or a Hitchcock flick."[42]

To accompany the film, the Beatles released a six-song double EP in Britain, before releasing an expanded full-length album that added previous releases such as "All You Need Is Love," "Penny Lane," and "Strawberry Fields Forever." It is significant that both "Penny Lane" and "Strawberry Fields" appeared on this album. The reader will recall that Lennon and McCartney had originally intended them for *Sgt. Pepper* because of their associations with the Beatles' childhoods in Liverpool. Once they had released those songs as singles, they abandoned that concept for the album, but it seems they returned to it for *Magical Mystery Tour*. Tony Bramwell, a childhood friend and close confidante of the Beatles, recalled, "Paul visualized the film as being the kind of day out we all remembered from our childhood in Liverpool, when our mums would see an ad in the window of the local news agent for a mystery coach trip."[43] Although lacking in narrative, nostalgia suffuses the film, as does the childlike sense of play and free reign given to the imagination so characteristic of childhood.

In fact, Kathryn Cox has argued that not only does nostalgia represent one of the major subtexts of the film, but that it also answered a particular need in the British psyche at the time of its release. She holds that "Memory, mythology, and history stabilize creative efforts in *Magical Mystery Tour*. Specifically, the soundtrack and the film demonstrate the Beatles' engagement with the postwar dream and the embrace of nostalgic memory."[44] At this point, Winston Churchill was gone, as was the British Empire, and Britain was in thrall to the United States, at the time engaged in the highly controversial and unpopular war in Vietnam. Moreover, British society had undergone a series of rapid and unsettling changes that left many people feeling unmoored and laid the groundwork for a revival of conservatism that would reach its apex with the rise of Margaret Thatcher at the end of the 1970s. As it turned out, *Sgt. Pepper* had not so much offered a new vision for a society compelled by the values of the counterculture to adopt alternative lifestyles as it had merely opened a window into a temporary escape, one readily identifiable with summertime, which began shortly after its release. By Christmas, itself a time of nostalgia and traditional values, the Beatles had returned to their roots and, in doing so, had transported the rest of Britain along with them. Perhaps the lack of narrative structure was not what had so disturbed British viewers of the film when it first aired, but some unconscious recognition of the loss of innocence and childlike wonder they could not relocate given the state of Britain and the world as 1967 ended.

If people in Britain did not like the film, this did not stop them from listening to the music. For example, within days of the film's showing on the BBC, the *South Wales Gazette* reported that the most frequently played song at Boyd's Record Bar was "Hello, Goodbye," which had been released as a single at the end of November and featured on the soundtrack album for *Magical Mystery Tour*. The title song for the film was the third most played song at Boyd's, with only Wales's own Tom Jones's "I'm Coming Home" sandwiched between the two Beatles numbers. The double EP with songs from the film reached the # 2 spot on the British charts.

Critics had varying opinions on the album. Mike Jahn, writing in the *Saturday Review*, called it "easily their best album." He wrote that *Magical Mystery Tour* was "a marvelous step in a very personal direction for the Beatles—one that they communicate well—and that is enough."[45] Writing in the *Outlook*, the student newspaper at Monmouth College in New Jersey, Joyce Matthews thought the album "left something to be desired," continuing that "After *Sgt. Pepper* one can only be let down by *Magical Mystery Tour*."[46] Yet she found value in such lyrics as "I am he as you are he as you are me and we are all together," from "I am the Walrus" and she asserted that "The Fool on the Hill" contained both a good melody and meaningful lyrics concerning one man who knows the truth facing the ignorance of the world.[47] In Britain, Norman Jopling gave the album a mixed review in the *Record Mirror*, as one can see from his contradictory analysis of individual songs. He described the song "Magical Mystery Tour" as "a shouting, loud effective item with a hollow overall sound and an unusually different piano ending." He found "Your Mother Should Know" a "corny little tune," but one whose atmosphere was "fantastic." While "The Fool on the Hill" was "a thoughtful reflective type of number," Jopling described "Flying," the Beatles' first instrumental, as "a ponderous medium pace effort which becomes strangely exhilarating."[48]

The criticism the Beatles endured over *Magical Mystery Tour* did not follow them with the release of their next film, a feature-length cartoon called *Yellow Submarine*, inspired by the 1966 song from *Revolver*. Nor did it significantly diminish the popularity of the Beatles, if it did so at all, especially in the United States. However, 1968 would prove an even more challenging year for the Beatles and the world than 1967 had. The Beatles temporarily sought refuge in India as an escape from the world's problems and their own. Meanwhile, the Vietnam War would escalate still further with a major new initiative on the part of the North Vietnamese called the Tet Offensive. As the war escalated, so did the tensions and unrest in Britain, the United States, and around the world, which exploded in the most revolutionary and politically charged year of the decade.

CHAPTER 8
1968: REVOLUTION, ROCK MUSIC, AND THE BEATLES; THE WHITE ALBUM IN HISTORICAL CONTEXT

The Spirit of '68: Paris, London, and New York

The year 1968 included many of the most dramatic and seminal moments of the 1960s, including attempted revolutions in France and Czechoslovakia; student demonstrations and protests in Britain, the United States, and numerous other countries around the world; and the chaotic violence during the youth protests at the Democratic National Convention in Chicago that summer. In January, the Tet Offensive, a surprisingly successful attack on US forces in South Vietnam by the North Vietnamese Communists, compelled people to realize that peace there was not on the horizon. The year also witnessed the assassinations of Martin Luther King Jr. and Robert F. Kennedy, and the continuation of race riots in the United States, now linked to an ascending Black Power movement. King's death on April 4 deprived the Civil Rights movement of a moderate voice in a volatile racial environment, while Kennedy's death two months later provided yet another shock to the fragile American psyche and ended the best chance for a propeace candidate to gain the White House in November.

The year marked a turning point for so many reasons, not the least of which was the coming of age of the baby boom generation, as its first members turned 23 years of age. The ballooning numbers of young people between the ages of 18 and 23 combined with the affluence of the postwar period to send record numbers of students to colleges and universities. In France, for example, 8 million people, over 16 percent of the population, fell within this narrow age range.[1] In response, new universities had started to spring up, including the satellite campus of the University of Paris at Nanterre, a suburb west of the city, founded in 1964. It seemed convenient for the French government to tuck away a sizable portion of the burgeoning baby boom generation in such newly created educational spaces to alleviate pressure on the job market temporarily, but these same spaces provided students with a sense of freedom and entitlement that gave them the confidence with which to challenge the established order. Another problem at Nanterre included the presence of outsiders, squatters, and drug sellers who frequented the dormitories intended exclusively for students. Authorities at the University decided to crack down not only on these interlopers but also on the practice of male and female cohabitation, which was in direct violation of university regulations. The students responded with demonstrations that escalated into direct and violent confrontations with the police. The University of Paris decided to close the Nanterre campus temporarily and transferred disciplinary hearings for offending students from Nanterre to the Sorbonne, located near the center of Paris.

When the student protests switched from Nanterre to Paris, the authorities' ham-fisted response exacerbated the situation and divided French society along class lines. Student demonstrations erupted and quickly turned violent, with revolutionaries erecting barricades in the streets in a time-honored tradition that went back to the French revolutions of the nineteenth century. French police arrested six hundred students and on May 3 the Sorbonne closed for the first time since its foundation in the twelfth century.[2] While French students found in the events of 1968 an outlet for their restlessness and dissatisfaction with the soulless conditions and complacency of modern life that some young people had railed against since the 1950s, French workers saw the opportunity to seek redress for their grievances. Strikes erupted throughout France, with some workers taking control of their workplaces, shutting down much of the country's economy. Workers in the aircraft, chemical, and automobile industries went out on strike, including a massive one at the Renault automobile factories just outside of Paris. Then, the revolution collapsed even more quickly than it started, partly because the anarchic ethos of the rebels did not admit of any kind of proficient, centralized leadership, leaving the rebellion to devolve into its various factions, none of which proved effective on its own. It had left its mark on France though and helped define a generation.

France represented only an extreme example of a wave of protests that swept across the world, from Poland to Mexico. In Germany, those who protested referred to themselves as the 68ers, further stressing the importance of this year in European youth culture. Italy, like Germany, experienced numerous student protests, which began even before the outburst of revolutionary activity in France. Across continents, young people seemed to find common ground in their desire to expose hypocrisy and corruption, to condemn abuses of power, whether by capitalist or communist governments, and especially to express their opposition to the American war in Vietnam. Rock and roll and the Beatles had provided a temporary outlet for their energy and frustration, but these could not appease young people indefinitely, especially once they became politically conscious and had so many readily available targets against which to direct their righteous anger.

In the early 1960s, college students in the United States could join the freedom riders in the south or they could march in support of Civil Rights, but the passage of the Civil Rights and voting rights acts had taken some of the steam out of the movement even before the assassination of Martin Luther King Jr in April. King's death deprived the movement of its leader, leaving Black Power advocates in the ascendancy. Even if King had lived, racial tensions would certainly have increased, as King himself had begun to focus on the issue of poverty and economic issues; he had also started to come to the realization that love and nonviolence alone might not be enough to achieve his objectives for an equal and just society.

Protests took a milder form in Britain than they did elsewhere, but there as well students bristled at government control and limited funding for universities, even as the protest movement as a whole focused mainly on opposition to the Vietnam War. However, since British students did not face conscription into military service, they did not turn out in the same numbers or exhibit quite the same level of desperation as their male American counterparts, who were subject to a draft. British students did have the legacy of the British Empire with which to contend, including the persistence of racist attitudes at home, often tied to immigration from many of Britain's former colonies around the world. Student demonstrations in Britain in 1968 followed the example of the October 1967 anti-Vietnam War protests, the momentum of which carried over into the following year. Student protests early in the year occurred at several British universities, including Oxford and Cambridge. The defense secretary, Denis Healey, almost had his car overturned by angry students while at Cambridge for a speaking engagement in March. On June 12, students staged a series of sit-ins at the campuses of more than ten universities and art colleges across Britain. Around two hundred students at Hull University occupied administration buildings and prevented the vice chancellor from gaining access to his office. Historians of the period have tended to downplay the seriousness of student protests in Britain, but those students who did engage in political activism shared many of the same concerns and exhibited many of the same characteristics as those of their generation engaged in similar protests around the world.

The student protest movement in the United States, like those in Paris and London, grew out of the generational struggle in which the authorities who represented the establishment—politicians, university administrators, and the police—appeared as the enemy. The struggle occurred, not just over the Vietnam War but also over other abuses of power and any laws or regulations that restricted the personal freedom of young people. Their concerns included limits on free speech, restrictions on visiting hours for members of the opposite sex in college dorms, and enforcement of laws against recreational drugs like marijuana and LSD. On January 17, 1968, at the State University of New York at Stony Brook, in one of the first major drug raids on a college campus in the United States, police officers, after having planted undercover agents on campus, entered student dorm rooms at 5:00 a.m. and arrested twenty-seven students and nine visiting nonstudents for sale and possession of drugs. Students at the time accused the police of using "Gestapo" tactics. One university official described "a generation gap," not just between administrators and students but also among administrators and faculty. "There's a concern for the kids' reputations, but a hard line feeling that they did break the law," one faculty member told the *New York Times*.[3] Tom Noce, who was a student there at the time, said the raid shocked him. He recalled losing his job working security at a campus gatehouse because he gave free passes several months later to a number of hippies who had come to stage a mock raid lampooning the activities of the police in the first raid.[4] Police officers arrived in time to prevent the mock raid from occurring, but the hippies stayed on campus without interference to entertain students for hours with some sarcastic skits and a folk-rock music concert.

In the United States, underground newspapers contributed to the radicalization of students and other young people, while incidents such as those at Stony Brook did not reflect well—in their minds anyway—on university officials or the police. In New York, the major center of student protest became Columbia University. At Columbia, student antagonism toward university officials stemmed less from specific regulations or the students' own concerns than they did over the Vietnam War and issues of perceived social injustice perpetrated by the university. Specifically, student opposition to the administration focused on the university's participation in military research designed to support US activity in Vietnam and efforts to expand the campus at the expense of nearby parks and low-income housing intended for the residents of Harlem. According to a survey done in 1968, Columbia had already displaced some 7,500 people from their homes, with planned acquisitions threatening to evict another 10,000.[5] Student demonstrations and occupation of administration buildings led Columbia to close its campus on April 26 (one of a number of US colleges and universities forced to do the same thing that spring). When the students refused to relent or leave the occupied buildings, administration called in the police, who arrested 692 people, most of whom were Columbia students, while breaking limbs and cracking a few heads in the process. In his seminal work on the 1960s, Todd Gitlin credits events at Columbia for ending civility between the student movement and its opponents.[6] This new reality manifested itself with resounding force at the Democratic National Convention in Chicago that August, where clashes between the Chicago police and the National Guard on the one side and antiwar demonstrators on the other led to hundreds of injuries on both sides and nearly seven hundred arrests.

In 1968, Norman Mailer published an unconventional book called *Armies of the Night*, which presented two versions of the October 1967 antiwar demonstration in Washington, the first half in the form of a novel ("The History as Novel") and the second half in the form of Mailer's historical account ("The Novel as History"). The book, more than anything, provides a first-hand account of the generation gap that existed in the United States at the time, while also detailing the opposing positions on the Vietnam War between the prowar "hawks" and the antiwar "doves." Mailer specifically identified a gap between those brought up since the 1950s, who experienced the world in a profoundly different way from the immediately preceding generations. Rebellious youth took exception to the war and other specific targets, but they also implicitly attacked an entire set of values they believed antithetical to the best interests of humanity and their own future. They did not buy into the entire premise of the Cold War, and from France to the United States, they found leaders like Charles de Gaulle and Lyndon Johnson hopelessly out of touch with their values and concerns. As the student activist Mark Rudd wrote to Columbia University President Grayson Kirk during the student protests there in 1968, "We can point, in short, to our meaningless studies, our identity crisis and our repulsion with being cogs in your corporate machines as a product of and reaction to a basically sick society."[7]

The various protests and demonstrations that erupted throughout 1968, then, were not merely a response to the specific events of that year but a culmination of revolutionary attitudes that had seeped into youth culture going back at least a decade, coinciding with the formation and rise of the Beatles. The Beatles played a dominant role in that culture, at least in Britain and the United States. In 1968, established British groups like the Beatles, the Who, and the Rolling Stones remained preeminent, but they faced increasing competition from American groups like the Jimi Hendrix Experience, Big

1968: Revolution, Rock Music, and the Beatles

Brother and the Holding Company (featuring Janis Joplin), the Doors, and the Band. That February, the Beatles went to India, members of the group staying for varying lengths of time, before returning to England to make one of their most important albums, which they called simply *The Beatles* (although it quickly became known as the White Album because of its all-white cover). In the meantime, the rock world underwent a profound transformation largely of the Beatles' own making. By 1968, some of those same groups the Beatles had influenced now threatened to surpass them.

The Year 1968 in Rock History: From San Francisco to London[8]

In late December 1967, Bob Dylan helped set the tone for the coming year. Following an eighteen-month hiatus after he suffered a somewhat mysterious motorcycle accident (the details of which remain in dispute), he released an album called *John Wesley Harding*. This album was a surprisingly placid and country-driven affair far removed from either his earlier protest music or the electronic rock music he had introduced at the 1965 Newport Folk Festival. Rock historian Barry Hoskyns writes, "When Bob Dylan's *John Wesley Harding* appeared early in 1968, its sparse Nashville sound and biblical imagery confirmed his apparent retreat from the exploding plastic counterculture."[9] Recorded in Nashville, Dylan's new album drew rave reviews, hailed as being on the cutting edge of the folk-rock movement, with perhaps a greater emphasis on folk or even country, which was influencing one future direction of rock music. Richard Goldstein thought that in this album Dylan demonstrated that he "realized that country and western music ... still possessed the charm, earthiness, and emotionalism that rock had 'outgrown.'"[10] The album marked a significant moment in the development of the new genre called folk-rock that Dylan had pioneered. The Byrds' *Sweetheart of the Rodeo* (1968) very much followed in the same vein and displayed a marked discontinuity from their relatively mellow folk-rock sound as they, too, veered dramatically toward traditional country.

Other emerging artists in 1968 pointed in the same direction toward the infusion of folk music into the rock scene. In March, the Canadian folk balladeer, Joni Mitchell, released her debut album, *Song to a Seagull*. Neil Young and Steven Stills with Buffalo Springfield and David Crosby with the Byrds were already developing the folk-rock sounds they would employ so successfully when they later merged, along with Graham Nash of the Hollies, to form the super group CSNY (Crosby, Stills, Nash, and Young). The album that probably best exemplified the trend in the direction of folk-rock came from Bob Dylan's backup band, formerly known as the Hawks but now simply calling themselves the Band. Released in July, their album *Music from Big Pink* wowed critics and signaled a new direction for popular music. The Band took their inspiration from Dylan, but they also drew on their own experience as Canadian outsiders traveling through the United States and noticing things people raised there might be taking for granted, like weight of history that included the legacy of slavery and the Civil War. They infused their particular brand of folk-rock with elements of traditional Americana, blues, gospel, and soul music. Prominent rock critic Greil Marcus later wrote of the album:

> There is a conviction here that every way of life practiced in America from the time of the Revolution on down still matters—not as nostalgia, but as the necessity of someone's daily life—and the music, though it never bends to any era, never tries for any quaint support of a theme, seems as if it would sound as right to a gang of beaver trappers as it does to us.[11]

Reviewing the album soon after its release, Richard Goldstein wrote, "The vocals are immediately appealing. To an old rockabilly fan, the falsetto work and the harmonies will seem deeply satisfying because they are so basic and so real. That same authenticity applies to the band's music as well. They won't blow your mind the first time around, but that's not what they're after."[12] Meanwhile, folk singer-songwriters like Joan Baez, Leonard Cohen, and Phil Ochs continued to enjoy success, as did Simon and Garfunkel with the release of their 1968 album, *Bookends*.[13] Perhaps giving a nod to the influence of the Band and others, even Pete Townshend of the Who told Jann Wenner in an interview for *Rolling Stone* published in September, "When I write today, I feel that it has to—this is incredible, man—I feel that it has to tell a little story."[14]

These trends seemed at odds with much of the pop music that had topped the charts in recent years, including the popular Motown sound, which had been one of the most important musical influences on the Beatles, who a few years earlier had covered songs by groups such as the Miracles and the Marvelletes. It may have been premature to proclaim Motown dead in 1968, as Chris Welch came close to doing in *Melody Maker* in August, but it had certainly hit a lull. Welch noted that the previously unassailable Motown label, Tamla, accustomed to producing many hit records from such artists as the Supremes, the Four Tops, Stevie Wonder, and Martha and the Vandellas, had only one song in the top thirty at the time. Dave Godin, who founded the Tamla Motown Appreciation Society, told Welch, after disbanding the society, "Personally, I don't think Motown is what it used to be. They have tended to stick too much to a set formula." "The Supremes are dead," Godin asserted.[15]

However, if some Motown acts suddenly found themselves struggling to achieve chart success, soul music was alive and well in the person of Aretha Franklin, who had switched labels and recording studios a year earlier and scored two top five albums on the Atlantic label in 1968, *Lady Soul* in January and *Aretha Now* in June. The latter landed her on the cover of *Time* magazine, its only cover that year devoted to a singer or a band. *Time* described her vocals as containing

> a direct, natural style of delivery that ranges over a full four octaves, and the breath control to spin out long phrases that curl sinuously around the beat and dangle tantalizingly from blue notes. But what really accounts for her impact goes beyond technique: it is her fierce, gritty conviction. She flexes her rich, cutting voice like a whip; she lashes her listeners—in her words—"to the bone, for deepness."[16]

1968: Revolution, Rock Music, and the Beatles

While Aretha was not only keeping soul music alive but also taking it to new heights, Los Angeles had developed an exceptional music scene that revolved around folk clubs like the Troubadour and the Ash Club, but which now faced competition from more rock-oriented clubs like the Whiskey-a-Go-Go and others along the famed Sunset Strip. The strip became the hot spot for all the young musicians and anyone associated with the music scene in Los Angeles, especially those living or hanging out in the fashionable hippie-laden Laurel Canyon neighborhood, which attracted everyone from groupies to the area's biggest music superstars.[17] Furthermore, rock had become big business in Southern California. Jerry Hopkins noted in *Rolling Stone* in June 1968 that "more acts are 'discovered' or 'created' in LA and more records are cut in LA than in almost all other cities of the world combined."[18] While the City of Angels boasted local groups such as the Byrds, the Doors, Buffalo Springfield, and even the Monkees, other groups and artists flocked there, both the amateurish and professional, including Joni Mitchell, Neil Young, and Linda Ronstadt, as well as the Mamas and the Papas, and the future members of the Eagles. Derek Taylor, former press officer for the Beatles who had moved to California and become the publicist for a number of bands, including the Byrds and the Beach Boys, said of Los Angeles: "Everyone you know or like wants to come here. Even the Beatles, who never go anywhere."[19] Paul Rothschild, a talent scout for Elektra Records, described the scene: "As each day goes by, the dress gets weirder, the friendships get deeper, and the streets get more packed. People meet each other at parties, in the parks, everybody's carrying an instrument, and groups form out of serendipity."[20]

Still, arguably the most exceptional music scene in the country was taking place in San Francisco, where Jefferson Airplane, the Grateful Dead, Santana, Quicksilver Messenger Service, Sly and the Family Stone, and Creedence Clearwater Revival were among the acts thriving or emerging in the Bay Area. Rock promoter Bill Graham's Fillmore West club in San Francisco became the central showcase for many area acts, and he expanded his influence when he opened up his Fillmore East in Greenwich Village in New York City. Record companies, in a rush to capitalize on what they belatedly recognized as the huge commercial potential for rock and roll, hurried to sign Bay Area acts after the hugely successful Monterrey Pop Festival in 1967, with the results beginning to show up on the charts the following year. Creedence Clearwater Revival's self-titled first album failed to crack Billboard's top fifty, but their cover of Dale Hawkins's 1957 hit "Suzie Q" reached # 11 on the singles charts and they broke through with two top ten albums in 1969. Sly and the Family Stone had a # 1 hit in the United States in 1968 with "Everyday People," with many more hits to follow. Jefferson Airplane had already come to national attention the previous year, while the Grateful Dead made a conscious decision not to follow their lead in embracing the corporate music industry and continuing to focus on live performances and playing the role of a "community band."[21] They tried to resist the commercialization of their music during a period in which New York record producers swarmed to the city to take advantage of the San Francisco music scene, leading to the promotion and commercial success of newer groups like the Steve Miller Band (originally the Steve Miller Blues Band). However, the Dead were not averse to making money and did finally sign with Warner/Reprise, even as they remained true to their musical roots, and did not allow the company to force them to compromise their ideals. Meanwhile, Clive Davis of CBS records was signing Janis Joplin's band, Big Brother and the Holding Company, for the huge sum of $250,000.[22]

The two California music scenes converged in early March when Jefferson Airplane performed at the Melodyland theatre near Disneyland in Anaheim, with the Grateful Dead performing as the opening act. The concert received a scathing review from Bill Wasserzieher in the *Long Beach Press-Telegram*. Wasserzieher described the Grateful Dead's thirty-minute opening set as "just two very long, mostly instrumental songs," while the Jefferson Airplane's performance, marred by an unexplained early exit by an apparently angry Marty Balin, the reviewer found simply "bizarre." Wasserzieher, drolly implying that San Francisco's musical reputation might be slightly overblown, ended his review by suggesting, "Maybe we're just too conservative in Orange County for hip San Franciscans."[23]

By contrast, a concert in Los Angeles two weeks later by the British super-group Cream, consisting of the blues guitarist impresario Eric Clapton, bassist and lead vocalist Jack Bruce, and the talented and expressive drummer Ginger Baker, received rave reviews from Tony Leigh writing for *KRLA Beat*. Leigh described Cream as "the best England has to offer" (a knock on the Beatles?), while writing of the concert, "With a strong blues orientation and a jazzman's ear for improvisation, the Cream created some of the most dynamic music heard anywhere."[24] Jon Landau had slammed Cream in a famous review in *Rolling Stone*, taking aim at Eric Clapton's pretentious and derivative blues-guitar solos in particular. Leigh completely contradicted Landau's assessment based on what he heard at the live performance he reviewed:

> Critics in their infinite wisdom have been known to be wrong before—and the Cream's performance proved that. Their original concept behind the formation of the group was to eliminate any weak links and to obtain maximum personal freedom within the confines of a group. Although this concept could have resulted in exhibitionist performances by the three, it in fact did not. Solo performances by each member of the group were beautifully in evidence, but they were still always part of the greater whole.[25]

Fans seemed to agree with Leigh rather than Landau—Cream's 1968 album, *Wheels of Fire*, which went to # 3 in Britain, rose to the top of the charts in the United States.

If British groups like Cream and Led Zeppelin, which would release its first album in January 1969, continued the success of the British invasion pioneered by the Beatles, the Rolling Stones, and the Who, by contrast American groups had a harder time breaking through in Britain. Just to name a few examples, Sly and the Family Stone's "Everyday People," a # 1 hit in the United States, only made it to # 36 in Britain. Aretha Franklin's 1967 hit, "Chain of Fools," made it to # 2 at home but only to # 37 on the UK charts. Tommy James and the Shondells, who originated in Michigan, had numerous hits in the United States, among them "Hanky Panky," I Think We're Alone Now," and "Sweet Cherry

Wine," but they had a hard time breaking through in Britain, only achieving success there with the infectious rocker "Mony Mony." After selling four million records in the United States, James was at a loss to explain his group's lack of international success. "I think it's possibly the type of record we've been doing that has been responsible for our lack of success in Britain," he said in a July 1968 interview, without explaining what he meant by that. However, perhaps his admiration for the Beatles offers a clue. He said, "I dig the Beatles to death. I know that's what people always say and it sounds corny, but I consider the Beatles to be just the most talented group in terms of music, creativity and composing in the world." Perhaps British audiences did not respond to pop rock groups like the Shondells because their smooth, polished sound had failed to keep pace with the creativity of the Beatles on albums like *Revolver* and *Sgt. Pepper*, while British fans could also enjoy homegrown emergent groups like Cream and established groups like the Rolling Stones, who were still going strong. In fact, the Rolling Stones gave their first concert in almost two years in Britain in May 1968. "Mony Mony" was the exception that proved the rule, reaching the top spot on the British charts in 1968. It would remain the Shondells' only hit on that side of the Atlantic, despite the fact that they released nine more singles before the group disbanded in 1970, including one that reached # 1 in the United States ("Crimson and Clover") and another that made it to # 2 ("Crystal Blue Persuasion").

An exception in this regard was Jimi Hendrix, another product of the West Coast hailing from Seattle, who recorded his third and final album with the Jimi Hendrix Experience in New York and London in 1967, released as *Electric Ladyland* in October 1968, a month before the Beatles' White Album came out. His first album, 1967's *Are You Experienced?*, which reached # 5 in the United States, actually made it to # 2 on the UK charts. His second album, *Axis: Bold as Love*, and *Electric Ladyland* both scored chart success in Britain; the former ascending to # five while the latter reached # six. British cultural historian Dominic Sandbrook has asserted that talented guitarists like Eric Clapton, Jimi Hendrix, and Jeff Beck had more interest in displaying their musical virtuosity to a minority of aficionados than in exerting an influence over the younger generation as a whole, a criticism also voiced at the time by critics such as Jon Landau and Robert Christgau.[26] This was probably true of Beck, but Sandbrook may have underestimated the inspirational creative impact of Hendrix and Clapton, especially considering their chart success on both sides of the Atlantic. For example, Clause Assante had just come out of the army with concerns about racial politics and Jimi Hendrix fascinated him. Hendrix, he said, "went out and did his own thing with the music and the clothes and he let his hair grow and I loved him and I loved his music. And then black people were getting on his case like he was catering too much to white people and creating white music." Assante continued, "I guess you just got to be free to do what you have to do. There is always going be somebody who's going to say you're not doing the right thing."[27] In other words, the creativity and expressiveness of artists like Hendrix and Clapton provided their own inspiration for a generation that valued personal freedom and coined the phrase "do your own thing."

Meanwhile, a group of brothers who had grown up in England before their family moved to Australia in 1955 was also transforming rock music by 1968. The band, the

The Beatles and the 1960s

Bee Gees, featuring Barry, Robin, and Maurice Gibb, formed in 1958, around the same time as the Beatles. They also began recording in 1963, again, about the same time the Beatles did. Although they enjoyed some modest success in Australia, unlike the Beatles, it took until 1967 for them to break through in the United States, reaching # 1 that year with the tender ballad, "Massachusetts." They set the stage for success in Britain in April 1968 with a standout appearance at the Royal Albert Hall in early April and had two top ten hits there that year, "I've Got to Get a Message to You" and "I Started a Joke." Derek Boltwood, writing in *Melody Maker*, called their Royal Hall performance "one of the most ambitious pop concerts ever," an ambition he proclaimed "beautifully and successfully fulfilled."[28] They had their first number one song in Britain two years later with "How Can You Mend a Broken Heart." Both "I've Got to Get a Message to You" and "I Started a Joke" were also ballads more in the folk-rock vein, though the chorus on the former accelerates considerably and the group musters considerable power as it drives home the central "message" of the song.

Finally, one further development in the history of rock music that occurred around this time deserves notice. The emergence of FM radio stations, such as KMPX in San Francisco, contributed to the growth in popularity of album rock and the freedom of rock musicians to depart from the standard top forty pop format favored by AM stations. In March 1968, Robert Shelton wrote a review of a group called the New York Rock 'n' Roll Ensemble in which he referred to the emergence of what he called "Bach rock" groups. He cited Procol Harum's 1967 hit "Whiter Shade of Pale" as a prototype song and the Beatles' *Rubber Soul* as a prototype album for the merger of classical and rock music. FM led to a dramatic increase in the sale of rock albums, many of which now featured longer tracks that departed from the traditional pop format of the three-minute single, but not everyone applauded that development. Richard Goldstein, for example, expressed his concern in a *New York Times* piece written in February that "Today's rock creator is free to pursue his vision through any mode he chooses, and he may rant or whisper for as long as he deems necessary."[29] By August, Goldstein was describing progressive rock as "musically advanced but emotionally barren."[30] Meanwhile, a young rock musician just beginning to play in bands around the Jersey Shore also took notice of this development and was not pleased. In 1975, Bruce Springsteen while on tour in Europe told a Swedish interviewer, "AM radio was fine right up until about 1967 when FM came in and started to play long cuts, and you could see the disappearance of the really good three-minute single. So the music that got me was what was on AM from 1959 to 1965."[31]

An understanding of the trends in rock music of this year might seem like a rather long digression from a consideration of the reception of the Beatles, but it is central to understanding how the Beatles' audience perceived them. While rock music continued to evolve, expand, and attract new talent, the Beatles found themselves in a position of having to respond to those changes or become yesterday's news. In short, the Beatles now faced tougher competition for the ears of the listener of rock music; for example, when the White Album did finally come out one reviewer compared it unfavorably to recent music by American groups such as Jefferson Airplane and Blood, Sweat and Tears.[32]

The year 1968 was especially significant in this regard because the Beatles went almost a full year between the release of *Magical Mystery Tour* and the White Album. Therefore, fans and critics anticipated the latter to an even greater degree than usual for a new Beatles' album, both because of the time that had lapsed since their previous album and because of the rapidly changing rock scene. However, in August the Beatles did release a single that contained two of their most iconic songs: "Hey Jude," written by Paul McCartney to assuage the feelings of John Lennon's 5-year-old son Julian about his parents' impending divorce, and a song John had written in India called "Revolution," an appropriate title for 1968 but also a misleading one.

Rock and the Politics of Protest

In 1982, a Beatles fan simply identified as K. J. from San Francisco wrote in a letter published in Marc Catone's book, "The Beatles served as our parents when our real parents lost their credibility. They gave us morals (as evidenced by their early words against the war in Vietnam), clothes, drug styles ... a sensibility. They gave us a feeling of what success could be without selling out."[33] The year 1968 would put to the test the feeling young people had that they could rely on the Beatles as moral guides on issues such as Vietnam when, while so many youth engaged in protests and demonstrations worldwide, the Beatles sat idly by and even seemed to implicitly denounce such political activism in their song "Revolution." The political assassinations of that year, the race riots, and the Vietnam War all made young people feel unsafe in an increasingly violent year. As John Lennon tried to reassure his listeners in the song that "it's gonna be all right," many of those same listeners would have had a deep foreboding that this would not in fact be the case. The song came out just as violence erupted in Chicago and young radicals continued to put their bodies on the line for the sake of bringing about change, with Lennon singing that, though we all "want to change the world," when it came to violence or destruction you could count him (and presumably the other Beatles) out.

The Rolling Stones had a much more radical reputation than that of the Beatles, reinforced by their 1968 tribute to the student demonstrations in London, "Street Fighting Man." Dominic Sandbrook notes the Stones not only did not engage in political activism themselves but they actually led conventional lives, "with Jagger the man-about-town and friend of the aristocracy, and Richards the bibliophile and war-film buff in his Sussex manor house."[34] Keith Richards reaffirmed this point in his 2010 autobiography:

> Suddenly we were being courted by half the aristocracy, the younger scions, the heirs to some ancient pile, the Ormsby-Gores, the Tennants, the whole lot. I've never known if they were slumming or we were snobbing. They were very nice people. I decided it was no skin off my nose. If somebody's interested, they're welcome. You want to hang, you want to hang.[35]

Furthermore, for all of the favorable comparisons "Street Fighting Man" garnered when compared to Lennon's seemingly more moderate "Revolution," Jagger's main conclusion in his song was that "in sleepy London town there's just no place for a street fighting man." Judging from the refusal of disk jockeys to play "Street Fighting Man" while the Beatles' "Revolution" was ubiquitous on AM airwaves in late summer 1968, listeners had completely misinterpreted the former. Even esteemed *New York Times* critic Richard Goldstein quotes the line, "The time is right for a palace revolution" out of context.[36] In the song, Jagger actually sings, "*Think* the time is right for a palace revolution, but where I live the game to play is compromise solution." How is this any different from Lennon singing, "But when you talk about destruction, don't you know that you can count me out?"

The fact is that, however much political radicals expected rock musicians to rally behind their cause, as British rockers began catering to a more mature audience and abandoning their teenage fans, they revealed themselves as singularly unprepared to do that. While pop songs aimed at teenage audiences continued to dominate the charts, British groups like the Beatles, the Rolling Stones, and the Kinks opted for a more psychedelic vibe that did not easily translate into top forty material but that mostly lacked political content as well. David Simonelli writes that, because rock musicians had introduced middle-class youth to working-class attitudes, "in 1968, musicians like John Lennon, Mick Jagger, Pete Townshend and Ray Davies were supposed to line themselves up behind the coming revolution."[37] As it turned out, these artists for the most part were doing anything but. In 1968, Pete Townshend had the following to say about what role rock and roll should play in young people's lives:

> Mother has just fallen down the stairs, dad's lost all his money at the dog track, the baby's got TB. In comes the kid with his transistor radio, grooving to Chuck Berry. He doesn't give a shit about mom falling down the stairs. … It's a good thing that you've got a machine, a radio that puts out rock and roll songs and it makes you groove throughout the day. … When you are listening to a rock and roll song the way you listen to "Jumpin' Jack Flash," or something similar, that's the way you should really spend your whole life.[38]

When asked if the Beatles were revolutionaries, Paul McCartney famously told a 1968 interviewer that the Beatles were, in fact, "the world's number one capitalists."[39] McCartney admitted that he saw the value in going to Vietnam to entertain, but knew he would never get around to it and rather than being a hypocrite, he preferred to keep his political opinions to himself.[40] Dominic Sandbrook even portrays the shift to album rock of groups such as Pink Floyd, Cream, and Led Zeppelin as primarily driven by commercial considerations, as the result of a marked drop in the singles market.[41]

Not that rock groups were necessarily against lending their talents to causes in which they believed, a trend that would accelerate greatly in the 1980s highlighted by the *Live Aid* concerts held in London and Philadelphia in 1985. In 1968, when revolutionary activist Abbie Hoffman was planning his Festival of Life in conjunction with plans for his Youth International Party to descend on Chicago to protest the Democratic National

Convention, he secured commitments from Country Joe and the Fish, the Steve Miller Blues Band, Blood, Sweat and Tears, and the Nitty Gritty Dirt Band, among others. These rock and roll groups would have supplemented planned appearances by folk singers such as Phil Ochs, Pete Seeger, Richie Havens, and Judy Collins. However, when Hoffman failed to obtain permits for his festival from the Chicago police, most groups backed out of their commitments although Phil Ochs and a few other acts did show up and perform. The acts descending on Chicago included the Michigan-based hard rock band MC5, who would become best known for their 1969 antiestablishment song "Kick out the Jams," which would reach # 30 in the United States.

Chicago proved a dividing line for the political activists among the counterculture because it forced a kind of reckoning with how far young people were willing to go and how much they were willing to fight to change the system. In August, with tension building and revolution in the air throughout the summer of 1968, with cities ablaze and tensions heightened by the assassinations of the spring, the Beatles song "Revolution" seemed out of step with the times. After Chicago, that no longer seemed the case. In his memoir, Richard Goldstein wrote about the Chicago experience, "The moment of our victory in the streets was also when we had to confront the consequences of our acts. Did we really want our country to fall apart? That was the question Chicago presented, and for most of us the answer was a definitive, if unarticulated, no."[42] This was, of course, the answer that John Lennon had already anticipated on behalf of his generation, even though in one verse of the slower version of the song called "Revolution 1" that appeared on the White Album he ambiguously added a faint "count me in" after he sang "count me out" on destruction.

That moment when radicalized young people began to realize the consequences of their actions affected people in different ways. Ivan Bell was a freshman at New York University at the time and he recalled exactly when that moment of realization came for him.

> The war protests were going on in 1968, I was just marching along, just locking hands with a whole bunch of other students, and all these people lining the parade route were just locals, from the city. They were not terribly well to do and I remember that I saw a bunch of young children, young as five, six, seven years of age screaming at us protesters and screaming "dirty hippies" and a lot of profane based phrases. And you look at this five-year-old kid who is really just modelling what their parents are screaming, and that's when you realize we're in a whole lot of really deep shit here because these kids are too young to have thoughts of their own. Here we have parents that are so violently opposed to protest and one of the great phrases of the time was "Just give peace a chance," and all we wanted to do was stop them from killing people.[43]

Bell seemed to recognize that hate had become endemic in the country, that its political divisions might just be too wide to breach. James Vignapiano had an even more traumatic awakening to this reality, though in his case it increased his revolutionary ardor. His recall of his transformative moment is worth quoting at length:

I went to an anti-war demonstration on Wall Street and I'll never forget it. A whole bunch of us went and it was right in front of the federal building and I remember construction workers coming there after their lunch hours and [they] just started beating people. I was one of them and I was running trying to get down the stairs on National Street and the subway platform so they wouldn't drag me up and kill me because I saw the beatings that the guys were getting. I was grabbing as many friends and we ran down to the subway station and the train pulled up. We just jumped on whatever train, I didn't even know if this train would take us home. I remember when we got on the train people were just looking at us with their eyes wide open, like we were some type of freaks when all we were doing was demonstrating against the war. Luckily, there was no problem on the train but I still remember how I felt they were looking at me. I said you know what this is bigger than me and I really got involved after that. Whatever demonstration they had locally as long I could get there, I was there, but yeah that sort of changed me. You know when I was running for my life in my own city, you know what I mean, that sort of changed me.[44]

Claude Assante, even though he served in the army, said he understood the antiwar message of groups like Country Joe and the Fish, who in 1967 had come out with their satiric "I-Feel-Like-I'm-Fixin'-to-Die Rag." He understood people who asked the question, "Who are these politicians in the government telling you that you had to go over there and fight and risk your life or kill people you don't even know?" On the other hand, he knew there were "enough people around that I remember who thought that you were unpatriotic [if you opposed the war]." Like many of his generation, maybe as a veteran more than most, Assante felt this division acutely, but said he was too busy trying to find himself to resolve this fundamentally unbridgeable division.

Where did all of this leave the Beatles? Did their fans feel betrayed by the antirevolutionary song "Revolution"? No and yes. When Joyce Matthews reviewed "Revolution" in September for Monmouth College's student newspaper, the *Outlook*, she analyzed the song mainly from a musical perspective. Echoing the criticisms of the direction of contemporary rock music made by Goldstein and, later, Springsteen, Matthews took note of "the feeling that pop was getting too complicated for the ordinary listener" and praised the Beatles for returning to "the hard rock style with the hard guitar opening, steady beat, hand clapping between verses, and, most notably, the definite ending."[45] Conversely, some students at colleges and universities around the country were still furious at the Beatles after Chicago. J. Roman Babiak, writing in the [University of] *Michigan Daily*, also in September, wondered if perhaps the Beatles had come to represent "the personalization of our repressed desires to get a job like dad's."[46] Others, however, saw no contradiction between the connection they felt with the Beatles and their political activism. Vignapiano recalled:

There was always this element in the Beatles music, they were so mystical, I remember when all this stuff hit the news about playing the albums backward and if you look on the album cover, you see whatever you see or don't see. That just added to me, an element of surrealism of The Beatles and again [I felt] my journey was also going in alignment [with theirs].[47]

On the one hand, this alignment had little to do, though, with any overt stance that the Beatles had taken, unlike in places like Germany where the "Krautrock" movement took a strong antiauthoritarian stance in support of the 68ers' revulsion at Germany's Nazi past.[48] On the other hand, it could have had everything to do with the kind of music the Beatles were making by 1968. In his 2017 doctoral dissertation, Jordy Cummings writes about the connection between music and politics in 1968. He argues:

In 1967 and 1968, the era of militant—and in some places (Vietnam, South and Central Africa) military—struggle against capitalism and imperialism, this could not be discursively framed in a simple four chord song with a verse/chorus/verse structure. Rather it had to be implied sonically, by allusion, by double meaning, a practice common in what we now know as classical music.[49]

Beatles fans had little idea of what kind of music they might expect from the group's next album, although the Beatles had released two singles in 1968 that might have provided some clues. We have already discussed "Revolution," which appeared on the other side of the comforting and soothing music and lyrics of "Hey Jude." Joyce Matthews called "Hey Jude" "the complete opposite of 'Revolution.'" If "Revolution" was a return to old-time rock and roll, "Hey Jude" seemed more representative of the trend toward album-oriented rock, a single that clocked in at 7 minutes and 11 seconds. Babiak found the two songs so reactionary he said they made him wonder if Lyndon Johnson actually owned Apple Records, speculating that, "Next we will hear a direct statement from the Beatles godhead ordering all American males between 18 and 22 to go directly to Vietnam." Many people might have agreed with Babiak's assessment, especially based on the lyrics of "Revolution," which criticized those "who go around carrying pictures of Chairman Mao" and "those who want money for minds that hate." Conversely, though, the music might have sent a different message. Devin McKinney wrote, "'Revolution' has subversive meaning precisely because the words, all ideology speak aphorisms, while the music, all instinct, howls violence."[50]

Earlier in the year, the Beatles had released "Lady Madonna," with George Harrison's Indian-inspired "The Inner Light" as its B-side. "Lady Madonna," like "Revolution," was a rock and roll number with an iconic guitar riff at the beginning, dealing with social commentary centering on the plight of the single, working mother. The title of Harrison's "The Inner Light" came from an Indian religious philosophy called Samkhya (meaning "discrimination"), which taught that the inner light one perceived in meditation provided a glimpse into a more authentic version of the self that freed one from illusion and thus contributed to one's spiritual evolution.[51] The song was in keeping with George's interest in both Indian music and philosophy and signaled a position of withdrawal rather than engagement with the world and its current problems. According to Babiak, this would not cut it for the circumstances in which his generation found itself. "The Beatles wish to mesmerize us into a world of idiotic irrelevance—which has always been their forte," he wrote. To him, the Beatles wanted "a world where everyone walks about repeating 'love' and 'it will be all right' for seven minutes to lull themselves into a false sense of security and well being."[52]

Despite Babiak's critique and the anger directed toward the Beatles from some quarters when "Revolution" came out, neither the Beatles' antirevolutionary stance in that song nor the excessive length of "Hey Jude" prevented the record from becoming the most popular single the Beatles ever released. It spent nine weeks at # 1 on the Billboard charts, two weeks longer than "I Want to Hold Your Hand" had four years earlier at the height of Beatlemania. As they had from the beginning, the Beatles provided their audience with a sense of liberation from the status quo, without politically radicalizing their young fans or advocating anything like the violent overthrow of the established order. Still, especially in the politically charged environment of 1968 and in the context of the exploding world of rock music and a plethora of new challengers for their fans' attention, any album the Beatles released was likely to be a referendum on their continued relevance and success, especially after the grief they had taken over the film *Magical Mystery Tour*. The Beatles prepared for the making of the White Album largely by withdrawing from the world and tapping further into their own creative energies. The difference was that this time they did so less as a group and more as individuals, unknowingly reflecting a trend that would soon come to permeate the rock universe.

The Making of the White Album: The Beatles in India

In February 1968, George Harrison gave an interview to Nick Jones of *Rolling Stone*, in which he tried to explain what he hoped the Maharishi Mahesh Yogi would do for him:

> Discipline is something that we don't like, especially young people where they have to go through school and they put you in the army and all that discipline. But in a different way I've found out it's very important because the only way those [Indian] musicians are great is because they've been disciplined by their guru or teacher, and they've surrendered themselves to the person they want to be.

Describing the state referenced in his song "The Inner Light," Harrison continued, "If you can contact that absolute state you can just tap that amazing source of energy and intelligence. Everything in life works out better because everybody is happier with themselves."[53] Just two weeks after Harrison's interview appeared, there followed one with Ravi Shankar, the famous Indian musician who had taught George to play the sitar. Sue Clark asked Shankar about the influence the Maharishi was having on the Beatles. Shankar responded in measured tones, saying he thought anyone who does something good deserves praise and acknowledging the possibility that the Maharishi might have a positive influence on the Beatles and the other show business personalities he had started to attract, which included the young Hollywood star Mia Farrow and the English folk singer Donovan. At the same time, however, Shankar admitted he did not know the Maharishi very well and pointed out that many roads exist that might lead to peace and spiritual fulfillment.[54] Just as Shankar had willingly instructed Harrison in the sitar, while affirming that it took a lifetime of discipline to master the instrument, he may have looked with skepticism on the many young Westerners thinking that a small dose of meditation and Indian philosophy would lead to any kind of spiritual depth. Yet the fact that in the mid- to late 1960s, many young people did develop an interest in Eastern religions as part of the counterculture indicated a profound dissatisfaction with Western commercialism and militarism and the search for a more meaningful set of values. We should not easily discount this phenomenon, or the Beatles' contribution to it.[55]

John Lennon, who would later voice his skepticism about Western religion in songs such as "Imagine" and "God," explained what the Beatles hoped to get out of Transcendental Meditation this way: "It's no gospel, Bible-thumping, singalong thing, and it needn't be religion if people don't want to connect it with religion. It's all in the mind. It strengthens understanding and makes people more relaxed. It's not just a fad or a gimmick, but the way to calm tensions down." Paul was searching for something beyond money and fame as well. He described the feeling at the time as one of, "Yeah, well, it's great to be famous, it's great to be rich—but what's it all for?"[56]

Whatever impact the Maharishi had on the Beatles' spiritual lives, their trip and prolonged stay at his ashram in Rishikesh had a profound impact on the White Album. For one thing, they wrote most of the songs in India, where they only had access to guitars and did not have George Martin available to provide them with different instruments or employ his technological wizardry. Therefore, many of the songs on the White Album, including "Rocky Raccoon," "Blackbird," and "Don't Pass Me By," among others, reflect the trend toward more folk and country influences in rock music seen in the work of Bob Dylan, the Byrds, and the Band, among others. Yet the Beatles as usual did not just stick to one style or genre and once again surpassed their peers in the variety and eclecticism of the types of music from which they drew. The White Album, in fact, would contain a perfect blend of musical styles and sensibilities that could at once serve as a critique of a bitter year ("While My Guitar Gently Weeps," "Why Don't We Do It in the Road," and "Piggies") and decidedly undercut that critique with the sincerity of songs like "I Will," "Julia," and "Mother Nature's Son." Only "Revolution 1" and "Happiness Is a Warm Gun," John Lennon's response to the assassination of Robert Kennedy, carried overt political commentary on the events of 1968.

Ringo Starr, whose constitution did not respond well to Indian food, left India at the beginning of March before the other Beatles, followed by Paul by the end of the month and John and George in April. They had individually written many of the songs that would wind up on the album, but it took them until May to regroup and make it back into the studio. Between the four of them, including Starr's "Don't Pass Me By," the group came to the studio with almost three dozen songs, most of which they had written while in India.

The album made slow progress but in July, the Beatles' cartoon feature film *Yellow Submarine* premiered in Britain; it came out in the United States in November, about two weeks before the release of the White Album. The soundtrack included four new songs by the Beatles and eight that they had previously recorded. The new songs on the album were "Only a Northern Song," "All Together Now," "It's All Too Much," and "Hey Bulldog." The soundtrack also included such classics as "Eleanor Rigby," "Nowhere Man," and "All You Need Is Love." In August, Paul McCartney told Alan Smith that the Beatles had needed time to get used to recording again, explaining the delay in the release of their next album. Paul did let on that the Beatles were intending to get back to doing "rockers" and that he had been influenced by music he had heard on a recent trip to Los Angeles.[57] However, Paul, who would contribute such rock-oriented songs as "Helter Skelter," Birthday," and the Beach Boys-inspired "Back in the U.S.S.R.," may have been mainly speaking for himself.

When interviewed for the *Beatles Anthology*, Harrison recalled, "There was also a lot more individual stuff and, for the first time, people were accepting that it was individual. I remember having three studios operating at the same time: Paul was doing some overdubs in one, John was in another and I was recording some horns or something in a third."[58] Yet even this statement testifies to the level of involvement each of them had in producing the album, which Beatles authority Ken Womack has argued was a much more collaborative effort than is normally portrayed.[59] Even if some of the album represented a return to rock and roll, the Beatles had long passed the stage where they would simply go into a studio and play a bunch of songs together as a band to record an album.

The Beatles, too, had begun to drift apart in their personal lives since returning from India. John had acquired a new love interest, a Japanese conceptual artist named Yoko Ono, and insisted on her presence in the studio, where she felt free to comment on the creative efforts of the band, something to which the other three Beatles were definitely not accustomed. He also had acquired a new drug habit, making his presence and state of mind somewhat more unreliable, thus pushing Paul even further in the direction of taking leadership of the group and the album. Yet Paul had taken on a number of side projects himself, including playing bass on recordings by Donovan and James Taylor. Rock historian Walter Everett calls 1968 "a time of simultaneous rejuvenation and dissolution for the Beatles."[60]

The Beatles finished recording the double album in October, a month in which they laid down the final tracks for "Honey Pie," "Savoy Truffle," "Martha My Dear," "Long Long Long", "I'm So Tired," "The Continuing Story of Bungalow Bill," and "Why Don't We Do It in the Road." The last song recorded was a solo effort by John Lennon, his tribute to his mother, "Julia." While this song is poignantly sad, Lennon's other contributions were either bitter ("Sexy Sadie"), wearisome ("I'm So Tired"), or downright depressing ("Yer Blues"). Although "Happiness Is a Warm Gun" was John's response to the assassination of Bobby Kennedy, the song's references and strong sexual content give it a much broader frame of reference, while making the song no less dark. "Sexy Sadie" John originally wrote about the Maharishi after his friend Alex Mardas circulated almost certainly false rumors of the guru engaging in sexual impropriety with one or more of his female guests. The rumors led to John's early departure from the ashram, but he wisely changed the title of the song so as not to implicate the Maharishi directly without a shred of proof regarding the allegations against him. The most controversial and experimental track on the album, a more than eight-minute sound collage called "Revolution 9," was almost entirely John's effort, probably inspired by Yoko's avant-garde approach to her own art. George and Ringo had little to do with it, contributing only a few vocal sound effects, while Paul was in New York during its recording.

George Martin did not think that all thirty songs belonged on the album ("some of them weren't great," he said), but he could not convince the Beatles who for some reason seemed to want to divest themselves of almost everything they had written in India. Among the songs they left off the White Album were "Polythene Pam" and "Mean Mr. Mustard," both of which wound up on the Beatles' last recorded album, *Abbey Road*, and "Junk" and "Teddy Boy," which Paul McCartney included on his first solo album in 1970. Martin thought it might be better to select the best tracks for a single album, but ended up deferring to the Beatles who thought otherwise. Opinions still vary on which choice should have prevailed. For every Ken Womack, who sees the album as "a magisterial, seamless whole,"[61] there is a Dominic Sandbrook who sees it as "a disorganized, sprawling mess."[62] Womack compares the album to an impressionist painting and, indeed, when you listen to the album with an open mind and a willingness to accept it as a work of art, the album can redefine the experience of listening to a rock album. The White Album is full of surprising contrasts, such as the transition from "Glass Onion" to "Ob-La-Di, Ob-La-Da," jarring insertions, such as "Wild Honey Pie" and "Helter Skelter," and nostalgic camp like "Martha My Dear" and "Honey Pie." Whatever its flaws, the album has become a Leviathan in the rock canon, the tenth greatest rock album of all time, according to *Rolling Stone*. But how did people receive it when it first came out, in the political and musical context of late 1968, after everything the year had brought in both of these arenas?

Contemporary Reactions to the White Album

The controversy in radical student circles in the United States centering on the Beatles' single "Revolution" did not destroy the Beatles' vast popularity, but it did put another dent in their armor following the criticism the group had endured over their film, *Magical Mystery Tour*. As a number of events over the past several years, such as John's "more popular than Jesus" comment and Paul's admission that the group took LSD, had proven, the Beatles were no longer immune to criticism. They did not receive universal praise for the White Album, but it went a long way toward reestablishing their preeminence in the rock universe and to add to the counterculture cachet they enjoyed with their fans. Jann Wenner of *Rolling Stone* may have been guilty of hyperbole when he said the album contained "every part of extant Western music through the all-embracing medium of rock and roll," but he insisted that the LP made "such categorical and absolute statements … imperative."[63]

For some contemporaries, the auditory experience involving such a wide range of genres on the album became a major part of its appeal. When Lenny Mandel talked about first hearing the album in 1968, he stressed the difference in songs like "Dear Prudence," "Happiness Is a Warm Gun," and "Back in the U.S.S.R.," three songs that alone ran the gamut from beautiful folk ballad to a song that itself encompassed a wide range of musical elements to an upbeat rock and roll number. Mandel also commented on the stories contained in songs like "Rocky Raccoon" and "The Continuing Story of Bungalow Bill" and the variety of songs on the album that stood up well to repeat listening. Mandel stated, "The album to me had many different genres that I sat there just listening to it over and over again."[64] Whatever one thought of it, one was not going to get bored listening to the White Album.

Len Pniewski, who was 17 at the time, claimed he scraped together the $9.50 required to buy the album in Greenwich Village the day it came out and became the first on his block to own it. What he most remembered noting at the time was the level of experimentation in which the Beatles still engaged. While the album contained its fair share of folk and blues material, as well as hard rock songs like "Helter Skelter," he saw the Beatles as going in a different direction from most American groups still focused on bringing melody into the pop hits played on AM radio. "Some songs [on the White Album] were very likeable," he said, "while others were quite abstract and experimental." He emphasized that no particular song defined the album, even if many would point to George's "While My Guitar Gently Weeps" as perhaps the best song on it.[65]

Michael Halbreich saw the album as just another example of how different each Beatles' album was from their previous one. Even so, he was shocked by what he heard when he first put the White Album on his turntable. "I didn't think that there was anything that was going to rival *Sgt. Pepper*, but the White Album did." His reaction to the album turned out to be a synthesis of later opposing viewpoints about whether the album represented a true group effort or the product of individual contributions that presaged the breakup of the band. He recalled:

> I could hear for the first time all of the individual talents of the Beatles, working together in a fabulous, cohesive, harmonic way. And the music had turned into something so much more complex and so much more creative, so advanced. It was just another album that just made me say where does it end?[66]

Halbreich's point was that now he could hear the evolution, not just of the Beatles as a group but as individuals, which to him suggested an unlimited potential. "As an album, I think it's a masterpiece," Halbreich affirmed. "I think the Beatles outgrew the ability of deejays and radio stations to even understand them. I just think the Beatles outgrew radio," he said.

Perhaps they did. The main purpose of poetry and music might be to evoke feelings and conjure images in the mind of the reader or listener, but it helps if art bears some connection to the world of the audience or speaks to them in their own vernacular so they can relate to it in however loose a manner. The main problem with much of the rock music of 1968, according to Richard Goldstein, was that it "lacked any relationship to recognizable experience."[67] While the Beatles were expanding to the outer limits of their creativity, in doing so did they leave their fans behind? If deejays could not adequately understand them, as Halbreich asserted, and did not play tracks from the White Album on AM radio, could their fans really be expected to follow them down the rabbit hole of the White Album? Charles Manson tried and it led him to engineer a murderous spree by several members of his brainwashed hippie coterie. The obscure lyrics did lend themselves to wildly varying interpretations; John Lennon even lampooned the tendency of Beatles fans to puzzle over hidden meanings in their lyrics in the song "Glass Onion." After listening to the album, Barry Miles wrote in the *International Times*:

> Naturally those who think they are the fool on the hill, who deciphered a secret message from "A Day in the Life" by playing it at 16 revs backwards, who discovered that "Hey Jude" was a message to Dylan asking him to do more live performances, and who found that almost every track on the last 3 albums have been about drugs, will have a field day here: *Beatles* is loaded with open-ended lines just waiting for someone to decipher![68]

Rebecca Duncan remembers breaking down the album with her friends and arguing about which side they liked best. To her, the length and variety of the album proved an obstacle to absorbing or even listening to the whole thing. "Every song was so different and we barely got to the fourth side," which she called "the Revolution stuff" because of the presence of both "Revolution 1" and "Revolution 9," which dominate a side that also contained the songs "Honey Pie," "Savoy Truffle," "Cry Baby Cry," and the lullaby "Good Night," which concludes the album. "Nobody I knew," she remembered, "really wanted to sit through all that; it sounded a little weird, but we spliced apart every song and picked up every bit of gossip. We wondered whether Martha was really about Paul McCartney's dog and my older brother and I brought home [whatever we heard] from friends at school [that] we shared with each other." Indeed, the Beatles had remained an obsession for devoted fans like Duncan, and it helped that she was not alone. She remembered attending a church camp in New England the following year and everyone bonding over their interest in the White Album. Specific memories included everyone knowing the words to "Rocky Raccoon," the Beatles' "Birthday" now playing whenever anyone had a birthday, and a friend explaining to her that "Back in the U.S.S.R." was actually a satire, which she says was her first introduction to the very idea or possibility of satire, which came as a revelation. "Ok, 'she thought,' they weren't thrilled about being in the USSR; they are making fun of it."[69]

James Vignapiano pointed out that much of what we later learned about the Beatles during that time people did not know in the months following the album's release. He recalled, "We sort of knew about Yoko because she was already in the air, but most Beatles fans at the time did not know she had a bed brought into the studio or that certain members of the band only played on particular tracks." His reaction to the album at the time was one of "what a great idea, just a plain white cover and a double album with song after song after song." He said the album just grabbed him from the beginning with "Back in the U.S.S.R.," and although some people regard some of the songs as rather flimsy, he liked them all. He said simply, "I loved the White Album, and considered it my favorite album after *Revolver*."[70]

If the songs on the album received little play on AM radio, they figured in the heavy rotation of deejays on FM radio and, as a Beatles album, certainly had the attention of rock critics. The whole album also managed to place # 22 *on the singles chart* in Britain the week of its release, an unprecedented development for an album.[71] Goldstein, despite his reservations about the music of the period generally and some past reservations about the Beatles, gave the White Album a favorable review when it came out, calling it "a major success" that contained "the most satisfying collection of Beatle songs since 'Revolver'" and was "far more imaginative than either 'Sergeant Pepper' or 'Magical Mystery Tour.'" Goldstein did not think the album perfect, but to him "this album is so vast in its scope, so intimate in its detail, so skillful in its approach, that even the flaws add to its flavor."[72] Thomas Crocker, reviewing the album for the *Daily Princetonian* at Princeton University, called the album "an expansive potpourri of juvenilia, parody, and mindless sophistication" that contained "many solid songs and a handful of outstanding ones" even if it did not possess "the unity and finesse of *Sgt. Pepper's*." Mike Jahn in another *New York Times* review agreed that the Beatles' new album was "not nearly as good as *Sgt. Pepper's*."[73] Alan Smith of *New Musical Express* did not like all the songs and called "Revolution 9" an earsore, but in his view, "those who ignore 26 or 27 generally superb tracks for the sake of three or four duds are, at the least, misguided."[74]

Despite the lack of unanimity in contemporary verdicts on the album revealed in these interviews and reviews, one observation does suggest itself. In spite of the presence of "Revolution 1" on the album, the White Album was definitely not seen as being political in the way in which the Rolling Stones' *Beggars Banquet* was, which was released just two weeks later. Crocker, to cite just one example, called *Beggars Banquet* "gutsy" and "the Stones at their best," giving it a much more unequivocal endorsement than he did the White Album. However, we have already seen that the Rolling Stones did not quite deserve their reputation as political radicals, based on either their personal lives or their music. Even an edgy song like "Sympathy for the Devil" says that the devil has been around for "a long, long time," the implication being that there was little the student revolutionaries of the 1960s could do to eradicate his presence and build the new utopia so many of them dreamed of. In another song from *Beggars Banquet*, "Salt of the Earth," Mick Jagger proposes a toast to "the hard workin' people" but admits, "They don't look real to me."

Both albums, in fact, proved a fitting way to end 1968, testifying to the chaos that prevailed in society and the political arena, the continued presence of evil in a world spun out of control, and social divisions the inspired youth of the period found impossible to bridge, despite their high ideals. Those divisions had contributed to the collapse of the Paris revolution in 1968, the failure of the student movement in the United States to effect significant change and end the war, and the lack of impact of rock music or musicians on Britain's hidebound and rigid class structure. Fans and critics listening to the White Album may have subconsciously found its variety and obscure meaning appealing because it reproduced the lack of direction and certainty present in the times and in their own lives. The decade was not over though, and 1969 would bring one last moment of hope that young people could come together to create a better world and one last triumph of harmony and beauty from the Beatles, as students began to turn away from the violent stance so many had begun to take the previous year. In October 1968, a month before the release of the White Album, Geoff Martin, president of the National Union of Students, released a statement to the *New York Times* in which he said, "The trend to violence must be halted. Ignore the demonstration, it won't help the Vietnamese people. … These political hooligans, many of whom are not students, admit they want a 'weekend revolution.'"[75] Revolutionary ideals had become widespread among youth across various countries in the late 1960s, but the will and the means to translate these into action were running scarce.

CHAPTER 9
1969: WOODSTOCK, THE BEATLES, AND THE END OF THE 1960S

"Revolutionaries Who Have to Be Home by 7:30"

Radical political activity, including over hundred separate incidents of arson, bombings, and attempted bombings, increased dramatically in the last two years of the 1960s. This number does not even include the countless number of bomb threats that led to evacuations of schools and other venues. Buildings at colleges and universities were among the main targets because so many young political radicals lived on college campuses, but high schools, government buildings, and public utilities like electrical towers became symbolic targets as well.[1] While the Vietnam War and the government's conduct of it remained the main sources of discontent, many young people by the end of the decade had developed a strong animosity toward the establishment as a whole and any form of authority, ranging from university officials to high school teachers and administrators, from the local police to the Pentagon.

The Beatles themselves had contributed to the protest movement and the radicalization of youth in the United States, despite the fact that they were not particularly outspoken on political issues, their "Revolution" single notwithstanding. Even in the early stages of their career, they had not only taken a stand against segregation and racial discrimination in the south but had covered a number of Motown artists, showing an appreciation for African American music. They had emerged as leaders of the counterculture and advocates of peace, love, and experimentation with drugs by the time of *Sgt. Pepper*. In 1967, Paul persuaded the Beatles to pay for a full-page ad in *The London Times* advocating the proposition that "The Law against Marijuana is Unworkable in Principle and Unworkable in Practice."[2] George Harrison had caustically lampooned the establishment with songs like "Taxman" and "Piggies," while introducing Indian spirituality to the consciousness of Western youth. They made known their opposition to the Vietnam War any time a reporter asked them about it, even if they did not go out of their way to denounce it prior to 1969.

The year 1969 unofficially opened on January 19 with the inauguration of President Richard M. Nixon and a simultaneous march on Washington organized by a group calling itself the National Mobilization Committee. Nixon's election not only spoke to the disgruntlement of the American people with the status quo, the rising crime rate, and the proliferation of urban riots but also resulted from the support of many Southern Democrats who abandoned their party because of unhappiness over the Civil Rights legislation passed during the Johnson administration. Nixon could have gained even more popularity and silenced many of his critics if he had immediately taken steps toward ending the war in Vietnam, but this he refused to do, mainly because he, like Johnson, did not want to be the president who conceded military defeat in a foreign war. He did not have the vision to see the inevitability of US defeat and instead stubbornly clung to his slogan of "Peace with Honor." Nixon ended up fighting two separate wars and employing essentially a defensive strategy in each. On the one hand, he tried to hold off the Communist forces of Ho Chi Minh in Vietnam long enough to force a negotiated peace in which the United States could avoid conceding defeat. On the other hand, he fought a war at home in which he tried to quell domestic dissent and political opposition by maintaining an "enemies list" and directing the resources of the White House to undermine his critics and those opposed to the war. The antiwar movement had become just as much of a story as the war itself and attracted just as much press coverage, much to Nixon's chagrin.

Todd Gitlin has calculated that over three hundred demonstrations occurred on college campuses in the spring of 1969, "a quarter of them marked by strikes or building takeovers, a quarter more by disruption of classes and administration, a fifth accompanied by bombs, arson, or the trashing of property."[3] The radical leaders of the student movement hoped substantive change was on the horizon and that continued pressure from the left would lead the instruments of state to collapse, ushering in a freer and more democratic society. Even in the midst of such activity, there were signs, though, that some students had started to adopt the more moderate stance toward political change advocated in John Lennon's 1968 song, "Revolution." An early sign of disillusionment resulting from the failures of the previous year's demonstrations, especially the debacle at the Democratic National Convention in Chicago, was the paltry turnout for the staged protest at Nixon's inauguration in January. In February, the antiwar organization, the American Friends Service Committee, attracted only half as many people to a sponsored event as they had just a year prior.[4] In March, members of the Harvard chapter of Students for a Democratic Society (SDS) occupied several administrative building to protest the continuing presence of the ROTC (Reserve Officer Training Corps) program on campus, forcefully banishing several deans in the process. This action drew criticism from other students at Harvard and elsewhere. The Monmouth College student newspaper, for example, published an editorial condemning the Harvard students' "strong-armed tactics."[5] Later that spring, when the SDS chapter at Columbia University attempted to provoke an uprising on campus, most students remained apathetic. Asked by a reporter why the revolt failed, Columbia graduate student Terry Tao replied, "You can't just have a revolution every week." Tao said, "Last year's spectacle was a shock to most students."[6] The strength of the student protest movement in Britain had slowly dissipated, as well; the British government took it as a positive sign in 1969 that no militant candidates claimed victory in the student elections at the London School of Economics, one of the hotbeds of radical activity in the 1960s.[7]

Although young people might have become disillusioned with the SDS and other radical groups, the antiwar movement was bound to last as long as the war did. Moreover, signs also existed that proved the radical political views of college students had filtered down to their younger contemporaries, including the formation of many radical groups at high schools, most notably the New York High School Student Union, which brought together radically inclined students from all over the city. In addition, a group of honors students from various high schools in New York got together to establish a radical student newspaper, *The High School Free Press*, to address the issues most important to their contemporaries. When they criticized the principal of one high school in Queens, the principal suspended anyone caught, or even anyone he suspected of, possessing a copy of the paper.

In many ways, those working on the paper remained typical high school students; when journalist Nicholas Pileggi visited their makeshift pressroom, he found them dining on "fried clams, popcorn, ice cream, barbecued chicken, potato chips, oranges, apples, Fritos, halvah, candy bars, processed cheese, packaged cake and peanuts." As the staff worked to get their latest issue out, Dana Driskell, an African American student from Bronx Science and Stuyvesant High School working on an article on the teachers union, checked the clock because he had to "be home by 7:30."[8] Yet the serious concerns of these students very much reflected those of their generation, including the draft, birth control, and even abortion, and the paper published phone numbers students could call to get advice on these issues, as well as numbers for those seeking free legal assistance. These "revolutionaries who had to be home by 7:30" ensured that many of the ideals and social changes of the 1960s would carry over into the next decade and beyond. Indeed, at the time, Tom Hayden, one of the founders of SDS and one of the most prominent political activists of the 1960s, thought high school students more radical than their college-age counterparts.

Two other groups picked up the revolutionary mantle as the decade grew to a close: African Americans and women. The politicization of American college students had really begun with their participation in the Civil Rights movement in the early 1960s and had only shifted its focus toward the draft and the Vietnam War since the middle of the decade. However, improved race relations and an end to racial discrimination remained high on the radical agenda. In July, a British newspaper explained to its readers "the passions behind the student revolution are extremely unlikely to subside without a peaceful accommodation between whites and blacks."[9] While students at Columbia in 1969 reacted with apathy to the demonstrations there compared to a year previously, in May African American students at Southern University in Baton Rouge responded with enthusiasm to demonstrations inspired by one of their alumni, the Black radical leader H. Rap Brown. The state police, supported by six hundred members of the National Guard, answered the summons to maintain order on the campus before the administration came to an agreement with the students that largely calmed the revolt. The Black High School Coalition in New York City sponsored a student walkout on the anniversary of the assassination of Malcolm X in February; over 2,000 students complied in support.[10] Throughout the country, African American students began to demand the creation of Black Studies Departments at colleges and universities and to advocate for the hiring of more minority faculty and staff. Beyond the halls of academia, the Black Panther Party for Self-Defense, founded in 1966 by Huey Newton and Bobby

Seale, proposed to answer violence with violence and advocated that African Americans arm themselves against the police, which they saw as posing a real threat to the lives of innocent people solely based on racial profiling.

In the same year as the founding of the Black Panther Party, several hundred women (and men), including the feminist pioneer Betty Friedan, author of the groundbreaking manifesto *The Feminine Mystique*, established the National Organization of Women (NOW) in order to promote full equality for women in American society and civil rights for women both at home and abroad. In the 1960s, women had often taken a subordinate position to male leadership of radical organizations like SDS or the Student Non-Violent Coordinating Committee (SNCC) and in the counterculture more generally, which had promoted free love partly to make women less reluctant to have sex before marriage. However, the decade raised the political consciousness of women and by the end of it, they began to develop their own agenda to address their specific concerns, revolving around gender equality in the workplace and in society more generally, an end to sexual harassment, access to traditionally male careers and positions of authority, and reproductive freedom. The 1960s had brought about positive changes for women, but as is often the case, small improvements led to rising expectations. These changes prepared the way for the feminist movement, one of the most prominent forces for social change in the 1970s, a decade that symbolically began for women when Gloria Steinem introduced *Ms.* magazine in 1971.

In 1969, sides were drawing up. Liberals and student radicals who remained committed to social change drifted in increasingly more radical directions. In the United States, the stance of the Black Panthers forced left-wing white advocates to reconsider their position about violence and pushed them into either a more radical or more moderate position than they otherwise might have taken. In the UK, the Civil Rights movement accelerated in Northern Ireland, leading to a long struggle between the Provisional Irish Republican Army (PIRA) and first the Ulster police and then the British Army, resulting in more than three thousand deaths over the next three decades. Those opposed to social change reacted just as strongly and formed the basis for the conservative revolution that would occur in both Britain and the United States ten years later under Margaret Thatcher and Ronald Reagan, respectively. An editorial in the *Illustrated London News* on August 9, 1969, expressed the fear that "there is an element of deep social rebellion at work, leading to the conviction that all social restraints must be abolished, because society in its regulative role is anti-libertarian and therefore evil."[11] Taken by themselves, easier access to divorce for women, the abolition of laws making homosexuality a criminal offense, and the lowering of the age of majority to 18, all pieces of major social legislation in Britain in the 1960s, represented important reforms that extended rights to people badly in need of them. Taken together, conservatives saw them as undermining the social order and the beginning of a slippery slope toward moral relativism, if not anarchy.

As they had throughout the 1960s, the Beatles did not live and work outside of the context of these larger social trends and developments, nor did their fans. Could the Beatles remain relevant with younger fans who grew up in a different social milieu? Could they continue to respond with changes to the times with music that seemed to meet the needs of or at least seemed to resonate with their fans based on changes in their lives and the times? Coming off the release of the White Album and its tremendous commercial success (it was the best-selling Beatles' album to that date), the Beatles continued to struggle to balance their now adult personal lives and individual aspirations with the fans' expectations about what they would do next and their own reluctance to break up the band. If the White Album provided any indication of their future, it seemed to suggest that the group might be ready to return to its rock and roll roots if the Beatles were to survive as a group at all. The appearance on the album of the song "Revolution 1," a slower, alternative version of the controversial "Revolution" single, indicated a still moderate stance toward revolution, although John had introduced some ambiguity into the lyrics by adding an alternate "count me in" lyric.

The Beatles and Their Fans in 1969

Despite the tacked-on ambiguity in "Revolution 1" and the commercial success and critical acclaim generated by the White Album, there was a sense at the time that the Beatles had not responded directly enough to the revolutionary turmoil that had characterized 1968 or the political issues that had generated such upheaval. For example, Jon Landau wrote of the White Album. "The Beatles have used parody on this album precisely because they were afraid of confronting reality."[12] Undaunted, the Beatles wasted no time after the start of the new year in getting back to work, meeting at Twickenham Film Studios on January 2 to start their next project. They had decided to film the recording sessions for their next album and release a documentary film based on them, tentatively titled *Get Back*.

The title came from a new song written by Paul McCartney that not coincidentally spoke to the kind of music the Beatles intended to include on the album. Having gone about as far as they could go in the direction of experimental music with "Revolution 9," the Beatles decided they would reclaim their joy in making music by returning to the sound of rock and roll that had inspired them to learn instruments and join a band in the first place. Unfortunately, the only joy they found together was when they were actually making music, as tensions rose within the group on a personal level, at times to an almost unbearable degree. By February, rumors circulated that the band was breaking up, that John and George had engaged in a fistfight, and that Apple Records was approaching bankruptcy. George, while denying the fistfight, did not exactly soothe any concerns that not all was right in Beatleland. "There was no punch-up," Harrison told *Rolling Stone*. "We just fell out. We got over the punch-up bit when we were in Liverpool. We just stopped speaking. When we fall out, we say more by keeping quiet."[13] Even without the disagreements, it took a while for the Beatles to adjust to playing together again.

Lennon revealingly said:

> It's like an athlete; you really have to keep playing all the time to keep your hand in. And we'd been off for months, and we'd suddenly come into the studio and be

expected to be spot on again. It would take us a few days getting loosened up and playing together and so therefore The Beatles musically weren't as together as in the last few years.[14]

Why the Beatles even agreed to a film project that would require additional time in the studio and why they would allow filming during a time of increasing strains in their personal relationships remains something of a mystery. The answer seems to lie mainly in Paul's ability to cajole the group into continuing to work together and coming up with the idea for the project that would force them to do that. Aside from Paul, the other three Beatles mainly appear more bored than quarrelsome in the documentary film eventually released under the same title as their 1970 album, *Let It Be*. Yet there were times things went beautifully and the men still enjoyed playing together, the most famous example being the impromptu rooftop concert the Beatles performed at their Apple Corps headquarters on Savile Row in London on January 30. Derek Taylor called the concert "the first good, big, positive story without any snags for months and months."[15] Paul had hoped to convince the group to return to live performing as yet another way of recapturing their youthful enthusiasm for rock and roll, but, after considering several possible venues, the group lacked the energy and inclination to travel anywhere beyond their own studio, hence the concert on the roof.

Meanwhile, the Beatles continued to pursue their own lives, relationships, and career projects. McCartney was more involved in writing, producing, and recording other artists, such as Mary Hopkin, who had a hit produced by Paul in 1968 with an English version of a traditional Russian song called "Those Were the Days." Hopkin had another hit in 1969 with the McCartney-penned "Goodbye." John and Yoko had already released their own album, the highly experimental and controversial *Two Virgins*, with an infamous photograph of the nude couple on the cover. Ringo Starr continued to pursue a movie career, starring in the film "The Magic Christian," which featured as part of its soundtrack another song written by McCartney that became a hit on the Apple label for the group Badfinger. After a hospital stay caused by tonsillitis that lasted about a week in February, Harrison endured an arrest on marijuana charges the following month and was busy trying to save his own marriage, threatened mainly by his infidelity. Nonetheless, he also remained busy professionally, pursuing a solo album and writing "Old Brown Shoe," which became the B-side for "Get Back."

Both John and Paul got married about a week apart in March 1969, Paul giving up the fancy-free life of a bachelor for Linda Eastman, an American photographer well known on the English rock scene whose father, Lee Eastman, Paul would unsuccessfully try to push for as the group's manager. Knowing that their wedding would attract something of a media circus, John and Yoko decided to capitalize on the event and invite the press to what they called a "bed-in" for peace in their Amsterdam hotel room, shattering conventions as if they were champagne glasses. The press was generally friendly with John and Yoko at this point, but, when they staged a similar bed-in in Montreal in June, the newlyweds received a strange and awkward visit from the curmudgeonly cartoonist Al Capp that encapsulated the generational conflict of the Beatles era.

1969: Woodstock, Beatles, and End of the 1960s

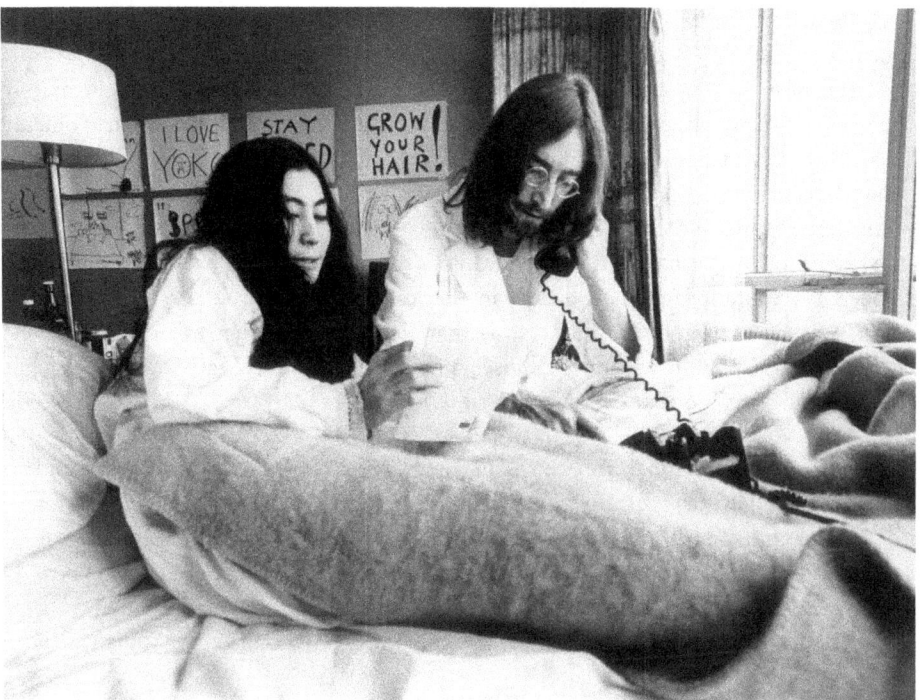

Figure 9.1 *John Lennon and Yoko Ono at the Hilton Hotel in Amsterdam, March 25, 1969. Courtesy of Bridgeman Images.*

Al Capp had become famous during the Great Depression for introducing his cartoon strip, *Li'l Abner*, set in the fictional rural village of Dogpatch, that by the Second World War reached almost 100 million readers and was beloved by many of them. Capp had once championed liberal values, including women's rights, but had become increasingly conservative during the 1960s. He became an outspoken critic of the antiwar demonstrations of the times and therefore had little sympathy with Lennon's calls for world peace. Dropping in on John and Yoko in Montreal, Capp facetiously introduced himself as a "Neanderthal fascist," before confronting the couple with a copy of their controversial *Two Virgins* album cover on which John and Yoko both appeared in full frontal nudity. Capp congratulated them for proving to the world that they both had pubic hair and remarked angrily, "Only the shyest people in the world would take pictures like this." He accused John of staging the bed-ins for publicity to increase record sales and chastised him for presuming to think that he could speak on behalf of the human race, saying, "You don't speak for me." The worst moment of the exchange came, however, when Capp directly insulted Yoko, telling John, "You've got to live with that? I can see why you want peace; God knows you can't have much." Discussing the incident years later for *The Beatles Anthology*, Paul McCartney commends John for preserving his tranquility with a heroic effort not to punch Capp in the face. McCartney says, "John really wants to deck him but you can see he controls himself. I think John behaved very well there, because the guy is actually slagging off Yoko—and that's the one thing you don't do."[16]

Capp also took umbrage with John's comparison of himself to Christ in a song released earlier that year called "The Ballad of John and Yoko." John and Paul had quickly recorded it in April on their own because the other two Beatles were unavailable at the time, George abroad and Ringo on the set of *The Magic Christian*. Singing "They're gonna crucify me" did create a fair amount of controversy, but the song may have been the beginning of a turnaround in fans' attitudes toward Yoko, who had quickly acquired a negative reputation among Beatles fans because they perceived her as breaking up John's relationship with Cynthia, just as they later perceived her as breaking up the Beatles. Claude Assante was among those fans prepared to believe the worst of Yoko, but he eventually became a little more understanding.

> I felt so bad for Cynthia, you know. But they were young when John married and all of a sudden, he was thrown into his slice of fame and fortune. So I felt bad for her and I have to tell you, in the beginning I wasn't a real happy person about Yoko's being with the band as much, but then later on in life, I started thinking, you know what, if they really love each other, that's what's important and I'm all for that. I am all for people being happy or being in love and trying to find their own way in life.[17]

The Beatles were starting to teach their fans through their lives as well as through their music.

Len Pniewski, who turned 18 in 1969, had grown up with the Beatles. He said he learned to appreciate the positive value of change from the Beatles. "Just like the Beatles progressed from 'I Want to Hold Your Hand' to 'Lady Madonna' to 'Let It Be,' I was maturing along with their music," he stated.[18] Assante said, "I just wanted to keep seeing what they were going to do next. It was just fascinating. You knew you didn't have to like everything on an album, but you knew there was always going to be stuff that you liked on [one of their] albums."

However, Allen Sorrentino remembered that many people thought the Beatles were beginning to fade by 1969, citing the proliferation of other groups making music he found just as relevant and interesting. Citing Blood, Sweat and Tears, Three Dog Night, and the Who, in particular, Sorrentino thought these groups were "cutting into the Beatles' popularity" somewhat.[19] Janet Nugent, who we encountered as a rabid Beatles fan in earlier chapters, graduated from high school in 1969 and said she was not as much in the Beatles "wave" as she had been earlier. "I had real people to have crushes on," she recalled. She continued, "Certainly there was still a reverence for them. I mean there would never not be. I just moved out of it a little bit." Jane Barnes, who like Nugent had seen the Beatles in concert at a young age, remembered still thinking the Beatles relevant in 1969, but for different reasons than they had been earlier.

> I think back when they first came to the United States and they first became popular I think they helped to sort of usher in or make more mainstream rock

and roll music. I think the cultural relevance as we got into the late 60s was more because they were figures that people would listen to for things other than music, for example, John and Yoko and the peace movement. George Harrison was very much into the peace movement also. Even though they spoke as individuals, they were still known as the Beatles. At best, their message became more political, more international, and more global and their message was different [from when they started]. So I think they were still very culturally relevant in the late 60s but in a different way.[20]

Ed Eichler combined the perspectives of Pniewski and the others in summoning up his memories of the Beatles in 1969. He affirmed that the "She Loves You" era was over, and the Beatles had stayed relevant through their trip to India and their adapting to the psychedelic phase of the late 1960s. Nevertheless, like Sorrentino, he thought other groups had started to supersede the Beatles in his estimation, as had singer-songwriters such as James Taylor. Eichler played guitar in a professional band at the time and said he had one rule: if he could not sing the song, he would not play the song. One song he never played was "Revolution." "John Lennon's musical contributions at that time became in my mind very unpleasant to listen to," he recalled.[21] Tom Noce agreed with Eichler and Sorrentino, to a point. While Noce held that the Beatles were not quite as relevant by 1969 as they had been earlier in their career, he believed it was "not so much that they were going bad or were not as cool, but I think the surge of the other groups in music just boiled over in that period."[22] He cited Led Zeppelin as a prominent example, while Eichler thought another group had eclipsed the Beatles, one comprising former members of three different rivals of the Beatles, namely the Byrds, Buffalo Springfield, and the Hollies. The three men who left these respective groups simply combined each of their last names to become the group known as Crosby, Stills and Nash.

The Summer of '69

"As a result there is this thing, this very together musical product, a sliding, swirling whirligig of sheer, often exonerating music," Mark Williams wrote in his May 1969 review of the eponymously named first album, *Crosby, Stills and Nash*.[23] David Crosby, Stephen Stills, and Graham Nash had all tired of their commitments to their previous bands, but all had contractual obligations they needed to overcome in order to play the music they wanted to play with their newly discovered musical soulmates. After overcoming these difficulties with the help of their manager, David Geffen, they went on to form one of the most successful music partnerships of all time. All three of them wrote songs in slightly different styles, giving their music enough variety to make it of intrinsic interest, while the compatibility of their voices and musical interpretations of their material made the three of them an almost perfect combination. In *The Foundations of Rock*, musicologist Walter Everett effuses, "No listener to 'Suite: Judy Blue Eyes' can miss hearing how the perfect harmonies of Nash and Crosby offer Stills the balm that can soothe his anguish, as each of his blues-laden solo expressions of pain is replaced by confident, hopeful, and even joyous vocal exaltations in the major mode."[24] As songwriters, although there was a fair amount of overlap among the three, Nash tended more toward a pop sensibility in songs like "Marrakesh Express" and "Teach Your Children," despite the fact that he had left the Hollies largely because they had become too formulaic and refused to expand beyond the pop genre that had brought them success. Stills inclined more toward blues-rock, but he was capable of writing songs in a range of styles, as exhibited by his contributions to CSN's first album, which included the soft rock masterpiece "Suite: Judy Blue Eyes" and the beautifully lilting folk-rock tune "Helplessly Hoping." Crosby, who had his roots in folk and folk-rock, inclined in that direction, as can be seen in the softer, haunting tones of a song like "Guinnevere," but his "Wooden Ships" is one of the best tracks on the first album and falls more into the blues-rock category, with elements of jazz and even hard rock. The blend of musical styles and the near perfection with which the three sang and played together—something they all said was evident from the first time they did—made the band a worthy competitor of if not a successor to the Beatles. The release of their album on May 28, 1969, two days after Memorial Day, set the stage for a summer of great music. The first single from the album "Marrakesh Express" came out in July, joining a soundtrack for the summer that included Neil Diamond's "Sweet Caroline," "I'd Wait a Million Years" by the Grass Roots, and the Beatles' "Get Back," a single that received radio airplay throughout the summer even though it was released in April.

If the formation of Crosby, Stills, and Nash and the release of their brilliant first album represented the first major development in the rock music world shaping the summer of 1969, the second was the death of Rolling Stones' guitarist Brian Jones, following his ouster from the group that had made him famous. The coroner ruled that Jones had drowned while under the heavy influence of drugs and alcohol. Jones died in his swimming pool on a day when he and his Swedish girlfriend, Anna Wohlin, were entertaining friends, Frank Thorogood and Janet Lawson, at his Sussex estate, previously owned by famed Winne the Pooh author A. A. Milne. Years later, Thorogood confessed on his deathbed to murdering Jones, though Keith Richards expresses skepticism in his autobiography about this claim. The coroner found no evidence of foul play, while all those present at the time acknowledged that Jones's faculties were impaired. Lawson said she had unsuccessfully tried to convince both men not to swim in their condition.

The brash Jones had a penchant for self-sabotage and a personality ill-equipped to deal with the headiness of fame and celebrity, but he told Don Short of the *Daily Mirror* that he looked upon his dismissal from the Stones as an opportunity to return to playing the music for which he had the most passion, namely classic rhythm and blues.[25] At his funeral service in his native Cheltenham, the Rector Hugh Evans Hopkins said, "Brian was a rebel. He had little patience with authority, convention and tradition. In this he was typical of many of his generation who have come to see in the Rolling Stones an expression of their whole attitude of life."[26] Jones's lifestyle had led to drug addiction and arrests, claims from three teenage girls that he had fathered their children, and bouts of depression that sometimes made it difficult for him to function, all of which eventually became too much for the two coleaders of the Stones, Keith Richards and Mick Jagger. Jones had resented the fact that the group focused mainly on recording the songs of Richards and Jagger at the expense of his own. Richards later wrote of Jones:

> I never saw a guy so much affected by fame. The minute we'd had a couple of successful records, zoom, he was Venus and Jupiter rolled into one. ... The minute the chicks started screaming, he seemed to go through a whole change, just when we didn't need it, when we needed to keep the whole thing tight and together.[27]

Richards, along with fellow Stones members Bill Wyman, Charlie Watts, and Jones's replacement Mick Taylor, attended the funeral; Mick Jagger presumably would have attended as well had he not been in Australia at the time.

Only two weeks after Jones's death, the Rolling Stones with Jagger gave a concert in Hyde Park. They had previously agreed to perform there as the third in a series of rock concerts filmed by Granada television for broadcast in the UK. The first two televised concerts had featured the LA band the Doors in London and country singer Johnny Cash's legendary performance at San Quentin State Prison in California. The Rolling Stones' concert in Hyde Park followed one earlier that summer by Eric Clapton's new group, Blind Faith; estimates of the crowd size for the Rolling Stones ranged from 250,000 to 400,000 people. Music critic Geoffrey Cannon compared it to the sixteenth-century meeting between King Henry VIII of England and King Francis I of France known as the Field of the Cloth of Gold. Cannon wrote, "If anyone doubts that the Stones are world No. 1 band, they weren't at Hyde Park."[28] Later that month they affirmed their status as rock icons with the release of one of their biggest hits, "Honky Tonk Women," that featured the sublime "You Can't Always Get What You Want" on the B-side. The Stones did not release their next album, *Let It Bleed*, until December, but their single that summer went to number one in both Britain and America.

Of course, the highlight for many people that summer had nothing to do with music or popular culture. At 10:56 p.m. (EDT) on July 20, American astronaut Neil Armstrong became the first human being ever to set foot on the surface of the moon. By 1969, most Americans had viewed any number of launches into space; the generation that came of age during the 1960s will remember teachers bringing in their small black-and-white portable televisions so that students could watch each blast-off from Cape Canaveral. The moon landing, however, captured the public imagination in ways that even an astronaut rocketing through space never did. In the context of the protracted struggle in Vietnam, the constant news of the latest casualties from that war, and the demonstrations against it, the moon landing did briefly provide a boon to American patriotism and some respite from the day-to-day calamities afflicting the nation. Having previously witnessed the triumphs of the Soviet Union in the launching of the satellite Sputnik and sending Yuri Gagarin up as the first man in space, Americans could rejoice for a change in a symbolic victory in the Cold War. As Patricia Lepis, a resident of Brooklyn, stated at the time, "It's the greatest thing that could happen to this country. It's definitely an American triumph."[29] Not everyone felt that way, but the moon landing became a memorable moment in American history and culture, even if the history of that summer (and the following decades) seemed to belie Neil Armstrong's famous quote that he had taken "one small step for man, one giant leap for mankind."

Significantly, a surprise hit by Zager and Evans called "In the Year 2525 (Exordium and Terminus)" sat at the top of the charts in the United States on the day Neil Armstrong walked on the moon. The song, the only hit by the duo, enumerated the problems unbridled technological innovation would inflict upon humankind centuries in the future, including machines that would make our arms and legs obsolete and a daily pill that would control "everything you think, do, and say." Following it on the charts, perhaps equally significantly, were Oliver's "Good Morning Starshine" from the pop musical *Hair* at # 2 and the song "Spinning Wheel" by Blood, Sweat and Tears, a song that started with the lyric "what goes up must come down."

The counterculture remained an important force in the summer of 1969. However, the hippie dream of the dawning of a new age of Aquarius filled with love and peace had already started to sour on many people. Echoes of dissent sounded even before two famous and seemingly diametrically opposed events took place in August 1969—the Hollywood murders committed by members of Charles Manson's hippie commune and the Woodstock Music and Arts Festival in Bethel, New York. For example, in July, *Time* magazine complained about the new permissiveness in sex, which along with the pill (or perhaps because of it) had brought about significant changes in sexual behavior. What really concerned the magazine, though, was the transformation of sex into a spectator sport. *Time* was not so much concerned with pornography per se, which would always have its niche, but with the legitimation of Andy Warhol's underground movies and popular films such as *I Am Curious (Yellow)*, which the magazine labeled "about as erotic as *Das Kapitol*."[30] The *Time* article reflected larger concerns that had been brewing for years about the lack of morals and discipline in society more generally, in addition to the more outlandish examples flaunted in the face of the public cited in the magazine. Men wearing long hair, women going braless, the proliferation of drug use among high school and college students, tie-dyed clothing, and new musical genres of psychedelic and acid rock all represented symbols in a culture war that involved more than the divisions over Vietnam.

Also in July, an episode played out in Massachusetts that also had profound political and cultural resonances. That incident involved another tragedy within the Kennedy family, although this one did not involve the death of one of the Kennedys but that of a young woman named Mary Jo Kopechne. Kopechne had been a passenger in a car driven by Edward (Teddy) Kennedy, the younger brother of President John F. Kennedy and Senator Robert Kennedy, both of whom fell to assassins' bullets earlier in the decade. The younger Kennedy was himself a rising political star in his own right, when the car he was driving plunged off a small bridge on Chappaquiddick Island in Massachusetts. Not only did Kennedy abandon the scene of the accident and Kopechne, who drowned, but he also failed to report the accident to the police until nine hours later. When Kennedy began appearing in public shortly thereafter wearing a neck brace, skeptics viewed this as a shameless attempt to distract attention from the real victim of the accident, even though it is certainly plausible that Kennedy might have sustained such an injury. The scandal dominated political conversation in Washington, making it seem as if people had already forgotten the moon landing less than two weeks after its occurrence. Kennedy ended up pleading guilty to a misdemeanor for leaving the scene of an accident and went on to a long and successful career as a US senator.

Whatever missteps Kennedy had taken at Chappaquiddick, a far more heinous crime eclipsed them a few weeks later with the brutal murders on the night of August 8–9 of actress Sharon Tate, who was in the ninth month of her pregnancy, along with four other victims. The murders occurred at the home of Tate and her absent husband, director Roman Polanski, in Benedict Canyon in Los Angeles. The victims also included 25-year-old Abigail Folger, whose family manufactured Folger's coffee; a 33-year-old Polish author named Wojciech Frykowski; the 36-year-old hairstylist of many Hollywood celebrities, Jay Sebring; and Steven Parent, a friend of the Polanski's caretaker. Police found a bloodbath with the bodies mutilated from repeated stabbings, bullet holes throughout the living room's walls and ceiling, and an X carved into Tate's stomach.

The plan for these outrageous murders turned out to have originated in the mind of an ex-con-turned-hippie-cult-leader named Charles Manson. Manson, a petty criminal since his youth, had obtained his freedom from prison, despite his own recommendation against parole, in 1967, after which he headed for the Haight-Ashbury District in San Francisco in the year of the summer of love. Possessing a certain amount of charisma and offering runaway girls a sense of belonging, family, and community, he began to attract a following that laid the groundwork for the commune he would shortly establish in Los Angeles, where he headed in the hopes of launching a music career. Manson played the guitar and wrote songs that hinted at enough talent that Neil Young passed one of his tapes along to the record producer Terry Melcher at his label, Reprise, while Dennis Wilson changed the first line and title of one of Manson's songs and recorded it with the Beach Boys. Manson had called the song "Cease to Exist," which Wilson changed to "cease to resist" in the lyric while renaming the song "Never Learn Not to Love." Nevertheless, this was as close as Manson got to a career in the music industry.

We will never know for sure of course if Manson might have become a productive and creative force had he enjoyed the success he craved. Nevertheless, the combination of Manson's own feeling of rejection and his apparent resentment at the success of the Beatles, along with what he perceived as hidden messages aimed at him personally in the White Album, sent him over the edge of psychopathy. Extracting meaning from the lyrics of songs such as "Blackbird" and "Helter Skelter," the delusional Manson became convinced that he should foment a race war that would lead to the destruction of Western Civilization, after which he would arise from an underground existence to lead humanity into a new golden age. By this time, he had established such a hold over the minds of the members of his "family" that he had the ability to exploit their psychological dependence on him to the point where they committed these ghastly murders under his command, though Manson did not personally participate in the killing spree. For this reason, some have argued that Charles "Tex" Watson, who played more of a central role in actually

The Beatles and the 1960s

carrying out the murders, deserves as much or more ignominy as Manson acquired from the killings.

The Tate murders actually were the second in three separate murder scenes enacted by Manson's followers, the first that of an associate of Manson, named Gary Hinman, against whom Manson held a grudge because Hinman refused to share an inheritance with him. The last victims were grocery store owner Leno LaBianca and his wife Rosemary, whom the assailants stabbed forty-one times. At this scene, the murderers provided the first clues that the killings had something to do with the White Album, as the murderers had smeared the words "Healter (sic) Skelter," "Rise," and "Death to Pigs" in blood inside the house, referencing the songs "Helter Skelter," "Blackbird," and "Piggies" from that disk. The Beatles thus would forever be connected to one of the most infamous and darkest crimes in American history, though they, of course, had no direct involvement.

Nor did the Beatles participate in the other event from August that helped to define not only the summer of '69, but the entire period as well—the Woodstock Music and Arts Festival held in Bethel, New York, from August 15 to 18. However, their presence still exerted itself in powerful and tangible ways, reinforcing their centrality to this decade of revolution and social change.

The Beatles at Woodstock

Woodstock attracted an estimated half a million people, completely overwhelming any measures at restricting entrance exclusively to ticket holders and turning it into essentially a free concert for most of those who attended. The festival lasted from Friday night until early Monday morning and featured a lineup that included folk performers like Joan Baez and Arlo Guthrie; traditional rock bands like the Who, Creedence Clearwater Revival, and Blood, Sweat and Tears; and practitioners of psychedelic rock such as Jefferson Airplane, Sly and the Family Stone, and Jimi Hendrix. Other notable acts included Janis Joplin, the Grateful Dead, and Country Joe and the Fish. However, Woodstock became symbolic of the 1960s not primarily for the music played there. More important to the legend was the surprisingly peaceful and good-spirited nature of the crowd in the midst of food shortages, a lack of sanitary facilities, no real effective measures in place for crowd control, and a torrential downpour that turned the sloping hill in front of the stage into a giant mudslide. Surviving on love, drugs, and food donated by local residents and businesses, the hippies at Woodstock created a scene quite unlike any before or since. It was as much a product of its time as *Sgt. Pepper* or the moon landing, moments that can only occur once.

The first night of the festival opened with a set by African American folk-singer Richie Havens, who had been a Beatles fan since he first heard someone playing "I Want to Hold Your Hand" from two rooms away in 1964. Havens' set at Woodstock included three Beatles covers—"With a Little Help from My Friends," "Hey Jude," and "Strawberry Fields Forever"—and thus ensured that the Beatles would have a presence at the festival, even in their absence. Not many other performers did Beatles covers during

1969: Woodstock, Beatles, and End of the 1960s

Figure 9.2 *Fans watching first act Richie Havens opening the Woodstock Music Festival, Bethel, New York, August 15, 1969. Courtesy of Getty Images.*

the festival, probably because most of the acts, many of them from San Francisco and the West Coast, saw the festival as an opportunity to present their own material to a mass audience. The festival did prove a boon to the careers of some, including the folk-pop singer Melanie, who wrote one of her biggest hits, "Lay Down (Candles in the Rain)" about her experience at Woodstock, Latino rock star Carlos Santana, whom many festival goers heard for the first time that weekend, and the rock and roll revivalists Sha Na Na. However, Crosby, Stills and Nash, joined on stage for this concert by their friend, future bandmate Neil Young, did include a cover of "Blackbird," in their set, and Joe Cocker's unique interpretation of "With a Little Help from My Friends" largely defined his set. In fact, Cocker's version of that song from *Sgt. Pepper* became one of the signature performances of the weekend, along with Jimi Hendrix's iconic reinterpretation of "The Star-Spangled Banner" in the very last set of the weekend and Country Joe McDonald's performance of his antiwar satire, "I-Feel-Like-I'm-Fixin'-to-Die-Rag."

Although the covers performed at Woodstock, especially the one by Joe Cocker, represented one aspect of the Beatles' presence at Woodstock, they were not the only ways in which the Beatles' presence manifested itself there.[31] Along with the Monterrey Pop Festival, the Beatles' 1967 satellite broadcast of "All You Need Is Love" provided an important backdrop for Woodstock. Woodstock did not set a precedent in the same way as Monterrey or the Hyde Park concerts of Blind Faith and the Rolling Stones, which first approximated the kind of size crowd expected at Woodstock, although these had actually been presaged by the Beatles' 1965 concert at Shea Stadium. Nevertheless, the

The Beatles and the 1960s

Beatles' enlistment of the rock community in 1967 to spread a message of peace and love to the world called attention to the ways in which musicians could reach a mass audience and promote an ideal that might actually succeed in changing the world for the better.

The Beatles' message of harmony and togetherness merged perfectly with the ethos prevalent at Woodstock and with the counterculture's emphasis on communalism more generally. The Beatles had charmed their fans throughout their career largely because they had performed as part of a group, seemingly lacking the inclination to assert themselves individually to pursue their own professional agenda. Lennon and McCartney shared songwriting credit, even for songs like "Yesterday" entirely composed and performed by Paul, with Beatles fans none the wiser. This helps to explain why fans would take it so hard when the band did break up and why some fans and critics disliked the White Album, which represented more distinct individual styles and contributions than earlier Beatles' albums. In that sense, Woodstock evoked more the positive vibes of the Summer of Love and *Sgt. Pepper* than the more radical, discordant tones set by 1968 and a number of songs on the White Album.

Arguably, no one in the period had done more to shape popular consciousness among the youth of America than the Beatles had. "It is no exaggeration to claim that the Beatles changed everything, and not just for young folk musicians, but for young people of all sorts throughout North America, Britain, and the world," music historian Richie Unterberger has asserted.[32] The very young people who clogged traffic and flocked to Woodstock in droves had grown up listening to not only "She Loves You" and "Help!" but also *Rubber Soul*, *Revolver*, and *Sgt. Pepper*. As Lenny Mandel, who attended the festival, put it, "There was nobody who was there who did not understand the Beatles. ... They were a driving force in all the changes I lived through."[33] Another attendee, David Scher, said, "I'm not going to say that because of the Beatles there was a Woodstock," but he did acknowledge "the influence they had on the music that was constantly developing."[34] Indeed, those who attended the festival came to Woodstock to hear musicians, many of whom were there themselves because of the impact of the Beatles or who were at least heavily influenced by them. Robbie Robertson, whose group, the Band, played on Sunday of the festival, cited songs on *Revolver* like "Eleanor Rigby" and "Taxman" as special influences.[35] John Fogerty of Creedence Clearwater Revival claimed to have gone straight to the record store to buy every record with the name "Beatles" on it after seeing them perform on the *Ed Sullivan Show*.[36] Ravi Shankar, the Indian musician who had taught George Harrison to play the sitar, also performed at the festival, his presence there largely the result of the Beatles having introduced Indian music to fans of Western rock music. According to rock historian Robert Santelli,

> Most of us knew nothing about Indian music. We probably wouldn't have been interested in Indian music at all had not the Beatles introduced the sitar and other components. Ravi Shankar's credibility really extends from George Harrison and the other Beatles who had gone to India and had expressed interest not only in the music, but also in the philosophical offerings that the culture of India gave to the West so he comes with instant credibility.[37]

Had the Beatles themselves performed at Woodstock, their physical presence might have actually undermined the influence they did exert over the spirit of the festival by making it more about them and their celebrity and less about the ideals for which they had stood and inculcated in the generation most represented there. In that regard, the absence of the Rolling Stones and Bob Dylan also contributed somewhat to the goals of the organizers, including Michael Lang, according to whom "Woodstock was not intended to be about any one band or group of bands. It was about the people—and the ideas and music interwoven through their lives."[38] Even so, there was some speculation that the Beatles might show up, fueled partly by the rooftop concert that some fans took as an indication that they might resume touring or at least be open to giving other live performances. Even though no possibility existed for the Beatles as a group to appear at Woodstock, the possibility existed that one or more of them could be charmed into performing. John Lennon expressed an interest in appearing with his new ad hoc group, the Plastic Ono Band, but a recent marijuana charge led to visa problems he did not think he could address in time. A month later, the Plastic Ono Band did give a live performance at the Toronto Rock and Roll Festival. Beatles fans at Woodstock did not know it at the time, but by the time the festival kicked off, the Beatles had just finished recording their final album, which would arrive in stores at the end of September. They called it, simply, *Abbey Road*.

Here Comes the Sun: *Abbey Road*

The release of *Abbey Road* on September 26, 1969, was another remarkable event that in many ways marked not only the culmination of the Beatles' spectacular career as a group but also of the decade they had played such a large role in defining. From the opening track, John Lennon's rock and roll, Chuck Berry-inspired "Come Together" through the beautifully arranged medley that comprised most of Side Two to the final snippet of a song called "Her Majesty," the Beatles somehow managed to make an album that would surpass the expectations of even their most ardent fans. The group had managed to set aside the incredibly tense feelings that had led to the temporary scuttling of the "Get Back/Let It Be" project to work together toward making arguably their finest album. As Ringo Starr put it, "After the *Let It Be* nightmare, *Abbey Road* turned out fine. The second side is brilliant. Out of the ashes of all that madness, that last section is for me one of the finest pieces we put together."[39]

In fact, the Beatles somehow managed to segue remarkably quickly from the collapsed sessions into those for the new album. The sessions for what would become *Abbey Road* began at the beginning of July after only a two-month hiatus for the band. At the time, the Beatles had no particular explanation for how this had happened. George Harrison told a reporter in an interview given right before the album's release, "Well, we had Get Back in the can, but one day we just decided that we'd like to do a newer album. There was no particular reason—we just wanted to use some of our newest songs."[40] Harrison had good reason for wanting to use two of his: his compositions "Something" and "Here Comes the Sun" would become two of the most identifiable songs the Beatles ever recorded; many fans consider them the best two songs on *Abbey Road*. Barry Miles suggests that John and Paul had perhaps rediscovered the joy of working together during the recording of John's song, "The Ballad of John and Yoko."[41] Whatever the reasons for wanting to do a new album, before George Martin would agree to produce it, McCartney had to convince him the Beatles were willing to cede some control back to him and that they would return to making records as they used to do. He also had to convince the other Beatles to go along with those conditions. He probably simply neglected to tell them the full extent of his conversations with Martin about the project.

McCartney showed up alone at the first session to begin recording a song he had written called "You Never Give Me Your Money," the lyrics of which reflected the Beatles' growing dissatisfaction with their financial situation, as well as foreshadowing the brewing conflict over who would manage the Beatles and future control over the Beatles' earnings. George and Ringo followed him into the studio the following day and the three began work on the rest of the album. John remained AWOL for a few weeks after he, Yoko, and their son Julian narrowly survived a serious automobile accident in Scotland on July 1. Still, even John began the project with a great deal of enthusiasm and he worked more collaboratively with Paul on the project than has been generally thought. Things went well for the first month of recording, with the collection of songs and partial songs that would constitute the medley on Side Two taking shape by the end of the month.

As had become the norm, however, Lennon proved the most difficult to corral and get him to apply himself to the painstaking task of making an album. In May, Lennon made the blithe comment to Alan Smith of *New Musical Express*: "I'm not really interested in the production of our records. In fact, I wish I didn't have to go through that whole thing, going through the production and balancing the bass and all that."[42] Even after his return from the accident, Lennon was not there for every session and when he did attend, he had Yoko to keep him company and offer him support. When a pregnant Yoko had a double bed brought into the studio from Harrods so she could comply with her doctor's orders for bedrest after the couple's accident and still be present for recording sessions, this only exacerbated the tensions in the studio over her presence there. Still, although John eventually soured on the second side of *Abbey Road*, rather than stall the process, he helped to bring it to fruition. George Martin said, "Even on the second side, John helped. He would come in and put his little bit in, and have an idea of sewing a bit of music into the tapestry." Of the group's work on the album as a whole, Martin stated, "Everybody worked frightfully well, and that's why I'm very fond of it."[43]

Although Simon Reynolds has called the White Album "eclectic in a way that had never been seen in rock before,"[44] rock music historian and Beatles expert Walter Everett points out that on *Abbey Road*, the medley alone contains a multitude of genres, including "R & B, Blues, Hard Rock, Soft Rock, Music Hall, Classical, Lullaby, and an everyman sing-a-long." Everett, the author of a two-volume work on *The Beatles as Musicians*, has studied and analyzed the album from seemingly every musical angle and argues "the reason the music sounds great to us is because it is constructed in particularly interesting ways." He notes, for example, that musically "there is more cohesion in the non-medley songs on the album than on the medley songs."[45]

The first side of *Abbey Road* opened with "Come Together," which John had written originally for use by Timothy Leary in his campaign for governor of California. Despite its status as the first track on the album, the Beatles actually recorded the song late in the sessions, after John had fully recovered from the injuries sustained in the car crash. The first side continues with George's "Something," which was inspired by a James Taylor song called "Something in the Way She Moves" and written as an ode to his wife, Pattie. Then followed two McCartney numbers, "Maxwell's Silver Hammer," a light-hearted pop tune with incongruously dark lyrics, and the Swamp Pop-influenced "Oh! Darling." Kit O'Toole has traced the influence of Swamp Pop on the Beatles and argues that "Oh! Darling" meets almost every criteria for songs identified as belonging to that genre, including its "tripleting honk-tonk piano," "emotional lovelorn lyrics," and "dramatic lead vocals."[46] Ringo's contribution to the album enters the sequence here in the form of the delightful "Octopus's Garden," ahead of the hard rock vibes of Lennon's "I Want You (She's so Heavy)," which abruptly ends Side One after running for almost eight minutes. Originally, the two sides were supposed to be opposite to the final arrangement, with this song coming at the end of the album, but the decision in the final stages of mastering to switch the two sides has shaped how generations of fans have perceived the album. Instead of concluding the album with a sudden end to a song not particularly beloved by most Beatles fans, the group gave their audience a satisfying ending with the Medley, concluding with "The End" and its admonition to remember, "The love you take is equal to the love you make."

Harrison's jewel "Here Comes the Sun" opens Side Two, followed by "Because," a song that Lennon based on "Beethoven's "Moonlight Sonata" and the first complete Beatles song to feature three-part harmonies since "Yes It Is."[47] Then comes the famous Medley, consisting of "You Never Give Me Your Money," "Sun King," "Mean Mr. Mustard," "Polythene Pam," "She Came in through the Bathroom Window," "Golden Slumbers," "Carry That Weight," and "The End." Ken Womack has argued that, in constructing the medley, the Beatles did not invent a new departure in rock and roll but rather kept up with the times instead in a year marked by the release of the famous rock opera *Tommy* by the Who. Womack also cites an obscure 1967 album called *Teenage Opera* by Keith West, a single from which appealed to Paul McCartney, as another example of the genre that anticipated what the Beatles would do with the medley on *Abbey Road*.[48]

In addition to these influences, however, the idea came from the desire of Paul and John in particular to make some use of songs they had started but never got around to completing. As Paul explained, "I think it was my idea to pull all the spare bits together, but I'm a bit wary of claiming these things. I'm happy for it to be everyone's idea. Anyway, in the end, we hit upon the idea of medleying them all and giving the second side a sort of operatic structure—which was great because it used ten or twelve unfinished songs in a good way."[49] At least at first, John was completely onboard. He confided to Alan Smith, "Paul and I are now working on a kind of song montage that we might do as one piece on one side. We've got two weeks to finish the whole thing so we're really working at it."[50]

His later efforts to disassociate himself from it were, therefore, somewhat disingenuous. Finally, McCartney liked the idea of showing what the Beatles could do with the form and putting their own stamp on it, proving himself more than up to the task.

What made *Abbey Road* so significant was not only the quality of the songs that appeared on the album but the manner in which they were recorded, using eight-track recording and solid state electronics, giving the album a fuller, more polished, although to some more artificial, sound. With Geoff Emerick returning to engineer the album and the use of new technology like the Moog synthesizer, the album acquired a smoother and richer tonality, making it sound mellower, according to Emerick.[51] Furthermore, Walter Everett explains, "the guitars and the bass were now running directly through DIT [Digital Imaging Technician] boxes, rather than being miked up at the amp." Emerick did not especially like this particular recording technique because he thought it distracted from the power of the amp and made the sound "wishy-washy," but, as Everett notes, "he acceded to the Beatles' desires."[52] This change in the sound of the Beatles' music would turn off some diehard fans, but most adjusted to the Beatles' new sound just fine.

Finally, Ian Macmillan's cover photograph of *Abbey Road* itself became a masterpiece of late-1960s popular culture. The photograph, taken on August 8, depicts the four Beatles striding soberly in single file across the crosswalk at the intersection in front of the Abbey Road studio. John leads the procession in a white suit and white shoes, followed by Ringo and Paul in dark suits, with George trailing behind in jeans and a denim shirt. Ringo wears black shoes; Paul is barefoot and holds a cigarette in his right hand. The tree-lined street recedes into the background, a white Volkswagen Beetle parked on the curb on the left, with other parked vehicles visible in the distance. The Fab Four walk away from the studio, an appropriate and symbolic image for the last album the group would ever record. It would not take long, however, for Beatles fans to begin noticing and searching for other symbols on the cover, as well as other Beatles albums and covers, leading them to the seemingly impossible, yet, to them, inevitable conclusion that Paul McCartney was actually dead.

CHAPTER 10
LET IT BE: CONTEMPORARY RESPONSES TO THE BEATLES' LAST ALBUMS AND THE BREAKUP OF THE BEATLES

"Paul Is Not Dead": The Beatles as News

In the autumn of 1969, Beatles fans were no more ready to confront the encroaching reality of the Beatles' breakup than was the Woodstock generation the end of the 1960s, despite all of the horrific events that had occurred during the decade. The attempt to forestall reality can often result in an effort to escape from it; such proved to be the case when Beatles fans latched onto a weird rumor that blew up at that time that Paul McCartney was dead. What made the rumor even odder was that, according to Russ Gibb, a deejay at WKNR-FM in Detroit who was one of the first to go public with it in a major media outlet, Paul had actually died three years earlier. Gibb had picked up the story from an article written by a University of Michigan student named Fred LaBour. According LaBour, the Beatles had replaced Paul with a look-alike named William Campbell, who apparently just happened to have abilities as a bass guitarist and songwriter that equaled if they did not surpass those of McCartney himself. Rumors of Paul's death had actually preceded the furor surrounding the subject that arose after LaBour's article and the radio broadcast on WKNR. According to J. Marks, a journalist who collaborated with Linda Eastman (the future Linda McCartney) on a project that brought them in close proximity to the Beatles in 1966, she was informed at a party where the Beatles were present that the person attending as Paul was not actually Paul, who had recently died.[1] This anonymous source, whom Marks identified only as someone close to the Beatles, allegedly told her that Jane Asher had agreed to cooperate with the ruse temporarily to help the group out, but that she would soon announce her breakup with the fake Paul. When Asher and McCartney did split shortly thereafter, it gave Marks some pause, she wrote. Then, in April 1969, an aspiring folk singer named Terry Knight released a song called "Saint Paul." In retrospect, the song seemed to foreshadow the rumors of Paul's death that would emerge later in the year. Knight had been to London for an audition with Apple Records, but nothing came of it, mainly because Paul seemed to forget about him in the midst of internal feuding among the Beatles at that time. Knight, who would go on to a fabulously successful career as manager and producer for the American hard rock band Grand Funk Railroad, was from Detroit, the same city from which Gibb would broadcast the news of Paul's death just months after the release of his song.

Gibb made his pronouncement on October 10 and by the end of the month, a number of news outlets had begun to cover the story, creating interest in the subject and sparking a dramatic increase in record sales from the Beatles' old catalog. In fact, Tony Bramwell blamed the Beatles' new manager, Allen Klein, for not doing more to scotch the rumors once he saw the effect they had on the band's sales.[2] A story on McCartney's reported death appeared in the *Aberdeen Evening Express* in Scotland on October 22. *The New York Times* published the story on the same date, quoting a representative of the Beatles dignifying the rumor with the reply that it was "a load of old rubbish."[3] The college radio station at Georgetown University played every Beatles song since 1966 and concluded that they left no doubt about the death of the Beatles' left-handed bass guitar player. Radio station WABC in New York pulled deejay Roby Young off the air in the middle of a broadcast as he detailed the reasons fans should believe their Beatles idol was dead. Fans flooded the Apple phone lines with inquiries and began to hold vigils outside of McCartney's London home, while Tony Bramwell and others did their best to repudiate the rumors.

Space precludes detailing the hundreds, if not thousands, of supposed clues that hinted at McCartney's death, but some of the more prominent or frequently mentioned included their decision to stop touring in 1966 and their failure to inform anyone of that decision until after the date when Paul supposedly died. Fans reported hearing John saying, "I buried Paul," at the end of "Strawberry Fields Forever." (Peter Brown made the wry comment in his autobiography that "As much as this might have been John's sentiments at the time, it was hardly true."[4]) The original butcher cover with dismembered dolls and slabs of bloody raw meat seemed to signal something seriously wrong and fit in with the theory of a decapitated Paul. On the cover of *Sgt. Pepper*, the other three Beatles stand at an angle as if to support Paul's body, which faces directly forward. In this same photo, Paul holds a black instrument, while the other three hold brass instruments. Fans began to see the rectangular flowerbed on the cover as a grave; the word "Beatles" spelled out over the alleged grave supposedly signals that Paul's death is also the demise of the band, as fans knew it. Paul is supposedly the subject of the line, "He blew his mind out in a car" in "A Day in the Life." "Glass Onion's" numerous references to other Beatles songs led fans to consider it full of clues to Paul's death, especially the line, "the Walrus was Paul," referring back to "I am the Walrus," which was interpreted as a symbol of death.

The procession on the cover of *Abbey Road* loomed particularly large among those perpetrating the rumor. John, dressed in white, leads the procession as the preacher, with Ringo dressed in his suit serving as a pallbearer and George in his denim performing the task of the gravedigger. The barefooted Paul is, of course, the corpse, with a cigarette, commonly known as a "coffin nail," in one hand. Beatles fans found many more supposed clues on the back cover of the album, as well as on other Beatles songs and album covers, enough to raise some doubts even in the minds of reasonable people. Tony Bramwell, who had known Paul since childhood, did not help matters when he called a Burlington, Ontario, radio station posing as Paul to deny the rumors, only to have it blow up in his face when two separate voice analyses of the brief interview concluded that the voice on the phone did not belong to Paul.[5] The whole controversy became enough of a news story that *Life* magazine dispatched a crew to Paul's farm in Scotland to ascertain the truth.

Paul's initial response to the rumors of his death was to stonewall the press and refuse to cope with the story, which he regarded as just a gigantic hassle. Defiant, he seemed to feel no special burden to prove that he was alive, which to him seemed perfectly self-evident. When the team from *Life* showed up at his farm, a hotheaded McCartney at first attempted to chase them off his property, before he quickly realized how the photographs taken of his ill-considered outburst might appear in the press. He then reversed course, promising an exclusive interview with photographs in exchange for the exposed film of those already taken, an offer too good for the journalists to pass up. This resulted in a cover story and interview that appeared in *Life* on November 7, 1969, titled "Paul is still with us."

Although Paul's interview and photo shoot with *Life* dispelled the rumors for many fans, others would cling to the belief that the real McCartney had died in 1966. A group called the Mystery Tour released a song based on the rumors called "The Ballad of Paul" in November 1969 and whole radio and television specials explored the phenomenon, including an infamous TV trial hosted by the famous American defense attorney, F. Lee Bailey. The rumor has had no shortage of supporters, even in recent years. Nicholas Kollerstrom, a Holocaust-denier who has pushed a number of conspiracy theories in his writings, published a book called *The Life and Death of Paul McCartney 1942–66* in 2015, the same year writer and film-maker David Malocco came out with his own accumulation of clues to McCartney's death in his book, *The Beatles Conspiracy*. In 2020, Paolo Baron and Ernesto Carbonetti published a graphic novel called *Paul Is Dead: When the Beatles Lost McCartney*, though they raise the possibility that McCartney faked his own death. In an epilogue, they also emphatically deny that they believe the death rumors, which they call "the most absurd nonsense the entertainment world has ever given birth to."[6]

When twenty-first-century authors and conspiracy theorists continue to try to unearth and piece together evidence to prove that Paul died in 1966, they miss the point entirely of the historical significance of the "Paul is dead" phenomenon. The main questions hovering over the controversy are why so many Beatles fans seemed to embrace the rumors with such enthusiasm in the first place and why they were so determined to find in the clues supposedly embedded in Beatles album covers and song lyrics evidence that one of their idols was actually dead. If one considers the Beatles' relationship with their fans as comparable to an actual romantic relationship, an answer suggests itself. It seems that, just as many people fall into unhealthy, codependent relationships, the same might have been true in terms of what many Beatles fans brought to their relationship to the group. In other words, some fans were so in love with the Beatles that they could hardly envision their lives continuing without them. Once a relationship ends and the thing one has most feared has happened, the individual afflicted with a codependent personality has no choice but to accept it and move on, unless they are so mentally unstable that they end their own life or perpetrate violence against the person who has left the relationship. However, in those final stages before a breakup occurs but when it seems painfully obvious that it will, the suffering becomes particularly intense and fear rather than love motivates the codependent individual. In the autumn of 1969, fans feared that the Beatles would break up—they had not done so yet, but there were many signs that they would. Paul's death rumors fed that fear at the same time they helped to alleviate it—if Paul had already died, that would make it easier to accept the breakup of a group that had already lost one of its key members. Fans might want to believe that they had given their love to an imposter for the past few years because it would make it easier to stop loving someone who was not who they thought he was.

We can also see the parallels between the fans' relationship with the Beatles and a romantic relationship in that one way to cope with a breakup is to cling to the hope or illusion that one day one might get back together with their lost love. Such a hope is not always an illusion; people do reunite all the time and sometimes bands do. For years, there was speculation that the Beatles would get back together. Surely, the breakup must be temporary. It did not make any sense to Beatles fans that the group would simply abandon them.

Why do people react so strongly to breakups when the phenomenon is so common? They do so because the end of any relationship, romantic or otherwise, is a subtle reminder of death and impermanence. Things change and once a stage of one's life is gone forever, it brings us a step closer to the final stage: death. How many times do we hear people going through a divorce say that it is easier to go through a death than a divorce? Beatles fans could have thought it would be easier to go through the breakup of the Beatles and the end of their relationship with the band, if the most beloved Beatle, Paul, were actually dead. Furthermore, Devin McKinney suggests that Beatles fans did not just fear the breakup of the Beatles but rather the failure of their own generation—the death of their hopes and aspirations. McKinney writes, "Technology could disseminate the rumor, deductive inquiry enlarge it, but nothing short of surrender to the fantastic world would explain the hole this generation was sinking into—the ultimate failure it felt impending."[7]

Another explanation of the "Paul is dead" phenomenon could lie in the ways in which the Beatles fandom approximated a religion for many people. Karen Armstrong has studied various religious traditions worldwide and written widely about them in a number of well-received books on the subject. She has observed that new religions frequently arise in times of hopelessness and despondency.[8] For example, Confucianism emerged in a violent and anarchical period of Chinese history known as the era of the warring states. Christianity, while originating during the age of the powerful emperor, Augustus, triumphed in the fourth century, a period associated with the decline of the Roman Empire. One of the main premises of this book is that we need to understand the career and reception of the Beatles in the context of a period of widespread social change, revolution, war, violence, and unrest. Ill at ease with conventional religion, many young people, as John Lennon surmised, did find hope in a band they could idolize and look to for guidance and inspiration. The Beatles, like any religious movement, allowed their fans to feel connected to something larger than themselves. If the Beatles albums did become scripture for their fans, it makes sense that they would carefully scrutinize them for hidden messages and meanings in much the same way people have dissected the Bible through the centuries. In the analysis Beatles fans applied to the cover of *Abbey Road*, Paul becomes the Messiah (even though John was the one who actually compared himself to Christ and at one point went so far as to announce to the group that he was Jesus). Richard Goldstein writes about the "Paul is dead" phenomenon, "Truth was not the point—it was all about the feeling of doom projected onto a beloved star."[9] In this context, the albums through the White Album became the Beatles' Old Testament and *Abbey Road*, the album just before the rumors take off, the latest revelation or the New Testament. This was exactly the interpretation offered by Fred LaBour, the person regarded as most responsible for setting off the frenzy in the United States over Paul's death.[10]

Finally, it is possible that the focus on McCartney's death spoke to a larger fascination with death that seemed to characterize the Woodstock generation as much as its hopeful message of peace and togetherness. Such a preoccupation comes through in the music of groups like the Doors and Crosby, Stills, Nash, and Young, in addition to its presence in a number of songs by the Beatles. The tragic early deaths of rock stars, going back to the plane crash that killed Buddy Holly, Richie Valens, and the Big Bopper in 1959 and continuing with the premature deaths of Brian Jones, Janis Joplin, Jim Morrison, and Jimi Hendrix, among others, certainly reinforced the precariousness of life and the vulnerability of the young. That Paul could have died in a car crash did not strain credulity; Richard Manuel of the Band suffered a broken neck and almost died in a wreck in August 1968, while Lennon had his famous accident earlier in 1969.

However, the main cause for a sense of morbidity among the young derived from the Vietnam War and the thousands of young American men and Vietnamese civilians losing their lives as a result. It was in the fall of 1969 that, while the McCartney death rumors swirled around, Americans became more aware of the full horrors of the My Lai Massacre, an atrocity in which Lieutenant William Calley Jr. and at least twenty-five American soldiers executed 109 civilian Vietnamese villagers. As disturbing as this event already was and as much as it served as yet another indictment of the American presence in Vietnam, *Time* magazine hit on a particularly unsettling aspect of the massacre in an article published in early December 1969. The article stated, "according to the ample testimony of their friends and relatives, the men of C Company who swept through My Lai were for the most part almost depressingly normal. They were Everymen, decent in their daily lives, who at home in Ohio or Vermont would regard it as unthinkable to maliciously strike a child, much less kill one."[11] This realization could have forced young Americans to confront the fact that they, in the same circumstances, might have acted just as heinously. Rather than facing up to this tragedy, they perhaps found it easier to look away and divert their attention to another alleged calamity to which they could perhaps more directly relate—the death of a rock and roll idol in an automobile crash.

Finally, fans were doing something else when they sought out Beatles' records for clues to Paul's mysterious fate. They were claiming the Beatles' music, lyrics, and album covers for themselves, just as Charles Manson had done, and decided they would interpret what they meant without any help from the Beatles. Not all fans who played the game believed

Paul was actually dead; some thought it a hoax perpetrated by the Beatles to generate interest, drive up sales, or simply to provide amusement for their fans. Nevertheless, no matter how much of a distraction the "Paul is dead" conspiracy provided for Beatles fans in the fall of 1969, they could not forestall their having to cope with the more undeniable news that would come in 1970 that the Beatles were in fact breaking up. Before further considering the reasons for the breakup of the Beatles and the fans' reaction to that news when it finally arrived, we need to consider the reaction to the last two albums released by the Beatles, *Abbey Road* and *Let It Be*, both of which provide some context for the news of the band's split and its impact.

Contemporary Responses to *Abbey Road*

Although the Beatles recorded *Let It Be* before their work on *Abbey Road*, the fans received *Abbey Road* first and this influenced the way they would view both albums. Although Beatles aficionados and sticklers for detail insist on viewing *Abbey Road* as the last Beatles album and there are good reasons for doing so, many fans did not view it that way at the time and some were not even so sure that *Let It Be* would constitute their final release as a group. The reputation of *Abbey Road* has been hurt somewhat by some of the pronouncements made by John Lennon in the years after the album's release, mainly related to his denigration of Paul's "Maxwell's Silver Hammer" and the Medley on Side Two, although we have seen that John was completely onboard with the project from the outset. Lennon's comments seem to have originated in bitterness associated with the Beatles' breakup and resentment toward McCartney for getting too much credit for the Beatles' success in the later years of the group.

The album did receive some lackluster reviews upon its release, in addition to others that were more glowing. Disagreements among critics began with the very first song on the album, "Come Together," described by Andrew Wilson as a "boring, deliberately obscure Lennonramble." By contrast, Lon Goddard praised the song for its "excellent and subtle combination of bass, vocal hiss and piano."[12] Alan Smith called "Come Together" "probably the funkiest thing the Beatles have ever done."[13] John Mendelsohn would write in *Rolling Stone* that "'Come Together' is John Lennon very nearly at the peak of his form; twisted, freely-associative, punful lyrically, pinched and somehow a little smug vocally."[14]

Wilson, who considered the entire first side "a disaster area," went on to excoriate every song on it:

> "Something" is George Harrison at his most saccharinely, excessively sentimental; "Maxwell's Silver Hammer" is an oldtimey singalong about a lovable murderer; "Oh! Darling" is a third-rate Elvis imitation; "Octopus's Garden" is an ever-so-cute Ringo toysong; and "I Want You (She's no heavy)" is an awful eight minutes of John screaming and "heavy" guitars repeating the same riff past the point of redundancy.[15]

Other reviewers seemed not to be listening to the same songs. Goddard praised "Something" as "another beautiful Harrison composition" that leaps scales in its heavy orchestral arrangement, then drifts down to George's simple but effective guitar style," and Smith called it a "floating, aching melody, virtually about the best thing he's ever written, sadness in a crying blend of piano and strings." In Goddard's view, "drooling rock ballads have never been so good" as McCartney's "Oh! Darling" and Harrison's mellifluous "Here Comes the Sun" had an "excellent melody" that "creates one of the best atmospheres present on the record." Of the famous Medley, Mendelsohn wrote, "That the Beatles can unify seemingly countless musical fragments and lyrical doodlings into a uniformly wonderful suite, as they've done on side two, seems potent testimony that no, they've far from lost it, and no, they haven't stopped trying."

Perhaps responding to the length and complexity of the White Album, Chis Welch called *Abbey Road* "just a natural born gas, entirely free of pretension, deep meanings or symbolism."[16] Perhaps for the same reasons, Mike Jahn found the album "rather dull," though he did not seem to regard this as an entirely bad thing. "*Abbey Road* may be dull compared with *The Beatles*," he wrote, "but it is much less overloaded with the phony ostrich-plume frills that made a large portion of that album seem unnecessary."[17] Goddard thought *Abbey Road* "every bit as good as the last three." A reviewer in the *Thanet Times* concluded that the songs on *Abbey Road* "are all of the usual high standard which should see the album at the top of the LP charts immediately."[18] Alan Smith called it "beautiful blistering, music," describing the album as "something of *Revolver*" and "something all its own," saying, "It exceeds the double album and parts of it touch the heights of *Sergeant Pepper*."[19] Geoffrey Cannon considered the album's strengths and weaknesses and concluded: "*Abbey Road* contains talent comparable with any other Beatles album, but nevertheless is a slight matter. Perhaps to their own relief, the Beatles have lost the desire to touch us. You will enjoy Abbey Road. But it won't move you."[20] Mike Gormley echoed this sentiment when he wrote, "There is no doubt it's a tremendous LP, but, except for a spot here and there, they've done it all before."[21]

In short, then, the main complaint of the critics seemed to be that the Beatles had failed to surprise the public as they had done with most, if not all, of their previous albums. Here they had given their fans a nice record to listen to but not one that would revolutionize popular music as *Sgt. Pepper* had done. Gormley, for example, wrote, "On top of a very good album, we expected inventiveness. We got the good LP part." Was it asking too much for the Beatles to do more, a group that had practically defined inventiveness when it came to popular music in the decade and that had perhaps taken that as far as they could, or at least as far as they wanted to take it? Did they not have a right to go back to the type and styles of music they liked best, even as they transformed them into entirely new creations? In the light of the above criticisms of the LP, can we legitimately regard *Abbey Road* as the Beatles' best album? Has it acquired that reputation because people now know that it was the last album they ever recorded? Should we even consider these criticisms fair and accurate descriptions of the album? For example, far from seeing a lack of innovation, Chris Welch in his review wrote, "While production is simple compared to past intricacies, it is still extremely sophisticated and inventive."[22]

Were the other reviewers perhaps expecting too much from the Beatles? Jahn stated in his review, "It is much less flossy and grandiose than the Beatles' last effort, but is endlessly more satisfying for just that reason. Throughout the album the Beatles mix sweet, melodic songs featuring elaborate, sometimes overly-slick harmony, with earthy rock songs built on a heavy blues or boogie foundation."[23] Should that not have been enough? For most fans, it seems it was.

Whatever critics thought of it—and even Wilson acknowledged that the release of any Beatles album was "an event"—fans could not wait to get their hands on a copy. The album had advance sales of 190,000 copies.[24] In the United States, the album reached # 1 by October 4 and spent a total of eighty-one weeks on the *Billboard* charts, seventeen of them occupying the top of the charts. What did fans think when they received their copies? Did fans still think the Beatles as relevant as they had been in the middle years of the decade? Did the album enhance their appreciation of the group or detract from it? Nick Ercoline said that, if anything, he became a bigger fan of the group after *Abbey Road*, which became his favorite Beatles album. Explaining why he liked *Abbey Road* so much, he related the timing of the album's release to where he was in his own life:

> I think as they grew musically and [gained] maturity, that they were able to express themselves musically a little bit better than they had when they were younger. "I Want to Hold Your Hand," "She Loves You," and songs like that were geared more for sixteen-year-olds and teenyboppers. When they went through the *Sgt. Pepper* era and they started to get into the psychedelic things, it was different; it wasn't the same type of music we were used to, it wasn't your typical dance band music. It was something that you probably sat around, smoked a joint, listened to, and just grooved out on. By 1970, I was 21-years-old and certainly thinking of a lot about what was going to happen in my lifetime and I had a more mature feeling towards their music.[25]

Claude Assante said he loved the album and played it all the time once he brought home his copy. However, he did say he found "Maxwell's Silver Hammer" "a little bit disturbing," wondering why the Beatles would choose to include a song about a serial killer who commits gruesome murders on the album. Interestingly, he singled out for praise Lennon's "I Want You (She's So Heavy)," despite, or perhaps because of, its length. "I don't care how long it is," he stated. "I'm not anxious for it to end. I just sort of go with it."[26] Michael Halbreich remembered, "*Abbey Road* to me, from the moment I played the album the first time, was a beautiful rock opera. I thought it was just incredible. And I tried doing everything I could to dissect it at the time."[27] Michael McEntarfer agreed and singled out the Medley for special praise. "I loved *Abbey Road*—it was the disciplined masterpiece that The White Album and *Let It Be* could have been. The Medley on Side Two stood out immediately. Abbey Road may be their finest album."[28]

Jane Barnes said, while she would be hard-pressed to pick her favorite Beatles album, she loved all the songs on *Abbey Road* and bought it as soon as it came out. She was still very much as into the Beatles as she had been when she saw them at Comiskey Park in

Chicago a few years earlier. However, less than a year later, she said, she had lost interest in the Beatles' next LP and did not bother to obtain a copy of *Let It Be*. [29] For many Beatles fans, *Abbey Road* would be the last Beatles album, not because the group recorded it last but because it in many ways marked the culmination of their fandom much more than *Let It Be* did. Was this because Beatles fans like Barnes had outgrown the group? Were fans distancing themselves from the Beatles because of their impending breakup? Alternatively, was there something in *Let It Be* that simply made it an anticlimactic end to the Beatles' stellar career?

Let It Be

When the Beatles abruptly stopped working on the "Get Back/Let It Be" sessions, they had not decided to scrap the project completely, but merely to postpone the release of the proposed film and album until at least December. However, after the recording of *Abbey Road*, which the Beatles seemed to realize would be their swan song, they lost some interest in seeing the "Let It Be" project through to its fruition. The engineer Glyn Johns had prepared some preliminary mixes from the session, but the group did not deem these suitable for release. Although anything Lennon said later needs taking with a grain of salt, he claimed that he actually favored the release of the Glyn Johns version "because it would break the Beatles."[30] At the time, at least, no one took the idea seriously, if John did actually propose it. George Martin had absented himself from most of the sessions for *Let It Be*, which he considered unprofessional and undisciplined. He had only minimal involvement with the project, so Allen Klein brought in producer Phil Spector to apply his magic and finish off the album. However, when Spector applied his "Wall of Sound" approach to the album, the individual Beatles lost whatever connection they had left to the album as a whole, even though they all made contributions to the final product, some as late as the month before its release. Spector eliminated two songs from the mix made by Johns, including Lennon's "Don't Let Me Down," which wound up as the B-side for "Get Back," and McCartney's "Teddy Boy," which Paul included on his first solo album. Of all the Beatles, Paul disliked the finished product that resulted from Spector's heavy hand the most, perhaps because he disliked Klein so much (see below); he particularly complained about the addition of strings and backing choral arrangements to his sentimental ballad, "The Long and Winding Road." Both Lennon and Harrison seemed fine with the album as released and both asked Spector to work on future solo projects with them.

There were certainly some good songs on *Let It Be*. It was amazing, really, that the Beatles had come up with so many new songs essentially within two months of completing the voluminous White Album. Ringo particularly liked "Get Back," which he called "a kick-ass track" but his other favorite song from the sessions, "Don't Let Me Down," did not make it on to the album.[31] The album also includes Paul's soulful title track and a delightful song called "Two of Us." McCartney claimed to have written the song for his wife Linda, but the lyric obviously reflects more on his relationship with John, who sings harmony with Paul on the track. Their "voices wrapped around each other like security blankets, established a disarming performance that recalls the synergy of earlier albums," in the words of Bob Spitz.[32] The group's desire to get back to their rock and roll roots comes through in "One after 909," an early Lennon-McCartney composition that makes an agreeable appearance on the album, although the pub ditty "Maggie Mae" seems mostly filler.

In the film, the rock and roll vibe definitely comes through in their live performance on the rooftop at Savile Row, where they performed two takes of "I've Got a Feeling" and "Don't Let Me Down," in addition to "One after 909," "Dig a Pony," and three takes of "Get Back." All these songs lent themselves particularly well to live performance in contrast to the heavily dubbed material the Beatles had produced in recent years. Finally, the album also included an improvisational track called "Dig It," George's lilting and romantic "For You Blue," and John's angelic "Across the Universe," a leftover from the White Album sessions. In terms of lyrical content, the most socially relevant tracks were probably "Get Back," in which McCartney parodied words of the anti-immigrant stance of the xenophobic British politician Enoch Powell ("get back to where you once belonged") and Harrison's "I Me Mine." George said he wrote the song about the death of his ego after taking LSD, but it seems to speak to the selfish, individualistic impulses then overtaking the band, including his own. The lyric presaged the ethos of the coming decade, which author Tom Wolfe later dubbed the period of "the me generation."

The Beatles allowed the release of the film documentary, *Let It Be*, directed by Michael Lindsay-Hogg, in order to fulfill their commitment to United Artists, which had deemed the group's involvement with *Yellow Submarine* insufficient to count toward their contractual obligation. It is certainly unique among Beatles films in that the film simply shows the Beatles rehearsing and playing music in the studio, ending with their famous rooftop concert at their Apple headquarters in London. The film focuses mainly on Paul and John, with occasional shots of George, Ringo, and Yoko. In fact, Yoko gets a great deal of screen time, probably because she never left John's side so that it was nearly impossible to film one without the other, although some shots do focus on her exclusively as if she were another member of the band. Unlike in the recording sessions for the White Album, however, Yoko made no positive contributions to the songs that would appear on this album, according to Lennon biographer Tim Riley.[33] George appears somewhat surly while Ringo just looks bored. Harrison, who at one point left the group during the sessions, took umbrage at both the constant presence of Yoko by John's side and what he perceived as Paul's overbearing bossiness. The film includes one scene of John and Yoko making out and another of the couple dancing while George plays "I Me Mine." Paul appears enthusiastic throughout, even on George's songs "I Me Mine" and "For You Blue." John actually seems surprisingly engaged on most of the numbers. However, he has lost much of his past bravado, while his disheveled and emaciated appearance framed by his long untended hair makes him a curious rather than a commanding figure. McCartney's role as the leader of the band seems clear in the film, although he has also let himself go a bit, having gained some weight and let his hair and untrimmed beard grow out.

Billy Preston, an accomplished keyboardist whom the Beatles had first met in Hamburg, always looks like he is having a good time jamming with the most famous band in the world. In the words of George Martin, "Billy Preston was a great help and a very good keyboard guy, and his work on 'Get Back' alone justified him being there."[34] Preston's contribution was especially important to the sound of the band since the Beatles had decided to eschew overdubs and studio trickery for the sound on the album. There was no question, however, of Preston officially joining the Beatles; as Bob Spitz points out, "there was no room in the band for a 'fifth Beatle' … The Beatles had a legacy to protect."

The band plays over two dozen songs in the film, ranging from "Be-Bop-a-Lula" and "If I Fell" to "Give Peace a Chance" and "Maxwell's Silver Hammer." The film includes songs from both *Sgt. Pepper* and the White Album and still only represents a tiny fraction of the music the Beatles wrote and played that month. Walter Everett and Tim Riley have identified 249 songs, including fifty-two new compositions the group played in January 1969.[35] In short, Lindsay-Hogg ended up directing a new kind of documentary with no narration or structure, other than its culmination in the rooftop concert, that provides a fascinating look at the Beatles at work with very little pretense or artifice. One of the best parts of the film is seeing the reactions of passersby and people in the neighborhood, including a number of befuddled constables, when they realize the Beatles are playing on the roof. One well-dressed, middle-aged man, oblivious to the historical importance of the moment, regards it as "quite an imposition to disrupt all the businesses in the area."

If the film broke some new ground, however, the album failed to do so. As Stephanie Fremaux points out, the filming of the sessions had an effect on the recording process and ultimately on the resulting album. It also, she argues, contributed to the band's breakup:

> And rather than capture the band working more naturally as individuals or pairs in the studio, the artificial nature of the space (Twickenham film studios in London) and the façade of the band all rehearsing and collaborating together at the same time, in the same room, like they used to do, starts to force the cracks in the group's already fragile unity.[36]

If *Abbey Road* drew some criticism for its lack of innovation, the critics at least split on that issue, whereas *Let It Be* represented a kind of hodgepodge that displayed some of the strengths of the Beatles and included a few iconic songs but did nothing to steer music in a new direction.

This does make it a bad album in the same way that most of the reviewers who criticized *Abbey Road* for not living up to the Beatles' previously high standards still thought it a good album. *Let It Be* was made by a band whose members each already had one foot out the door and even the joy that they could obviously still find in making music together became a rarer event and not enough to heal relationships on the verge of fracturing. They pulled together to make *Abbey Road* after they had recorded *Let It Be*, but the feeling the former would probably be the last album they would make together made it easier for them than during the filming and recording of *Let It Be*, which, as Fremaux pointed out, forced a togetherness that they no longer felt. At least, with the making of *Abbey Road*, they could go back to working individually or in smaller combinations for much of the time. By the time that the group released *Let It Be*, the 1960s had ended, the Beatles had broken up, and *Abbey Road* had been an enormously satisfying effort to most Beatle fans. Therefore, the response to *Let It Be* came in a context entirely different from that of any previous Beatles album.

Contemporary Responses to *Let It Be*

The Beatles released the album *Let it Be* on May 8, 1970; the film came out five days later in the United States and twelve days later in the UK. Two months earlier, on March 6, they had released "Let It Be" as a single, with the novelty song, "You Know My Name" (Look up the Number) as the B-side. As for the album, Paul McCartney was not the only one who thought Phil Spector had done the Beatles a disservice by overproducing the album. John Mendelsohn in his review for *Rolling Stone* wrote that Spector had transformed several "rough gems" on what he thought could have been "the best Beatles album in ages" into "costume jewelry." Mendelsohn also echoed Paul's complaint about what Spector had done to "The Long and Winding Road." He described it as

> virtually unlistenable with hideously cloying strings and a ridiculous choir that serve only to accentuate the listlessness of Paul's vocal and the song's potential for further mutilation at the hands of the countless schlock-mongers who will undoubtedly trip all over one another in their haste to cover it. A slightly lesser chapter in the ongoing story of McCartney as facile romanticist, it might have eventually begun to grow on one as unassumingly charming, had not Spector felt compelled to transform an apparently early take into an extravaganza of oppressive mush. [37]

Alan Smith of *New Musical Express*, correctly assuming this would be the last Beatles album, called *Let it Be* "a cheapskate epitaph, a cardboard tombstone, a sad and tatty end to a musical fusion which wiped clean and drew again the face of pop music." He asked, "Can this minicollection of new tracks, narcissistic pin-ups and chocolate box dressing really be the last will and testament of the once-respected and most-famous group in the world?" Smith took particular issues with the inclusion of such throwaways as "Maggie Mae" and "Dig It" on the album, in addition to three previously released songs ("Get Back," "Let It Be," and "Across the Universe").[38]

Among Beatles fans, Alan Chevat remembered thinking that the Beatles' last album paled in comparison with the Rolling Stones' *Let It Bleed*, which they had released the previous December. He said by 1970 many in his circle of friends at Stony Brook University had tired of the Beatles, thinking they had become too soft.[39] Chevat indicated that he had no trouble shifting his musical allegiance to the Rolling Stones and the Grateful Dead around the time the Beatles broke up, highlighted by what he saw as the difference between the edgier *Let It Bleed* and the more conventional mix of soft rock and rock and roll songs on *Let It Be*. Michael McEntarfer looked at the album more from the perspective of someone who had played music professionally and found the album wanting. "I'm not a fan of the little asides and fragments of songs that fall in between the otherwise great songs. ... It's messy and that bugs me." He added, however, "My wife is four years younger than me and *Let it Be* was her first Beatles experience and it's her favorite."[40]

Deirdre McEntarfer was not alone in her favorable impression of the album. A review in the *New York Times* opined that the lyric of the song "Let It Be" had taken "rock and the Beatles into a new era," while finding that of "Across the Universe" equally compelling.[41] Michael Halbreich called *Let It Be* "a beautiful album" and said he found some of the songs on it "absolutely magnificent." Halbreich considered *Let It Be* one of his favorite albums, though he did think it unfortunate that it came out after *Abbey Road* because of the presumption of many fans that the last Beatles album should be their best one and the heavy burden this placed on it.[42] James Vignapiano called *Let It Be* "a tremendous album" and particularly liked that the Beatles had returned to their familiar rock and roll roots.[43] Len Pniewski recalled that he liked the later Beatles albums, including *Let It Be*, just as much as their earlier albums.[44]

As for the film, it also received some mixed reaction. As hard as the reviewer Alan Smith was on the album, he was much more enamored with the film *Let It Be*. He calls it "a sharp and fascinating insight into the minds of the Beatles and the finest musical excursion they have ever committed to film," advising that "no fan, follower, listener or committed or casual voyeur of the Beatles" should miss it.[45] The *Acton Gazette* agreed, suggesting that all Beatles fans should see the film if for no other reason than "it may be the last occasion we see these four masters of music together again."[46] A review that appeared in the *New York Times* described the film as "none too artfully made," but the reviewer found the film "arresting" nonetheless. The reviewer praised the music in the film in particular. However, he also observed, "The very helter-skelter, unstudied nature of the picture provides a revealing close-up of the world's most famous quartet, playing, relaxing and chatting."[47] Smith even used his review to highlight the inadequacy and weakness of the album compared to the quality of the music that appeared in the film.

Vignapiano, who played in a band, said he watched the film and could tell just by the way the Beatles were looking at each other during the rooftop concert that they knew they were not going to continue to play together much longer. He thought that realization enabled them to commit to rocking and rolling the way they did in that mini-concert. The time gap between that concert and the release of the film, by which time fans were more aware of the impending breakup of the band, might have influenced Vignapiano's impression when he watched the film.

Others thought they could tell the band was breaking up just by listening to the album. *The New York Times* review stated:

> Interestingly enough, from all the wealth of choice implied in this free-association music, the core sadness of the album lies in its references to being lost, trains, traveling, and, as in the blues poetry of early twentieth-century Northbound

blacks, long roads. Even the harmonies of "Winding Road" wander tellingly along like water down a pane to resolve home at last on the words "your door."[48]

Writing in the school newspaper at the University of California in San Francisco, a student named Michael Jackson came to one conclusion after listening to *Let It Be*: the Beatles were through. Unlike the individual nature of the tracks that many listeners heard on the White Album, however, Jackson thought this message came loud and through in the lyrics of the songs, especially "Get Back," "For You Blue," and "Two of Us." "This is what they've been leading up to for the past six years—they are now alone with themselves," Jackson wrote.[49]

The Beatles Break Up and the Fans React

Once historians know that some particular event has occurred, they find it too convenient to search the past and find causes or explanations for the inevitability of that event, which often actually hinges on contingent factors unique to the immediate period when the event occurs. This is a fair criticism, one leveled at historians by Nassim Taleb in his 2007 book *The Black Swan: The Impact of the Highly Improbable*. Historians thus need to be careful in assessing the long-range causes of events, whether dealing with wars, revolutions, or the breakup of rock groups.

Yet Taleb's concept of a "black swan," which has since entered the lexicon as a highly improbable event that no one could have predicted in advance, may not apply to the breakup of the Beatles, which, as devastating as it was to fans, might have actually occurred even sooner than it did. "Bands tend to devolve," David Crosby said in a recent interview, discussing the breakup of other bands from the period such as Buffalo Springfield and his own group, the Byrds.[50] The legendary record producer Clive Davis said, "Nobody expects groups to stay together except the group and their fans. The managers, the professionals—they know those groups aren't going to stay together."[51]

In retrospect, it is easy to make much of the relatively short time that the Beatles were together, especially when compared with the longevity of groups like the Rolling Stones and the Who, which lasted decades. However, for the Beatles themselves, it seemed like they were together for a very long time and a better question than what led to their breakup might be how they managed to hold together for as long as they did given all the fissiparous forces that threatened to pull them apart. John Lennon said as much when he stated,

> I've compared it to a marriage a million times, and I hope it's understandable for people that aren't married or in any relationship. It was a long relationship. It started many, many years before the American public or the English public knew us. Paul and I were together since he was fifteen and I was sixteen.[52]

Nevertheless, there were clearly specific factors that contributed to the breakup of the Beatles, as natural an occurrence as this might have been. Certainly, one cause of the Beatles' breakup—perhaps the main cause—was the desire of each of the Beatles to pursue their own solo careers, at least Paul, John, and George. In the case of Ringo, he may have simply recognized the warning signs and decided he had better get busy with his own projects and songwriting to prepare for a post-Beatles career. By the time *Let It Be* came out in May, Paul had already released his first solo album, *McCartney*, as had Ringo (*Sentimental Journey*). John had already released the controversial *Two Virgins* with Yoko, as well as a live album and two singles, "Instant Karma (We All Shine On)" and "Cold Turkey," with the Plastic Ono Band. Aside from Ringo, Larry Kane suggests that, remarkably, each of the other three Beatles thought the group was holding them back. "John, Paul, and George all believed that they could do better alone," he said.[53]

Many people today would scoff at that idea, but when Jann Wenner asked McCartney in 1970 if he had any songs on his new solo album that were as good as "Let It Be" or "Hey Jude," Paul's response was, "I can never tell. But I know that on this record there are some great tracks."[54] However, even at the time, a reviewer in *Time* magazine found on Paul's solo album, *McCartney*, "nothing to match his past pop classics, particularly 'Yesterday', 'Michelle', and 'Hey Jude'."[55] A reviewer for the *Daily Mirror* did see enough promise though, to think, "Paul will, at some time or another, write some great new compositions to compare with 'Yesterday'."[56]

The desire to pursue solo careers may have led the Beatles to decide to go their separate ways regardless of the numerous other factors frequently cited to explain their breakup. Even if this is true, however, the breakup could have been far more amicable and perhaps delayed at least a bit longer had personal and business relationships not started to fray among them. In his book on creative partnerships, *The Powers of Two*, Joshua Wolf Shenk identifies two types of causes that contribute to the end of a relationship, which he calls wedges and stumbles. He defines a wedge as "whatever gets between two people or exacerbates an ongoing challenge,"[57] while stumbles result from the inability of the pair to clear obstacles that might stand in the way of their path. The main source of friction came from the Beatles' need for a new manager, with George and Ringo siding with John in his predilection to hire Allen Klein, who had previously managed the Rolling Stones, while Paul favored Linda's father, Lee Eastman, and was adamantly opposed to Klein. In an interview with Jann Wenner of *Rolling Stone* published on April 30, McCartney bluntly stated, "The thing is that I am not signed with Allen Klein because I don't like him and I don't think he is the man for me however much the other three like him."[58] Shenk thinks the most common wedge that comes between two people is a third person; while many at the time and since have seen Yoko as the person who came between Paul and John, in reality the person who formed the main wedge in their relationship was actually Allen Klein.

While Yoko, then, was not the decisive wedge that broke up the band, her presence in the studio and her tendency to insert her input into the recording process, which had always been taboo for the Beatles, certainly did create additional tension. Outside the studio, Paul got along well with Yoko and he had no objections to John's relationship with her, except perhaps subliminally based on his own previous closeness with John. Besides, McCartney had also gotten married and was starting a new life, so his relationship with

Linda was at least as responsible as John's relationship with Yoko for the split between the two Beatles, based on the simple fact that the two men had now embarked upon separate lives with the people with whom they had fallen in love. In 1970, when Paul was asked why the Beatles were breaking up, he replied, "Personal differences, business differences, musical differences, but most of all because I have a better time with my family."

Even so, Paul hedged his bets. When asked whether he was starting a new solo career or merely taking a rest from the Beatles, he replied, "I don't know. Time will tell. Being a solo album means it's the 'start of a solo career'—and not being done with the Beatles

Figure 10.1 *Paul and Linda McCartney on their lonely farm near the fishing town of Campbeltown, the day after McCartney started High Court proceedings to seal the final breakup of the Beatles, January 5, 1970. Courtesy of Getty Images.*

means it's a rest. So it's both."⁵⁹ As previously stated, Paul simply could not abide Klein nor could he ever understand why John had become so infatuated with him to the point that he put their friendship and the future of the band at risk because of him. This raises the possibility that not Klein, but Lennon was the main immediate culprit in the breakup, as suggested by writer Dominic Sandbrook. Sandbrook wrote, "In the end, though, it was John Lennon who broke up the Beatles. ... Many of his friends thought that Ono brought out Lennon's worst qualities, exacerbating his already considerable egotism and self-absorption, but he would not hear a word against her."⁶⁰ Mikal Gilmore, writing about the Beatles' breakup in *Rolling Stone* in 2009, agrees. According to Gilmore:

> John Lennon—who until *Abbey Road* and *Let It Be* had written most of the Beatles' masterpieces and defined their greatest depths—could no longer bear to divide up his brilliance with Paul McCartney. The Beatles could withstand whatever tensions Yoko Ono brought them. They might have endured Allen Klein. But the Beatles could not survive John Lennon. His anxiety was simply too vast.⁶¹

These perspectives suggest the possibility that John's insistence that the Beatles hire Klein for their manager was the symptom rather than the cause of his fallout with Paul.

Lennon's growing animosity toward McCartney could have been rooted in his partner's growing leadership role within the band, usurping the position once held by John, and the accompanying credit Paul increasingly received for the Beatles' success. Thus, another source of friction involved Paul's control over the group and creative differences about what they would record. For example, McCartney had refused to consider putting Lennon's song "Cold Turkey" on a Beatles album, even though John had lobbied him to do so. Paul did not think the song, which deals with Lennon's method of attempting to overcome his heroin addiction, fit the Beatles' image, but to John's mind they had long before started to put individual tracks on their albums and he did not think Paul should treat this one any differently.⁶² In addition, George had long bristled at his tertiary role within the group and had no desire to continue to perform in the shadow of Lennon and McCartney, neither of whom had ever deigned either to write songs with him or to include him in their exclusive songwriting partnership. Many of these issues predated the dispute over who would manage the Beatles, which merely proved to be a tipping point.

In fact, the need for a new manager had arisen in the first place in the context of the dubious business practices at Apple, the corporation the Beatles had decided to establish to assert control over their financial affairs in the aftermath of Brian Epstein's death. Instead of allowing Robert Stigwood to step in, the Beatles decided they would be better off running things on their own. Epstein had made Stigwood a partner to manage some of his other acts and Stigwood had expected to assume control over the Beatles when Epstein died. Unfortunately, the Beatles lacked the experience to run a business on their own. Too many hangers-on and individuals who simply did not have the Beatles' best interests at heart had managed to enmesh themselves in the daily operations of Apple Corps, which soon began hemorrhaging money. Nor was their attempt to establish a concomitant Apple Foundation for the Arts much more successful, despite its support of talents like James Taylor and Mary Hopkin. As George's wife Pattie Boyd tells it, "The offices were bombarded with every manner of artistic endeavor—not just tapes, but clothing, paintings, drawings, novels, plays, poems, sculpture, designs—everything you could think of—and most of it was rubbish."[63] In short, Epstein's death had caused the Beatles to stumble and they never quite managed to get past it as a group, partly because he was the one neutral arbiter of disputes among the Beatles. In addition, although he made a number of bad business deals that cost the Beatles a great deal of money, he at least spared them from handling business themselves, something at which they proved ill-equipped to do despite their best intentions and hard work. The frustrations born of this business dispute seeped into their personal relationships; it seems Paul could not be bothered to attend George's twenty-sixth birthday celebration at the Harrisons' new home at Friar Park. John and Ringo, however, both attended.[64]

Despite these and other indications that the individual Beatles did not see themselves as a group, the news of their breakup still came as a jolt to millions of fans around the world. Paul officially announced the breakup of the group in an interview that appeared in papers on April 10, in which he also stated that he could not foresee a time when he and John would resume writing songs together. *Time* magazine, reporting on the breakup, supposed "England might have been less shocked to find Buckingham Palace transformed into the Royal Arms Motel."[65] Nick Ercoline recalled, "At first, I didn't believe it, probably because how can you break something that was so successful?" "That's kind of crazy," he thought to himself.[66] Michael Halbreich compared the breakup of the Beatles to a death in the family. "It rips your heart out," he said. "You knew something very important that will never be again had been taken from us."[67] Larry Kane, who despite his friendship with the Beatles has always tried to maintain a reporter's objectivity in discussing them, when asked to remember his reaction to the Beatles' breakup, said simply, "I was very sad; I thought they would never break up." He quickly qualified that statement by saying that maybe in that last year he did, but not the group he had known in the mid-1960s.[68]

Of course, by 1970 the Beatles were no longer the same group they had been, nor were the individual Beatles the same. Perhaps even more importantly, the times had changed as well. Jane Barnes harked back to that time and said, "I can remember the first time I heard that rumor I was pretty much in disbelief. Somebody told us and I was like 'oh no, no, no that's not gonna happen, that couldn't happen, they wouldn't do that.' Then when it became reality it felt almost to me like the end of an era." Her reaction probably mirrored those of millions of fans, disappointed but not devastated by the news. However, Barnes continued, saying, "I was a senior in high school [in 1970] and I had been following them from sixth grade, but I was beginning to transition at that point and so I thought, 'well, this is part of life and [it was time to] move on to something else. I was saddened by it but I wasn't distraught over it.'"[69]

In *The Powers of Two*, Shenk questions whether creative partnerships ever truly break up, based on the idea that their legacy continues in the products they created that continue to exercise an influence on others in perpetuity. George Harrison suggested as much when he said, "The Beatles can't ever really split up because as we said at the time we did split up, it doesn't really make any difference. The music is there, the films are all there. Whatever we did is still there and it always will be."[70] James Vignapiano explains, however, why such an explanation would not have satisfied Beatles fans at the time. At 20 years of age, he was mature enough, like Barnes, to handle the news of the breakup of his favorite band, but he still mourned the loss of the additional great music they might have made together. He describes his reaction and that of others he knew:

> Look at the volume of stuff that these guys put out, and their talent and the writing and the different types of music and then all of a sudden after six years it just ended. It bothered us, it bothered people who I knew, it bothered fellow musicians I knew, people who were Beatles fans. We didn't have another album to look forward to in another two or four months; that stopped. The music was still there, of course, and you could still listen to [their] music but waiting for the new chapter, waiting on what they were going to do next—that was over. So yeah, [the breakup] bothered a lot of people. In the 60s there were plenty of bands, but as far as the Beatles went, it did bother people that we had six years and then it was over.[71]

Vignapiano is right, of course, about the Beatles' contribution to popular music in an era when it exercised an outsized influence on culture and society, but in addition, the breakup of the Beatles went beyond just the absence of a single musical group in a period full of them. The Beatles had been a conspicuous presence at a time of tremendous social and cultural change, much of which they had helped to shape or even create.

Having said that, it is clear that the breakup did not affect all fans the same way. For everyone who felt disappointed or even devastated, others did not quite go along with the apotheosis of the group that appears in the remembrances of many fans from the time. "At that point, I didn't really care," Alan Chevat said, when asked how he reacted at the time to the news of the breakup. "I was getting into more edgy stuff," he remembered.[72] Len Pniewski said, "Certainly, I felt bad. But it was inevitable. They were all going their separate directions, they had changed musically, and certainly [their] personal lives were involved."[73] Ivan Bell stated, "It didn't upset me, but I was 19-years-old so I didn't really have any empathy or anger if any of the Beatles were going off and doing their own thing." However, he did remember others who felt differently, adding, "I recall that people were crying in the streets that 'Oh my God how can The Beatles break up?' "[74]

Another possible factor in the Beatles' breakup derives from a theory that arose at the time and has drawn attention from at least some more recent writers: the trend away from the collective mentality that appealed to the young generation in the more idealistic decade of the 1960s toward a more individualistic, cynical worldview that young people tended to adopt in the 1970s. Astonishingly, this interpretation existed as early as April 1970 when an article in *Time* magazine on the Beatles' breakup took note of "a de-escalation of what might be called rock music's group consciousness and a rising enthusiasm for solo artistry."[75] If this trend began even before the dissolution of the Beatles, their breakup must surely have contributed to it, given the outsized influence the group had exercised over popular culture for the past eight years. In the 1960s, "everyone thought of the group as the strongest unit for success," according to Clive Davis.[76] By 1970, there were already indications that this was no longer the case. In addition to the Beatles, Paul Simon and Art Garfunkel had split up to pursue solo careers, while singer-songwriters such as James Taylor, Carly Simon, Joni Mitchell, Jackson Browne, and Carole King soon began to dominate the pop charts. Crosby, Stills, Nash, and Young would retain their individual names as part of their new super-group, and each would release multiple solo albums in the 1970s in addition to the work they did in various combinations with one another. David Browne writes about this development in his book, *Fire and Rain: The Beatles, Simon & Garfunkel, James Taylor, CSNY, and the Lost Story of 1970*. He traces the decline of group albums, including the Beatles' *Let It Be*, and the rise of solo albums, including those by individual members of the Beatles on the charts that year. In his opinion, "The rise of the solo album embodied the new self-reliance and self-absorption: the I Don't Need Anyone Else But Myself, Thanks, statement."[77] By the middle of the decade, rock critic Greil Marcus would write, "What, in the sixties, looked like a chance to find new forms of political life, has been replaced by a flight to privacy and cynicism; the shared culture that grew out of a love affair with the Beatles has collapsed (not without their help) into nostalgia and crackpot religion."[78] The dissatisfaction many people had started to feel toward the new decade perhaps reinforced this nostalgia for the 1960s and nurtured the hopes that the Beatles might get back together. It also affected fans' response to the solo careers of the individual Beatles and fueled their search for groups who might aspire to become their successors.

CONCLUSION
POST-1960S POLITICS AND THE ABSENCE OF THE BEATLES

The Morass of the 1970s

On April 29, 1970, nine days before the Beatles released *Let It Be*, the United States launched an invasion of Cambodia, representing an expansion of the Vietnam War. At this point, a majority of the American public still supported President Richard M. Nixon and trusted him to conclude the war successfully. Both the actions of the Nixon administration in Southeast Asia and the continued support for them by a large swathe of the American people led dissenters to despair and further exacerbated the divisions within the country. Then, on May 4, the National Guard fired on student protesters attacking the reserve officers training building on the campus of Kent State University in Ohio. They shot thirteen students, four of whom died. Ten days later on May 14, police opened fire on Black protesters at Jackson State University in Mississippi, killing two and wounding twelve. Ivan Bell said the Kent State shootings drove him "into a fury" and that college students began to realize the strength and nature of the forces confronting them. However, he said he also realized "that there were students all across the country, across the world at that point who were standing up. I felt proud that I had made my voice known and I also knew that it is the youth on college campuses that was the oven that cooks a lot of protests and radical movements."[1] Bell certainly was not alone; demonstrations erupted at over four hundred colleges and universities and 100,000 people marched in Washington in protest against the killings.

Meanwhile, even as Nixon and the chief architect of his policy in Vietnam, Secretary of State Henry Kissinger, ostensibly moved toward peace, they did so while alternating overtures toward negotiations with the Viet Minh with a scorched earth policy that drew comparisons with the Thirty Years War that devastated seventeenth-century Germany. The number of bombs dropped and the damage they caused actually increased in the later years of the war, approaching the kind of destruction witnessed in cities like Dresden toward the end of the Second World War. For example, US bombing in 1972–3 practically destroyed Hanoi, the capital of North Vietnam.

In Britain, Nixon's strategy in Vietnam posed no less a dilemma for the government of the Conservative Prime Minister Ted Heath (1970–74) than it had for his predecessor, Harold Wilson. Wilson had continued to believe Nixon's assurances the United States would leave Vietnam by 1972—assurances Heath inherited but without a real fallback plan should those promises not materialize. Although in Britain the large-scale demonstrations of the 1960s had died down, Heath still could afford neither to alienate the United States nor to seem too supportive of its actions in Cambodia and

Vietnam that remained deeply unpopular with the British electorate. In May 1972, a group of thirty MPs, academics, and trade union leaders signed a telegram delivered to the American ambassador in London calling for the United States to withdraw from Vietnam. The statement read, "We demand now an end to American aggression in Vietnam; a stop to the bombing; the withdrawal of all American military forces and a peaceful settlement that allows the Vietnamese people to govern themselves in peace, freedom and democracy."[2] Such acts may not have had a large effect, but, combined with continued dissent at home, they did serve as a reminder of how deeply unpopular this war had become.

Given the way in which Vietnam had put such an enormous strain on Lyndon Johnson during his presidency and caused him to drop out of the race for reelection in 1968, it is perhaps somewhat surprising that Richard Nixon survived the continuation of the war through his first term. American actions in Southeast Asia during his presidency had only widened divisions within the country, which at times seemed at the point of unraveling. Nixon, however, continued to tap into concerns about law and order among the electorate that had helped him win in 1968. His landslide victory over George McGovern in 1972 constituted part of the backlash against the excesses of the 1960s that would last into the 1980s and beyond. Many people in both Britain and the United States felt that they had had enough of the eccentricities of youth and their confrontational stance toward both the political establishment and traditional social mores. Little did they know in the early 1970s how much more rebellious youth could become and the ways in which some young people in the punk movement would be dressing and adorning themselves by the end of the decade.

Although the Vietnam War wound down to its ignominious end by 1975, its exorbitant costs had exacted a heavy toll on the US economy, which became afflicted with high inflation rates throughout the decade. Meanwhile, an oil embargo imposed by the Arab states in 1973 doubled the price of a valuable commodity essential to American prosperity and the country's way of life, meaning gas shortages and the beginning of the so-called energy crisis. The cost of living doubled between 1970 and 1979, by which time interest rates had risen to almost 20 percent and unemployment to almost 8 percent.[3] Economic conditions were even worse in Britain where labor strife led to an industrial crisis, weakening its already declining economic position. In 1972 alone, strikes resulted in the loss of an estimated 23 million working days, the largest number since 1926, the year of a General Strike.

In addition to the economic downturn and the dragging on of the Vietnam War, the Watergate scandal that resulted in the downfall of Richard Nixon, who resigned on August 8, 1974—the only president in history to do so—created further disillusion and cynicism, especially among young people. Although the new president, Gerald Ford, pardoned Nixon for his crimes, many of the conspirators and high-level officials from the Nixon White House did go to jail, including his attorney general, John Mitchell, who served nineteen months in prison. Yet these developments only confirmed what many people felt a few years earlier with the onset of a new decade. In 1971, John Lennon said, "The dream is over. I'm not just talking about the Beatles. I'm talking about the generation thing. It's over, and we gotta—I have personally gotta—get down to so-called reality."[4] However, when a new generation turned their heads toward reality, they did not like what they saw any better than their counterparts in the previous decade had.

Youth politics went to two extremes in the 1970s. Left-wing political groups became more radical in the 1970s; the more extremist groups included the Baader-Meinhof gang in West Germany, the Red Brigades in Italy, and the Weather Underground in the United States. However, a kind of reactionary sentiment also set in, even among youth, who sought to revive the angry energy of the youth rebellion that gave rise to rock and roll in the first place in the 1950s. In Britain, a resurgence of the Teddy Boys became a phenomenon of angry youths imitating their counterparts from that earlier era, who had dressed in costumes emanating from the early twentieth century. The Teddy Boys of the early 1970s served as a precursor to the emergence of punk rock later in the decade. Writing in *Rolling Stone* in March 1972, Jerry Hopkins estimated the number of Teddy Boys in England at that time as perhaps twenty thousand. Hopkins equated this revival with a desire on the part of young people to return to what seemed like the relatively simpler times of the 1950s, including the music of the period. That meant returning to more primitive or original rock and roll *before the Beatles*. Hopkins quoted one Teddy Boy as saying, "We bloody loathed the Beatles. They absolutely murdered all the originals—Carl Perkins' 'Matchbox,' 'Long Tall Sally,' the rest. We remembered how much better the originals were."[5]

A key moment in 1970s Britain occurred on January 12, 1976, when the quintessential punk rock group the Sex Pistols made a profanity-laced appearance on the television show, *Today*, hosted by Bill Grundy. As raunchy as John Lennon could be in private, he never went nearly so far in thumbing his nose at the establishment as the Sex Pistols did in this episode, which made his comments comparing the Beatles' popularity to Jesus look like nothing. Grundy would tell the group after their appearance, "I never want to see you again," though the feeling was probably mutual. Although the Sex Pistols would soon implode as a group because of their self-destructive tendencies, they became a galvanizing force for the most significant movement in rock music in the decade. Writing a year-end review of the music scene of 1977, Carol Clerk described it as "the year when punk rock and the new wave grabbed the business by its throat and shook the living daylights out of it."[6] The Sex Pistols had been joined by successful punk rock bands, including the American band the Ramones and English bands like the Clash and the Damned, who included a cover version of the Beatles' "Help!" among their repertoire.

The Conservative Party victory that elevated Margaret Thatcher to the position of prime minister in the UK in 1979 and the election of the conservative Republican Ronald Reagan as US president in 1980 seemed to mark a decisive defeat for values championed by many young people in the 1960s. Many conservative people in both countries shared a feeling that parents, teachers, and society in general had become far too permissive. They felt this had led to a lack of rules or standards necessary to hold families and the social fabric together. However, the social changes of the 1960s proved longer lasting and more resilient than the developments discussed so far in this chapter would imply. Despite the economic downturn, the boom of the 1960s still provided a rise in the standard of

The Beatles and the 1960s

living for most people who lived through the 1970s in the West far above what most people had known in the 1950s, not to mention how bad conditions were in the 1930s or 1940s. Furthermore, civil rights legislation in the United States, the decriminalization of homosexuality in Britain, legislation making divorce easier and the loss of some of the stigma associated with it, and changes in hairstyles and dress codes for men and women were just some of the many social changes that did not disappear at the end of the decade. The 1960s also brought greater levels of sexual freedom and the beginnings of a women's movement, not to mention the mainstream acceptance of marijuana for recreational use. As Arthur Marwick stated about the trend toward conservative politics by the end of the 1970s, "whatever the political changes, the consequences of what happened in the sixties were long-lasting; the sixties cultural revolution in effect established the enduring cultural values and social behavior for the rest of the century."[7]

The Beatles Go Their Separate Ways

Even though the Beatles broke up in 1970 and all four Beatles had highly visible solo careers in the succeeding decade, it did not take long for nostalgia to kick in as the demand for the music of the Beatles as a group remained high. The show "Beatlemania" opened on Broadway in March 1977 and ran for 1,006 performances until it closed in October 1979. A 28-year-old Beatle fan wrote to Marc Catone in 1982, "When you consider that a bunch of clones can go on stage and pack them in as the show, 'Beatlemania,' has (and in a poor way, one I disapprove of) that proves that The Beatles could still marshal people and their imaginations."[8] For true Beatles fans who had been around for their career, there could be no mere substitute for the real thing. If it took until 1977 for imitation-Beatles to take the stage, it was because for most of the decade fans kept hoping for the real thing: that the Beatles would reunite and that the dream had not ended with *Let It Be*.

The possibility that the Beatles might reunite became one of the biggest nonstories of the decade. People and the press constantly speculated about the prospects of a Beatles reunion, with each of the individual Beatles asked about the subject in almost every interview they gave. Journalists, disk jockeys, and fans then carefully parsed and scrutinized each word said on the subject to see if it raised the percentage of the likelihood upward or downward. Paul was perhaps most coy about it, but even John failed to rule it out on a number of occasions. Ringo probably would have been amenable, but George, finally out of the shadow of Lennon and McCartney, turned out to be the least inclined to entertain the possibility. Paul and John, at least, came close to reuniting following a famous segment on *Saturday Night Live* on April 24, 1976, in which producer Lorne Michaels offered the Beatles $3,000 to appear on the show. McCartney and Lennon happened to be watching the show together at John and Yoko's apartment, where Paul and Linda were visiting. They briefly considered going down to the studio that night before deciding it was probably too late to do so.

However much Beatles fans longed for such a reunion—and there is no doubt that they did, quite fervently—most of them eventually learned to go on with their lives and perhaps even to understand the reasons why a reunion might not happen and might not even be a good idea. Opinions varied; most Beatles fans thought that whatever they might do together again would be fantastic. However, Beatles fan Mark Angellini said, "I thought eventually they'd get over it [and] eventually do another record. Of course, since then I've come to realize they really couldn't. All they could do is rehash anything they've done and what would be the point?"[9] Wade Lawrence remembered, "I think the whole world expected them to [reunite]. We couldn't imagine a world without the Beatles, but then some of their solo projects were spectacular successes." Lawrence also noted, however, that other of their solo projects "were spectacular failures."[10]

John Lennon remained the most politically engaged of the four Beatles during the 1970s, though more so earlier in the decade when he wrote songs such as "Power to the People," "Imagine," and "Working Class Hero." He also continued to wrestle with his personal demons, writing about his parents in the song "Mother," his disenchantment with all forms of religion in "God," and his fractured relationship with Paul McCartney in "How Do You Sleep?" In addition, though, he still wrote love songs to Yoko such as "Oh Yoko!" and about love more generally as in "Jealous Guy," both of which appeared on his 1971 album, *Imagine*. Alan Smith gave the album a glowing review in *New Musical Express*, calling it "superb. Beautiful. One step away from the chill of his recent total self-revelation, and yet a giant leap towards commerciality without compromise. The songs have structure, direction and melody; guts, sensitivity and class."[11] John himself thought the album one of the best things he had ever done, and deservedly so. Smith attributes the success of the album though to the fact that McCartney's influence pervades the album, supporting Shenk's idea that the pair had never really broken up. Both John and Paul would testify to the inner critic in their head belonging to their former partner that helped make their music better and push it away from the exaggerated tendencies each often fell prone to on their own—Paul to the more saccharine side of pop and John to the rougher edges of rock. John believed that whenever he did something good, it raised the stakes for Paul and pushed him to do something as good or better, so that both careers in fact did continue to benefit from the rivalry between the two. Although there were significant gaps in Lennon's recording career in the 1970s, he still produced an enviable body of work and ended on a high note with an album he did with Yoko in 1980 called *Double Fantasy*—tragically the last album he would have a chance to record.

From the very beginning of Paul McCartney's solo career with the release of 1970's *McCartney*, critics compared his work with that of the Beatles and found it wanting. In *Rolling Stone*, Landon Winner called it "distinctly second-rate" and Richard Williams criticized the album for its "sheer banality," with the exception of the standout "Maybe I'm Amazed."[12] It is unclear if such reviews shattered McCartney's confidence, but he withdrew to his farm in Scotland, fell into a deep depression, and spent his time grappling with what he would do with the rest of his life now that he was no longer in the Beatles. It seems that he needed to mourn the loss of his bandmates and cope with losing the one signifier that had given him his identity for the past decade or more—that of being a Beatle. In Paul's own words:

> It was a pretty good job to have lost—The Beatles. My whole life since I'd been seventeen had been wrapped up in it; so it was quite a shock. I took to my bed, didn't bother shaving much, did a lot of drinking. "What's it matter?" you know. You hear about guys who've been made redundant doing that. Just staying in a lot, not wanting to go out, not wanting to socialize. So I lost the plot there for a little while—for about a year, actually—but luckily Linda's very sensible and she said, "Look, you're OK. It's just the shock of The Beatles and all of that." I was thinking: "Well, can I ever write and sing again? What does anyone want with an out of work bass-player?" It hit me pretty hard.[13]

Thus, with the help of his wife Linda, he eventually came out of his funk and decided to put together a new band, convincing Linda to join him despite her limited musical experience and rudimentary abilities. They headed to New York for a recording session that resulted in the album *Ram* and the single "Another Day," which made it to number two in the UK and number five in the United States. By the end of the year, he had formed the band Wings, which by 1973 already had several hits that included "C Moon," "Hi, Hi, Hi," "My Love," and the title song for the James Bond film, *Live and Let Die*. In concert, Paul eschewed performing Beatles songs with his new group, determined to let his new band and music stand on their own. The album *Band on the Run* made it to number one in both the UK and the United States and garnered a Grammy nomination for album of the year. In some ways, the album marked the high point of McCartney's post-Beatles career, even though he would release many more albums and record with Michael Jackson, Stevie Wonder, and Kanye West, among others. C. C. from New York City, one of the letter writers who wrote to Catone for his 1982 book, offered a particularly harsh assessment, but one similar to that of many other Beatles fans. The letter bluntly stated:

> Paul McCartney's solo music has never done much for me. *Band on the Run* was his brightest achievement to date, but otherwise his music is blah stuff. I'm astonished at Paul's inane hogwash he calls music. My Heavens! Can this be the same person who composed *Yesterday, Michelle, Fixin' A Hole*, and *Sgt. Pepper's Lonely Hearts Club Band*? Now he writes such drivel, the standards he set in his hey-day beat him everytime, I keep hoping he'll come around, but I don't think it's likely.[14]

Mark Angellini said he thought McCartney's early solo work was "horrible" and that he was mostly interested in John Lennon because of his rebellious streak. McCartney offered a defense of his work in his 1976 hit "Silly Love Songs," which made it to number one in the United States and number two in the UK. Paul's enormous post-Beatles output is too large to evaluate here, but it is worth pointing out that, despite the critics, he has remained enormously popular. Even his 2019 album *Egypt Station* contains some of his best work and has received much critical praise.

Conclusion

Although George Harrison continued to make albums and occasional live appearances, he did not appear to be any happier on his own than he had been with the Beatles, at least at first. His wife, Pattie Boyd, who ended up leaving him for his close friend Eric Clapton, wrote in her memoir, "George didn't really like going out—he hated being recognized—so we stayed in that great house and became gradually detached from reality. We didn't listen to the radio because George wouldn't let us, and we didn't have newspapers, and the people who came to see us were either musicians or worked for Apple."[15] However much he yearned to stand on his own, it became a difficult adjustment for Harrison without the structure belonging to the group provided him. His moody response to his changed circumstances clearly contributed to the end of his marriage to Boyd. Of all the Beatles, it seemed as though George, so anxious to prove himself without the Beatles, had the hardest time finding his footing. Angellini said that he just found George Harrison's solo work "odd because it didn't sound like rock and roll to me," though he conceded that *All Thing Must Pass* had "a lot of good stuff on it."[16] George did in fact enjoy some early success, especially with *All Things Must Pass* (1970) and the album *Living in the Material World* (1973). The former went Platinum six times over and reached number one in both the United States and the UK. However, Harrison never managed to replicate the success of these albums with any of his subsequent efforts. His reputation also took a hit when he had to go to court to answer plagiarism charges for "My Sweet Lord," by far his most popular single, for its similarities to a 1963 hit called "He's So Fine" by the girl group the Chiffons. However, his 1973 single "Give Me Love (Give Me Peace on Earth)" made it to the top of the US charts, while reaching number eight in the UK. He also helped Ringo Starr write one of his biggest hits, the song "Photograph," and cowrote with Mal Evans another nice song for Ringo called "You and Me (Babe)." Probably his best album after *All Things Must Pass* is 1976's *Thirty Three and a Third*, which received a good critical reception and rose to number eleven in the United States, although for some reason it never made it past number 35 in the UK. Although still capable of turning out a respectable pop tune like "Crackerbox Palace," he continued to take his music seriously and see it as an opportunity to get across his messages aimed at spiritual enlightenment and personal growth. On *Rubber Soul*, he had admonished Beatles fans to "Think for Yourself"; now he told his listeners to "See Yourself" and your own flaws instead of fixating on those of others.

Ringo Starr has gone on to an extremely prolific career that has included twenty studio albums and forty-one singles, some of them quite successful. However, in reviewing the 1973 album *Ringo*, Alan Betrock might have summed up Ringo's entire musical output by writing the album was "definitely worth having, that's for sure, but the main problem with Ringo is that it's uneven." As a solo artist, Ringo suffered from having been in the Beatles, the toughest act to follow in the history of music. As Betrock pointed out, "The Beatles rarely, if ever, made an uneven album, and Ringo has now joined the rest of the Beatle spinoff LPs with a product that is a pastiche of greatness and mediocrity, of vibrancy and staleness … if you will, of the sublime and the ridiculous."[17] Starr has tended to make enjoyable albums, including those dating from this century, that probably deserve more credit and attention than they receive. They include 2008's *Liverpool 8* and 2010's *Y Not*;

the title song of the former celebrates the history of the Beatles, while on the latter "The Other Side of Liverpool" is a steady rocker that reveals the dark environment in which Ringo grew up. This dark song was something of an exception for Ringo; Nick Ercoline accurately stated, "If you actually listen to [Ringo's] music it's really pretty much happy music."[18] Michael Halbreich noted that with the onset of the Beatles Channel on Sirius/XM Satellite Radio, "Ringo is starting finally, all these years later to get his due. I think that there is more appreciation for what he did, what he does and what he's doing than there has ever been before."[19]

The response of Beatles fans to their solo careers, of course, varied, but a couple of patterns emerge from the interviews conducted for this book, in conjunction with contemporary reviews. First, no one argued that any of the Beatles' solo work as a whole rivaled the music they produced as members of the group, but some found value in it for its own sake. For example, Michael Halbreich said:

> I knew that in this case the whole was always to me going to be greater than the sum of the parts, [but] I'm not sure if that ultimately was true or not, because John put out some absolutely magnificent music as [did] George. Oh, my God! Talk about continued growth and experimentation in music and these guys are unbelievable. You could see Paul striving constantly for something new, something more, a new twist. To this day, I think Paul was looking constantly for, "What's my next twist on the way I produce something, or write something, or sing something?"[20]

On the other hand, Larry Kane stated emphatically, "None of them could ever equal what they did together."[21] Ivan Bell acknowledged that the song "Imagine" had a large impact on him, but other than that, he was not particularly interested in the Beatles' solo careers in the 1970s. He described Paul's solo career as unspectacular, and said, "In later years we all discovered that [the individual Beatles] were very good and very talented musicians and songwriters and lyricists, but I don't think that any of their respective individual careers made any dent on me."[22]

Second, although many male fans of the Beatles seemed to agree with Roy Auerbach, who said he probably followed John Lennon's career more closely than he did the others, Beatles fans as a group tended to follow each member of the group to some degree. Despite John's eccentricities, he still seemed closest to someone fans could relate to, largely because his music was a bit less commercial than that of Paul or Ringo but more accessible than much of George's output. By contrast, however, Jeff Ayers said he continued to follow the careers of each of the Beatles quite closely, buying their albums and at least giving a chance even to albums he did not end up caring for so much. He singled out John's work with the Plastic Ono Band as his favorite among the efforts of the individual Beatles, although he also very much liked George Harrison's *All Things Must Pass*. Wade Lawrence called *All Things Must Pass* "a phenomenal album." Ayers said he favored Lennon's work "a little more" than that of the other Beatles. However, he still thought, as most do, that the Beatles were better together, "especially Lennon and McCartney with their writing because individually you could hear the impact they had on each other when they get together and played."²³ Nick Ercoline also acknowledged following the careers of each of the individual Beatles after the group broke up. He described George Harrison as "a very good guitar player who was very good not only as a musician but also as a lyricist." Ercoline said he followed Lennon's solo career and that of Paul McCartney with his new band, Wings, and that, although Ringo Starr's career was perhaps not as good as that of the other three nor was he as popular as they were, he was still a Beatle and people still wanted to see him and buy his music.²⁴

In short, individually the four Beatles wrote many great songs and put out a few great albums, but, as Kane said, they would never replicate what they had done as a group. Nor would the Beatles dominate the culture of the 1970s as they had the 1960s, even if their individualism was largely in step with the ethos of the new decade.

Successors to the Beatles?

With the breakup of the Beatles and the ascendance of the introspective singer-songwriter in the early 1970s, was there any room for potential successors to the Beatles who bore any resemblance in term of their creative output or the impact that they had on music fans? The short answer to that question is no, but it might be worth considering briefly several candidates who might have had the combination of the talent and the appeal to fill that role.

In 1967, an English literature student named Donald Fagen met guitarist Walter Becker at Bard College in upstate New York and the two formed a friendship that ultimately resulted in the creation of their group, Steely Dan. They broke through in 1972 with their debut album, *Can't Buy a Thrill*, which included two smash singles, "Do It Again" and "Reelin' in the Years." Music historian Bill Avant actually did compare them to the Beatles, writing, "One temptation is to see Steely Dan as what the Beatles ... might have sounded like if the music had been made by Woody Allen-ish wiseass Jewish kids from New York, instead of witty lads from the U.K."[25] Roy Auerbach said the only other group that ever rivaled the way he felt about the Beatles was Steely Dan when he was in his twenties. He said both the Beatles and Steely Dan "really somehow fit who I was or represented who I was at the time and seemed to change along the same kind of parallel path to where I was going."[26] Other bands in the 1970s achieved tremendous popular success, the Eagles being one prominent example, but none matched the creativity, growth, and literate, evocative lyricism that matched the distinctive sound, at once both infectious and unique, of Steely Dan. The Eagles served as the leading practitioners of the new genre of country rock that had emerged out of the 1960s, with influences like Buck Owens and the Buckaroos out of Bakersfield, California. Their sound resembled the easy vibes of the singer-songwriter movement and lacked the musical diversity of a group like Steely Dan, who infused rock with jazz and blues influences but did so in such a way that they transcended any easily recognizable genre other than rock. This also made them similar to the Beatles, who put songs as diverse as "Helter Skelter," "Ob-la-di, Ob-la-da," and "Honey Pie" on the same album.

The Beatles and the 1960s

In retrospect, Steely Dan might deserve consideration as the best candidate for successor to the Beatles, except they never rose to quite the heights the Beatles had in dominating their decade among their peers. Steely Dan also made more use of studio musicians to polish their sound, whereas the Beatles did so only occasionally such as with the use of strings on songs like "Yesterday" and "She's Leaving Home" or employing Billy Preston in the "Get Back" sessions. Perhaps most importantly, Steely Dan did not match their times quite as well as the Beatles did in that singer-songwriters dominated the first half of the 1970s, disco and punk rock the second half, with Steely Dan just there providing relief from both on stellar albums such as *Countdown to Ecstasy*, *Katy Lied*, and most impressively *Aja*. In the end, while the Beatles receive practically universal recognition as the greatest band ever, the reservations of Rolling Stones fans notwithstanding, Steely Dan frequently (and unjustifiably) does not even receive mention in the discussion. For example, in 2003 VH1 came out with a book of what their experts considered the 100 Greatest Albums of all time. They ranked *Revolver* number one and included five Beatles' albums in the top eleven.[27] No Steely Dan album made the list. It would therefore be difficult to anoint them as *the* successor to the Beatles, even though in many respects they were *a* successor to the Beatles.

Of course, after the Beatles had broken up, both their two biggest British rivals, the Rolling Stones and the Who, continued to carve out their legacies in the rock universe. Of the two, the Who continued to stretch themselves more while the Rolling Stones mainly just continued to operate like a fine-tuned rock machine, although they did make some effort to adjust to the times such as their foray into disco with songs like "Miss You," "Shattered," and "Emotional Rescue," all the while beginning to show their age. By contrast, in 1979, Jay Cocks, writing in *Time*, suggested that the Who had

> sustained—indeed, defined—the vaunting, unstable strength that is the soul of rock, the barefoot boogie along the keen edge of the blade … The music remains intact, inviolate. No other group has ever pushed rock so far, or asked so much from it. No other band has ever matched its sound, a particular combination of sonic onslaught and melodic delicacy that is like chamber music in the middle of a commando raid.[28]

Since the Beatles no longer played together as a group, the Who had perhaps done the most to carry their mantle forward. However, as was the case with Steely Dan, while their music remained strong and continued to appeal to their fans, it would be hard to argue that the Who embodied the ethos of the 1970s in the way the Beatles had that of the 1960s, even if they did embody "the soul of rock." Their music would remain a staple of FM rock stations, like WNEW in New York, which adopted the slogan "Where Rock Lives," but they did not come close to dominating the charts the way the Beatles had in the 1960s and had only a handful of singles that came close to being hits in the decade.

Certainly, bands founded a little later like Led Zeppelin and Pink Floyd had their devout followers, but they both remained more an acquired taste and mostly lacked the

Conclusion

universal appeal the Beatles had. Some might argue for Queen, which also had a large and devoted following and a number of successful singles and albums, but they never dominated the charts the way the Beatles had and soon blended in with other similar arena rock bands such as Journey and Foreigner. Female rock groups, pioneered by the Runaways and female rock stars like Joan Jett (originally the bass player for the Runaways), Pat Benatar, and Chrissie Hynde of the Pretenders have great cultural significance as pioneers paving the way for the success of someone like Madonna, but, again, unlike the Beatles, did not dominate the larger youth culture of an entire generation.

The fact that there were so many other famous and successful rock stars and bands not even mentioned here testifies to the point that no one dominated the 1970s as the Beatles did the 1960s. However, among bands, perhaps we might consider one final candidate as a possible successor to the Beatles, another British group with a two-syllable name. The Police had five number one hits and two more singles that reached number two in the UK between 1979 and 1983 and drew much of their inspiration from their Liverpudlian predecessors. In fact, their lead singer and bass guitarist Sting acknowledged that "The Beatles were formative in my upbringing, my education. They came from a very similar background: the industrial towns in England, working class; they wrote their own songs, conquered the world. That was the blueprint for lots of other British kids to try to do the same."[29] The Police followed that blueprint and had great success with it at home, but did not duplicate that success in the United States, which the Beatles had used to catapult themselves to worldwide acclaim and even hysteria. Only 1983's "Every Breath You Take" reached the top of the charts in the States. Furthermore, although longevity need not be the only factor in a band's cultural importance, the Police did not even remain together as long as the Beatles did, with only Sting among the three band members, which also included Andy Summers and Steward Copeland, having great success as a solo artist.

Given the predominance of solo artists in the 1970s, it might make sense to consider whether one of the most successful of these might deserve designation as the successor of the Beatles. The primary candidate from England would have to be Elton John, while the most logical American candidate would perhaps be Bruce Springsteen. Elton John is one of rock's true superstars who in the 1970s played to enthusiastic sold-out arenas and, in collaboration with his lyricist Bernie Taupin, flooded the marketplace with a prodigious number of albums and singles, many of them enormously successful. There is no question about his musical talent, showmanship, or popular appeal. However, he did not come close to having the kind of far-reaching influence the Beatles did, especially after about 1973. That year he released his double album, *Goodbye Yellow Brick Road*, a masterpiece that indicated Elton might be an artist who would challenge and grow along with his audience the way the Beatles had. Instead, it marked a high point or creative peak he never quite reached again. As his career went on, it seemed he and Taupin settled for writing the kind of songs that would follow a formula for pop success, straying from the kind of meaningful folk and country-influenced rock and reflective and insightful lyrics that characterized early albums such as *Tumbleweed Connection* and *Madman across the Water*. Already by 1973, the duo had written many of their best songs, some of which did have commercial appeal, including "Tiny Dancer," Levon," "Rocket Man," and "Daniel," just to name a few. However, in 1975 Taupin conceded, "We never want to write songs that tell an audience what to do. We don't know enough about the world to preach to people. We take ourselves seriously, but the music has to be listenable."[30] By the time the pair returned to the kind of music and lyrics found on those early albums in 2001 with *Songs from the West Coast* and 2004's *Peachtree Road*, most of Elton's fans would rather continue listening to "Crocodile Rock" or "Bennie and Jets" than buy and explore their new material. *Songs from the West Coast* did sell better in the UK, Elton's native land, than it did in the United States. Nevertheless, one measure of its reception is in the lack of success of its follow-up, *Peachtree Road*, the lowest selling album of Elton's career, despite good critical reviews and songs as good as those on *West Coast* or any of his early albums.

Bruce Springsteen labored early in his career under such appellations as "the next Dylan" and "the future of rock and roll," which came from a quote in a review by his eventual manager Jon Landau, who wrote, "I saw the future of rock and roll and its name is Bruce Springsteen." Springsteen has far surpassed the Beatles in terms of the length of his career, the extent and diversity of his output, and the number of times he has reinvented himself. He has always had a large and passionately devoted fan base, on whom his music and lyrics have exercised an impact every bit as profound as that of the Beatles did on theirs. Springsteen came along a time that was not only post-Beatles but also one during which rock fans were looking for a new voice to infuse energy into rock and roll as the Rolling Stones and the Who got older. They also needed someone to inject some raw energy into the popular music scene dominated by the placid, easygoing sounds of the new breed of singer-songwriters. Springsteen answered those needs but still operated in too diverse a marketplace and came too close to sounding like a voice from the past to speak for all of the young people in the 1970s the way the Beatles seemed to do in their decade. As Kim Fowley, the manager of the all-female punk band, the Runaways, said in an interview with late-night talk show host Tom Snyder in 1977, "I feel it's a vacuum because we're living in a fragmented '70s where there's so many different things happening that there isn't one Beatles or one Elvis Presley." It did not help that at that time Springsteen was in the middle of a three-year period without releasing a record because of a bitter financial quarrel with his manager, Mike Appel. The initial hype surrounding him turned some fans and critics off, as did his appearance on the covers of both *Time* and *Newsweek* after the release of his 1975 album, *Born to Run*. It took until 1984 and his *Born in the USA* album and tour for him to achieve massive commercial success, but even then he retained an ambivalent relationship with superstardom, wanting success but on his own terms. In this ambivalence, he does resemble the Beatles somewhat, and he could be considered a worthy successor as an artist, but he simply was not someone as followed or beloved by as wide a segment of the population as the Beatles were. In fact, many music fans among the late baby boomers and early Generation Xers preferred punk, new wave, or alternative rock music even at the height of Springsteen's own popularity.

Conclusion

Perhaps the most logical candidate as a successor to the Beatles would be the ex-Beatle Paul McCartney. As an ex-Beatle, he had the potential to attract a similarly huge following, his band Wings did appeal to younger fans in the 1970s, and he remained an evolving creative force throughout his career. He also has done more than anyone to keep alive the legacy of the Beatles' music in concerts, which he started performing live again after the turn of the century and because he has remained capable of producing music that sounds like the Beatles, perhaps never more so than on his 2019 album, *Egypt Station*. Yet even if *Egypt Station* might approximate something like what a Beatle record would have sounded like in 2019, both the times and the music industry have changed so much that no matter the quality it would not get the airplay or have the opportunity to reach the ears of millions of listeners. Those who wished to become familiar with the album would primarily be restricted to those who actively sought it out because they were already fans of the Beatles or McCartney. The significance of the Beatles, then, ultimately does not lie in their music, as suggested by the 2019 film *Yesterday*, which implies that their music was so transcendent that the Beatles songs would be universally popular no matter when they were released or who sang them, both highly dubious propositions. It lies rather in the times in which they flourished and the reception of their music by the generation to whom they spoke and sang.

Perhaps the true successors to the Beatles were not any single band like Steely Dan or rock musician like Elton John or Bruce Springsteen, but the collective wave of acoustic-oriented singer-songwriters that defined the 1970s for so many people. The list would include, among others, Paul Simon, Joni Mitchell, Jackson Browne, Carole King, Gordon Lightfoot, Carly Simon, James Taylor, David Crosby, Graham Nash, and Neil Young. In many ways, they followed the Beatles' example in exploring their inner life and working out their feeling about many of their issues within their lyrics. Any number of Beatles songs from the 1960s would have fit well into the singer-songwriter ethos of the 1970s, among them "Yesterday," "In My Life," "Nowhere Man," "I Will," or "You've Got to Hide Your Love Away." In fact, Beatles' covers in the 1970s included Cher's "The Long and Winding Road" (1973), Anne Murray's "You Won't See Me" (1974), David Bowie's "Across the Universe" (1975), Bryan Ferry's "She's Leaving Home" (1976), and Earth, Wind and Fire's highly original interpretation of "Got to Get You Into My Life" (1978). However, with a few exceptions such as the fabulously talented and successful Linda Ronstadt, for the most part music fans in the 1970s and beyond preferred artists who wrote their own songs, just one of many important legacies left by the Beatles. The most popular of the bunch might have been James Taylor, whose mental instability and serious drug problems only made him a more sympathetic figure, but Taylor's songs did not vary enough from the mellow groove that characterized early hits like "Fire and Rain" and "Carolina in My Mind." In this regard, he differed from Jackson Browne and especially Neil Young, who varied their styles more than Taylor ever did, but only to become more pop-oriented and commercially successful in the case of Browne or to alienate a significant portion of his fans in the case of Young. Collectively, these singer-songwriters helped to define their generation, but none ever emerged from the pack to rival the influence of the Beatles.

The Beatles and the 1960s

The Long-Term Significance of the Beatles and Their Breakup

The Beatles stood alone for six years atop the rock universe and achieved fame, success, and a reputation that exceeded any group or solo artist that came before or after them. Others have come close—Elvis Presley, the Rolling Stones, perhaps Michael Jackson—though even these superstars do not quite measure up to the Beatles in terms of their enduring fame and popularity or in the influence that they had over their time. Elvis Presley's career and musical output were much more uneven and Elvis did not remain true to himself in the same way that the Beatles did, extending to their decision to split at the height of their powers. Furthermore, Elvis did not write his own songs, made too many B-movies, and exercised little artistic control over either his records or his films. The Rolling Stones had a huge fan base and created a musical legacy that is arguably as good, or almost as good, as that of the Beatles. However, they benefited from working in the Beatles' shadow in the 1960s, which freed groups like the Stones and the Who to push limits and explore new territory without the burden of being the standard-bearer for their generation. Many of their fans turned to them in reaction to the popularity of the Beatles as an act of rebellion and contrariness. There was plenty of room for both, contrary to the somewhat contrived Beatles vs. Stones rivalry—contrived partly because they did not see themselves in competition with one another and partly because most people who liked rock and roll in the 1960s liked and listened to both groups. Michael Jackson, his dubious moral legacy aside, was as much renowned for his dancing and theatricality as his music, however great the latter might have been. Furthermore, his music at no time was nearly as ubiquitous as that of the Beatles was in the 1960s and has been ever since.

The Beatles had once huge advantage over Presley and Jackson in that they belonged to a group in which the other members could identify with and understand the costs and pressures of fame that they all experienced, burdens that Presley and Jackson largely bore alone, despite Jackson's background singing with a musical family since a very young age. Jackson's family was not with him at the height of his fame and success when he chose isolation and refuge in the secluded privacy of Neverland as had Presley at Graceland, Jackson with his cohort of prepubescent admirers, and Presley with the Memphis Mafia.

The Beatles held it together long enough to set an example not only for contemporary rock groups, many of which formed because of their influence, but also to impact the entire direction of pop and rock music in the decades that followed. Whether this influence was good or bad depends on one's taste in music and the criteria for evaluating their legacy. The punk rockers, for example, hated the Beatles because they had taken rock too far away from its initial purity and simplicity. Nevertheless, as Wade Lawrence asserted, "every bit of music in the 70s owes everything to the Beatles. You can't look at ELO (Electric Light Orchestra) without the Beatles."[31] Syd Barrett, who cofounded the progressive rock band Pink Floyd, revered the Beatles and knew how to play many of their songs, while David Paich who cofounded the successful American rock band Toto, said, "I always tried to pattern ourselves after The Beatles and Fleetwood Mac. I thought it would be better to have more talent and more songwriters."[32]

Conclusion

The Beatles' career provided not only a template for other rock groups but also for any individual seeking to navigate the pitfalls of growing into adulthood and managing a career, relationships, friendships, the expectations of society, and the temptations of drugs, sex, or sheer laziness. In the case of John and Paul, people might learn from their experience, both positive and negative, coping with grief and childhood issues of abandonment. In addition, as Joshua Wolf Shenk has argued, the creative partnership of Lennon and McCartney provides a model for the powers and advantages of collaborating with another person on any endeavor, with additional lessons for anyone in a relationship with a partner.[33] It is easy to forget how young the Beatles were when they got together and when they broke up. In retrospect, that they stayed together as long as they did and managed the creative output they shared with the world in the maelstrom of both the personal changes that come with the transition to adulthood and the social and revolutionary turbulence of the decade in which they thrived is nothing short of astonishing.

Yet the Beatles as THE BEATLES was also a creation of their fans and the times. This book has argued that, in addition to the Beatles themselves, the Beatles' reception in the 1960s was an important component of the history of that time. Through the voices included in this book, we begin to get a sense of how important the Beatles were in the lives of those coming of age during this time. These included the voices not just of the Beatlemaniacs who screamed their lungs out in 1963 and 1964, but also those who were just curious and interested participants in the youth culture and issues of their generation for whom the Beatles became a cultural touchstone throughout the decade. As Greil Marcus wrote of the Beatles and their influence in 1975, "They understood, finally, that they could affect the lives of kids all over the world. The fact that they succeeded tells us how much big pop ambitions are worth; everyone who might conceivably read this book has been changed for the better because of what the Beatles did."[34]

For Beatles fans, the end of the 1970s came not just with the rise to power of Margaret Thatcher and Ronald Reagan but also, and perhaps primarily, with the death of John Lennon, just as the breakup of the Beatles marked a symbolic end to the 1960s ten years earlier. Long-time WNEW disk jockey Richard Neer summed up the tragedy as well as anyone has:

> Those of us he had touched were outraged at the waste of it all, that a man with so much yet to give was cut down, just as he was starting to get his life on track again. The bitterness of the split with McCartney was dissipating, and his music was taking on a more optimistic tone. He'd reconciled with Yoko and was revisiting the joys of parenthood with a boy he absolutely adored. Just as his life and art were about to enter a happier phase, his mortal being was cashiered in a pool of blood outside his Dakota apartment.[35]

A death always affects those left behind, especially that of someone who meant as much to people as John Lennon had. Both McCartney and Harrison honored John with songs that paid tribute to their friendship and shared Beatles past in "Here Today" and "All

Those Years Ago," respectively. Elton John and Bernie Taupin honored Lennon in the desolately moving "Empty Garden (Hey Hey Johnny)." Michael Halbreich spoke for all Beatles fans when he said, "John's death was a shock every bit as great as the Beatles breaking up, every bit as great as any death I ever heard of in my lifetime."[36] He compared the breakup of the Beatles to having one's parents getting divorced. As with the death of a divorced parent, John's death ended any possibility of a reconciliation. It made the end of the Beatles permanent, in addition to removing a figure beloved by rock music fans all over the world. In a way, though, the Beatles never really ended and they have remained popular to this day among people of all generations. Their musical and cultural legacy has not only remained large in the twenty-first century, but their impact on the decade of the 1960s helped to bring about revolutionary political and social changes that still reverberate a half century later and will be felt for a long time to come.

NOTES

INTRODUCTION

1. Marc A. Catone, *As I Write This Letter: An American Generation Remembers the Beatles* (Ann Arbor, MI: Greenfield Books, 1982).
2. Philip Norman, *Shout!: The Beatles and Their Generation*, revised ed. (New York: Simon & Schuster, [1981] 2003), xxi.

CHAPTER 1

1. G. Reynolds, "A Wind Analysis for the Northern Irish Sea," *Quarterly Journal of the Royal Meteorological Society* 82, no. 354 (1956): 469. https://rmets.onlinelibrary.wiley.com/doi/abs/10.1002/qj.49708235410 (accessed June 13, 2019).
2. *The Beatles Anthology* (San Francisco, CA: Chronicle Books, 2000), 25.
3. Barry Miles, *Paul McCartney: Many Years from Now* (New York: Henry Holt, 1997), 4.
4. Tim Riley, *Lennon: The Man, the Myth, the Music—the Definitive Life* (New York: Hyperion, 2011), 3.
5. *The Beatles Anthology*, 25.
6. David Kynaston, *Austerity Britain: 1945–1951* (New York: Waller, 2008), 592.
7. Colin MacInnes, *Absolute Beginners* (London: Allison & Busby, [1959] 2011), 30–1.
8. Ibid., 21, 32.
9. *The Beatles Anthology*, 7.
10. Miles, *Paul McCartney*, 6.
11. Ibid., 19.
12. Ibid.
13. Ibid., 11–12.
14. *The Beatles Anthology*, 18.
15. Miles, *Paul McCartney*, 18–19.
16. Riley, *Lennon*, 36.
17. *The Beatles Anthology*, 9.
18. Ibid., 34.
19. Ibid., 37.
20. Ibid., 34.
21. Cynthia Lennon, *John* (New York: Crown, 2005), 12.
22. Elijah Wald, *How the Beatles Destroyed Rock "N" Roll: An Alternative History of American Popular Music* (Oxford: Oxford University Press, 2009), 175.

Notes

23. David R. Shumway, "Watching Elvis," in *American Popular Culture and the Beatles*, ed. Kenneth Campbell (San Diego, CA: Cognella Press, 2019), 23–8.
24. Norma Coates, "Elvis from the Waist Up and Other Myths: 1950s Music Television and the Gendering of Rock Discourse," in *American Popular Culture and the Beatles*, ed. Kenneth Campbell (San Diego, CA: Cognella Press, 2019), 58.
25. Riley, *Lennon*, 50.
26. Brian Ward, "'By Elvis and All the Saints' Images of the American South in the World of 1950s British Popular Music," in *American Popular Culture and the Beatles*, ed. Kenneth Campbell (San Diego, CA: Cognella Press, 2019), 94.
27. Bob Groom, "'Whose Rock Island Line'? Originality in the Composition of Blues and British Skiffle," in *American Popular Culture and the Beatles*, ed. Kenneth Campbell (San Diego, CA: Cognella Press, 2019), 115.
28. Riley, *Lennon*, 46.
29. *The Beatles Anthology*, 27.
30. Kenneth Womack, *Long and Winding Roads: The Evolving Artistry of the Beatles* (New York: Bloomsbury, 2007), 10.
31. Miles, *Paul McCartney*, 27.
32. David Pritchard and Alan Lysaght, *The Beatles: An Oral History* (New York: Hyperion, 1998), 14.
33. G. Barry Golson, ed., *The Playboy Interviews with John Lennon and Yoko Ono*, conducted by David Sheff (New York: Playboy Press, 1981), 117.
34. *The Beatles Anthology*, 20.
35. Pritchard and Lysaght, *The Beatles*, 13–14.
36. Ibid., 12.
37. Peter Ames Carlin, *Paul McCartney: A Life* (New York: Simon & Schuster, 2009), 27.
38. Golson, *Playboy Interviews*, 117.
39. Jonathan Gould, *Can't Buy Me Love: The Beatles, Britain, and America* (New York: Three Rivers Press, 2007), 34.
40. *The Beatles Anthology*, 29.
41. Ibid., 12.
42. Miles, *Paul McCartney*, 21.
43. Ibid., 36.
44. *The Beatles Anthology*, 23.
45. Ibid., 31.

CHAPTER 2

1. Raphael Gross, "Relegating Nazism to the Past: Expressions of German Guilt in 1945 and Beyond," *German History* 25, no. 2 (2007): 220, 223. doi:10.1177/0266355406075715 (accessed July 17, 2019).
2. Wilhelm Roepke, "New Germans Must Shape the New Germany: Those of Good Faith Must Re-Educate Their People and Make Their Country a Democratic Federation. Shaping a New

Germany Shaping a New Germany," *New York Times*, October 13, 1946, 120. https://ezproxy.monmouth.edu/login?url=https://search-proquestcom.ezproxy.monmouth.edu/docview/107731089?accountid=12532 (accessed July 16, 2019).

3. Tony Judt, *Postwar: A History of Europe since 1945* (New York: Penguin Books, 2005), 58.
4. Ibid., 22.
5. Ibid., 155.
6. Ibid., 158.
7. Ibid., 61.
8. Drew Middleton, "West Germany Is Making Strides Toward Industrial Rehabilitation," *New York Times*, January 4, 1950, 50. https://ezproxy.monmouth.edu/login?url=https://searchproquest-com.ezproxy.monmouth.edu/docview/111377242?accountid=12532 (accessed July 16, 2019).
9. Ania Kruke, "Western Integration vs. Reunification? Analyzing the Polls of the 1950s," *German Politics & Society* 25, no. 2 (2007): 43–4, 49. doi:10.3167/gps.2007.250204 (accessed July 16, 2019).
10. Judt, *Postwar*, 274.
11. Bob Spitz, *The Beatles: The Biography* (New York: Little, Brown, 2005), 206.
12. Hunter Davies, *The Beatles* (New York: W. W. Norton, [1968] 2009), 75.
13. J. Arthur, "Hamburg Strives to Keep Booming," *New York Times*, February 2, 1958, 88. https://ezproxy.monmouth.edu/login?url=https://search.proquest.com/docview/114389008?accountid=12532 (accessed July 16, 2019).
14. Linde Apel, "Voices from the Rubble Society: 'Operation Gomorrah' and Its Aftermath," *Journal of Social History* 44, no. 4 (2011): 1020. doi:10.1353/jsh.2011.0041 (accessed July 16, 2019).
15. Ernest Leiser, "Germany's Wide-Open City," *Saturday Evening Post*, June 3, 1950, 49. https://search-ebscohostcom.ezproxy.monmouth.edu/login.aspx?direct=true&db=a9h&AN=19631963&site=ehos t-live&scope=site (accessed July 16, 2019).
16. "Rebuilt Hamburg a Political Issue: Both Socialists and Bonn Claim Credit for Restoring German City after Bombing," *New York Times*, October 29, 1953, 16. https://ezproxy.monmouth.edu/login?url=https://search.proquest.com/docview/112694555?accountid=12532 (accessed July 16, 2019).
17. Arthur, "Hamburg Strives to Keep Booming," 88.
18. "Hamburg Fears for Port Trade: Rivalry between Economic Blocs of Europe Thought Harmful to Business," *New York Times*, July, 26, 1959, 67. https://ezproxy.monmouth.edu/login?url=https://search-proquestcom.ezproxy.monmouth.edu/docview/114753074?accountid=12532 (accessed July 16, 2019).
19. Devin McKinney, *Magic Circles: The Beatles in Dream and History* (Cambridge, MA: Harvard University Press, 2003), 28.
20. Leiser, "Germany's Wide-Open City," 49.
21. Pritchard and Lysaght, *The Beatles*, 43.
22. Lennon, *John*, 51.
23. Sam Leach, *The Rocking City: The Explosive Birth of the Beatles* (Merseyside: Pharaoh Press, 1994), 44.
24. *The Beatles Anthology*, 45.

Notes

25. Pete Best and Patrick Doncaster, *Beatle! The Pete Best Story* (London: Plexus, 1985), 33.
26. Pauline Sutcliffe and Douglas Thompson, *The Beatles' Shadow: Stuart Sutcliffe & His Lonely Hearts Club* (London: Pan Macmillan, 2002), 88.
27. Pritchard and Lysaght, *The Beatles: An Oral History*, 45.
28. *The Beatles Anthology*, 48.
29. Ibid., 45.
30. McKinney, *Magic Circles*, 36.
31. David Fricke, "Paul McCartney Looks Back: The Rolling Stone Interview," *Rolling Stone*, August 10, 2016. https://www.rollingstone.com/music/music-features/paulmccartney-looks-back-the-rolling-stone-interview-102797/ (accessed July 19, 2019).
32. Pritchard and Lysaght, *The Beatles*, 40.
33. Sutcliffe and Thompson, *The Beatles' Shadow*, 76.
34. *The Beatles Anthology*, 49.
35. Carlin, *Paul McCartney*, 62–3.
36. Best and Doncaster, *Beatle!*, 39.
37. Astrid Kirchherr and Max Scheler, *Yesterday: The Beatles Once Upon a Time* (New York: Vendome Press, 2007), 6.
38. Qtd. in Steven D. Stark, *Meet the Beatles: A Cultural History of the Band That Shook Youth, Gender, and the World* (New York: HarperCollins, 2005), 96.
39. Spitz, *The Beatles: The Biography*, 222.
40. Riley, *Lennon*, 133.
41. Sutcliffe and Thompson, *The Beatles' Shadow*, 110.
42. *The Beatles Anthology*, 53.
43. Sutcliffe and Thompson, *The Beatles' Shadow*, 155.
44. Gould, *Can't Buy Me Love*, 95.
45. *The Beatles Anthology*, 56.
46. Stark, *Meet the Beatles*, 80.
47. Leach, *The Rocking City*, 175.
48. Spitz, *The Beatles*, 421.
49. *The Beatles Anthology*, 62.
50. Lennon, *John*, 52.
51. *The Beatles Anthology*, 49.
52. Pritchard and Lysaght, *The Beatles*, 97–8.
53. Best and Doncaster, *Beatle!*, 165–6.
54. Pete Shotton and Nicholas Shaffner, *John Lennon: In My Life* (New York: Stein and Day, 1983), 71.
55. Leach, *The Rocking City*, 174.
56. Pritchard and Lysaght, *The Beatles*, 98.
57. Kirchherr and Scheler, *Yesterday*, 8.
58. See Gillian Garr, "Girl Groups," in *American Popular Culture and the Beatles*, ed. Kenneth Campbell (San Diego: Cognella, 2019), 64–87.

Notes

59. Leach, *The Rocking City*, 175.
60. Riley, *Lennon*, 125.
61. Gould, *Can't Buy Me Love*, 126.
62. *The Beatles Anthology*, 72.

CHAPTER 3

1. Mark Jarvis, *Conservative Governments: Morality and Social Change in Affluent Britain 1957–1964* (Manchester: Manchester University Press, 2005), 101.
2. "Excerpts from Lord Denning's Report on the Implications of Profumo Scandal," *New York Times*, September 26, 1963, 14. https://ezproxy.monmouth.edu/login?url=https://searchproquest-com.ezproxy.monmouth.edu/docview/116463012?accountid=12532 (accessed November 27, 2019).
3. Qtd. in "Briton Under a Cloud: John Dennis Profumo He Fits Classic Mold 'Third Time Lucky': A New Career," *New York Times*, June 8, 1963, 13. https://ezproxy.monmouth.edu/login?url=https://search-proquestcom.ezproxy.monmouth.edu/docview/116468352?accountid=12532 (accessed November 27, 2019).
4. Frank Mort, *Capital Affairs: London and the Making of the Permissive Society* (New Haven, CT: Yale University Press, 2010), 281.
5. Arthur Marwick, *The Sixties: Cultural Revolution in Britain, France, Italy, and the United States, c.1958–c.1974* (Oxford: Oxford University Press, 1998), 479.
6. Mort, *Capital Affairs*, 282.
7. Riley, *Lennon*, 198.
8. David, Griffiths, "Screaming Lord Sutch: Two Sides of Sutch," *Record Mirror*, March 23, 1963. http://www.rocksbackpages.com/Library/Article/screaming-lord-sutch-two-sidesof-sutch (accessed October 9, 2020).
9. Paul McCartney, "A Little Bare," *Mersey Beat*, September 6, 1962. http://triumphpc.com/mersey-beat/archives/littlebare.shtml (accessed August 15, 2019).
10. Ian MacDonald, *Revolution in the Head: The Beatles' Records and the Sixties* (New York: Henry Holt, 1994), 12.
11. D. A. Coleman, "Population," in *British Social Trends since 1900*, ed. A. H. Halsey (Houndmills: Macmillan, 1988), 71.
12. Jeffrey Weeks, *Sex, Politics and Society* (London: Longman, 1981), 252.
13. Mark Donnelly, *Sixties Britain: Culture, Society and Politics* (Harrow: Pearson Longman, 2005), 116.
14. Weeks, *Sex, Politics and Society*, 249.
15. Frank Mort, "Striptease: The Erotic Female Body and Live Sexual Entertainment in Mid-Twentieth-Century London," *Social History* 32, no. 1 (2007): 29. http://www.jstor.org.ezproxy.monmouth.edu/stable/4287394 (accessed November 27, 2019).
16. Bernard Hollowood, "This Is the Satire That Is: 'That Was the Week That Was' Has Caused a Sensation on British TV with Its Mockery of Everything and Everybody—But Is such Irreverence Satire or Sadism?," *New York Times Sunday Magazine*, July 7, 1963, 7. https://ezproxy.monmouth.edu/login?url=https://search-proquestcom.ezproxy.monmouth.edu/docview/116537655?accountid=12532 (accessed November 27, 2019).

Notes

17. Martin Pugh, *State and Society: A Societal and Political History of Britain since 1870*, 5th ed. (London: Bloomsbury, 2017), 389.
18. John Benson, *Affluence and Authority: A Social History of Twentieth Century Britain* (London: Oxford University Press, 2005), 169.
19. John Savage, *Teenage: The Creation of Youth Culture* (New York: Viking, 2007), 448, 450.
20. Alan Smith, "At a Recording Session with the Beatles," *Mersey Beat*, January 3, 1963. http://triumphpc.com/mersey-beat/archives/recording-session.shtml (accessed August 15, 2019).
21. Brian Epstein, "Beatles Record at EMI," *Mersey Beat*, September 20, 1962. http://triumphpc.com/mersey-beat/archives/beatles-emi.shtml (accessed August 15, 2019).
22. Spitz, *The Beatles*, 357.
23. Qtd. in Carlin, *Paul McCartney: A Life*, 80.
24. Smith, "At a Recording Session."
25. Rodney Nevitt, "Abbey Road and the History of Beatles' Album Cover Design," Paper Presented at Come Together: Fifty Years of Abbey Road Symposium, Rochester, NY, September 27–29, 2019.
26. J. P. Bean, *Joe Cocker: The Authorized Biography* (London: Omnibus Press, 1990), 15.
27. Rob Sheffield, *Dreaming the Beatles: The Love Story of One Band and the Whole World* (New York: HarperCollins, 2017), 39.
28. Walter Everett, *The Beatles as Musicians: The Quarry Men through* Rubber Soul (Oxford: Oxford University Press, 2001), 145–6.
29. *The Beatles Anthology*, 93.
30. Graham Nash, *Wild Tales: A Rock & Roll Life* (New York: Three Rivers Press, 2013), 49.
31. Kevin Howlett, *The Beatles at the Beeb: The Story of Their Radio Caree*r (London: BBC, 1982), 12.
32. Kevin Howlett, *The Beatles: The BBC Archives, 1962–1970* (New York: HarperCollins, 2013), 54.
33. See Everett, *The Beatles as Musicians* and Womack, *Long and Winding Roads*.
34. Qtd. in Marwick, *The Sixties*, 108.
35. Qtd. in Mark Lewisohn, *Tune In: The Beatles: All These Years, Volume 1* (New York: Three Rivers Press, 2013), 178.
36. Qtd. in Ian Inglis, "'I Read the News Today, Oh Boy': The British Press and the Beatles," *Popular Music & Society* 33, no. 4 (2010): 551–2. doi:10.1080/03007761003694373 (accessed December 6, 2019).
37. Maureen Cleave, "Why the Beatles Create All That Frenzy," *Evening Standard*, February 2, 1963. https://www.rocksbackpages.com/Library/Article/why-the-beatles-create-allthat-frenzy (accessed December 6, 2019).
38. Peter Jones, "The Beatles: With the Beatles (Parlophone)," *Record Mirror*, November 9, 1963. https://www.rocksbackpages.com/Library/Article/the-beatles-iwith-the-beatlesi-Parlophone (accessed December 6, 2019).
39. Wald, *How the Beatles Destroyed Rock "N" Roll*, 231.
40. Pritchard and Lysaght, *The Beatles*, 117.
41. Ibid., 118.
42. Jones, "The Beatles: With the Beatles."

43. Ibid.
44. John Fogerty and Jimmy McDonough, *Fortunate Son: My Life, My Music* (New York: Little, Brown, 2015), 95.
45. Gary Berman, *"We're Going to See the Beatles!": An Oral History of Beatlemania* (Santa Monica, CA: Santa Monica Press, 2008), 33.
46. Leach, *The Rocking City*, 130.
47. Nash, *Wild Tales*, 48.
48. Cleave, "Why the Beatles Create All That Frenzy."
49. Ian Inglis, "Ideology, Trajectory & Stardom: Elvis Presley & The Beatles," *International Review of the Aesthetics and Sociology of Music* 27, no. 1 (1996): 68. doi:10.1080/03007761003694373 (accessed December 5, 2019).
50. Howlett, *The Beatles at the Beeb*, 10.
51. Reprinted in Barry Miles, *The British Invasion: The Music, the Times, the Era* (New York: Sterling, 2009), 64.
52. Peter Brown and Steven Gaines, *The Love You Make: An Insider's Story of the Beatles* (New York: McGraw Hill, 1983), 104.
53. Ibid.
54. David Fowler, *Youth Culture in Modern Britain 1920–1970* (London: Palgrave Macmillan, 2008), 168.
55. Pritchard and Lysaght, *The Beatles*, 124.
56. *The Beatles Anthology*, 92.
57. Ibid., 109.
58. Pritchard and Lysaght, *The Beatles*, 126.
59. Fowler, *Youth Culture in Modern Britain*, 168.
60. Frederick Lewis, "Britons Succumb to 'Beatlemania,'" *New York Times*, December 1, 1963, 398. https://ezproxy.monmouth.edu/login?url=https://search-proquestcom.ezproxy.monmouth.edu/docview/116384951?accountid=12532 (accessed December 6, 2019).

CHAPTER 4

1. Melissa Davis, "A Conceptual Analysis of the Reception of the Beatles in America, February 1964" (MA diss., Liverpool Hope University, Liverpool, 2010), 17.
2. Lawrence Wright, *In the New World: Growing Up in America from the Sixties to the Eighties* (New York: Vintage Books, [1987] 2013), 64.
3. Davis, "A Conceptual Analysis," 40.
4. E.W. Kenworthy, "Russell Is Ready for Rights Fight: Says Southern Senators Will Battle Bill around the Clock," *New York Times*, February 20, 1964, 15. https://ezproxy.monmouth.edu/login?url=https://search-proquestcom.ezproxy.monmouth.edu/docview/115678928?accountid=12532 (accessed December 20, 2019).
5. "Humphrey, at Jersey Seminar, Says Civil Rights Bill Will Pass," *New York Times*, March 15, 1964, 66. https://ezproxy.monmouth.edu/login?url=https://search-proquest-com.ezproxy.monmouth.edu/docview/115706456?accountid=12532 (accessed December 20, 2019).

Notes

6. "Clay Takes a Jab at Civil Rights Bill," *New York Times*, May 20, 1964, 11. https://ezproxy.monmouth.edu/login?url=https://search-proquestcom.ezproxy.monmouth.edu/docview/115523920?accountid=12532 (accessed December 20, 2019).
7. Larry Kane, personal interview, January 20, 2020.
8. "Wallace, in Dallas; Scores Prayer Ban and Civil Rights Bill," *New York Times*, June 24, 1964, 15. https://ezproxy.monmouth.edu/login?url=https://search-proquestcom.ezproxy.monmouth.edu/docview/115856694?accountid=12532 (accessed December 20, 2019).
9. Walker Percy, "Mississippi: The Fallen Paradise," *Harper's Magazine*, April 1965, reprinted in *Voices in Our Blood: America's Best of the Civil Rights Movement*, ed. Jon Meacham (New York: Random House, 2001), 327.
10. Marwick, *The Sixties*, 268.
11. Brian L. Ott and Robert L. Mack, *Critical Media Studies: An Introduction* (Malden, MA: Wiley-Blackwell, 2010), 222.
12. Lewis, "Britons Succumb to 'Beatlemania'", 398.
13. Amanda Krause, Adrian North, and Lauren Hewitt, "Music Selection Behaviors in Everyday Listening," *Journal of Broadcasting & Electronic Media* 58, no. 2 (2014): 306–23. doi:10.1080/08838151.2014.906437 (accessed January 30, 2019).
14. Michael Frontani, *The Beatles: Image and the Media* (Jackson: University of Mississippi, 2007), 3.
15. Richie Havens and Steve Davidowitz, *They Can't Hide Us Anymore* (New York: Avon Books, 1999), 136.
16. Spitz, *The Beatles: The Biography*, 442.
17. Jane Barnes, personal interview, January 18, 2019.
18. Miles, *The British Invasion*, 56.
19. Evan Davies, "Psychological Characteristics of Beatle Mania," *Journal of the History of Ideas* 30, no. 2 (1969): 280. www.jstor.org/stable/2708439 (accessed December 30, 2019).
20. Robert G. Pielke, *Rock Music in American Culture: The Sounds of Revolution* (Jefferson, NC: McFarland, 2012), 34.
21. Quoted in Richard D. Freed, "Beatles Stump Music Experts Looking for Key to Beatlemania," *New York Times*, August 13, 1965, 17. https://ezproxy.monmouth.edu/login?url=https://search.proquest.com/docview/116940266?accountid=12532 (accessed December 21, 2020).
22. Barnes, personal interview.
23. Larry Kane, *Ticket to Ride: Inside the Beatles; 1964 Tour That Changed the World* (Philadelphia, PA: Running Press, 2003), 172.
24. Catone, *As I Write This Letter*, 10.
25. Dominic Sandbrook, *White Heat: A History of Britain in the Swinging Sixties* (London: Little, Brown, 2006), 112.
26. Andre Millard, "Beatlemania," in *American Popular Culture and the Beatles*, ed. Kenneth Campbell (San Diego, CA: Cognella, 2019), 162.
27. Spitz, *The Beatles*, 356–7.
28. Davis, "A Contextual Analysis," 31.
29. Kane, personal interview.
30. Millard, "Beatlemania," 161.

31. Stark, *Meet the Beatles*, 3.
32. Susan Douglas, *Where the Girls Are: Growing Up Female with the Mass Media* (New York: Three Rivers Press, 1994), 114–20.
33. Barbara Ehrenreich, Elizabeth Hess, and Gloria Jacobs, "Beatlemania: Girls Just Want to Have Fun," in *American Popular Culture & the Beatles*, ed. Kenneth Campbell (San Diego, CA: Cognella, 2018), 178–9.
34. Douglas, *Where the Girls Are*, 116.
35. Sandbrook, *White Heat*, 693.
36. Stark, *Meet the Beatles*, 133.
37. Katie, Kapurch, "The Wretched Life of a Lonely Heart: Sgt. Pepper's Girls, Fandom, the Wilson Sisters, and Chrissie Hynde," in *Roll Up for the Mystery Tour!: The Beatles, Sgt, Pepper, and the Summer of Love*, ed. Kenneth Womack (Lanham, MD: Lexington Books, 2017), 148.
38. Ibid., 148, 151.
39. Ibid., 180.
40. Rebecca Duncan, personal interview, January 21, 2019.
41. Ehrenreich, Hess, and Jacobs, "Beatlemania," 180.
42. Douglas, *Where the Girls Are*, 116.
43. Barnes, personal interview.
44. Bob Neaverson, *The Beatles Movies* (London: Cassell, 1997), 4.
45. Steven Glynn, *The British Pop Music Film: The Beatles and Beyond* (London: Palgrave Macmillan, 2013), 91.
46. Peter Jones, "The Beatles: A Hard Day's Night (Dir: Richard Lester)," *Record Mirror*, July 11, 1964. http://www.rocksbackpages.com/Library/Article/the-beatles-ia-hard-days-nightidir-richard-lester (accessed January 1, 2020).
47. Peter Jones, "The Beatles: A Hard Day's Night (Parlophone)," *Record Mirror*, July 11, 1964. http://www.rocksbackpages.com/Library/Article/the-beatles-ia-hard-days-nightiparlophone (accessed January 1, 2020).
48. Duncan, personal interview.
49. James Vignapiano, personal interview, April 2, 2019.
50. Bob Schiffer, personal interview, March 12, 2019.
51. McKinney, *Magic Circles*, 64.
52. Womack, *Long and Winding Roads*, 89.
53. Walter Everett, *The Foundations of Rock: From "Blue Suede Shoes" to "Suite: Judy Blue Eyes"* (Oxford: Oxford University Press, 2009), 48.
54. Nash, *Wild Tales*, 113.
55. Quoted in Richie Unterberger, *Turn! Turn! Turn!: The '60s Folk-rock Revolution* (San Francisco, CA: Backbeat Books, 2002), 66.
56. Quoted in Unterberger, *Turn! Turn! Turn!*, 66.
57. Michael McEntarfer, Written Response to Author's Questionnaire, October 2019.
58. Bill Harry, "The Beatles, Mary Wells, Sounds Incorporated, Tommy Quickly: Apollo Theatre, Ardwick, Manchester, Mersey Beat," October 22, 1964. https://www.rocksbackpages.com/Library/Article/the-beatles-mary-wells-sounds-incorporated-tommy-quickly-apollo-theatre-ardwick-manchester (accessed January 1, 2020).

Notes

59. Kane, personal interview.
60. Nick Ercoline, personal interview, February 7, 2019.
61. Ivan Bell, personal interview, February 19, 2019.
62. Peter Orenzoff, personal interview, March 6, 2019.
63. Geoffrey Cannon, "Pop Music Democratised," *New Society*, December 3, 1964. https://www.rocksbackpages.com/Library/Article/pop-music-democratised- (accessed January 1, 2020).
64. Theodor Strongin, "Musicology," *New York Times*, February 10, 1964, 53. https://searchproquestcom.ezproxy.monmouth.edu/hnpnewyorktimes/docview/115680530/805622AA5FC24ED4PQ/1?accountid=12532 (accessed January 1, 2020).
65. Gill Faggen, "Beatles: Plague or Boon for Radio?," *Billboard*, October 10, 1964, 16. https://books.google.com/books?id=0CAEAAAAMBAJ&pg=PA16&dq=The+Beatles&hl=en&sa=X#v=onepage&q=The%20Beatles&f=false (accessed January 1, 2020).

CHAPTER 5

1. Marwick, *The Sixties*, 264.
2. Harold Wilson, *The Labor Government 1964–1970: A Personal Record* (London: Weidenfeld and Nicolson, 1971), 125.
3. Ben Pimlott, *Harold Wilson* (London: HarperCollins, 1992), 351.
4. Thomas E. Mullaney, "The Week in Finance: Market Takes British Monetary Ills in Stride Despite Weakness of Pound Week in Finance: Weakness in Pound," *New York Times*, August 8, 1965, F1. https://ezproxy.monmouth.edu/login?url=https://search-proquestcom.ezproxy.monmouth.edu/docview/116957013?accountid=12532 (accessed January 23, 2020).
5. "Cheering Too Soon," *Birmingham Daily Post*, August 12, 1965, 7. https://www.britishnewspaperarchive.co.uk/viewer/bl/0002135/19650812/494/0019 (accessed January 30, 2020).
6. Alan Smith, "The Beatles: John Lennon Slams The Critics," *New Musical Express*, August 6, 1965. http://www.rocksbackpages.com/Library/Article/the-beatles-john-lennon-slamsthe-critics (accessed October 13, 2020).
7. Jeremy Thamer, "The Radical Left and Popular Music in the 1960s," in *Preserving the Sixties: Britain and the "Decade of Protest"*, ed. Trevor Harris and Tonia O'Brien Castro (London: Palgrave Macmillan, 2014), 91.
8. David Simonelli, *Working Class Heroes: Rock Music and British Society in the 1960s and 1970s* (Lanham, MD: Lexington Books, 2013), 61.
9. Simon Winder, *The Man Who Saved Britain: A Personal Journey into the Disturbing World of James Bond* (New York: Farrar, Straus and Giroux, 2007).
10. Ibid., 97.
11. MacDonald, *Revolution in the Head*, 27.
12. Spitz, *The Beatles*, 550.
13. Kane, personal interview.
14. Paul Skellett, Simon Wells, and Simon Weitzman, *Eight Arms to Hold You: 50 Years of* Help! *and the Beatles* (New York: ACC, 2017), 12.

Notes

15. Elspeth Grant, "The Beatles Need Help," *The Tatler*, August 11, 1965, 36. https://www.britishnewspaperarchive.co.uk/viewer/bl/0001853/19650811/027/0036 (accessed January 30, 2020).
16. Quoted in Stephanie Fremaux, *The Beatles on Screen: From Pop Stars to Musicians* (New York: Bloomsbury Academic, 2018), 68.
17. Quoted in Gould, *Can't Buy Me Love*, 265.
18. Alan Smith, "The Beatles: John Lennon Slams the Critics," *New Musical Express*, August 6, 1965. https://www.rocksbackpages.com/Library/Article/the-beatles-john-lennon-slamsthe-critics (accessed January 24, 2020).
19. Candy Leonard, *Beatleness: How the Beatles and Their Fans Remade the World* (New York: Arcade, 2014), 82.
20. Fremaux, *The Beatles on Screen*, 67.
21. Grant, "The Beatles Need Help."
22. McKinney, *Magic Circles*, 59.
23. Neaverson, *The Beatles Movies*, 37.
24. Richard Green, "The Beatles: Help! (Parlophone)," *Record Mirror*, July 24, 1965. https://www.rocksbackpages.com/Library/Article/the-beatles-ihelpi-parlophone (accessed January 20, 2020).
25. "Teen Beat," *West Lothian Courier*, October 1, 1965, 8. https://www.britishnewspaperarchive.co.uk/viewer/bl/0002738/19651001/066/0008 (accessed January 20, 2020).
26. Ibid.
27. Robert Shelton, "Beneath the Festival's Razzle Dazzle," *New York Times*, August 1, 1965, X11. https://ezproxy.monmouth.edu/login?url=https://search-proquestcom.ezproxy.monmouth.edu/docview/116946218?accountid=12532 (accessed February 4, 2020).
28. Gerard DeGroot, *The Sixties: A Kaleidoscopic History of a Disorderly Decade* (Cambridge, MA: Harvard University Press, 2008), 177.
29. Peter Bart, "New Negro Riots Erupt on Coast," *New York Times*, August 13, 1965, 1. https://ezproxy.monmouth.edu/login?url=https://search-proquestcom.ezproxy.monmouth.edu/docview/116937262?accountid=12532 (accessed February 4, 2020).
30. Kane, *Ticket to Ride*, 201.
31. Pritchard and Lysaght, *The Beatles*, 199.
32. For example, "The Beatles: Is Beatlemania Dying?," *KRLA Beat*, August 7, 1965. https://www.rocksbackpages.com/Library/Article/the-beatles-is-beatlemania-dying (accessed February 12, 2020).
33. Pritchard and Lysaght, *The Beatles*, 197.
34. Ibid.
35. *Eight Days a Week* (2016) [Film] Ron Howard, USA: Apple Corps.
36. Janet Nugent, personal interview, March 7, 2019.
37. Barnes, personal interview.
38. Mark Slobin, "Rock 'n' Roll Race to the Top," *Michigan Daily*, August 3, 1965.
39. Bosley Crowther, "Pop Go the Beatles," *New York Times*, August 29, 1965, X1. https://ezproxy.monmouth.edu/login?url=https://search-proquest-com.ezproxy.monmouth.edu/docview/116732116?accountid=12532 (accessed February 13, 2020).

Notes

40. Michael McEntarfer, Written Response to Author's Questionnaire, October 2019.
41. Roy Auerbach, personal interview, January 22, 2019.
42. Barnes, personal interview.
43. Aaron Sternfield, "Rock + Folk +Protest=An Erupting New Sound," *Billboard*, August 21, 1965, 1. https://books.google.com/books?id=YCkEAAAAMBAJ&printsec=frontcover&dq=beatl es&hl=en&ppis=_c&sa=X&ved=2ahUKEwioudmSeLlAhVNwlkKHRjYBEQ4ChDoATAIegQICBAC#v=onepage&q=beatles&f=fals (accessed February 4, 2020).
44. Quoted in Craig Harris, *The Band: Pioneers of Americana Music* (Lanham, MD: Rowman and Littlefield, 2014), 37.
45. Mitchell Axelrod, *Beatletoons: The Real Story Behind the Cartoon Beatles* (Pickens, SC: Wynn, 1999), 16.
46. Quoted in Harris, *The Band*, 38.

CHAPTER 6

1. Walter Cronkite, *A Reporter's Life* (New York: Alfred A. Knopf, 1996), 293.
2. "A Kennedy Protest Dropped in Jackson," *New York Times*, March 16, 1966, 41. https://ezproxy.monmouth.edu/login?url=https://search-proquestcom.ezproxy.monmouth.edu/docview/117126329?accountid=12532 (accessed March 3, 2020).
3. Todd Gitlin, *The Sixties: Years of Hope, Days of Rage*, revised ed. (New York: Bantam Books, 1993), 141.
4. Quoted in Dan T. Carter, *The Politics of Rage: George Wallace, the Origins of the New Conservatism, and the Transformation of American Politics*, 2nd ed. (Baton Rouge: Louisiana State University Press, 2000), 273.
5. Harold H. Martin, "The Race of the Thousand Clowns," *Saturday Evening Post*, May 7, 1966, 26. https://search-ebscohostcom.ezproxy.monmouth.edu/login.aspx?direct=true&db=a9h&AN=17053597&site=ehos t-live&scope=site (accessed March 6, 2020).
6. Jeff Frederick, *Stand Up for Alabama: Governor George Wallace* (Tuscaloosa: University of Alabama Press, 2017), 140.
7. Ray Jenkins, "Mr. & Mrs. Wallace Run for Governor of Alabama," *New York Times*, April 24, 1966, 10. https://ezproxy.monmouth.edu/login?url=https://search- proquest-com.ezproxy.monmouth.edu/docview/117581147?accountid=12532 (accessed March 5, 2020).
8. John Kruth, *This Bird Has Flown: The Enduring Beauty of Rubber Soul, Fifty Years On* (Milwaukee: Backbeat Books, 2015), 13.
9. Brown and Gaines, *The Love You Make*, 197.
10. Quoted in Spitz, *The Beatles*, 590.
11. *The Beatles Anthology*, 196.
12. Everett, *The Beatles as Musicians*, 309.
13. Schiffer, personal interview.
14. Ed Eichler, personal interview, May 11, 2019.
15. Vignapiano, personal interview.
16. Tom Noce, personal interview, March 26, 2019.

Notes

17. McEntarfer, Written Response.
18. Eden, "The Beatles: Rubber Soul (Parlophone UK)," *KRLA Beat* (1966). The Beatles. Rock's Backpages. http://www.rocksbackpages.com/Library/Article/the-beatles-irubber-souli-parlophone-uk (accessed March 6, 2020).
19. "The Beatles: Rubber Soul," *Record Mirror*, December 4, 1965. The Beatles. Rock's Backpages. http://www.rocksbackpages.com/Library/Article/the-beatles-rubber-soul (accessed March 6, 2020).
20. Quoted in Kruth, *This Bird Has Flown*, 9.
21. Wade Lawrence, personal interview, April 4, 2019.
22. Richard Green, "The Beatles: Rubber Soul (Parlophone)," *Record Mirror*, December 11, 1965. The Beatles. Rock's Backpages. http://www.rocksbackpages.com/Library/Article/the-beatles-irubber-souli-parlophone (accessed March 6, 2020).
23. MacDonald, *Revolution in the Head*, 130.
24. Andrew Grant Jackson, *1965: The Most Revolutionary Year in Music* (New York: St. Martin's Press, 2015), 264.
25. *The Beatles Anthology*, 215.
26. McKinney, *Magic Circles*, 130.
27. "Beatles in Manila in Palace Mix-Up," *Liverpool Echo*, July 3, 1966, 1. https://www.british newspaperarchive.co.uk/viewer/bl/0000271/19660704/011/0001 (accessed March 10, 2020).
28. "Interest in the East Is Not a Gimmick," *Liverpool Echo*, August 16, 1966, 1. https://www.british newspaperarchive.co.uk/viewer/bl/0000271/19660816/082/0004 (accessed March 10, 2020).
29. Quoted in Catone, *As I Write This Letter*, 31.
30. Quoted in Maureen Cleave, "How Does a Beatle Live? John Lennon," *Evening Standard*, March 4, 1966. https://www.rocksbackpages.com/Library/Article/how-does-a-beatle-live-john-lennon (accessed March 10, 2020).
31. McKinney, *Magic Circles*, 325–7.
32. Schiffer, personal interview.
33. *The Beatles Anthology*, 223.
34. Quoted in Riley, *Lennon*, 322.
35. Mark Sullivan, "'More Popular Than Jesus': The Beatles and the Religious Far Right," *Popular Music* 6, no. 3 (1987): 313–26. www.jstor.org/stable/853191 (accessed March 10, 2020).
36. Auerbach, personal interview.
37. Schiffer, personal interview.
38. Tom Blazucki, personal interview, March 30, 2019.
39. Nugent, personal interview.
40. Lawrence, personal interview.
41. Gould, *Can't Buy Me Love*, 340.
42. Quoted in Catone, *As I Write This Letter*, 31.
43. McKinney, *Magic Circles*, 143.
44. Robbie Robertson, *Testimony: A Memoir* (Toronto: Alfred A. Knopf, 2016), 238.
45. Ibid.
46. Vignapiano, personal interview.

Notes

47. Ruth Mandel, personal interview, March 28, 2019.
48. Richard Green and Peter Jones, "The Beatles: *Revolver* (Parlophone)," *Record Mirror*, July 30, 1966. http://www.rocksbackpages.com/Library/Article/the-beatles-irevolveri-parlophone (accessed March 12, 2020).
49. "The Beatles: *Revolver*."
50. "The Beatles: *Revolver* (Capitol)," *KRLA Beat*, September 10, 1966. http://www.rocksbackpages.com/Library/Article/the-beatles-irevolveri-capitol (accessed March 12, 2020).
51. McKinney, *Magic Circles*, 137.
52. https://www.billboard.com/music/the-beatles/chart-history/HSI/song/337259 (accessed March 12, 2020).
53. Lenny Mandel, personal interview, May 13, 2019.

CHAPTER 7

1. Quoted in Simonelli, *Working Class Heroes*, 117.
2. Sandbrook, *White Heat*, 382.
3. Alden Whitman, "Toynbee Doubts U.S. Can Win War," *New York Times*, March 19, 1967, 5. https://ezproxy.monmouth.edu/login?url=https://search-proquestcom.ezproxy.monmouth.edu/docview/117748906?accountid=12532 (accessed March 28, 2020).
4. Richard Reeves, "U.S. Think Tanks: In Santa Barbara Dialogue Is the Thing," *New York Times*, June 13, 1967. https://ezproxy.monmouth.edu/login?url=https://search-proquestcom.ezproxy.monmouth.edu/docview/118057388?accountid=12532 (accessed March 28, 2020).
5. Stanley Karnow, *Vietnam: A History* (New York: Penguin Books, [1983] 1997), 501. Karnow put the numbers for the Vietnam War in 1967 as costing about 3 percent of national GNP, compared to 12 percent for the Korean War and 48 percent for the Second World War.
6. "The War: On Two Fronts," *Time*, March 17, 1967. http://content.time.com/time/subscriber/article/0,33009,836789,00.html (accessed March 29, 2020).
7. Miles, *Paul McCartney*, 125–6.
8. Jody Rosen, "The Day the Music Burned," *New York Times*, June 11, 2019.
9. *The Beatles Anthology*, 241.
10. Norman, *Shout!*, 325–6.
11. Miles, *Paul McCartney*, 306.
12. Stark, *Meet the Beatles*, 191.
13. Brian Southall, *Sgt. Pepper's Lonely Hearts Club Band: The Album, the Beatles, and the World in 1967* (Watertown, MA: Carlton Books, 2017), 40.
14. Everett, *The Foundations of Rock*, 73.
15. Ibid., 23.
16. "The Beatles: Sgt. Pepper's Lonely Hearts Club Band," *Hit Parader*, November 1967. The Beatles. Rock's Backpages. http://www.rocksbackpages.com/Library/Article/thebeatles-isgt-peppers-lonely-hearts-club-bandi-2 (accessed April 1, 2020).
17. "Pop Music: The Messengers," *Time*, September 22, 1967. http://content.time.com/time/subscriber/article/0,33009,837319,00.html (accessed April 1, 2020).

Notes

18. Ibid.
19. Richard Goldstein, "Recordings: We Still Need the Beatles, but ...," *New York Times*, June 18, 1967, 104. https://ezproxy.monmouth.edu/login?url=https://search-proquestcom.ezproxy.monmouth.edu/docview/117914811?accountid=12532 (accessed April 2, 2020).
20. Richard Goldstein, *Another Little Piece of My Heart: My Life of Rock and Revolution in the '60s* (New York: Bloomsbury, 2015), 53–4.
21. Catone, *As I Write This Letter*, 39.
22. Wald, *How the Beatles Destroyed Rock "N" Roll*.
23. MacDonald, *Revolution in the Head*, 21.
24. Sandbrook, *White Heat*, 438.
25. Orenzoff, personal interview.
26. Jon Landau, "Their Satanic Majesties Request," *Rolling Stone*, December 8, 1967, https://www.rollingstone.com/music/music-album-reviews/their-satanic-majesties-request-187464/ (accessed April 3, 2020).
27. Orenzoff, personal interview.
28. Stanton Green, personal interview, January 30, 2019.
29. *The Beatles Anthology*, 248.
30. Auerbach, personal interview.
31. "Youth: The Hippies," *Time*, July 7, 1967. http://content.time.com/time/subscriber/article/0,33009,899555,00.html (accessed April 3, 2020).
32. Goldstein, *Another Little Piece of My Heart*, 60.
33. Rob Landsman, Michael Dover, and Lee Weitzenkorn, "Workshops Probe War, Race, Hippies," *Michigan Daily*, October 6, 1967, 10.
34. Mandel, personal interview.
35. Gitlin, *The Sixties*, 244.
36. Ercoline, personal interview.
37. Susan Lydon, "New Thing for Beatles: Magical Mystery Tour: Paul, John, George and Ringo Board a Bus for Their Latest Trip," *Rolling Stone*, December 14, 1967. https://www.rollingstone.com/music/music-news/new-thing-for-beatles-magical-mystery-tour-44115/ (accessed April 6, 2020).
38. *The Beatles Anthology*, 272.
39. Tom Nolan, "The Beatles: Magical Mystery Tour (Apple Corps/BBC)," *Los Angeles Free Press* (1968). The Beatles. Rock's Backpages. http://www.rocksbackpages.com/Library/Article/the-beatles-imagical-mystery-touriapple-corpsbbc-2 (accessed April 8, 2020).
40. Don Short, "So We Boobed, Says Beatle Paul: The Inside Story of What Went Wrong with the Magical Mystery Tour," *Daily Mirror*, December 28, 1967. https://www.britishnewspaperarchive.co.uk/viewer/bl/0000560/19671228/023/0003 (accessed April 8, 2020).
41. Ross Bloomfield, personal interview, April 12, 2019.
42. Nolan, "The Beatles: Magical Mystery Tour."
43. Tony Bramwell, *Magical Mystery Tours: My Life with the Beatles* (London: Portico, 2005), 229.
44. Kathryn B. Cox, "Mystery Trips, English Gardens, and Songs Your Mother Should Know: The Beatles and British Nostalgia in 1967," in *New Critical Perspectives on the Beatles: Things*

Notes

We Said Today, ed. Kenneth Womack and Katie Kapurch (London: Palgrave Macmillan, 2016), 32.

45. Mike Jahn, "The Beatles: Magical Mystery Tour," *Saturday Review*, December 1967. The Beatles. Rock's Backpages. http://www.rocksbackpages.com/Library/Article/the-beatlesmagical-mystery-touri (accessed April 8, 2020).
46. Joyce Matthews, "*Magical Mystery Tour*," *The Outlook*, Monmouth College, February 16, 1968, 39.
47. Matthews, "*Magical Mystery Tour*," 39.
48. Norman Jopling, "The Beatles: Magical Mystery Tour," *Record Mirror*, December 1, 1967. The Beatles. Rock's Backpages. http://www.rocksbackpages.com/Library/Article/thebeatles-imagical-mystery-touri (accessed April 8, 2020).

CHAPTER 8

1. Judt, *Postwar*, 391.
2. Ian Kershaw, *The Global Age: Europe 1950–2017* (London: Viking, 2018), 231.
3. Francis S. Clines, "Students Decry Stony Brook Raid: Marijuana Arrests Likened to Those of Prohibition Era," *New York Times*, January 19, 1968, 22. https://ezproxy.monmouth.edu/login?url=https://search-proquest- com.ezproxy.monmouth.edu/docview/118359742?accountid=12532 (accessed April 27, 2020).
4. Noce, personal interview.
5. Mark Kurlansky, *1968: The Year That Rocked the World* (New York: Ballantine Books, 2004), 195.
6. Gitlin, *The Sixties*, 307.
7. Kurlansky, *1968*, 197.
8. The next two sections are partly adapted from my paper "Was the Rock Music of 1968 Revolutionary?" Paper Presentation, "The Beatles' THE WHITE ALBUM: An International Symposium," West Long Branch, NJ, November 9, 2018.
9. Barry Hoskyns, *Hotel California: The True-Life Adventures of Crosby, Stills, Nash, Young, Mitchell, Taylor, Browne, Ronstadt, Geffen, the Eagles, and Their Many Friends* (Hoboken, NJ: John Wiley, 2006), 59.
10. Richard Goldstein, "'Big Pink' Is Just a Home in Saugerties," *New York Times*, August 4, 1968, D20. https://ezproxy.monmouth.edu/login?url=https://search-proquestcom.ezproxy.monmouth.edu/docview/118316100?accountid=12532 (accessed October 2, 2018).
11. Greil Marcus, *Mystery Train: Images of America Rock "N" Roll Music*, 6th ed. (New York: Penguin, [1975] 2015), 50.
12. Goldstein, "'Big Pink' Is Just a Home," D20.
13. Kurlansky, *1968*, 182.
14. Jann S. Wenner, "Pete Townshend Talks Mods, Recording, and Smashing Guitars," *Rolling Stone*, September 14, 1968. https://www.rollingstone.com/music/music-news/pete-townshend-talks-mods-recording-and-smashing-guitars-79369/ (accessed May 5, 2020).
15. Chris Welch, "No Mo' Motown?," *Melody Maker*, August 10, 1968. Rock's Backpages. http://www.rocksbackpages.com/Library/Article/no-mo-motown (accessed May 5, 2020).

Notes

16. "Lady Soul Singing It Like It Is," *Time*, June 28, 1968. http://content.time.com/time/subscriber/article/0,33009,841340,00.html (accessed May 6, 2020).
17. For an excellent history of Laurel Canyon during this period and beyond, see Michael Walker, *Laurel Canyon: The Inside Story of Rock-and-Roll's Legendary Neighborhood* (New York: Faber and Faber, 2006).
18. Jerry Hopkins, "Inside the Los Angeles Scene," *Rolling Stone*, June 28, 1966. https://www.rollingstone.com/music/music-news/inside-the-los-angeles-scene-78698/ (accessed May 5, 2020).
19. Ibid.
20. Quoted in Fred Goodman, *The Mansion on the Hill: Dylan, Young, Geffen, Springsteen and the Head-On Collision of Rock and Commerce* (New York: Vintage Books, 1998), 56.
21. Nicholas van Hoffman, *We Are the People Our Parents Warned Us About* (Chicago: Quadrangle Books, 1968), 24.
22. Goodman, *Mansion on the Hill*, 77.
23. Bill Wasserzieher, "Jefferson Airplane, Grateful Dead: Melodyland, Anaheim CA," *Long Beach Press-Telegram*, March 14, 1968. Rock's Backpages. http://www.rocksbackpages.com/Library/Article/jefferson-airplane-grateful-deadmelodyland-anaheim-ca (accessed May 5, 2020).
24. Tony Leigh, "Cream, The Electric Prunes, Steppenwolf: Santa Monica Civic Auditorium, Los Angeles CA," *KRLA Beat*, March 23, 1968. Rock's Backpages. http://www.rocksbackpages.com/Library/Article/cream-the-electric-prunes-steppenwolfsanta-monica-civic-auditorium-los-angeles-ca (accessed May 5, 2020).
25. Ibid. Leigh, "Cream, The Electric Prunes, Steppenwolf."
26. Sandbrook, *White Heat*, 558.
27. Claude Assante, personal interview, March 29, 2019.
28. Derek Boltwood, "The Bee Gees: Royal Albert Hall, London," *Record Mirror*, April 6, 1968. Rock's Backpages. http://www.rocksbackpages.com/Library/Article/the-bee-gees-royalalbert-hall-london (accessed May 5, 2020).
29. Richard Goldstein, "Freedom Can Be Costly," *New York Times*, February 4, 1968, D26. https://ezproxy.monmouth.edu/login?url=https://search-proquestcom.ezproxy.monmouth.edu/docview/118291677?accountid=12532 (accessed September 28, 2018).
30. Goldstein, "'Big Pink' Is Just a Home," D20.
31. Christopher Phillips and Louis P. Masur (eds), *Talk about a Dream: The Essential Interviews of Bruce Springsteen* (New York: Bloomsbury Press, 2013), 31.
32. Mike Jahn, 'The Beatles: The Beatles [The White Album] (Apple)," *New York Times*, November 21, 1968. Rock's Backpages. http://www.rocksbackpages.com/Library/Article/the-beatles-the-beatles-the-white-albumapple (accessed May 6, 2020).
33. Catone, *As I Write This Letter*, 36.
34. Sandbrook, *White Heat*, 48.
35. Keith Richards and James Fox, *Life* (New York: Little, Brown, 2010), 202.
36. Richard Goldstein, 'Why Do the Kids Dig Rock?," *New York Times*, November 24,1968, H1. https://search-proquestcom.ezproxy.monmouth.edu/hnpnewyorktimes/docview/118456995/FA1524516D604FF 2PQ/1?accountid=12532 (accessed May 6, 2020).
37. Simonelli, *Working Class Heroes*, 143.

Notes

38. Quoted in Greil Marcus, *Lipstick Traces: A Secret History of the Twentieth Century* (Cambridge, MA: Belknap Press of Harvard University Press, 1989), 53–4.
39. Quoted in Peter Wiche, "Music, Dissidence, Revolution, and Commerce: Youth Culture between Mainstream and Subculture," in *Between Marx and Coca-Cola: Youth Cultures in Changing European Societies, 1960–1980*, ed. Axel Schildt and Detlef Siegfried (New York: Berghahn Books, 2006), 121.
40. Alan Smith, 'Beatles' Loose Habit of Recording," *New Musical Express*, August 17, 1968. Rock's Backpages. http://www.rocksbackpages.com/Library/Article/beatles-loose-habit-of-recording (accessed May 7, 2020).
41. Sandbrook, *White Heat*, 558.
42. Goldstein, *Another Little Piece of My Heart*, 181.
43. Bell, personal interview.
44. Vignapiano, personal interview.
45. Joyce Matthews, "Hey Jude/Revolution," *The Outlook*, Monmouth University, September 27, 1968, 8.
46. J. Roman Babiak, "Why the Beatles Really Stink," *Michigan Daily*, September 16, 1968, 2. This was not the first article to appear in the University of Michigan student newspaper equating the Beatles with reaction. An article appeared in March written by Ken Sanderson of the "Liberation News Service" that argued that the true meaning of the name "Beatles" derived from its pronunciation as "Beadles," a beadle being a name for a minor church official in Britain, thus betraying the Beatles' association with "petty bureaucracy." Ken Sanderson (Liberation News Service), "Reaction Revision in the BoBarty," *Michigan Daily*, March 19, 1968.
47. Vignapiano, personal interview.
48. O. Heilbronner, "Music and Protest: The Case of the 1960s and Its Long Shadow," *Journal of Contemporary History* 51, no. 3 (2016): 688–700.
49. Jordy Cummings, "Forces of Chaos and Anarchy: Rock Music, The New Left and Social Movements, 1964 to 1972" (PhD diss., University of York, Toronto, 2017), 10. https://yorkspace.library.yorku.ca/xmlui/bitstream/handle/10315/34468/Cummings_Jordan_L_2017_PhD.pdf?sequence=2&isAllowed=y (accessed May 7, 2020).
50. McKinney, *Magic Circles*, 221.
51. Karen Armstrong, *The Great Transformation: The Beginning of Our Religious Traditions* (New York: Alfred A. Knopf, 2006), 192.
52. Babiak, "Why the Beatles Really Stink."
53. Nick Jones, 'The Rolling Stone Interview: George Harrison—Part 2," *Rolling Stone*, February 24, 1968. https://www.rollingstone.com/music/music-news/the-rolling-stone-interviewgeorge-harrison-part-2-231245/ (accessed May 5, 2020).
54. Sue C. Clark, 'Ravi Shankar: The Rolling Stone Interview," *Rolling Stone*, March 9, 1968. https://www.rollingstone.com/music/music-news/ravi-shankar-the-rolling-stoneinterview-65247/ (accessed May 5, 2020).
55. For more on this topic, see B. Ireland and S. Gemie, "Raga Rock: Popular Music and the Turn to the East in the 1960s," *Journal of American Studies* 53, no. 1 (2019): 57–94.
56. *The Beatles Anthology*, 281.
57. Smith, "Beatles' Loose Habit of Recording."
58. *The Beatles Anthology*, 305.

Notes

59. Womack, *Long and Winding Roads*, 219.
60. Walter Everett, *The Beatles as Musicians:* Revolver *through the* Anthology (New York: Oxford University Press, 1999), 149.
61. Womack, *Long and Winding Roads*, 220.
62. Sandbrook, *White Heat*, 766.
63. Jann S. Wenner, "Review: The Beatles' 'White Album,'" *Rolling Stone*, December 21, 1968. https://www.rollingstone.com/music/music-news/review-the-beatles-white-album186863/ (accessed May 7, 2020).
64. Mandel, personal interview.
65. Len Pniewski, personal interview, June 15, 2019.
66. Michael Halbreich, personal interview, April 16, 2019.
67. Goldstein, *Another Little Piece of My Heart*, 134.
68. Barry Miles, "The Beatles: The Beatles (White Album)," *International Times*, November 29, 1968. http://www.rocksbackpages.com/Library/Article/the-beatles-ithe-beatles-whitealbumi (accessed May 7, 2020).
69. Duncan, personal interview.
70. Vignapiano, personal interview.
71. Alan Smith, 'The Beatles: The Beatles (The White Album)," *New Musical Express*, November 30, 1968. Rock's Backpages. http://www.rocksbackpages.com/Library/Article/the-beatles-ithe-beatlesi-the-whitealbum (accessed May 6, 2020).
72. Richard Goldstein, "The Beatles: Inspired Groovers," *New York Times*, December 8, 1968. https://ezproxy.monmouth.edu/login?url=https://search-proquestcom.ezproxy.monmouth.edu/docview/118417369?accountid=12532 (accessed May 6, 2020).
73. Jahn, "The Beatles."
74. Smith, "The Beatles."
75. Quoted in DeGroot, *The Sixties*, 361.

CHAPTER 9

1. Gitlin, *The Sixties*, 342.
2. John McMillan, *Beatles vs. Stones* (New York: Simon and Schuster, 2013), 157.
3. Ibid., 342.
4. Charles DeBenedetti, *An American Ordeal: The Antiwar Movement of the Vietnam Era* (Syracuse, NY: Syracuse University Press, 1990), 241.
5. "Let's Demonstrate," *The Outlook*, Monmouth University, March 18, 1969, 18.
6. "Columbia Students Tell of Anger Over Disruption," *New York Times*, May 3, 1969, 22. https://ezproxy.monmouth.edu/login?url=https://search-proquestcom.ezproxy.monmouth.edu/docview/118660056?accountid=12532 (accessed May 22, 2020).
7. Fowler, *Youth Culture in Modern Britain*, 163.
8. Nicholas Pileggi, "Revolutionaries Who Have to Be Home by 7:30.," *New York Times*, March 16, 1969, 6. https://ezproxy.monmouth.edu/login?url=https://searchproquest-com.ezproxy.monmouth.edu/docview/118496554?accountid=12532 (accessed May 22, 2020).

Notes

9. "Roots of the American Student Revolution," *Coventry Evening Telegraph*, July 15, 1969, 10. https://www.britishnewspaperarchive.co.uk/viewer/bl/0000769/19690715/107/0010 (accessed May 22, 2020).
10. Pileggi, "Revolutionaries Who Have to Be Home," 26.
11. "Package Dealers," *Illustrated London News*, August 9, 1969, 6. https://www.britishnewspaperarchive.co.uk/viewer/bl/0001578/19690809/046/0006 (accessed May 22, 2020).
12. Quoted in Jeffrey Roessner, "We All Want to Change the World: Postmodern Politics and the Beatles' *White Album*," in *Reading the Beatles: Cultural Studies, Literary Criticism, and the Fab Four*, ed. Kenneth Womack and Todd F. Davis (Albany: State University of New York Press, 2006), 149.
13. Rolling Stone Editors, "Apple Records Is Alive & Healthy in the UK: Beatle Split Rumor Untrue," February 15, 1969. https://www.rollingstone.com/music/music-news/applerecords-is-alive-healthy-in-the-uk-229497/ (accessed May 9, 2020).
14. *The Beatles Anthology*, 322.
15. Ibid., 321.
16. Ibid., 334.
17. Assante, personal interview.
18. Pniewski, personal interview.
19. Allen Sorrentino, personal interview, April 5, 2019.
20. Barnes, personal interview.
21. Eichler, personal interview.
22. Noce, personal interview.
23. Mark Williams, "Crosby, Stills & Nash: Crosby, Stills & Nash (Atlantic 588 189)," *International Times*, August 15, 1969. Rock's Backpages. http://www.rocksbackpages.com/Library/Article/crosby-stills--nash-icrosby-stills--nashiatlantic-588-189 (accessed May 26, 2020).
24. Everett, *The Foundations of Rock*, 392.
25. Don Short, "The Wild Pooh of Pooh Corner," *Daily Mirror*, July 4, 1969, 7. https://www.britishnewspaperarchive.co.uk/viewer/bl/0000560/19690704/051/0007 (accessed May 26, 2020).
26. "'Brian Jones was Rebel' Says Rector," *Coventry Evening Telegraph*, July 10, 1969, 41. https://www.britishnewspaperarchive.co.uk/viewer/bl/0000769/19690710/583/0041 (accessed May 26, 2020).
27. Richards and Fox, *Life*, 189.
28. Geoffrey Cannon, "The Rolling Stones, King Crimson, Family: Hyde Park, London," *New Society*, July 10, 1969. Rock's Backpages. http://www.rocksbackpages.com/Library/Article/the-rolling-stones-king-crimson-familyhyde-park-london (accessed May 26, 2020).
29. "The Moon: Awe, Hope, and Skepticism on Planet Earth," *Time*, July 25, 1969. http://content.time.com/time/subscriber/article/0,33009,901105,00.html (accessed May 26, 2020).
30. "Modern Living: Sex as a Spectator Sport," *Time*, July 11, 1969. http://content.time.com/time/subscriber/article/0,33009,901005,00.html (accessed May 26, 2020).
31. For an expanded treatment of this topic, see Kenneth L. Campbell, "The Beatles at Woodstock," *Popular Music and Society* 43, no. 2 (2019): 188–200.
32. Unterberger, *Turn! Turn! Turn!: The '60s Folk-Rock Revolution*, 65.

33. Mandel, personal interview.
34. David Scher, personal interview, March 19, 2019.
35. Robertson, *Testimony*, 238.
36. Fogerty, *Fortunate Son*, 95.
37. Quoted in Pete Fornatale, *Back to the Garden: The Story of Woodstock 1969* (New York: Simon and Schuster, 2009), 73.
38. Michael Lang and Holly George-Warren, *The Road to Woodstock: From the Man Behind the Legendary Festival* (New York: HarperCollins, 2009), 84.
39. *The Beatles Anthology*, 337.
40. Ritchie Yorke, "George Harrison Talks about The Beatles' Album, *Abbey Road*," *Detroit Free Press*, September 26. 1969. Rock's Backpages. http://www.rocksbackpages.com/Library/Article/george-harrison-talks-about-the-beatlesalbum-iabbey-roadi (accessed May 20, 2020).
41. Miles, *Paul McCartney*, 551.
42. Alan Smith, "Beatles Music Straightforward On Next Album: An Interview with John Lennon," *New Musical Express*, May 3, 1969. Rock's Backpages. http://www.rocksbackpages.com/Library/Article/beatles-music-straightforward-on-nextalbum-an-interview-with-john-lennon (accessed May 26, 2020).
43. *The Beatles Anthology*, 338.
44. Simon Reynolds, *Retromania: Pop Culture's Addiction to Its Own Past* (New York; Faber and Faber, 2011), 278.
45. Walter Everett, "The Mellow Depth of Melody in Abbey Road," Paper presented at Come Together: Fifty Years of Abbey Road Symposium, Rochester, NY, September 27–29, 2019. Quoted by permission.
46. Kit OToole, "From the Swamp to the Mersey: 'Oh! Darling' and Its Debt to Swamp Pop," Paper presented at Come Together: Fifty Years of Abbey Road Symposium," Rochester, NY, September 27–29, 2019.
47. Walter Everett, "The Beatles as Composers: The Genesis of *Abbey Road*, Side Two," in *Concert Music, Rock, and Jazz since 1945: Essays and Analytical Studies*, ed. Elizabeth West Marvin and Richard Hermann (Rochester: University of Rochester Press, 1995), 186.
48. Kenneth Womack, *Solid State: The Story of* Abbey Road *and the End of the Beatles* (Ithaca, NY: Cornell University Press, 2019), 96–7.
49. *The Beatles Anthology*, 37.
50. Smith, "Beatles Music Straightforward."
51. Womack, *Solid State*, 282.
52. Everett, *The Beatles as Musicians:* Revolver *through the* Anthology, 245.

CHAPTER 10

1. J. Marks, "No, No, No, Paul McCartney Is Not Dead: No, No, No, Paul McCartney Is Not Dead," *New York Times*, November 2, 1969, 13. https://ezproxy.monmouth.edu/login?url=https://search-proquestcom.ezproxy.monmouth.edu/docview/118632478?accountid=12532 (accessed June 8, 2020).

Notes

2. Bramwell, *Magical Mystery Tours*, 319.
3. "Beatle Spokesman Calls Rumor of McCartney's Death 'Rubbish,'" *New York Times*, October 22, 1969, 8. https://ezproxy.monmouth.edu/login?url=https://searchproquest-com.ezproxy.monmouth.edu/docview/118626161?accountid=12532 (accessed June 8, 2020).
4. Brown and Gaines, *The Love You Make*, 372.
5. Bramwell, *Magical Mystery Tours*, 320.
6. Ernesto Carbonetti and Paolo Baron, *Paul Is Dead: When the Beatles Lost McCartney* (Portland: Image Comics, 2020), Epilogue.
7. McKinney, *Magic Circles*, 277.
8. See especially, Armstrong, *The Great Transformation*.
9. Goldstein, *Another Little Piece of My Heart*, 134.
10. McKinney, *Magic Circles*, 279.
11. "My Lai: An American Tragedy," *Time*, December 5, 1969. http://content.time.com/time/subscriber/article/0,33009,901621,00.html (accessed June 8, 2020).
12. Lon Goddard, "The Beatles: Abbey Road (Apple Stereo PCS 7088)," *Record Mirror*, September 27, 1969. Rock's Backpages. http://www.rocksbackpages.com/Library/Article/the-beatles-iabbey-roadi-apple-stereopcs-7088 (accessed June 9, 2020).
13. Alan Smith, "The Beatles: Abbey Road Album Track-By-Track," *New Musical Express*, September 20, 1969. Rock's Backpages. http://www.rocksbackpages.com/Library/Article/the-beatles-iabbey-roadi-album-trackby-track (accessed June 9, 2020).
14. John Mendelsohn, "*Abbey Road*," *Rolling Stone*, November 15, 1969. https://www.rollingstone.com/music/music-album-reviews/abbey-road-181270/ (accessed June 9, 2020).
15. Andrew Wilson, "'Abbey Road': An Event," *Sounds* 93, no. 10, October 9, 1969.
16. Chris Welch, "The Beatles: Abbey Road (Apple)," *Melody Maker*, September 27, 1969. Rock's Backpages. http://www.rocksbackpages.com/Library/Article/the-beatles-abbeyroad-apple (accessed June 9, 2020).
17. Mike Jahn, "The Beatles: Abbey Road (Apple)," *New York Times*, October 4, 1969. Rock's Backpages. http://www.rocksbackpages.com/Library/Article/the-beatles-iabbeyroadi-apple (accessed June 9, 2020).
18. "Beatles Issue New 'Abbey Road' Album," *Thanet Times*, September 30, 1969, 10. https://www.britishnewspaperarchive.co.uk/viewer/bl/0002513/19690930/149/0010 (accessed June 9, 2020).
19. Smith, "The Beatles: Abbey Road."
20. Geoffrey Cannon, "The Beatles: Abbey Road (Apple)," *The Guardian*, October 8, 1969. Rock's Backpages. http://www.rocksbackpages.com/Library/Article/the-beatles-iabbeyroadi-apple-3 (accessed June 9, 2020).
21. Mike Gormley, "The Beatles: Abbey Road (Apple)," *Detroit Free Press*, September 30, 1969. Rock's Backpages. http://www.rocksbackpages.com/Library/Article/the-beatles-iabbeyroadi-apple-4 (accessed June 9, 2020).
22. Welch, "The Beatles: Abbey Road."
23. Jahn, "The Beatles: Abbey Road."
24. Womack, *Solid State*, 199.
25. Ercoline, personal interview.
26. Assante, personal interview.

Notes

27. Halbreich, personal interview.
28. McEntarfer, Written Response.
29. Barnes, personal interview.
30. Philip Norman, *John Lennon: The Life* (New York: HarperCollins, 2008), 608.
31. *The Beatles Anthology*, 318.
32. Spitz, *The Beatles: A Biography*, 813.
33. Riley, *Lennon*, 430.
34. *The Beatles Anthology*, 319.
35. Walter Everett and Tim Riley, *What Goes On: The Beatles, Their Music, and Their Time* (Oxford: Oxford University Press, 2019), 209.
36. Fremaux, *The Beatles on Screen*, 120.
37. John Mendelsohn, "Let It Be," *Rolling Stone*, June 11, 1970. https://www.rollingstone.com/music/music-album-reviews/let-it-be-2-187101/ (accessed June 9, 2020).
38. Alan Smith, "The Beatles: Let It Be (Apple)," *New Musical Express*, May 9, 1970. Rock's Backpages. http://www.rocksbackpages.com/Library/Article/the-beatles-let-it-be-apple (accessed June 9, 2020).
39. Chevat, personal interview.
40. McEntarfer, Response to Questionnaire.
41. "About the Beatles," *New York Times*, May 24, 1970, x29. https://ezproxy.monmouth.edu/login?url=https://search-proquestcom.ezproxy.monmouth.edu/docview/118975956?accountid=12532 (accessed June 9, 2020).
42. Halbreich, personal interview.
43. Vignapiano, personal interview.
44. Pniewski, personal interview.
45. Alan Smith, "Let It Be (Dir. Michael Lindsay-Hogg, United Artists)," *New Musical Express*, May 23, 1970. Rock's Backpages. http://www.rocksbackpages.com/Library/Article/iletit-beidir-michael-lindsay-hogg-united-artists (accessed June 9, 2020).
46. "Last Beatles," *Acton Gazette*, June 25, 1970, 26. https://www.britishnewspaperarchive.co.uk/viewer/bl/0002463/19700625/493/0026 (accessed June 10, 2020).
47. "Film: Beatles Together: 'Let It Be' Documents Recording Sessions," *New York Times*, May 29, 1970, 11. https://ezproxy.monmouth.edu/login?url=https://searchproquest-com.ezproxy.monmouth.edu/docview/118911994?accountid=12532 (accessed June 10, 2020).
48. "Article 1—no Title: About the Beatles," *New York Times* (1923–Current File), May 24, 1970. https://ezproxy.monmouth.edu/login?url=https://www-proquest-com.ezproxy.monmouth.edu/historical-newspapers/article-1-no-title/docview/118975956/se-2?accountid=12532 (accessed June 9, 2020).
49. Michael Jackson, "Beatles Get Back Home," *Synapse (UCSF Student Newspaper)*, October 20, 1969.
50. *Echo in the Canyon* (2018). [Film] Dir. Andrew Slater. USA: Greenwich Entertainment.
51. Goodman, *The Mansion on the Hill*, 80.
52. *The Beatles Anthology*, 317.
53. Kane, personal interview.

Notes

54. Jann S. Wenner, "Q&A: Paul McCartney," *Rolling Stone*, April 30, 1970. https://www.rollingstone.com/music/music-news/qa-paul-mccartney-177764/ (accessed June 11, 2020).
55. "Music: Hello, Goodbye, Hello," *Time*, April 20, 1970. http://content.time.com/time/subscriber/article/0,33009,944046,00.html (accessed June 11, 2020).
56. "Yesterday and Tomorrow by Paul McCartney," *Daily Mirror*, April 11, 1970, 7. https://www.britishnewspaperarchive.co.uk/viewer/bl/0000560/19700411/047/0007 (accessed June 11, 2020).
57. Joshua Wolf Shenk, *Powers of Two: Finding the Essence of Innovation in Creative Pairs* (Boston: Eamon Dolan/Houghton Mifflin Harcourt, 2014), 214.
58. Wenner, "Q&A: Paul McCartney."
59. "Paul Quits the Beatles," *Coventry Evening Telegram*, April 10, 1970, 55. https://www.britishnewspaperarchive.co.uk/viewer/bl/0000769/19700410/763/0055 9 (accessed June 11, 2020).
60. Sandbrook, *White Heat: A History of Britain in the Swinging Sixties*, 767.
61. Mikal Gilmore, "Why the Beatles Broke Up," *Rolling Stone*, September 2009, 94.
62. Womack, *Solid State*, 191.
63. Pattie Boyd and Penny Junor, *Wonderful Tonight: George Harrison, Eric Clapton and Me* (New York: Three Rivers Press, 2007), 125.
64. David Browne, *Fire and Rain: The Beatles, Simon & Garfunkel, James Taylor, CSNY, and the Lost Story of 1970* (Cambridge, MA: Da Capo Press, 2011), 87.
65. "Music: Hello, Goodbye, Hello."
66. Ercoline, personal interview.
67. Halbreich, personal interview.
68. Kane, personal interview.
69. Barnes, personal interview.
70. *The Beatles Anthology*, 354.
71. Vignapiano, personal interview.
72. Chevat, personal interview.
73. Pniewski, personal interview.
74. Bell, personal interview.
75. "Music: Hello, Goodbye, Hello."
76. Goodman, *Mansion on the Hill*, 80.
77. Browne, *Fire and Rain*, 298.
78. Marcus, *Mystery Train*, 83.

CONCLUSION

1. Bell, personal interview.
2. "Protest over Vietnam War," *Newcastle Journal*, May 15, 1972, 9. https://www.britishnewspaperarchive.co.uk/viewer/bl/0002240/19720515/116/0009 (accessed June 24, 2020).

Notes

3. David Chalmers, *And the Crooked Places Made Straight: The Struggle for Social Change in the 1960s* (Baltimore, MD: Johns Hopkins University Press, 1991), 174.
4. "One Man's Family of Rock," *Time*, March 1, 1971. http://content.time.com/time/subscriber/article/0,33009,878920,00.html (accessed June 30, 2020).
5. Jerry Hopkins, "Beatle Loathers Return: Britain's Teddy Boys: Rock and Roll Fashion Revivalists," *Rolling Stone*, March 2, 1972. https://www.rollingstone.com/music/musicnews/beatle-loathers-return-britains-teddy-boys-119244/ (accessed June 24, 2020).
6. Carol Clerk, "Year of the Bin-Liner," *Acton Gazette*, January 5, 1978, 8. https://www.britishnewspaperarchive.co.uk/viewer/bl/0002463/19780105/048/0008 (accessed June 25, 2020).
7. Marwick, *The Sixties*, 806.
8. Catone, *As I Write This Letter*, 4.
9. Angellini, personal interview, January 14, 2019.
10. Lawrence, personal interview.
11. Alan Smith, "John Lennon: Imagine (Apple)," *New Musical Express*, September 11, 1971. Rock's Backpages. http://www.rocksbackpages.com/Library/Article/john-lennonimagine-apple (accessed June 26, 2020).
12. Womack, *Solid State*, 224.
13. *The Beatles Anthology*, 349.
14. Catone, *As I Write this Letter*, 4–5.
15. Boyd and Junor, *Wonderful Tonight*, 167.
16. Angellini, personal interview.
17. Alan Betrock, "Ringo Starr: Ringo," *Phonograph Record*, 1973. Rock's Backpages. http://www.rocksbackpages.com/Library/Article/ringo-starr--ringo (accessed June 26, 2020).
18. Ercoline, personal interview.
19. Halbreich, personal interview.
20. Ibid.
21. Kane, personal interview.
22. Bell, personal interview.
23. Jeff Ayers, personal interview, February 19, 2019.
24. Ercoline, personal interview.
25. Bill Martin, *Avant Rock: Experimental Music from the Beatles to Björk* (Chicago: Open Court, 2002), 84.
26. Auerbach, personal interview.
27. Jacob Hoye, ed. *VH1's 100 Greatest Albums* (New York: Barnes and Noble Books, 2003).
28. Jay Cocks, "Rock's Outer Limits: Through Turmoil and Triumph, the Who Makes Music That Will Last," *Time*, December 17, 1979. http://content.time.com/time/subscriber/article/0,33009,920745,00.html (accessed June 30, 2020).
29. Quoted in Robert Brosh, *Rock History: The Musician's Perspective* (EBook: DDG Publishing, 2018), 58.
30. "Elton John: Rock's Captain Fantastic," *Time*, July 7, 1975. http://content.time.com/time/subscriber/article/0,33009,913239,00.html (accessed June 30, 2020).
31. Lawrence, personal interview.

Notes

32. Quoted in Brosh, *Rock History*, 208.
33. Shenk, *Powers of Two*, 192.
34. Marcus, *Mystery Train*, 91.
35. Richard Neer, *FM: The Rise and Fall of Rock Radio* (New York: Villard, 2001), 264.
36. Halbreich, personal interview.

SELECT BIBLIOGRAPHY

Apel, Linde. "Voices from the Rubble Society: 'Operation Gomorrah' and Its Aftermath." *Journal of Social History* 44, no. 4 (2011): 1020. doi:10.1353/jsh.2011.0041 (accessed July 16, 2019).
Axelrod, Mitchell. *Beatletoons: The Real Story behind the Cartoon Beatles*. Pickens, SC: Wynn, 1999.
Bean, J. P. *Joe Cocker: The Authorized Biography*. London: Omnibus Press, 1990.
The Beatles Anthology. San Francisco, CA: Chronicle Books, 2000.
Benson, John. *Affluence and Authority: A Social History of Twentieth Century Britain*. London: Oxford University Press, 2005.
Berman, Gary. *"We're Going to See the Beatles!": An Oral History of Beatlemania*. Santa Monica, CA: Santa Monica Press, 2008.
Best, Pete, and Patrick Doncaster. *Beatle! The Pete Best Story*. London: Plexus, 1985.
Boyd, Pattie, and Penny Junor. *Wonderful Tonight: George Harrison, Eric Clapton and Me*. New York: Three Rivers Press, 2007.
Bramwell, Tony. *Magical Mystery Tours: My Life with the Beatles*. London: Portico, 2005.
Brosh, Robert. *Rock History: The Musician's Perspective*. E-Book: DDG, 2018.
Brown, Peter, and Steven Gaines. *The Love You Make: An Insider's Story of the Beatles*. New York: McGraw Hill, 1983.
Browne, David. *Fire and Rain: The Beatles, Simon & Garfunkel, James Taylor, CSNY, and the Lost Story of 1970*. Cambridge, MA: Da Capo Press, 2011.
Campbell, Kenneth L. "The Beatles at Woodstock." *Popular Music and Society* 43, no. 2 (2019): 188–200.
Campbell, Kenneth L. "'You Say You Want a Revolution': The Beatles and the Political Culture of the 1960s." In *Roll Up for the Mystery Tour!: The Beatles, Sgt, Pepper, and the Summer of Love*, edited by Kenneth Womack, 161–73. Lanham, MD: Lexington Books, 2017.
Cannon, Geoffrey. "Pop Music Democratised." *New Society*, December 3, 1964. https://www.rocksbackpages.com/Library/Article/pop-music-democratised- (accessed January 1, 2020).
Carlin, Peter Ames. *Paul McCartney: A Life*. New York: Simon & Schuster, 2009.
Carter, Dan T. *The Politics of Rage: George Wallace, the Origins of the New Conservatism, and the Transformation of American Politics*. 2nd ed. Baton Rouge: Louisiana State University Press, 2000.
Catone, Marc A. *As I Write This Letter: An American Generation Remembers the Beatles*. Ann Arbor, MI: Greenfield Books, 1982.
Chalmers, David. *And the Crooked Places Made Straight: The Struggle for Social Change in the 1960s*. Baltimore, MD: Johns Hopkins University Press, 1991.
Coates, Norma. "Elvis from the Waist Up and Other Myths: 1950s Music Television and the Gendering of Rock Discourse." In *American Popular Culture and the Beatles*, edited by Kenneth Campbell, 43–63. San Diego, CA: Cognella Press, 2019.
Cox, Kathryn B. "Mystery Trips, English Gardens, and Songs Your Mother Should Know: The Beatles and British Nostalgia in 1967." In *New Critical Perspectives on the Beatles: Things We Said Today*, edited by Kenneth Womack and Katie Kapurch, 31–50. London: Palgrave Macmillan, 2016.
Cronkite, Walter. *A Reporter's Life*. New York: Alfred A. Knopf, 1996.

Select Bibliography

Cummings, Jordy. "Forces of Chaos and Anarchy: Rock Music, The New Left and Social Movements, 1964 to 1972." PhD diss., University of York, Toronto, 2017. https://yorkspace.library.yorku.ca/xmlui/bitstream/handle/10315/34468/Cummings_Jordan_L_2017_PhD.pdf?sequence=2&isAllowed=y (accessed May 7, 2020).

Davies, Evan. "Psychological Characteristics of Beatle Mania." *Journal of the History of Ideas* 30, no. 2 (1969): 273–80. www.jstor.org/stable/2708439 (accessed December 30, 2019).

Davies, Hunter. *The Beatles*. New York: W. W. Norton, [1968] 2009.

Davis, Melissa. "Beatlemania." In *The Beatles in Context*, edited by Kenneth Womack, 71–97. Cambridge: Cambridge University Press, 2020.

Davis, Melissa. "A Conceptual Analysis of the Reception of the Beatles in America, February 1964." MA diss., Liverpool Hope University, Liverpool, 2010.

DeBenedetti, Charles. *An American Ordeal: The Antiwar Movement of the Vietnam Era*. Syracuse, NY: Syracuse University Press, 1990.

DeGroot, Gerard. *The Sixties: A Kaleidoscopic History of a Disorderly Decade*. Cambridge, MA: Harvard University Press, 2008.

Donnelly, Mark. *Sixties Britain: Culture, Society and Politics*. Harrow, England: Pearson Longman, 2005.

Douglas, Susan. *Where the Girls Are: Growing Up Female with the Mass Media*. New York: Three Rivers Press, 1994.

Doyle, Tom. *Man on the Run: Paul McCartney in the 1970s*. New York: Ballantine Books, 2013.

Echo in the Canyon. [Film] Dir. Andrew Slater. USA: Greenwich Entertainment, 2018.

Ehrenreich, Barbara, Elizabeth Hess, and Gloria Jacobs. "Beatlemania: Girls Just Want to Have Fun." In *American Popular Culture & the Beatles*, edited by Kenneth Campbell, 166–82. San Diego, CA: Cognella Press, 2018.

Eight Days a Week. [Film] Ron Howard. USA: Apple Corps, 2016.

Everett, Walter. "The Beatles as Composers: The Genesis of Abbey Road, Side Two." In *Concert Music, Rock, and Jazz since 1945: Essays and Analytical Studies*, edited by Elizabeth West Marvin and Richard Hermann, 172–218. Rochester: University of Rochester Press, 1995.

Everett, Walter. *The Beatles as Musicians: Revolver through the Anthology*. New York: Oxford University Press, 1999.

Everett, Walter. *The Beatles as Musicians: The Quarry Men through Rubber Soul*. Oxford: Oxford University Press, 2001.

Everett, Walter. *The Foundations of Rock: From "Blue Suede Shoes" to "Suite: Judy Blue Eyes."* Oxford: Oxford University Press, 2009.

Everett, Walter, and Tim Riley. *What Goes On: The Beatles, Their Music, and Their Time*. Oxford: Oxford University Press, 2019.

Fogerty, John, and Jimmy McDonough. *Fortunate Son: My Life, My Music*. New York: Little, Brown, 2015.

Fornatale, Pete. *Back to the Garden: The Story of Woodstock 1969*. New York: Simon and Schuster, 2009.

Fowler, David. *Youth Culture in Modern Britain 1920–1970*. London: Palgrave Macmillan, 2008.

Frederick, Jeff. *Stand Up for Alabama: Governor George Wallace*. Tuscaloosa: University of Alabama Press, 2017.

Fremaux, Stephanie. *The Beatles on Screen: From Pop Stars to Musicians*. New York: Bloomsbury, 2018.

Fricke, David. "Paul McCartney Looks Back: The Rolling Stone Interview." *Rolling Stone*, August 10, 2016. https://www.rollingstone.com/music/music-features/paulmccartney-looks-back-the-rolling-stone-interview-102797/ (accessed July 19, 2019).

Frontani, Michael. *The Beatles: Image and the Media*. Jackson: University of Mississippi, 2007.

Select Bibliography

Garr, Gillian. "Girl Groups." In *American Popular Culture and the Beatles*, edited by Kenneth Campbell, 64–87. San Diego, CA: Cognella Press, 2019.

Gilmore, Mikal. "Why the Beatles Broke Up." *Rolling Stone*, September 2009, 46–57, 94.

Gitlin, Todd. *The Sixties: Years of Hope, Days of Rage*. Revised ed. New York: Bantam Books, 1993.

Glynn, Steven. *The British Pop Music Film: The Beatles and Beyond*. London: Palgrave Macmillan, 2013.

Goldstein, Richard. *Another Little Piece of My Heart: My Life of Rock and Revolution in the '60s*. New York: Bloomsbury, 2015.

Golson, G. Barry (ed.). *The Playboy Interviews with John Lennon and Yoko Ono, conducted by David Sheff*. New York: Playboy Press, 1981.

Goodman, Fred. *The Mansion on the Hill: Dylan, Young, Geffen, Springsteen and the Head-On Collision of Rock and Commerce*. New York: Vintage Books, 1998.

Gould, Jonathan. *Can't Buy Me Love: The Beatles, Britain, and America*. New York: Three Rivers Press, 2007.

Graziani, David. *Mix It Up: Popular Culture, Mass Media, and Society*. New York: W. W. Norton, 2010.

Groom, Bob. "Whose 'Rock Island Line'? Originality in the Composition of Blues and British Skiffle." In *American Popular Culture and the Beatles*, edited by Kenneth Campbell, 114–25. San Diego, CA: Cognella Press, 2019.

Gross, Raphael. "Relegating Nazism to the Past: Expressions of German Guilt in 1945 and Beyond." *German History* 25, no. 2 (2007): 219–38. doi:10.1177/0266355406075715 (accessed July 17, 2019).

Halberstam, David. *The Children*. New York: Random House, 1998.

Halsey, A. H. *British Social Trends since 1900*. Houndmills: Macmillan, 1988.

Harris, Craig. *The Band: Pioneers of Americana Music*. Lanham, MD: Rowman and Littlefield, 2014.

Havens, Richie, and Steve Davidowitz. *They Can't Hide Us Anymore*. New York: Avon Books, 1999.

Heilbronner, O. "Music and Protest: The Case of the 1960s and Its Long Shadow." *Journal of Contemporary History* 51, no. 3 (2016): 688–700.

Hoffman, Nicholas van. *We Are the People Our Parents Warned Us About*. Chicago: Quadrangle Books, 1968.

Hoskyns, Barry. *Hotel California: The True-Life Adventures of Crosby, Stills, Nash, Young, Mitchell, Taylor, Browne, Ronstadt, Geffen, the Eagles, and Their Many Friends*. Hoboken, NJ: John Wiley, 2006.

Howlett, Kevin. *The Beatles at the Beeb: The Story of Their Radio Career*. London: BBC, 1982.

Howlett, Kevin. *The Beatles: The BBC Archives, 1962–1970*. New York: HarperCollins, 2013.

Inglis, Ian. "Ideology, Trajectory & Stardom: Elvis Presley & The Beatles." *International Review of the Aesthetics and Sociology of Music* 27, no. 1 (1996): 53–78. doi:10.1080/03007761003694373 (accessed December 5, 2019).

Inglis, Ian. "'I Read the News Today, Oh Boy': The British Press and the Beatles." *Popular Music & Society* 33, no. 4 (2010): 549–62. doi:10.1080/03007761003694373 (accessed December 6, 2019).

Jackson, Andrew Grant. *1965: The Most Revolutionary Year in Music*. New York: St. Martin's Press, 2015.

Jarvis, Mark. *Conservative Governments: Morality and Social Change in Affluent Britain 1957–1964*. Manchester: Manchester University Press, 2005.

Judt, Tony. *Postwar: A History of Europe since 1945*. New York: Penguin Books, 2005.

Select Bibliography

Kane, Larry. *Ticket to Ride: Inside the Beatles; 1964 Tour that Changed the World*. Philadelphia, PA: Running Press, 2003.

Kapurch, Katie. "The Wretched Life of a Lonely Heart: *Sgt. Pepper's* Girls, Fandom, the Wilson Sisters, and Chrissie Hynde." In *Roll Up for the Mystery Tour!: The Beatles, Sgt, Pepper, and the Summer of Love*, edited by Kenneth Womack, 137-60. Lanham, MD: Lexington Books, 2017.

Karnow, Stanley. *Vietnam: A History*. Revised ed. 1983. New York: Penguin Books, 1997.

Kenny, Francis. *The Making of John Lennon*. Bloomington, IN: Red Lightning Books, 2018.

Kershaw, Ian. *The Global Age: Europe 1950-2017*. London: Viking, 2018.

Kirchherr, Astrid, and Max Scheler, *Yesterday: The Beatles Once Upon a Time*. New York: Vendome Press, 2007.

Krause, Amanda, Adrian North, and Lauren Hewitt. "Music Selection Behaviors in Everyday Listening." *Journal of Broadcasting & Electronic Media* 58, no. 2 (2014): 306-23. doi:10.1080/08838151.2014.906437 (accessed January 30, 2019).

Kruke, Ania. "Western Integration vs. Reunification? Analyzing the Polls of the 1950s." *German Politics & Society* 25 no. 2 (2007): 43-67. doi:10.3167/gps.2007.250204 (accessed July 16, 2019).

Kruth, John. *This Bird Has Flown: The Enduring Beauty of Rubber Soul, Fifty Years On*. Milwaukee: Backbeat Books, 2015.

Kurlansky, Mark. *1968: The Year That Rocked the World*. New York: Ballantine Books, 2004.

Kynaston, David. *Austerity Britain: 1945-1951*. New York: Waller, 2008.

Kynaston, David. *Family Britain: 1951-1957*. New York: Walker, 2009.

Kynaston, David. *Modernity Britain, 1957-62*. New York: Bloomsbury, 2014.

Lang, Michael, and Holly George-Warren. *The Road to Woodstock: From the Man Behind the Legendary Festival*. New York: HarperCollins, 2009.

Leach, Sam. *The Rocking City: The Explosive Birth of the Beatles*. Merseyside: Pharaoh Press, 1994.

Lennon, Cynthia. *John*. New York: Crown, 2005.

Leonard, Candy. *Beatleness: How the Beatles and Their Fans Remade the World*. New York: Arcade, 2014.

Lewisohn, Mark. *Tune In: The Beatles: All These Years, Volume 1*. New York: Three Rivers Press, 2013.

MacDonald, Ian. *Revolution in the Head: The Beatles' Records and the Sixties*. New York: Henry Holt, 1994.

McKinney, Devin. *Magic Circles: The Beatles in Dream and History*. Cambridge, MA: Harvard University Press, 2003.

McMillan, John. *Beatles vs. Stones*. New York: Simon and Schuster, 2013.

Marcus, Greil. *Lipstick Traces: A Secret History of the Twentieth Century*. Cambridge, MA: Belknap Press of Harvard University Press, 1989.

Marcus, Greil. *Mystery Train: Images of America Rock 'N' Roll Music*. 6th ed. New York: Penguin, [1975] 2015.

Martin, Bill. *Avant Rock: Experimental Music from the Beatles to Björk*. Chicago: Open Court, 2002.

Marwick, Arthur. *The Sixties: Cultural Revolution in Britain, France, Italy, and the United States, c.1958-c.1974*. Oxford: Oxford University Press, 1998.

Meacham, Jon (ed.) *Voices in Our Blood: America's Best of the Civil Rights Movement*. New York: Random House, 2001.

Miles, Barry. *The British Invasion: The Music, the Times, the Era*. New York: Sterling, 2009.

Miles, Barry. *Paul McCartney; Many Years from Now*. New York: Henry Holt, 1997.

Millard, Andre. "Beatlemania." In *American Popular Culture and the Beatles*, edited by Kenneth Campbell, 147-65. San Diego, CA: Cognella Press, 2019.

Mort, Frank. *Capital Affairs: London and the Making of the Permissive Society*. New Haven, CT: Yale University Press, 2010.

Mort, Frank. "Striptease: The Erotic Female Body and Live Sexual Entertainment in Mid-Twentieth-Century London." *Social History* 32, no. 1 (2007): 27–53.

"Music: Hello, Goodbye, Hello." *Time*, April 20, 1970. http://content.time.com/time/subscriber/article/0,33009,944046,00.html (accessed June 11, 2020).

Nash, Graham. *Wild Tales: A Rock & Roll Life*. New York: Three Rivers Press, 2013.

Neaverson, Bob. *The Beatles Movies*. London: Cassell, 1997.

Neer, Richard. *FM: The Rise and Fall of Rock Radio*. New York: Villard, 2001.

Norman, Philip. *John Lennon: The Life*. New York: HarperCollins, 2008.

Norman, Philip. *Shout! The Beatles and Their Generation*. Revised edn. New York: Simon and Schuster, [1981] 2003.

Ott, Brian L., and Robert L. Mack. *Critical Media Studies: An Introduction*. Malden, MA: Wiley-Blackwell, 2010.

Pielke, Robert G. *Rock Music in American Culture: The Sounds of Revolution*. Jefferson, NC: McFarland, 2012.

Pileggi, Nicholas. "Revolutionaries Who Have to Be Home by 7:30." *New York Times Magazine*, March 16, 1969. https://ezproxy.monmouth.edu/login?url=https://searchproquest-com.ezproxy.monmouth.edu/docview/118496554?accountid=12532 (accessed May 22, 2020).

Pimlott, Ben. *Harold Wilson*. London: HarperCollins, 1992.

Pritchard, David, and Alan Lysaght, *The Beatles: An Oral History*. New York: Hyperion, 1998.

Pugh, Martin. *State and Society: A Societal and Political History of Britain since 1870*. 5th ed. London: Bloomsbury, 2017.

Reynolds, Simon. *Retromania: Pop Culture's Addiction to Its Own Past*. New York: Faber and Faber, 2011.

Richards, Keith, and James Fox. *Life*. New York: Little, Brown, 2010.

Riley, Tim. *Lennon: The Man, the Myth, the Music—The Definitive Life*. New York: Hyperion, 2011.

Robertson, Robbie. *Testimony: A Memoir*. Toronto: Alfred A. Knopf, 2016.

Roessner, Jeffrey. "We All Want to Change the World: Postmodern Politics and the Beatles' White Album." In *Reading the Beatles: Cultural Studies, Literary Criticism, and the Fab Four*, edited by Kenneth Womack and Todd F. Davis, 147–58. Albany: State University of New York Press, 2006.

Sandbrook, Dominic. *Never Had It So Good: A History of Britain from Suez to the Beatles*. London: Abacus, 2005.

Sandbrook, Dominic. *State of Emergency: The Way We Were: Britain 1970–1974*. London: Penguin, 2011.

Sandbrook, Dominic. *White Heat: A History of Britain in the Swinging Sixties*. London: Little, Brown, 2006.

Savage, John. *Teenage: The Creation of Youth Culture*. New York: Viking, 2007.

Shaffner, Nicholas. *The British Invasion: The First Wave to the New Wave*. New York: McGraw Hill, 1983.

Sheffield, Rob. *Dreaming the Beatles: The Love Story of One Band and the Whole World*. New York: HarperCollins, 2017.

Shenk, Joshua Wolf. *Powers of Two: Finding the Essence of Innovation in Creative Pairs*. Boston: Eamon Dolan/Houghton Mifflin Harcourt, 2014.

Shotton Pete, and Nicholas Shaffner. *John Lennon: In My Life*. New York: Stein and Day, 1983.

Shumway, David R. "Watching Elvis." In *American Popular Culture and the Beatles*, edited by Kenneth Campbell, 22–42. San Diego, CA: Cognella Press, 2019.

Select Bibliography

Simonelli, David. *Working Class Heroes: Rock Music and British Society in the 1960s and 1970s*. Lanham, MD: Lexington Books, 2013.

Skellett, Paul, Simon Wells, and Simon Weitzman. *Eight Arms to Hold You:50 Years of Help! and the Beatles*. New York: ACC, 2017.

Southall, Brian. *Sgt. Pepper's Lonely Hearts Club Band: The Album, the Beatles, and the World in 1967*. Watertown, MA: Carlton Books, 2017.

Spitz, Bob. *The Beatles: The Biography*. New York: Little, Brown, 2005.

Stark, Steven D. *Meet the Beatles: A Cultural History of the Band That Shook Youth, Gender, and the World*. New York: HarperCollins, 2005.

Sullivan, Mark. "'More Popular Than Jesus': The Beatles and the Religious Far Right." *Popular Music* 6, no. 3 (1987): 313–26. www.jstor.org/stable/853191 (accessed March 10, 2020).

Sutcliffe, Pauline, and Douglas Thompson. *The Beatles' Shadow: Stuart Sutcliffe & His Lonely Hearts Club*. London: Pan Macmillan, 2002.

Thamer, Jeremy. "The Radical Left and Popular Music in the 1960s." In *Preserving the Sixties: Britain and the "Decade of Protest,"* edited by Trevor Harris and Tonia O'Brien Castro, 90–104. London: Palgrave Macmillan, 2014.

Turner, Steve. *Beatles '66: The Revolutionary Year*. New York: HarperCollins, 1966.

Unterberger, Richie. *Turn! Turn! Turn!: The '60s Folk-Rock Revolution*. San Francisco, CA: Backbeat Books, 2002.

Wald, Elijah. *How the Beatles Destroyed Rock "N" Roll: An Alternative History of American Popular Music*. Oxford: Oxford University Press, 2009.

Walker, Michael. *Laurel Canyon: The Inside Story of Rock-and-Roll's Legendary Neighborhood*. New York: Faber and Faber 2006.

Ward, Brian. "'By Elvis and All the Saints' Images of the American South in the World of 1950s British Popular Music." In *American Popular Culture and the Beatles*, edited by Kenneth Campbell, 93–113. San Diego, CA: Cognella Press, 2019.

Weeks, Jeffrey. *Sex, Politics and Society*. London: Longman, 1981.

Wiche, Peter. "Music, Dissidence, Revolution, and Commerce: Youth Culture between Mainstream and Subculture." In *Between Marx and Coca-Cola: Youth Cultures in Changing European Societies, 1960–1980*, edited by Axel Schildt and Detlef Siegfried, 109–27. New York: Berghahn Books, 2006.

Wilson, Harold. *The Labor Government 1964–1970: A Personal Record*. London: Weidenfeld and Nicolson, 1971.

Winder, Simon. *The Man Who Saved Britain: A Personal Journey into the Disturbing World of James Bond*. New York: Farrar, Straus and Giroux, 2007.

Womack, Kenneth. *Long and Winding Roads: The Evolving Artistry of the Beatles*. New York: Bloomsbury, 2007.

Womack, Kenneth. *Maximum Volume: The Life of Beatles Producer George Martin: The Early Years, 1926–1966*. Chicago: Chicago Review Press, 2017.

Womack, Kenneth. *Solid State: The Story of Abbey Road and the End of the Beatles*. Ithaca, NY: Cornell University Press, 2019.

Wright, Lawrence. *In the New World: Growing Up in America from the Sixties to the Eighties*. New York: Vintage Books, 1987.

"Youth: The Hippies," *Time*, July 7, 1967. http://content.time.com/time/subscriber/article/0,33009,899555,00.html (accessed April 3, 2020).

INDEX

Abbey Road 132, 163, 185–8, 190, 193, 194–7, 199–200, 201
"Across the Universe" 198, 200, 201
Adenauer, Konrad 24, 25, 26
Ali, Muhammad (*see* Clay, Cassius)
"All My Loving" 54
All Things Must Pass (Harrison) 215, 216
"All Together Now" 162
"All You Need is Love" 136, 143, 162, 183
Animals 52, 75, 82, 97
"And I Love Her" 74, 79
Angellini, Mark 213, 214, 215
"Anna (Go to Him) 51
"Another Girl" 96
Armstrong, Neil 179, 180
Asher, Jane 114, 115, 189
As I Write this Letter (Catone) 3, 117–18, 121, 134–5, 155, 212, 214
Aspinall, Neil 57, 117, 132
Assante, Claude 153, 158, 176, 196
audience reception theory 2, 66–7
Auerbach, Roy 103, 121, 123, 139, 216, 217
Ayers, Jeff 216

"Back in the U.S.S.R." 162, 164, 165, 166
Baez, Joan 150, 182
"Ballad of John and Yoko, The" 122, 176, 186
"Ballad of Paul, The" (Mystery Tour) 191
Band, The 149–50, 161, 184, 193
Barnes, Jane 69, 70–1, 76, 101, 103, 176–7, 196–7, 206
Barrow, Tony 49, 115
Beach Boys 113, 132–3, 138, 151, 162, 181
Beatlemania 55–9, 61, 66–77, 79, 83, 91, 94, 101
Beatles
    attitudes toward race 63–4
    attitudes toward women 111
    auditions with Decca and EMI 37
    BBC appearances 52, 55, 56
    breakup 176, 184, 189, 192, 194, 199 202–8, 212, 224
    comparison with other artists/groups 217–22
    drug use 31, 75, 94, 122, 140, 162, 169, 174, 198
    first US tour (1964) 67
    first U.S. visit (1964) 63–4, 66–7
    influence of Astrid Kirchherr 33–6
    influence of Brian Epstein 36, 39, 55, 57, 68
    influence of Bob Dylan 92, 111
    influence on other artists 223
    final US tour (1966) 120, 125
    MBE (Members of the British Empire) designation 90, 92, 102
    meeting with Elvis Presley 100
    meeting with Muhammad Ali 63
    name origins 21–2
    regrets about fame 36–7, 57–8
    rooftop concert (1969) 185, 198, 199, 201
    second US tour (1965) 100–1, 105, 111
    Shea Stadium concert 91, 101–2, 183
    television appearances 56, 59
    tensions before the breakup 173–4
    world tour (1966) 111, 115–16
    (*see also* Best, Pete; *Ed Sullivan Show*; Epstein, Brian; Harrison, George; Lennon, John; McCartney, Paul; Martin, George; Starr, Ringo; Sutcliffe, Stuart)
Beatles, The (television series) 104
Beatles, The (White Album) 123, 132, 149, 153, 154–5, 157, 160, 161–7, 173, 181, 182, 184, 195, 196
Beatles Anthology, The 11, 17, 35, 39, 138, 162, 175
Beatles for Sale 21, 85
"Because" 187
Bee Gees, The 153–4
"Being for the Benefit of Mr. Kite" 133, 134
Bell, Ivan 82, 157, 207, 209, 216
Berry, Chuck 15, 16, 20, 31, 32, 51, 64, 71, 104, 185
"Besame Mucho" 48, 51
Best, Pete 21. 30, 33, 35, 36–9, 55
Big Brother and the Holding Company 149, 152
"Birthday" 162, 165
"Blackbird" 64, 161, 181, 182, 183
Black Panther Party 171–2
Black Power 119, 145, 146
Blazucki, Tom 121
Blood, Sweat, and Tears 154, 157, 176, 180, 182
Bloomfield, Ross 142
"Boys" 50, 75
Bramwell, Tony 143, 190–1
Brown, Peter 56, 69, 112, 190
Browne, Jackson 208, 221
Buffalo Springfield 149, 151, 177, 202
"Bungalow Bill" 162
Byrds 98, 99, 149, 151, 161, 177, 202

"Can't Buy Me Love" 78, 79
Capp, Al 174–6

Index

"Carry That Weight" 187
Cavern Club 19, 36
"Chains" 51, 53, 75
Chappaquiddick, Massachusetts 180–1
Chevat, Alan 137, 200, 207
Chicago, Illinois; Democratic convention, 145, 148, 155, 156-7, 170
Civil Rights Act (1964) 61, 62, 64–5, 66, 84–5, 146
Civil Rights movement (U.S.) 17, 61–5, 84–5, 107–8, 119, 145, 146, 171
Clapton, Eric 152, 153, 179 (*see also* Cream)
Clay, Cassius 62–3
Cleave, Maureen 53, 54, 55, 118
Cocker, Joe 51, 183
"Cold Turkey" (Lennon/Ono/Plastic Ono Band) 203, 205
Cold War 10, 24–7, 59, 116, 148, 179
Columbia University 147–8, 170, 171
"Come Together" 185, 187, 194
"Continuing Story of Bungalow Bill, The" 162, 164
Country Joe and the Fish 157, 158, 182, 183
Cream 152, 153, 156
Creedence Clearwater Revival 151, 182, 184
Cronkite, Walter 107
Crosby, David 70, 80, 149, 177–8, 202, 221 (*see also* Byrds, The; Crosby, Stills, and Nash; Crosby, Stills, Nash, and Young)
Crosby, Stills, and Nash (CSN) 177–8, 183
Crosby, Stills, Nash, and Young (CSNY) 149, 193, 208
"Cry Baby Cry" 165

Daily Princetonian 68, 83, 102–3, 166
Dave Clark Five 75, 98
Davis, Clive 152, 202, 208
Davis, Melissa 72
"Day in the Life, A" 132, 138, 165, 190
"Day Tripper" 115, 140
"Dear Prudence" 164
"Dig It" 198, 200
Donegan, Lonnie 17
"Don't Bother Me" 54
"Don't Let Me Down" 197, 198
"Don't Pass Me By" 161
Donovan 161, 162
Doors 97, 140, 149, 151, 179, 193
Douglas, Susan 72, 73–4, 76
"Drive My Car" 114
Duncan, Rebecca 75, 79, 83, 165
Dylan, Bob 80–1, 82; 92, 99, 104, 123, 133, 149, 161, 165, 185

Eagles 151, 217
East Germany (*see* German Democratic Republic)
Eastman, Lee 174, 203

Ed Sullivan Show 59, 67, 68, 69, 70, 79, 80–1, 100, 184
Egypt Station (McCartney) 214, 221
Ehrenreich, Barbara 72, 75, 76
Eichler, Ed 112, 177
Eight Days a Week (film) 94, 101
"Eleanor Rigby" 5, 124, 132, 162, 184
Emerick, Geoff 132, 188
"End, The" 187
Epstein, Brian 36, 37, 38, 39, 48, 49, 55, 57, 63, 64, 68, 96, 116, 117, 120, 125, 141, 205–6
Ercoline, Nick 82, 140, 196, 206, 216, 217
Evans, Mal 215
Everett, Walter 1, 51, 52, 112, 133, 162, 177–8, 186–7, 188, 199

Fabian 16, 71
Federal Republic of Germany (West Germany) 24–7, 146, 159
"Fixing a Hole" 133, 138, 214
Fleming, Ian 59, 93
Fogerty, John 54, 70, 184 (*see also* Creedence Clearwater Revival)
"Fool on the Hill, The" 142, 144
"For No One" 125
"For You Blue" 198, 202
Foster, Marbie 81
France 28, 53, 61, 145, 148; student revolt 146
Franklin, Aretha 150–1, 152
Fremaux, Stephanie 96, 199
"From Me to You" 52, 54, 67

Garry, Len 17, 18, 19
German Democratic Republic (East Germany) 23, 28
Germany (*see* Federal Republic of Germany; German Democratic Republic)
Gerry and the Pacemakers 8, 38, 48, 52, 75, 94
"Get Back" 173, 174, 178, 197, 198, 199, 200, 202
"Getting Better" 132, 133, 138
Gibb, Russ 189–90
Gitlin, Todd 148, 170
"Glass Onion" 163, 165, 190
Glynn, Stephen 77–8
"God" (Lennon) 161, 213
"Golden Slumbers" 187
Goldstein, Richard 134, 139, 149, 150, 154, 156, 157, 158, 165–6, 193
"Good Day Sunshine" 124, 125
"Good Morning Good Morning" 132
"Good Night" 165
"Got to Get You into My Life" 124
Grateful Dead 98, 140, 151–2, 182, 200
Green, Richard 110, 113, 123

Index

Halbreich, Michael 164, 196, 201, 206, 216, 224
Hamburg, Germany 22, 26–9, 199
    Beatles 1966 visit 115
    Beatles' first trip to 30–4
    impact of the Second World War 27
    reputation 28
"Happiness is a Warm Gun" 161, 162, 164
"Hard Day's Night, A" 79
Hard Day's Night, A (film) 73, 76–80, 85, 94–5, 96, 103, 104, 125, 141
Hard Day's Night, A (LP) 79
Harrison, George 7, 9, 21–2, 30. 95, 173, 174, 190, 198, 203, 212
    after the Beatles 215
    childhood 13
    interest in Indian culture 117, 159, 160, 184
    musical abilities 20
    musical influences 17–18
    role in the Beatles 49, 205
    solo career 203, 215, 216–17
    songwriting 54, 111–12, 114, 124, 133, 159, 169, 174, 185–6, 187, 195, 198, 215
    (*see also* Beatles, The)
Harrison, Pattie (Boyd) 187, 206, 215
Havens, Richie 69, 70, 157, 182
"Hello, Goodbye" 144
"Help!" 92, 97, 104, 105, 184, 211
Help! (film) 90–1, 93–7, 98, 103–4, 105, 141, 143
Help! (LP) 91, 94, 96–7, 104, 105, 111, 113, 140
"Helter Skelter" 162, 163, 164, 181, 182, 217
Hendrix, Jimi 140, 148, 153, 182, 183, 193
"Here Comes the Sun" 185–6, 187, 195
"Here, There and Everywhere" 124, 125
"Her Majesty" 185
Herman's Hermits 52, 75
"Hey Bulldog" 162
"Hey Jude" 155, 159–60, 165, 182, 203
Ho Chi Minh 128, 129, 130, 170
Hoffman, Abbie 156–7
Hollies 52, 149, 177
Holly, Buddy 18, 21, 22, 71, 193
"Honey Pie" 162, 163, 165, 217
Hopkin, Mary 174, 206

"I'm Happy Just to Dance with You" 79
"I'm Looking through You" 114
"I'm Only Sleeping" 123
"I'm So Tired" 162
"I Am the Walrus" 144, 190
"If I Fell" 79, 199
"If I Needed Someone" 113
"I've Got a Feeling" 198
"I've Just Seen a Face" 114
"Imagine" (Lennon) 161, 213, 216
"I Me Mine" 198

Indra (club) 30, 31, 34
"I Need You" 96
"In My Life" 112, 114, 221
"Inner Light, The" 159, 160
"I Saw Her Standing There" 50
"I Should Have Known Better" 79
"It's All Too Much" 162
"I Wanna Be Your Man" 50, 54
"I Want to Hold Your Hand" 39, 66, 67, 69, 160, 176, 182, 196
"I Want You (She's So Heavy)" 187, 194, 196
"I Will" 161, 221
"I'll Follow the Sun" 21

Jackson, Michael 214, 222
Jackson State University 209
Jagger, Mick 82, 137, 155–6, 166, 179 (*see also* Rolling Stones)
Jefferson Airplane 98, 139, 151, 152, 154, 182
John, Elton 219–20, 224
Johnson, Lyndon B. 61, 64, 65–6, 91, 98, 127, 129–30, 148, 159 169–70, 210
Jones, Brian 178, 193
Jones, Peter 53, 54, 79, 123, 124
Jones, Tom 98, 144
Joplin, Janis 182, 193 (*see also* Big Brother and the Holding Company)
"Julia" 161, 162

Kane, Larry 63, 67, 69, 71, 72, 73, 82, 83, 95, 100, 101, 203, 206, 216, 217
Kapurch, Katie 75
Kaufman, Murray (Murray the K) 70, 82, 101
Keeler, Christine 41–3
Kennedy, Edward (Teddy) 180–1
Kennedy, John F.
    assassination 61–2, 65–6, 72
    support for Civil Rights 107–8
Kennedy, Robert 107–8, 109–11, 145, 161, 162
Kent State University 209
King, Carole 115, 208, 221
King, Jr., Martin Luther 4, 65, 107, 108, 119, 145, 146
Kinks 75, 156
Kirchherr, Astrid 28, 33–6, 38–9, 93
Klein, Allen 190, 197, 203, 205
Koschmider, Bruno 30, 31, 32
Kosygin, Alexei 128, 130

LaBour, Fred 189, 193
Lady Chatterley's Lover 45, 46
"Lady Madonna" 159, 176
Landau, Jon 137, 152, 153, 173, 220
Lawrence, Wade 113, 114, 121, 213, 216, 222
Leach, Sam 30, 36, 38, 39, 55
Leary, Timothy 97, 123, 187

Index

Led Zeppelin 152, 156, 177, 218–19
Lennon, Cynthia 9, 15, 30, 39, 176
Lennon, John 5, 27, 30, 193, 197, 198, 202, 210–11
  anti-war stance 130
  bed-ins for peace 174–6
  childhood 9, 12, 13, 15, 17
  comments on Christianity 118–21, 211
  death 223–4
  during *Abbey Road* sessions 186, 188
  musical ability, 17–18, 21
  musical influences 16–17
  reaction to criticism 96
  relationship with Paul McCartney 18–20, 21, 205, 213
  role in the Beatles 49, 205
  role in the Beatles' breakup 205
  role in *A Hard Day's Night* 78
  solo career 203, 213, 214, 216–17
  songwriting 97, 111–12, 114 131, 132–3, 155, 161, 162–3, 165, 185, 187 198, 213
  stage antics in Hamburg 27, 32
  views on the possibility of reuniting with the Beatles 212
  views on Transcendental Meditation 161
  vocal performances 51, 69
  (*see also* Beatles, The)
Lennon, Julia 13, 20
Lester, Richard 76, 94, 95, 96
"Let It Be" 21, 176, 200, 203
Let It Be (film) 198–201
Let It Be (LP) 185, 194, 196, 197, 199–201, 208
Let It Bleed (Rolling Stones) 179, 200
Levine, Robin 81
Lewisohn, Mark 15, 52
Lindsay-Hogg, Mark 198, 199
Little Richard 15, 16, 19, 20, 71
"Long Long Long" 162
"Long and Winding Road, The" 197, 200, 202
Los Angeles, California 99–100, 138, 151, 152, 162, 181 (*see also* Watts)
"Lovely Rita" 133
"Love Me Do" 21, 38, 39, 48, 49, 51 53, 56
"Love You To" 124, 133
"Lucy in the Sky with Diamonds" 5, 131, 133, 134, 136, 138

McCartney (McCartney) 203, 213
McCartney, Linda Eastman 174, 189, 198, 203–4, 214
McCartney, Paul
  after the Beatles 213–14
  attitude toward fame 161
  attitude toward the Vietnam War 130, 156
  childhood 9, 12, 13, 14–15, 17, 30
  considers leaving the Beatles 35–6
  death rumors 188, 189–94
  musical ability, 17–18, 21
  musical influences 17–18
  relationship with John Lennon 18–20, 21, 186, 213
  relationship with Stuart Sutcliffe 32–3
  role in the Beatles 49, 205
  role in Beatles' breakup 203–6
  solo career 56, 203, 213, 214, 216–17, 222
  songwriting 111–12, 114–15, 124, 132–3, 155, 198, 200
  (*see also* Beatles, The)
MacDonald, Ian 45, 94, 114, 135
McEntarfer, Michael 81, 103, 113, 196, 200–1
MacInnes, Colin 10, 45
McKinney, Devin 26, 28, 31, 80, 96, 116, 118, 121–2, 124, 159, 192
McMillan, Harold 41, 43, 78
"Maggie Mae" 198, 200
"Magical Mystery Tour" 144
Magical Mystery Tour (EP) 143, 144
Magical Mystery Tour (Film) 141–4, 160, 163
Magical Mystery Tour (LP) 143–4, 154, 166
Maharishi Mahesh Yogi 141, 160–1, 162–3
Mailer, Norman 148
Mamas and the Papas 138, 139, 151
Mandel, Lenny 164, 184
Mandel, Ruth 123, 125, 140
Manson, Charles 165, 180, 181–2, 193
Mao Zedong 130, 159
Marcos, Ferdinand 116–17
Marcos, Imelda 116–17
Marcus, Greil 113, 149, 208, 223
Marsden, Gerry (*see* Gerry and the Pacemakers)
Marshall Plan 23, 24
"Martha My Dear" 162, 163
Martin, George, 37, 39, 48, 49, 51–3, 92, 112, 131, 132, 133, 161, 163, 186, 197, 199
Marwick, Arthur 44, 87, 211
Matthews, Joyce 144, 158
"Maxwell's Silver Hammer" 187, 194, 196, 199
"Mean Mr. Mustard" 163, 187
Meet the Beatles 52, 82
Mendelsohn, John 194, 195, 200
"Michelle" 114, 203, 214
Michigan Daily 103, 121, 140, 158
Miles, Barry 14, 20, 70, 130, 165, 186
Millard, Andre 71, 72
"Misery" 51
Mississippi, University of 107, 110
Mitchell, Joni 149, 151, 208, 221
"Money (That's What I Want)" 53
Monkees 136, 151
Monterrey Pop Festival 139, 151, 183

Index

Morrison, Jim 97, 99, 193 (*see also* Doors, The)
"Mother Nature's Son" 161
Motown artists 54, 150

Nash, Graham 51, 55, 80, 149, 177–8, 221 (*see also* Crosby, Stills, and Nash; Crosby Stills, Nash, and Young; Hollies, The)
Neaverson, Bob 77, 96
Nixon, Richard M. 169–70, 209, 210
Noce, Tom 113, 147, 177
"Norwegian Wood (This Bird Has Flown)" 114
Nowhere Boy (film) 16–17
"Nowhere Man" 114, 132, 162, 221
Nugent, Janet 79–80, 83, 101, 121, 176

"Ob-la-di, Ob-la-da" 163, 217
Ochs, Phil 150, 157
"Octopus's Garden" 187, 194
"Oh! Darling" 187, 195
"Old Brown Shoe" 174
"One after 909" 21, 198
"Only a Northern Song" 162
Ono, Yoko 13, 162, 163, 165, 174–6, 177, 186, 198, 203–4, 213, 223
Orenzoff, Peter 82, 137–8
Osborne, John, *Look Back in Anger* 10, 46
O'Toole, Kit 187
Owen, Alun 76

"Paperback Writer" 122
Paris, France 98, 129, 145–6
Passover Plot, The (Schonfield) 118
"Penny Lane" 131, 143
Pet Sounds (Beach Boys) 132–3, 138
"Piggies" 161, 169, 182
Pill (birth control, Enovid) 46–7, 140, 180
Pink Floyd 156, 218–19, 222
"Please Mr. Postman" 54, 75
"Please Please Me" 39, 48, 49, 53, 54, 56, 67
Please Please Me 48–51, 52, 54
Pniewski, Len 164, 176, 177, 201, 207
Police, The 219
"Polythene Pam" 163, 187
Pop Art 50, 77, 90, 92–3
"P.S. I Love You" 21, 48, 51
Powers of Two, The (Shenk) 203, 206, 213
Presley, Elvis 13, 16–17, 21, 33, 55–6, 59, 67, 68, 71, 73, 76, 98, 100, 222
Preston, Billy 199, 218
Profumo Affair 41–4, 58

Quarrymen 18–20

Radio Luxembourg 11, 17
"Rain" 122

Reagan, Ronald 172, 211, 223
"Revolution" 5, 155–7, 158, 159–60, 163, 169, 170, 173, 177
"Revolution 1" 157, 161, 165, 166, 173
"Revolution 9" 163, 165, 166, 173
Revolver 116, 122–5, 136, 140, 153, 166, 184, 195
Richard, Cliff 55–6
Richards, Keith 9, 155, 178–9 (*see also* Rolling Stones)
Riley, Tim 19, 12, 17, 39, 44, 198, 199
Robertson, Robbie 105, 122, 123, 184 (*see also* Band, The)
"Rocky Raccoon" 161, 164, 165
Rolling Stones 54, 59, 75, 82, 83, 103, 134, 137–8, 148, 152, 153, 155–6, 166, 178, 183, 185, 200, 202, 203, 218, 220, 222
"Roll Over Beethoven" 53
Ronstadt, Linda 151, 221
Rory Storm and the Hurricanes 22, 30, 32
Rubber Soul 105, 111–15, 116, 122, 123, 132, 136, 140, 154, 184
Runaways 219, 220
"Run for Your Life" 114
Russell, Bertrand 130
Russell, Richard B. 62, 64

Sandbrook, Dominic 71, 135–6, 153, 155, 163, 205
San Francisco, California 97, 100, 138–9, 151, 152, 181
Santana, Carlos 151, 183
"Savoy Truffle" 162, 165
Scher, David 184
Schiffer Bob 79, 112, 118, 121, 137
"Sgt. Pepper's Lonely Hearts Club Band" 131–2, 138, 143, 214
Sgt. Pepper's Lonely Hearts Club Band 21, 75, 130–8, 141, 144, 153, 164, 166, 182, 183, 184, 190, 195, 196
Sex Pistols 211
"Sexy Sadie" 162
Sha Na Na 183
Shankar, Ravi 160–1, 184
"She Came in Through the Bathroom Window" 187
"She's Leaving Home" 75, 132, 134, 138, 218
"She Loves You" 51, 53, 54, 56, 67, 74, 177, 184, 196
"She Said She Said" 124
Shotton, Pete 12, 17, 19, 38
Simon, Carly 208, 221
Simon and Garfunkel 150, 208
Simon, Paul 208, 221 (*see also* Simon and Garfunkel)
Sly and the Family Stone 151, 152, 182
Smith, Alan 48, 49, 162, 166, 186, 187, 194, 195, 200, 201, 213
"Something" 186, 187, 194, 195
Sorrentino, Allen 176, 177

Index

Southern University 171
Spector, Phil 197, 200
Spitz, Bob 1, 26, 49, 69, 71, 95. 198, 199
Springsteen, Bruce 154, 158, 219, 220
Stark, Steven 2, 36, 72, 75
Starr, Ringo, 17, 22, 30, 95, 133, 161, 185, 190, 197, 198, 203 212
  acting career 174
  childhood 12, 13–14, 15
  joins the Beatles 37–9
  musical ability 39
  role in the Beatles 49, 50
  role in *A Hard Day's Night* 78
  solo career 203, 215–17
  songwriting 161, 187, 215–16
  (*see also* Beatles, The)
Steely Dan 217–18
Steve Miller (Blues) Band 151, 157
Stills, Steven 80, 149, 177–8 (*see also* Crosby, Stills, and Nash; Crosby Stills, Nash, and Young)
Sting 219
Stony Brook, State University of New York at 147, 200
"Strawberry Fields Forever" 131, 143, 182, 190
"Street Fighting Man" (Rolling Stones) 155–6
Students for a Democratic Society (SDS) 170, 171, 172
Suez Crisis 9, 10
"Sun King" 187
Sutcliffe, Stuart 13, 21–2, 30, 32–3, 34, 35; 36, 134

"A Taste of Honey" 51, 70
Taupin, Bernie 219–20, 224
"Taxman" 124, 169, 184
Taylor, James 162, 177, 187, 206, 208, 221
"Teddy Boy" (McCartney) 163, 197
Teddy Boys 15, 211
"Tell Me Why" 79
Tet Offensive 144, 145
Thatcher, Margaret 172, 211, 223
Their Satanic Majesties Request (Rolling Stones) 137, 138
"There's a Place" 74
"Think for Yourself" 113, 114, 215
"Ticket to Ride" 92, 96, 105
"Till There Was You" 54, 70
Tommy James and the Shondells 152–3
"Tomorrow Never Knows" 123, 125
Townshend, Pete 150, 156 (*see also* Who, The)
Toynbee, Arnold 127–31
Twiggy (Lesley Hornby) 73, 93
"Twist and Shout" 51, 54
"Two of Us" 197–8, 202
Two Virgins (Lennon-Ono) 174, 175, 203

U Thant 129, 130

Vaughan, Ivan 12, 17, 18
Vietnam War 4, 85, 91, 98, 110, 127–30, 132, 140, 143, 144, 145, 146, 147, 148, 155, 158, 159, 169–70, 171, 179, 193, 209–10
Vignapiano, James 79, 80, 103, 113, 123, 157–9, 165–6, 201, 207
Voorman, Klaus 28, 34, 35

"Wait" 114
Wald, Elijah 53, 135
Wallace, George C. 64, 107–11, 119, 125
Wallace, Lurleen 108–9, 111
Ward, Stephen 41–2, 43
Watergate 210
Watson, Charles "Tex" 180–1
Watts, Los Angeles, California 99–100, 107, 110, 119
"We Can Work It Out" 115, 140
Wenner, Jann 150, 163, 203
West Germany (*see* Federal Republic of Germany)
"What Goes On" 113
"When I'm Sixty-Four" 21, 75, 132, 133
"While My Guitar Gently Weeps" 161, 164
White Album (*see Beatles, The*)
Who, The 148, 150, 152, 176, 182, 187, 202, 218, 220, 222
"Why Don't We Do It in the Road" 161, 162
"Wild Honey Pie" 163
Williams, Alan 28, 30, 32, 49
Wilson, Harold 41, 43, 44, 50, 68, 78, 85, 87–90, 92, 93, 128, 130, 209
Wings 214, 217, 220
"With a Little Help from My Friends" 75, 132, 133, 138, 182, 183
"Within You, Without You" 133, 136
With the Beatles 32, 34, 50, 53–4
Womack, Kenneth 1, 52, 80, 162, 163, 187
Woodstock Festival 140, 180, 182–3
"The Word" 113

"Yellow Submarine" 124, 144
Yellow Submarine (film) 144, 162, 198
Yellow Submarine (LP) 162
"Yer Blues" 162
"Yes It Is" 187
"Yesterday" 74. 92, 96, 105, 184, 203, 214, 218, 221
Yesterday and Today 136, 140–1
"You're Going to Lose that Girl 1965" 74
"You've Got to Hide Your Love Away" 74, 92, 97, 105, 221
"You Know My Name (Look up the Number)" 200
"You Never Give Me Your Money" 186, 187
Young, Neil 80, 149, 151 181, 183, 221 (*see also* Crosby, Stills, Nash, and Young)
"Your Mother Should Know" 144
"You Won't See Me" 113, 114

www.ingramcontent.com/pod-product-compliance
Lightning Source LLC
Chambersburg PA
CBHW060946230426
43665CB00015B/2082